PROFESSIONAL
MICROSOFT® POWERPIVOT
FOR EXCEL® AND SHAREPOINT®

PROFESSIONAL

Microsoft® PowerPivot
for Excel® and Sharepoint®

PROFESSIONAL

Microsoft® PowerPivot
for Excel® and SharePoint®

Sivakumar Harinath
Ron Pihlgren
Denny Guang-Yeu Lee

Wiley Publishing, Inc.

Professional Microsoft® PowerPivot for Excel® and SharePoint®

Published by
Wiley Publishing, Inc.
10475 Crosspoint Boulevard
Indianapolis, IN 46256
www.wiley.com

Copyright © 2010 by Wiley Publishing, Inc., Indianapolis, Indiana

Published simultaneously in Canada

ISBN: 978-0-470-58737-9

Manufactured in the United States of America

10 9 8 7 6 5 4 3 2 1

For general information on our other products and services please contact our Customer Care Department within the United States at (877) 762-2974, outside the United States at (317) 572-3993 or fax (317) 572-4002.

Wiley also publishes its books in a variety of electronic formats. Some content that appears in print may not be available in electronic books.

Library of Congress Control Number: 2010928461

ABOUT THE AUTHORS

SIVAKUMAR HARINATH was born in Chennai, India. He has a Ph.D. in Computer Science from the University of Illinois at Chicago. His thesis title was "Data Management Support for Distributed Data Mining of Large Datasets over High-Speed Wide Area Networks." Harinath has worked for Newgen Software Technologies (P) Ltd; IBM Toronto Labs, Canada; National Center for Data Mining; and the University of Illinois at Chicago. He started as a Software Design Engineer in Test (SDET) at Microsoft in 2002 for the Analysis Services Performance Team, and is currently a Senior Test Manager in the SQL Server Analysis Services team. Harinath has co-authored *Professional Microsoft SQL Server Analysis Services 2005 with MDX* (Indianapolis: Wiley, 2006), *MDX Solutions: With Microsoft SQL Server Analysis Services 2005 and Hyperion Essbase* (Indianapolis: Wiley, 2006), and *Professional Microsoft SQL Server Analysis Services 2008 with MDX* (Indianapolis: Wiley, 2009). His other interests include high-performance computing, distributed systems, and high-speed networking. He is married to Shreepriya and has twins, Praveen and Divya. His personal interests include travel, games/sports (in particular, carrom, chess, racquetball and board games). You can reach him at Sivakumar.harinath@microsoft.com.

RONALD PIHLGREN is a native of Chicago, Illinois. He has a Bachelor of Science degree in Computer Science from DePaul University. A 15-year veteran at Microsoft, he is currently a Senior Test Manager on the SQL Server Analysis Services team, and has been a part of the project that became PowerPivot since it was in incubation. He was one of the principal technical reviewers for the book *Professional Microsoft SQL Server Analysis Services 2008 with MDX* (Indianapolis: Wiley, 2009). He has a blog at http://blogs.msdn.com/ronpih. This is his first book as an author.

DENNY LEE is a Senior Program Manager with Microsoft based out of Redmond, Washington, in the SQL Customer Advisory Team (SQLCAT) DW/BI Group. He has more than 13 years of experience as a developer and consultant implementing software solutions to complex online transaction processing (OLTP) and data warehousing problems. His industry experience includes accounting, human resources, automotive, retail, Web analytics, telecommunications, and healthcare. He helped create the first online analytical processing (OLAP) services reporting application in production at Microsoft. He co-authored *Professional Microsoft SQL Server Analysis Services 2008 with MDX* (Indianapolis: Wiley, 2009), *Professional Microsoft SQL Server 2000 Data Warehousing with Analysis Services* (Indianapolis: Wiley, 2001), and *Transforming Healthcare through Information* (New York: Springer, 2004). In addition to contributing to the SQLCAT Blog, SQL Server Best Practices, and SQLCAT.com, you can also review Lee's blog at http://dennyglee.com. Lee specializes in developing solutions for Enterprise Data Warehousing, Analysis Services, and Data Mining. He also has focuses in the areas of Privacy and Healthcare.

ABOUT THE TECHNICAL EDITOR

JOHN SIRMON is a Senior Escalation Engineer with the SQL Server Analysis Services Support team at Microsoft, based in the Microsoft Regional Support Center in Charlotte, North Carolina. He has worked for Microsoft since March, 2001, and began working with Microsoft SQL Server more than 10 years ago when he began his professional career as a consultant at PricewaterhouseCoopers. He has extensive development experience with Microsoft Visual Studio and all the components of the Microsoft BI Stack. His specialties include Analysis Services performance tuning, Reporting Services, SharePoint integration, and troubleshooting Kerberos authentication. Sirmon has presented on topics ranging from Reporting Services SharePoint Integration to Analysis Services at SQL Server PASS Summits and Microsoft TechReady conferences. He holds a Bachelor of Science degree in Business Administration from the Citadel. Sirmon holds Microsoft Certified Solution Developer (MCSD) and Microsoft Certified Database Administrator (MCDBA) certifications.

CREDITS

EXECUTIVE EDITOR
Robert Elliott

PROJECT EDITOR
Kevin Shafer

TECHNICAL EDITOR
John Sirmon

PRODUCTION EDITOR
Kathleen Wisor

COPY EDITOR
Christopher Jones

EDITORIAL DIRECTOR
Robyn B. Siesky

EDITORIAL MANAGER
Mary Beth Wakefield

MARKETING MANAGER
Ashley Zurcher

PRODUCTION MANAGER
Tim Tate

VICE PRESIDENT AND EXECUTIVE GROUP PUBLISHER
Richard Swadley

VICE PRESIDENT AND EXECUTIVE PUBLISHER
Barry Pruett

ASSOCIATE PUBLISHER
Jim Minatel

PROJECT COORDINATOR, COVER
Lynsey Stanford

COMPOSITOR
Jeffrey Lytle, Happenstance Type-O-Rama

PROOFREADERS
Jen Larsen, Word One
Michael Shaw, Word One

INDEXER
Johnna VanHoose Dinse

COVER DESIGNER
Michael E. Trent

COVER IMAGE
© Ben Blankenburg/istockphoto

ACKNOWLEDGMENTS

THE AUTHORS THANK SQLCAT, the SQL Server Analysis Services team, Excel team, and Excel Services team for their help and contribution to this book. The authors would like to specially thank Rob Collie, Howie Dickerman, Deva Kaladipet Muthukumarasamy, Amir Netz, Sergey Volegov, Dave Wickert, Lee Graber, John Hancock, Marius Dumitru, Jeffrey Wang, Karen Aleksanyan, Ashvini Sharma, Kathy MacDonald, Marcelo Blinder, Bogdan Crivat, Leon Cyril, and Thierry D'Hers for their key contributions and reviews for the book. The authors thank John Sirmon for technical review of the book, as well as Kevin Shafer for helping with all the logistics of technical editing and publishing, and keeping us on track for all the timelines. The authors finally thank Robert Elliott for all his support of this book, from initial proposal to final completion.

CONTENTS

PART IV: APPENDIX

INTRODUCTION

SELF-SERVICE BUSINESS INTELLIGENCE (BI) is hot! Companies are scrambling to provide easier-to-use tools to bring the benefits of BI to analysts and business decision makers at all levels of organizations. PowerPivot is Microsoft's entry into this fast-growing market.

Built on top of Microsoft's popular Office suite, PowerPivot extends Excel and SharePoint to create a self-service BI system that allows creation of applications inside Excel 2010, a server-side component that enhances SharePoint 2010 with the capability to share those applications across the organization, update them with the latest data, and monitor how people are using them.

This book describes all aspects of PowerPivot and shows you how to use each of its major features. It also provides insight into the design and development of this innovative product. By the time you are finished with this book, you will be well on your way to becoming a PowerPivot expert.

WHO THIS BOOK IS FOR

This book is for people who want to learn about PowerPivot end to end. You should have some rudimentary knowledge of databases and data analysis. Familiarity with Microsoft Excel and Microsoft SharePoint is helpful, since PowerPivot builds on those two products.

Part I of the book is for those who want an introduction to PowerPivot. It provides background on self-service BI and how PowerPivot fits into the picture. It also includes a quick end-to-end walk-through of the major features in PowerPivot for those who want to get their feet wet.

Part II is for those who want to understand the client half of PowerPivot — PowerPivot for Excel. This includes Excel power users who work with PivotTables day in and day out, and are curious about the additional capabilities PowerPivot can provide to them, as well as BI professionals who want to understand the details of what PowerPivot is and what you can do with it. If you are a business analyst, this section will be particularly relevant for you.

Part III of the book is for those who want to learn about the server side of PowerPivot. This includes IT professionals who want to learn about how to plan for, deploy, and maintain PowerPivot's server infrastructure. Since PowerPivot builds on SharePoint, SharePoint administrators who are responsible for adding PowerPivot to their SharePoint farm will find a wealth of information in this section of the book.

WHAT THIS BOOK COVERS

This book covers the first version of PowerPivot, which ships with SQL Server 2008 R2 and enhances Microsoft Office 2010. It provides an overview of PowerPivot and a detailed look at its two components: PowerPivot for Excel and PowerPivot for SharePoint. It explains the technologies that make up these two components, and gives some insight into why these components were implemented the way they were. Through an extended example, it shows how to build a PowerPivot application from end to end.

HOW THIS BOOK IS STRUCTURED

After discussing self-service BI and the motivation for creating PowerPivot, we present a quick, end-to-end tutorial showing how to create and publish a simple PowerPivot application. We then drill into the features of PowerPivot for Excel in detail and, in the process, build a more complex PowerPivot application based on a real-world case study. Finally, we discuss the server side of PowerPivot (PowerPivot for SharePoint) and provide detailed information about its installation and maintenance.

Chapter 1, "Self-Service Business Intelligence and Microsoft PowerPivot," begins Part I of the book. This chapter describes self-service BI and introduces PowerPivot, Microsoft's first self-service BI tool. It provides a high-level look at the two components that make up PowerPivot — PowerPivot for Excel and PowerPivot for SharePoint.

Chapter 2, "A First Look at PowerPivot," walks you through a simple example of creating a PowerPivot application from end to end. In the process, it shows how to set up the two components of PowerPivot (PowerPivot for Excel and PowerPivot for SharePoint), and describes the normal workflow of creating a simple PowerPivot application.

Chapter 3, "Assembling Data," starts off Part II of the book, and explains how to bring data into PowerPivot from various external data sources. It also introduces the extended example that you will build in this and subsequent chapters.

Chapter 4, "Enriching Data," shows how to enhance the data you brought into your application by creating relationships and using PowerPivot's expression language, Data Analysis eXpressions (DAX).

Chapter 5, "Self-Service Analysis," describes how to use your PowerPivot data with various Excel features, such as PivotTables, PivotCharts, and slicers to do analysis. Chapter 5 also delves further into DAX, showing how to create and use DAX measures.

Chapter 6, "Self-Service Reporting," shows how to publish your PowerPivot workbook to the server side of PowerPivot (PowerPivot for SharePoint), and make use of its features to view and update PowerPivot reports. It also shows how to use the data in a PowerPivot workbook as a data source for reports created in other tools such as Report Builder 3.0 and Excel.

Chapter 7, "Preparing for SharePoint 2010," is the first chapter in Part III of the book. It describes the components of SharePoint 2010 that are relevant for PowerPivot, and looks at how PowerPivot for SharePoint interacts with those components.

Chapter 8, "PowerPivot for SharePoint Setup and Configuration," provides instructions on how to set up and configure a multi-machine SharePoint farm that contains PowerPivot for SharePoint.

Chapter 9, "Troubleshooting, Monitoring, and Securing PowerPivot Services," gives tips on how to troubleshoot PowerPivot for SharePoint issues. It also shows how to monitor the health of your PowerPivot for SharePoint environment, and discusses relevant security issues.

Chapter 10, "Diving into the PowerPivot Architecture," describes at a deeper level the architecture of PowerPivot, both for client and server. It also explains the Windows Identity Foundation and discusses the use of Kerberos in the context of PowerPivot for SharePoint.

Chapter 11, "Enterprise Considerations," talks about common PowerPivot for SharePoint enterprise considerations: capacity planning, optimizing the environment, upgrade considerations, and uploading performance.

Appendix A provides instructions for setting up the data sources that are used to build the SDR Healthcare extended example in Chapters 3 through 6.

Additionally, one "bonus" element is available online at the book's companion Web site (see the later section, "Source Code"):

➤ Appendix B is a comprehensive DAX reference that describes all the DAX functions and provides code snippets that show how to use them. The content published in Appendix B has been provided by Microsoft.

WHAT YOU NEED TO USE THIS BOOK

To work through the examples in this book, you will need Microsoft Office Excel 2010 and Microsoft Office SharePoint 2010. You will also need PowerPivot for Excel (which is available as a free download) and PowerPivot for SharePoint (which is included in the Enterprise edition of Microsoft SQL Server 2008 R2). The Contoso BI Demo Database, available from the Microsoft Download Center, is needed for the Chapter 2 tutorial. Data that is needed for the extended BI Healthcare example is available on this book's www.wrox.com download site. Instructions for installing the data needed for the example are included in Appendix A.

CONVENTIONS

To help you get the most from the text and keep track of what's happening, we've used a number of conventions throughout the book.

Boxes with a warning icon like this one hold important, not-to-be-forgotten information that is directly relevant to the surrounding text.

The pencil icon indicates notes, tips, hints, tricks, or asides to the current discussion.

As for styles in the text:

➤ We *highlight* new terms and important words when we introduce them.

➤ We show keyboard strokes like this: Ctrl+A.

➤ We show filenames, URLs, and code within the text like so: `persistence.properties`.

➤ We present code in two different ways:

```
We use a monofont type with no highlighting for most code examples.
We use bold to emphasize code that is particularly important in the present
     context or to show changes from a previous code snippet.
```

SOURCE CODE

As you work through the examples in this book, you may choose either to type in all the code manually, or to use the source code files that accompany the book. All the source code used in this book is available for download at `http://www.wrox.com`. When at the site, simply locate the book's title (use the Search box or one of the title lists) and click the Download Code link on the book's detail page to obtain all the source code for the book. Code that is included on the Web site is highlighted by the following icon:

**Available for
download on
Wrox.com**

Listings include the filename in the title. If it is just a code snippet, you'll find the filename in a CodeNote such as this:

code snippet filename

 Because many books have similar titles, you may find it easiest to search by ISBN; this book's ISBN is 978-0-470-58737-9.

Once you download the code, just decompress it with your favorite compression tool. Alternately, you can go to the main Wrox code download page at `http://www.wrox.com/dynamic/books/download.aspx` to see the code available for this book and all other Wrox books.

ERRATA

We make every effort to ensure that there are no errors in the text or in the code. However, no one is perfect, and mistakes do occur. If you find an error in one of our books, like a spelling mistake or faulty piece of code, we would be very grateful for your feedback. By sending in errata, you may save another reader hours of frustration, and at the same time, you will be helping us provide even higher quality information.

To find the errata page for this book, go to `http://www.wrox.com` and locate the title using the Search box or one of the title lists. Then, on the book details page, click the Book Errata link. On this page, you can view all errata that has been submitted for this book and posted by Wrox editors. A complete book list, including links to each book's errata, is also available at `www.wrox.com/misc-pages/booklist.shtml`.

If you don't spot "your" error on the Book Errata page, go to `www.wrox.com/contact/techsupport.shtml` and complete the form there to send us the error you have found. We'll check the information and, if appropriate, post a message to the book's errata page and fix the problem in subsequent editions of the book.

P2P.WROX.COM

For author and peer discussion, join the P2P forums at `p2p.wrox.com`. The forums are a Web-based system for you to post messages relating to Wrox books and related technologies, and interact with other readers and technology users. The forums offer a subscription feature to email you topics of interest of your choosing when new posts are made to the forums. Wrox authors, editors, other industry experts, and your fellow readers are present on these forums.

At `http://p2p.wrox.com`, you will find a number of different forums that will help you, not only as you read this book, but also as you develop your own applications. To join the forums, just follow these steps:

1. Go to `p2p.wrox.com` and click the Register link.

2. Read the terms of use and click Agree.

3. Complete the required information to join, as well as any optional information you wish to provide, and click Submit.

4. You will receive an email with information describing how to verify your account and complete the joining process.

 You can read messages in the forums without joining P2P, but in order to post your own messages, you must join.

Once you join, you can post new messages and respond to messages other users post. You can read messages at any time on the Web. If you would like to have new messages from a particular forum emailed to you, click the "Subscribe to this Forum" icon by the forum name in the forum listing.

For more information about how to use the Wrox P2P, be sure to read the P2P FAQs for answers to questions about how the forum software works, as well as many common questions specific to P2P and Wrox books. To read the FAQs, click the FAQ link on any P2P page.

PART I
Introduction

1

Self-Service Business Intelligence and Microsoft PowerPivot

WHAT'S IN THIS CHAPTER?

➤ Reviewing SQL Server 2008 R2

➤ Understanding Self-Service Business Intelligence

➤ Getting to know PowerPivot

➤ Taking a look at PowerPivot applications

➤ Taking a look at PowerPivot for Excel

➤ Taking a look at PowerPivot for SharePoint

➤ Taking a look at the VertiPaq engine

PowerPivot is Microsoft's entry into the self-service business intelligence (BI) arena. PowerPivot was built with specific goals in mind, and this chapter will explain some of those goals. PowerPivot was also specifically designed not to address certain goals, and this chapter will also discuss those decisions as well. Some dependencies PowerPivot had on other groups and technologies (specifically, Microsoft Office, especially Excel and SharePoint) led to how it was designed and built. This chapter will explore those goals, dependencies, and decisions.

By the end of this chapter you will have a clear idea of the "what and why" of PowerPivot. Subsequent chapters will go into much greater detail on how to work with PowerPivot, and describe its features with the goal of helping you become a professional PowerPivot user who can get the most out of this innovative product.

SQL SERVER 2008 R2

PowerPivot is included in the R2 release of SQL Server 2008. The "R2" in the name might give you the impression that this release of SQL Server is a minor update to SQL Server 2008. If you thought that, you would be wrong. The 2008 R2 release includes major new functionality, including the following:

➤ Application and Multi-server Management capabilities, which provide the ability to manage a data environment that includes many servers

➤ Stream Insight, which supports building applications that do high-volume, complex event processing

➤ Master Data Services, which helps organizations manage and standardize their enterprise data across applications and systems.

➤ PowerPivot, Microsoft's self-service BI offering, which is the subject of this book.

SQL Server 2008 R2 was designed to be a BI-centric release of SQL Server, with a particular focus on self-service BI.

SELF-SERVICE BUSINESS INTELLIGENCE

If you ask different people to define *self-service business intelligence* (or *self-service BI*), chances are you will get different answers, depending on who you ask. That's because self-service BI is a new BI paradigm that is still being defined and created. It has not been around long enough to be standardized in the way that other paradigms like relational databases or even traditional BI has. And yet, it is also not an approach that is starting completely from scratch.

Many of the concepts in self-service BI sprang from earlier BI principles and practices. This book refers to those earlier BI paradigms as "corporate BI." Self-service BI, then, is something new, but it's also based on some things that came before. To help explain the relationship between corporate BI and self-service BI, consider another technological advancement that is familiar to many people — the move from command-line interfaces (CLIs) to graphical user interfaces (GUIs) in computer operating systems.

Earlier personal computer operating systems (such as MS-DOS) provided a very simple interface to users: the command line. This interface was text-based, as opposed to graphics-based, and allowed you to type in one line at a time. The response you got back was a single line of text, and perhaps a change in the state of the system that wasn't visible to you (the command-line user).

There were, of course, ways to get more friendly and capable applications on those operating systems, but in order to do it, you had to build everything yourself. The operating system didn't provide standardized components like graphical controls, easy-to-use interfaces to the file system, or a common way to talk to devices like printers. In that world, mere mortals (those without detailed computer knowledge and low-level programming skills) would need custom applications built for them in order to work with computers.

Back then, as you can imagine, the majority of people did not see the computer as an integral part of the way they did their jobs. People who could build the custom applications needed to make computers a part of the way people did their work were few and far between. Since you had to build all the functionality your application needed, applications took a long time to build. Even if you had an idea of how a computer application could help you do your job, unless you had the money to hire someone to build it, or had that highly specialized knowledge of how to implement it yourself, you wouldn't be able to realize your idea of a computer application that could help you do your job.

With the emergence of GUIs, operating systems provided a much richer set of common functionality that applications could make use of without having to implement all the low-level details themselves. For example, instead of having to write your own printer drivers for every printer you wanted to support in your application, you could simply rely on the printer drivers that were provided by the operating system. When coupled with new application-creation tools (such as Visual Basic), that allowed more people with less detailed knowledge and skill to build the applications that people wanted and needed in order to get their jobs done. Then you had the ingredients necessary to make computers an integral part of more and more people's daily lives. Many more people than before could realize the ideas they had about how computers could help them do their work.

GUIs, and the operating systems that supported them, were a completely new paradigm of how people interacted with computers. And yet, underneath were many of the same components that were there before GUIs came on the scene. They extended, augmented, and standardized what came before and allowed much greater capability for a larger variety of people than their predecessor, the command-line-based operating system.

Self-service BI aims to effect the same sort of paradigm shift in the BI world that modern operating systems did for general computer users. Here is what the state of BI looked like before the self-service concept:

➤ In order to build BI applications, you had to be a BI developer with highly specialized skills, or have enough money (or clout) to hire one. BI applications were generally custom-built.

➤ Once your BI application was built and deployed, it could be difficult to change in response to a change in the business situation or customer requirements.

➤ If you worked in the data center and were responsible for BI applications, chances were that you had to maintain every application in a separate way. Each one may have had its own special requirements for deployment, maintenance, backup, and so on.

➤ If you were an analyst needing to use data to make your business decisions but were not able to build the BI application you needed, you might have cobbled together data from various sources in an ad-hoc way in order to do your analysis. You probably used spreadsheets to do this. Once you did, your application and its data moved out of the realm of the corporate BI systems and into the wild and wooly world of desktop and laptop systems.

➤ As a result, your analytical data might have become disconnected from its source and, as a result, outdated as the source data changed. Refreshing your data, when it was possible, could be difficult and time-consuming.

➤ Since your data now lived in a spreadsheet file, when you shared it, you lost explicit control over it. If all or part of the data was confidential, you couldn't prevent those you shared it with from sharing it with unauthorized people.

Contrast that situation with Microsoft's vision of self-service BI, which it calls "managed self-service business intelligence," as implemented in PowerPivot:

➤ Anyone can easily build his or her own self-service BI applications using tools that they already know, starting with Microsoft Office Excel.

➤ Self-service BI applications are easy to update and modify. This can be done by the person who built them, even if that person isn't a BI application developer.

➤ If you work in the data center and are responsible for deploying and managing self-service BI applications, you can manage all your published applications in a common way. You have the tools you need to track usage, administer security, and deploy new hardware in response to the needs of the system.

➤ Your analytical data remains connected to its source. Refreshing your application from source data is easy, and can even be done automatically by the system.

➤ You can easily share data, but in a controlled way. Customers of your application can access it over the Web (internal or external) without needing anything other than a Web browser.

Microsoft's previous tag line for its BI products was "business intelligence for the masses." With self-service BI, that tag line can now be expanded to "business intelligence for the masses, by the masses." The Microsoft product that aims to make this possible is PowerPivot.

POWER PIVOT: MICROSOFT'S IMPLEMENTATION OF SELF-SERVICE BI

PowerPivot is made up of two separate components that work together:

➤ *PowerPivot for Excel* — PowerPivot for Excel is an Excel add-in that enhances the capabilities of Excel, enabling business analysts and Excel power users to create and edit PowerPivot applications.

➤ *PowerPivot for SharePoint* — PowerPivot for SharePoint extends Microsoft Office SharePoint Server to include the capabilities to share and manage the PowerPivot applications that are created with PowerPivot for Excel.

The next section describes what a PowerPivot application looks like.

PowerPivot Applications

At first glance, PowerPivot applications look just like Excel workbooks. And that they are, but they also include something more — PowerPivot data and metadata embedded in the workbook itself. This allows a PowerPivot-enhanced Excel workbook to contain much more functionality than can be contained in a regular Excel workbook that doesn't connect to external data sources. For example, PowerPivot workbooks can contain tables that are much bigger than Excel tables. Excel tables (in Office 2007 and beyond) can contain 1 million rows of data. PowerPivot tables inside an Excel workbook can contain tens or even hundreds of millions of rows of data, as shown at the bottom of Figure 1-1.

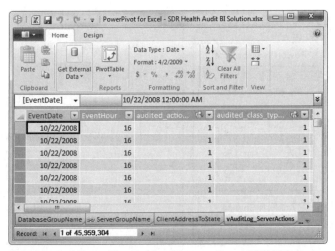

FIGURE 1-1: A PowerPivot table with more than 1,000,000 rows of data

The PowerPivot tables in the workbook make up the PowerPivot data mentioned previously. These tables can be joined together and then used as the source data for Excel PivotTables and PivotCharts, which can then be used for analysis and reporting.

PowerPivot applications can be shared among stakeholders, co-workers, management — anyone who wants to view or interact with them. To do this, you publish your PowerPivot workbook to Microsoft Office SharePoint Server. People can then browse and/or interact with your application using either the Excel client or a Web browser. You can also set up PowerPivot to automatically refresh your application from the source data either once or on a regular schedule.

To summarize, you can think of a PowerPivot application as an Excel workbook "on steroids." It gives you all the power of Excel, plus the greater analytical capability necessary to deliver true self-service BI.

Now, let's take a look at the two components that make PowerPivot applications possible.

PowerPivot for Excel

PowerPivot for Excel is the tool you use to create and edit PowerPivot applications. It supports integrating data from various external data sources, enriching that data with custom calculations and adding relationships between tables, as well as using that data to do analysis in Excel using features such as PivotTables and PivotCharts. PowerPivot for Excel is implemented as a managed Excel add-in that provides the user interface for working with PowerPivot data. Figure 1-2 shows the architecture of PowerPivot for Excel.

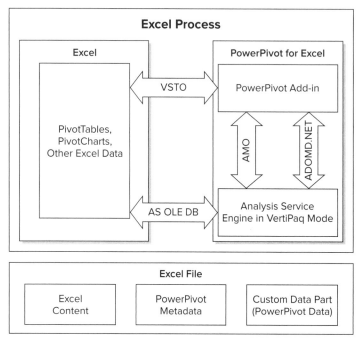

FIGURE 1-2: The architecture of PowerPivot for Excel

PowerPivot for Excel also includes the VertiPaq engine, a local, in-process version of the Analysis Services engine in VertiPaq mode (which is discussed later in this chapter). The PowerPivot for Excel add-in communicates with the VertiPaq engine via the traditional Analysis Services interfaces Analysis Management Objects (AMO) and ActiveX Data Objects Multi-Dimensional (ADOMD.NET). The add-in communicates with Excel via its object model using the Visual Studio Tools for Office (VSTO) managed interface. Excel communicates with the in-process VertiPaq engine via the Analysis Services OLEDB provider.

When you are working with PowerPivot for Excel, the PowerPivot data will reside in memory. But when you save your workbook, PowerPivot will store its data and metadata inside the Excel file, as shown in Figure 1-2. The in-memory database will be stored in a section of the file called the Custom Data Part (CDP). The writing of the CDP is done through a public interface that first appeared in Excel 2010. It allows applications to write and retrieve their own data inside an Excel file.

PowerPivot for Excel will also store metadata and workbook settings in XML streams inside the Excel file. This saved metadata allows PowerPivot to attempt to reconstruct a workbook's data model if the CDP data becomes corrupted. If the structure is successfully recovered, you may be able to refresh the workbook's external data, and recover the contents of the workbook.

PivotTables and PivotCharts are the main analytical tools in Excel. The PowerPivot add-in and VertiPaq engine work with Excel to provide you with the capability to use these tools to do your self-service BI analysis.

Microsoft wants to make it as easy as possible to get started with PowerPivot, so it is making this part of PowerPivot available as a free download on the Web. PowerPivot for Excel has the following prerequisites:

➤ *.NET 3.5 SP1* — Installation of this component is not needed on later operating systems like Windows 7, which includes it as part of the operating system itself. If you are installing on an older operating system such as Windows XP or Windows Vista, you will need to install .NET 3.5 SP1. Install this before installing Office 2010.

➤ *Excel 2010 + Office Shared Features* — PowerPivot for Excel requires Excel 2010. It will not install on earlier versions of Excel. Also, the architecture of PowerPivot for Excel must match the architecture of Excel itself. If you have 32-bit Excel installed, you must install the 32-bit version of PowerPivot for Excel. If you have 64-bit Excel installed, you must install the 64-bit version of PowerPivot for Excel.

When installing Office 2010, you must also install the Office Shared Features item along with Excel. This is because PowerPivot for Excel is a Visual Studio Tools for Office (VSTO) add-in and requires the VSTO run-time in order to work. Office Shared Features will install the VSTO run-time. If you install Excel without Office Shared Features, you will have to uninstall Excel and then re-install including Office Shared Features.

➤ *Platform Update for Windows Vista/Windows Server 2008* — PowerPivot for Excel requires this component if you are running on the Windows Vista or Windows Server 2008 operating systems. You can find more information about this prerequisite at `http://support.microsoft.com/kb/971644`.

Note that this component is installed via Windows Update. Also note that the Platform Update for Windows Vista/Windows Server 2008 is an important, rather than a critical, update. If you have set up Windows Update to only install critical updates, you may miss this.

➤ *Drivers for connecting to non-Microsoft data sources* — If you want to import data from data sources other than Microsoft data sources that are included with PowerPivot (such as Oracle, Teradata, or DB2), you must acquire and install those drivers and any related client components yourself. They are not included with PowerPivot for Excel. Importing data and more details on the data sources that are supported by PowerPivot will be covered in Chapter 3.

Note that there are also operating system requirements, as shown in Table 1-1.

TABLE 1-1: PowerPivot Operating System Requirements

OPERATING SYSTEM	REQUIREMENT
Windows XP	SP3 or greater, 32-bit only
Windows Server 2003 R2	32-bit or on WOW64 mode on 64-bit only
Windows Vista	SP2 or greater
Windows Server 2008	SP2 or greater
Windows 7	No special requirements
Windows Server 2008 R2	No special requirements

After you install the necessary prerequisites and PowerPivot for Excel, launch Excel. The first time you launch Excel after installing PowerPivot for Excel, you will see a dialog asking for confirmation that you want to install the add-in. Accept this dialog, and PowerPivot for Excel will load. You will notice that the Excel toolbar now has one new tab called PowerPivot, as shown in Figure 1-3. This tab is your entry point into PowerPivot for Excel.

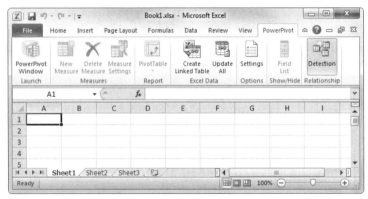

FIGURE 1-3: The PowerPivot tab in the Excel ribbon

If you click the PowerPivot Window button on the left side of the ribbon, the PowerPivot Window appears, as shown in Figure 1-4.

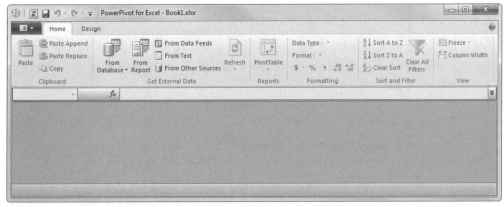

FIGURE 1-4: The PowerPivot Window

This is where you will import and work with analytical data in your PowerPivot application. You can think of the PowerPivot Window as the window into the PowerPivot data that is stored inside the workbook. Here is where you launch the import wizard, the tool that lets you import data from various data sources. These data sources include the following:

➤ Various relational data sources

➤ Data from Analysis Services and other PowerPivot workbooks

➤ File-based data from Microsoft Access, Microsoft Excel, and delimited text files

➤ Data feeds, which are syndicated sources of data that can be updated in a manner similar to RSS or Atom, including SharePoint 2010 lists and SQL Server Reporting Services reports (from SQL Server 2008 R2 and beyond)

You can also paste data from the Windows clipboard into a PowerPivot table if the contents of the clipboard are recognized by PowerPivot as tabular data. In addition, PowerPivot has the capability to create a PowerPivot table whose source data is a table in the Excel workbook. These two tables are linked such that if the Excel table is updated, the PowerPivot table will be updated as well, and the data will match. Chapter 3 goes into greater detail on all these methods of bringing data into PowerPivot.

As shown in Figure 1-2 earlier in this chapter, data imported into a PowerPivot workbook is stored inside the workbook itself. PowerPivot is capable of doing this because of a new feature in Excel 2010 that allows external applications (like Excel add-ins) to store custom data inside the Excel workbook. This is one of several reasons that PowerPivot requires Office 2010. (See the sidebar "Why PowerPivot Requires Office 2010.")

WHY POWERPIVOT REQUIRES OFFICE 2010

When the PowerPivot team made the decision to require Office 2010, influencing that decision were the features that were new to the 2010 release. These include the following:

➤ *The capability to embed custom data inside an Excel 2010 workbook file* — This allows PowerPivot data to be included in the PowerPivot workbook.

➤ *Slicers* — Slicers are a new type of control in Excel 2010. These controls make it much easier to filter analytical data in PivotTables and PivotCharts than in previous versions of Excel. PowerPivot for Excel includes enhancements to slicers over and above what is available in Excel without PowerPivot. Later chapters will examine this PowerPivot feature in more detail.

➤ *The Shared Service support in SharePoint 2010* — SharePoint 2010 has defined extensibility points that allow third-party applications to plug into the SharePoint infrastructure in a well-defined way that wasn't available in previous versions of SharePoint. In essence, they allow third-party applications to integrate with SharePoint in a way that is similar to the way Excel Services or SharePoint Search are integrated into SharePoint.

Another aspect of Office 2010 that PowerPivot benefits from is the availability of a 64-bit version. Since PowerPivot works with its data in-memory rather than from disk as in previous versions of Analysis Services (this aspect of PowerPivot is also examined in this chapter), the increased memory address space available to a 64-bit application is a real benefit when your analysis data gets large.

The PowerPivot team understood that requiring Office 2010 was a trade-off, and could limit (in some cases) the adoption of PowerPivot, but the team's eyes were on the future and on the increased capabilities that the latest version of Office enabled. The vision they had for PowerPivot required this.

After data is imported into PowerPivot, it appears in the PowerPivot Window as tables. Figure 1-5 shows the PowerPivot Window after a number of tables have been imported.

Tables in the PowerPivot Window appear similar to worksheets in an Excel workbook, but there is a difference. The table grid in the PowerPivot Window will only show the cells that include data. Also, every table gets its own sheet. In PowerPivot, the basic unit you work with is the table.

Another difference between PowerPivot data and data in Excel spreadsheets is that you can define relationships between tables. This allows much more powerful analysis than is possible in Excel worksheets using VLOOKUP. Relationships in PowerPivot and how to work with them will be discussed in Chapter 4, which will show how to work with PowerPivot data to build your self-service BI applications.

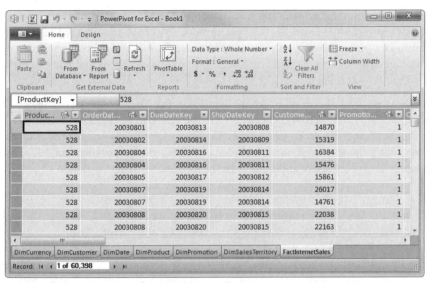

FIGURE 1-5: The PowerPivot Window with multiple tables imported

Yet another difference between PowerPivot and Excel is the sheer amount of data that can be included in a single table. In later versions of Excel, the number of columns and rows that can be included in a table was increased greatly to be able to have worksheets with up to 1 million rows of data. While this may seem like a lot, in the BI world, a table with 1 million rows of data is considered small or medium-sized. PowerPivot allows you to have tables that include tens or even hundreds of millions of rows of data.

Because PowerPivot is a part of Excel, and PowerPivot workbooks are Excel workbooks, you can leverage all the capabilities of Excel itself to do your analysis and reporting. Features such as PivotTables, PivotCharts, named sets, conditional formatting, and others are all available as you work with PowerPivot data.

Once you've built your PowerPivot application and you're happy with the capabilities it gives you to analyze your data and present it in an insightful way, you probably will want to share it with others. You now move into the realm of the other major component of PowerPivot — PowerPivot for SharePoint.

PowerPivot for SharePoint

PowerPivot for SharePoint installs on top of SharePoint 2010, and adds services and functionality to SharePoint to make PowerPivot workbooks first-class citizens of the SharePoint system. If you think of PowerPivot for Excel as the tool for creating and editing PowerPivot applications, PowerPivot for SharePoint is the tool that allows collaboration, sharing, and reporting. In addition, in conjunction with Excel Services, PowerPivot for SharePoint provides a "thin-client" capability for PowerPivot applications.

Because of the nature of SharePoint itself, installing PowerPivot for SharePoint is significantly more complex than installing PowerPivot for Excel. Hence, this introductory chapter won't spend time going into the details of PowerPivot for SharePoint installation. Those details will be presented in Chapter 8. For now, let's take a high-level look at the parts of PowerPivot for SharePoint so that you can get an idea of what it looks like and what it does.

PowerPivot for SharePoint consists of two main components that give SharePoint the capability of hosting PowerPivot applications. These two components are the *PowerPivot System Service* (the *PowerPivot Service* for short) and the *Analysis Services Service in VertiPaq mode* (or the *Analysis Services Service*). PowerPivot for SharePoint also includes a Web Service component that allows applications to connect to PowerPivot workbook data from outside the farm.

 In the following discussions, remember that references to the Analysis Services Service are actually references to Analysis Services in VertiPaq mode.

Figure 1-6 shows an overview of the components that make up the PowerPivot for SharePoint system.

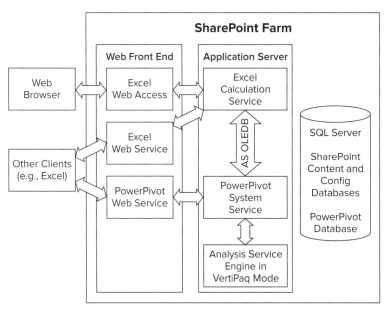

FIGURE 1-6: The components of PowerPivot for SharePoint

On the backend, PowerPivot for SharePoint includes one or more instances of the Analysis Services Service. These service instances are analogous to the traditional Analysis Services servers that you may be familiar with from previous versions of Analysis Services. Unlike those previous versions of Analysis Services, however, these services are under the control of the PowerPivot System Service. The PowerPivot System Service mediates the requests to load and work with the data in PowerPivot workbooks.

PowerPivot for SharePoint will load balance those requests among a pool of one or more Analysis Services Servers. If more requests come in than there are servers that can handle them, PowerPivot for SharePoint will unload the oldest unused workbooks in favor of the newest requests. You'll learn more about the VertiPaq mode of the Analysis Services engine later in this chapter.

When PowerPivot for SharePoint loads a workbook, it opens the workbook file (which, you will remember, contains the PowerPivot data store), extracts the PowerPivot data from the file, and sends it to an Analysis Services server that loads it as an in-memory analytical database. It also hooks up that server instance as an external data source to the corresponding published workbook. PowerPivot for SharePoint is smart about this. If more than one user requested a read-only copy of the same workbook, only one copy will be loaded, and the multiple workbooks will get connected to that single instance. This is just one of the ways that PowerPivot for SharePoint provides scalability for your self-service BI applications.

Note also, as shown in Figure 1-6, PowerPivot will create a database on the SharePoint farm's SQL Server to store various state information that must be queried from the different instances of the PowerPivot services.

PowerPivot for SharePoint also provides automatic data refresh from the source data of the workbook. Workbook owners can schedule this data refresh to happen at a periodic interval, or invoke a one-time refresh. When the time arrives to refresh the workbook, PowerPivot will load the data and tell the back-end server to reprocess it with the latest version of the source data. Once the data refresh is done, the workbook will be saved so that the next time a user asks for the workbook, it will contain up-to-date data. Figure 1-7 shows the Web page that allows scheduling of automatic data refresh.

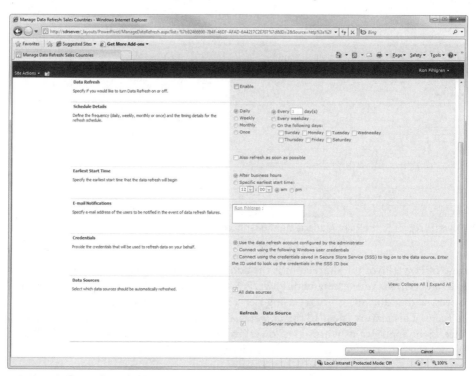

FIGURE 1-7: PowerPivot for SharePoint data refresh schedule page

As you may have guessed by now, PowerPivot for SharePoint has a lot of moving parts. A goal of the PowerPivot team was to make the management of the server side of PowerPivot easy. To do that, PowerPivot for SharePoint does extensive logging to SharePoint's Unified Logging Services (ULS) log. Becoming proficient at understanding ULS logs will give you a leg up on successfully managing and administering PowerPivot for SharePoint. Chapter 9 provides more detail on this.

The management dashboard is another feature of PowerPivot for SharePoint that helps in application management. The example shown in Figure 1-8 is a PowerPivot workbook that imports data from PowerPivot's usage database. It provides a helpful dashboard that gives the SharePoint administrators responsible for the server side of PowerPivot the capability to understand usage patterns of the PowerPivot applications that live in their SharePoint farm and to take appropriate action. High usage of a particular application, for example, may indicate that it is ready to be built out into a full-blown corporate BI application.

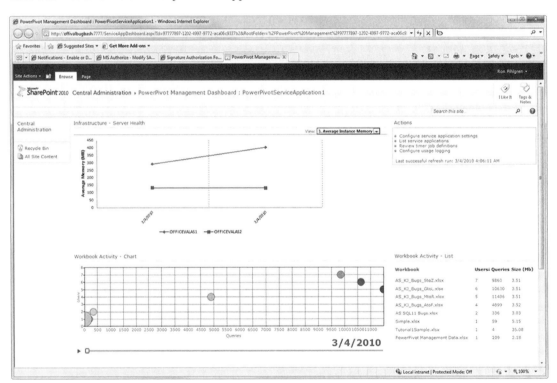

FIGURE 1-8: PowerPivot for SharePoint Management dashboard

Another feature of PowerPivot for SharePoint is the addition to SharePoint of a new type of document library designed to make working with PowerPivot applications pleasant. This includes the capability to browse that document library using rich views of the PowerPivot applications contained within them. This feature is called the *PowerPivot Gallery*. Figure 1-9 shows the default display of PowerPivot applications within the PowerPivot Gallery. Other views are also available. Figure 1-10 shows the carousel view of that same gallery.

CORPORATE BI AFTER POWERPIVOT

What happens to corporate business intelligence (corporate BI) after PowerPivot? The short answer is, "not much will change." PowerPivot was not designed to replace corporate BI. It was designed to add to it and bring the power of BI to people who don't have it today. It augments rather than replaces previous BI tools and techniques.

Analysis Services, SQL Server Management Studio, and BI Development Studio don't go away with the introduction of PowerPivot. Although the focus in this R2 release of SQL Server 2008 is on PowerPivot and self-service BI, future releases of SQL Server will add features that increase the usefulness and capability of the corporate BI side of the house.

There are capabilities corporate BI has that PowerPivot doesn't. For example, certain types of dimensions (such as parent/child dimensions) and certain features (such as writeback) are not available in PowerPivot applications. Furthermore, because of limitations in version one of PowerPivot, Workbooks cannot exceed 2 GB in size. Corporate BI databases in Analysis Services can be multiple terabytes in size.

It's important to realize these limitations of PowerPivot so that you don't try to use it in a way that it wasn't intended to be used and won't work. Understand the capabilities of each of the tools, and pick the right tool for the job.

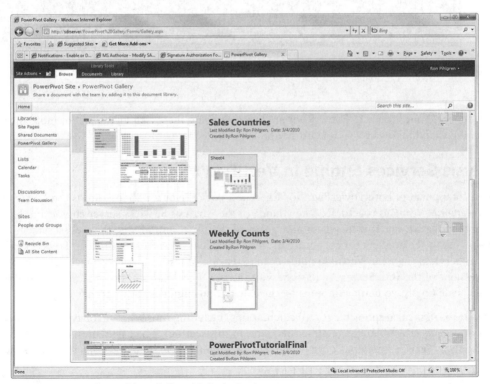

FIGURE 1-9: The PowerPivot Gallery (default view)

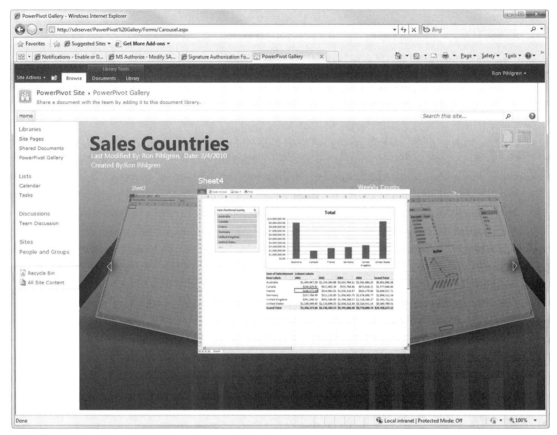

FIGURE 1-10: The PowerPivot Gallery (carousel view)

Being able to view your library of PowerPivot applications using these rich views is a lot more inviting and helpful than looking at a simple list of application filenames.

The Analysis Services Engine in VertiPaq Mode

A common component of both PowerPivot for Excel and PowerPivot for SharePoint is the *VertiPaq in-memory engine*. VertiPaq is actually a new mode of the Analysis Services server engine and has a number of innovative new features. It should be noted that, in a similar way that self-service BI is an extension (not a replacement) of corporate BI (see the sidebar, "Corporate BI After PowerPivot"), the Analysis Services engine in VertiPaq mode is an extension of (rather than a replacement for) the previous versions of the SQL Server Analysis Services server. The Analysis Services engine is still (as in the past) made up of two main components: the calculation engine and the storage engine.

The *calculation engine* is responsible for all calculations, including those that involve the new *data analysis expressions* (DAX) language (described later in this section). The calculation engine also supports Analysis Service's previous query language, *Multidimensional Expressions* (MDX). This allows traditional Analysis Services client applications (such as Excel) to work without modification against PowerPivot data. A third query language that the calculation engine supports is tabular queries, which it uses to talk to relational databases.

The *storage engine* component of the Analysis Services engine is responsible for the importing of data from external data sources, as well as the efficient storage and retrieval of data in response to requests from the calculation engine.

The key difference between the traditional mode of the Analysis Services server (called the *Multidimensional Online Analytical Processing,* or *MOLAP*, mode) and the new VertiPaq mode is where the data is stored when it is operated on.

In MOLAP mode, the data is stored on disk. This is the traditional mode of most typical database engines. It made sense that this was the only mode of storage when RAM was expensive and disk storage was relatively cheap. Relying on the normal amount of RAM in a typical system to hold all the data in large databases wasn't feasible in those days, especially for analytical data, where analysis is usually based on calculations against very large data sets.

In today's world, this is starting to not be the case. RAM in large quantities has become very cheap relative to where it was even just a few years ago. Now, having enough RAM to store large quantities of data in typical machines is much more feasible. When you can consider doing this, different capabilities become available. First, accessing data from RAM is much faster (orders of magnitude faster) than accessing data from disk. This allows higher performance when working with data than was possible before.

In the BI world, performance is king. Being able to interact with your data (that is, slicing and dicing in real time as ideas flow and questions about the data form) is a big part of the power of BI. Because of this, disk-based BI servers would do things like pre-aggregate data in anticipation of the way analysts would want to slice and dice it. If calculations could be done fast enough, though, having to do all that pre-aggregation with its attendant processing and storage requirements would not be necessary. This is one of the big advantages of an engine that works with data in-memory.

Although RAM has become much cheaper and more plentiful, it is still more costly than disk storage. It's not totally free! And there is a limit on the amount of RAM that systems can have. Clearly, you still must be cognizant of the amount of RAM you need and optimize your usage of it. The VertiPaq engine still must make the most of the RAM that is available.

Because of this, the VertiPaq mode also includes patented compression technology that is made possible by implementing what is called a *column-oriented store.* This means that, unlike traditional database storage engines that store data by rows, Analysis Services in VertiPaq mode stores data by columns. This allows much more effective compression of tabular data. VertiPaq compression rates depend on the nature of the data stored, but rates greater than 10:1 are common.

Another goal of self-service BI is to provide the capability to make building analytical applications much simpler than building analytical applications using corporate BI tools. With that in mind, the VertiPaq engine implements the new DAX expression language that allows self-service BI practitioners to create calculations in a manner very close to working with Excel formulas.

There are a couple of things to keep in mind about DAX.

First, PowerPivot is in its first version. In order to ship the first version in a reasonable timeframe, not all the functionality that the team would have liked to include is implemented in this first version of the product. The team believes that it has made the right trade-offs in terms of useful functionality and shipping this version of the product. You can expect DAX to grow in functionality in future versions of PowerPivot.

Second, although DAX expressions are designed to be similar to Excel formulas, they are different in a fundamental way. DAX is not designed to operate on single cells of data. It is designed to work on groups of data (such as columns) simultaneously. This is key to the way that BI analysis is done. So, when you write a DAX expression for a calculated column of a table, that expression will apply to that entire column for every row in the table. You'll learn much more about DAX in later chapters of this book.

INSIDE POWERPIVOT

PowerPivot was born from two 2006 Think Week papers by Amir Netz, who was at that time the Microsoft Business Intelligence partner-level architect. (As of the writing of this book, Netz has been made a Microsoft Distinguished Engineer.)

Think Weeks were dedicated periods of time that Bill Gates, when he was head of Microsoft, would take to immerse himself in reading and thinking about new trends and concepts that could impact the future direction of Microsoft. Microsoft employees were encouraged to write papers that would be a part of Gates' Think Week reading. Compelling Think Week papers could lead to allocation of resources to make new products and technologies happen. In the case of the papers that led to PowerPivot, this was the case.

The first paper was about the concept of a BI "sandbox"—a product that would allow much easier BI application creation in a defined and controlled space that would include a relational database, a multidimensional database, and a report generator. Although some of what was in that paper changed as PowerPivot grew (for example, the initial thought was that Microsoft Access would be the PowerPivot client), many of the ideas remain, and are core to what PowerPivot is today.

The second Think Week paper proposed an in-memory BI engine that took advantage of the emerging trends in computer hardware (such as falling RAM prices and multi-core processors) that would allow such an in-memory engine to be both possible and practical. The capabilities that such an engine would make possible included some of the features in the previous paper.

Both papers were well-received and a small incubation team was formed to explore the possibility of building a product incorporating the ideas in the papers. At the time, the project was called the "Sandbox Project" after the title of the first of the Think Week papers. This incubation team spent the second half of the SQL Server 2008 product cycle putting together specifications, designs, and plans under the code name "Gemini." Toward the end of the 2008 product cycle, the go-ahead was given to turn the project into a product, and the rest is history.

SUMMARY

This chapter examined the attributes of self-service BI and Microsoft's vision for self-service BI. It discussed Microsoft's first version of its self-service BI product, PowerPivot. It described the components that make up PowerPivot, and discussed the features of each of those components. The goal of this introductory chapter was to whet your appetite to learn more about this great new capability of self-service BI being introduced in Microsoft SQL Server 2008 R2.

Chapter 2 walks you through an example of using PowerPivot from end to end. This will give you a solid grounding in the entire PowerPivot product and prepare you for digging into greater detail in subsequent chapters.

2

A First Look at PowerPivot

WHAT'S IN THIS CHAPTER?

➤ Setting up and installing PowerPivot for Excel

➤ Using the `Contoso` sample database

➤ Importing data

➤ Enriching data

➤ Creating PivotTables/PivotCharts

➤ Setting up and installing PowerPivot for SharePoint

➤ Sharing PowerPivot workbooks

➤ Viewing workbooks in PowerPivot Gallery

In Chapter 1, you learned about the evolution of business intelligence (BI) and the shift to self-service analytics. Microsoft PowerPivot helps you to perform self-service analytics for the information producer and the information consumer. At the same time, PowerPivot provides the essentials for your IT department administrators to monitor and plan for enhancing the infrastructure based on usage.

As you learned in Chapter 1, PowerPivot contains two main components — an add-in for Excel 2010 (which helps you to work with Excel workbooks and components that integrate with Microsoft Office) and enhancements to SharePoint Server 2010 (which help you to view/analyze data in the PowerPivot workbooks efficiently, as well as monitor the usage of workbooks). As mentioned in Chapter 1, in this chapter and subsequent chapters, the PowerPivot add-in for Excel 2010 will be called PowerPivot for Excel, and the component integrating with SharePoint Server 2010 will be called PowerPivot for SharePoint.

This chapter first familiarizes you with Power Pivot for Excel and some of its key features by work-ing through a tutorial based on a sample relational database for SQL Server Analysis Services 2008 R2. The sample database is the new `Contoso` BI Demo database, and it can be downloaded from `http://www.microsoft.com/downloads/details.aspx?displaylang=en&FamilyID=868662dc-187a-4a85-b611-b7df7dc909fc`. This tutorial covers key features in PowerPivot for Excel, finally ending at creating a PowerPivot workbook that analyzes the data. As part of the tutorial, you will learn Data Analysis Expressions (DAX) that will help you create custom calculations on data you have imported into PowerPivot.

Once you have created the workbook with PowerPivot data, you would definitely want to share this with your co-workers/boss to show the cool report within Excel you have created. This chap-ter shows you how to share the workbook using SharePoint. You will learn about PowerPivot for SharePoint as part of this tutorial. PowerPivot for SharePoint helps you view, manage, and refresh PowerPivot workbooks efficiently.

By the end of this chapter, you will be familiar with PowerPivot for Excel and PowerPivot for SharePoint, the key components that constitute PowerPivot. You will see the creation of PowerPivot workbooks, along with simple DAX calculations that help in analyzing the data imported into PowerPivot.

POWERPIVOT FOR EXCEL

PowerPivot for Excel helps you integrate data from several data sources, create custom calculations, and create self-service BI applications via PowerPivot workbooks that can help you to analyze the data easily and efficiently. PowerPivot for Excel is a managed Excel add-in that is part of SQL Server 2008 R2 release. It is a free download from Microsoft, and can be downloaded from `http://www.microsoft.com/BI/`. PowerPivot for Excel has the capability of importing millions of rows of data and the capability to interactively work with them.

So, let's dive into a tutorial that shows you how to use PowerPivot to create a self-service BI application.

SETTING THE STAGE

As part of the PowerPivot and SQL Server Analysis Services 2008 R2, Microsoft provides a sam-ple database based on the (fictional) retail company called Contoso. You can download the sample relational database called `Contoso` from `http://www.microsoft.com/downloads/details.aspx?displaylang=en&FamilyID=868662dc-187a-4a85-b611-b7df7dc909fc`. Contoso is a global retail company selling various products in several countries via several stores. The company main-tains sales, inventory information for products, IT, and finance scenarios, as well as sales quota for each store.

In this tutorial, you import some of the tables from the `Contoso` database into Excel as Excel work-sheets to learn certain features of PowerPivot. As you follow the steps outlined here, you will build a self-service BI application designed for the executives of Contoso to compare their sales against their sales quota, as well as comparing inventory levels in various stores.

INSIDE POWERPIVOT

The walkthrough in this chapter uses a new sample database from Microsoft called the "Microsoft Contoso BI Demo Dataset for Retail Industry." As you see in this chapter's walkthrough, the tables in Contoso are quite a bit larger than previous sample databases from Microsoft. The FactOnlineSales table, for example, contains more than 12 million rows. This makes it ideal for showing how PowerPivot can work with large amounts of data; more than could be contained within an Excel worksheet.

This dataset contains both relational and multi-dimensional databases, and is designed to be larger and more comprehensive than the venerable AdventureWorks database that shipped alongside SQL Server 2005 and 2008, and is used in samples, tutorials, and demos far and wide. Unlike AdventureWorks, which was created by the SQL Server division, Contoso was created by the Office division. Also, unlike AdventureWorks, Contoso was designed exclusively to be a BI dataset. AdventureWorks was designed to be both an online transaction processing (OLTP) dataset and an online analytical processing (OLAP) dataset.

Early on in the development of Contoso, a program manager on the SQL Server Analysis Services team, Howie Dickerman, found out about the project. He began to work with the Contoso database in his early product demos, and provided a lot of feedback to the Contoso development team that really helped improve it as a dataset that could be used to demonstrate BI scenarios in general, and PowerPivot self-service BI scenarios in particular. This was one example of different teams at Microsoft working together to help make Office 14 and PowerPivot successful.

Setup and Installation

An important feature of Excel 2010 is support for the 64-bit processor architecture. You have the option to choose a 64-bit or a 32-bit install. If you will be working with large quantities of data, you should use the 64-bit version. If you install the 32-bit version of the product, you are limited to a maximum of 2 GB memory for Excel processes, and PowerPivot for Excel is also limited to a maximum of 2 GB memory.

To get started, follow these steps:

1. Install Excel 2010 from Office 2010 suite, along with the Office Shared Features. Installing Office Shared Features installs VSTO 4.0, which is needed as a prerequisite for PowerPivot for Excel. These install instructions are for the Windows 7 operating system. If you have an operating system other than Windows 7, you might need to install additional prerequisites before the PowerPivot for Excel install, as mentioned in Chapter 1.

2. Download and install PowerPivot for Excel, which is available at http://www.microsoft.com/bi/.

3. Install SQL Server from the SQL Server 2008 R2 release. Alternately, you can use an existing SQL Server 2008 instance.

4. Download the `Contoso` sample database `ContosoBIDemoBAK.exe` from `http://www` `.microsoft.com/downloads/details.aspx?displaylang=en&FamilyID=868662dc-` `187a-4a85-b611-b7df7dc909fc` and extract the `Contoso` relational backup file.

5. Connect to your SQL Server relational database server using SQL Server Management Studio and restore the `Contoso` retail sample database on your SQL Server instance.

6. Launch Excel 2010 from All Programs ➪ Microsoft Office ➪ Microsoft Excel 2010.

7. Open the `PowerPivotTutorial.xlsx` file provided with the Chapter 2 code download, which can be found on this book's companion web site at `www.wiley.com`. You will see two sheets in the workbook called `DimProductCategory` and `DimProductSubCategory`, which contain the data from the `Contoso` retail sample relational database. These have been included for this tutorial to demonstrate the copy/paste and linked tables features of PowerPivot, which you will learn about later in this chapter.

8. Switch to the PowerPivot tab in the Excel ribbon, as shown in Figure 2-1. From this PowerPivot tab, you can launch the PowerPivot Window. There are other commands in the PowerPivot tab that help you to build your BI application, which you will learn about in this chapter, as well as later in the book.

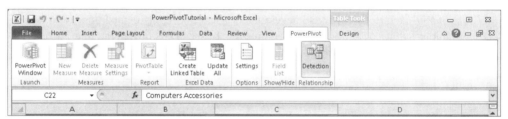

FIGURE 2-1 PowerPivot tab in Excel 2010

9. Click on the PowerPivot Window button and you will see the PowerPivot Window, as shown in Figure 2-2. The PowerPivot Window helps you with the key operations of importing data, filtering, and analyzing the data, as well as creating certain DAX calculations.

FIGURE 2-2 PowerPivot Window

Now that you have completed the setup and prerequisite steps, and have opened the sample tutorial spreadsheet with Contoso data, let's start to import and enhance the data. Let's build a self-service BI application for the Contoso company.

Importing Data

You can import data in several ways, including the following:

- ➤ From a relational database
- ➤ From SQL Server Analysis Services
- ➤ From Reporting Service reports
- ➤ From text files
- ➤ From a table in an Excel worksheet
- ➤ Pasting from the clipboard

Let's explore some of these in a bit more detail.

From a Relational Database

To import data from a relational database, follow these steps:

1. In the PowerPivot Window, click on the drop-down From Database button toward the left of the ribbon. Choose the From SQL Server option.

2. In the opening screen of the Table Import Wizard, specify the SQL Server instance name where you restored the `Contoso` relational database. Choose the `ContosoRetailDW` database name in the "Connect to a Microsoft SQL Server Database" dialog, as shown in Figure 2-3, and click Next.

FIGURE 2-3 Specifying the server and database name

3.   In the next dialog to appear, "Choose How to Import the Data," you are provided with two ways to import data: selecting from a list of tables and views, or specifying a query. In the former, PowerPivot retrieves the schema information from the data source and provides it as a list for you to select the tables and columns. In the latter, you can either enter the SQL query as a text, or design the SQL query using the query designer. Select the default value of "Select from a list of tables and views to choose the data to import" and click Next.

4.   In the next dialog, "Select Tables and Views," select the tables DimAccount, DimChannel, DimCurrency, DimCustomer, DimDate, DimEmployee, DimGeography, DimProduct, DimPromotion, DimSalesTerritory, DimStore, FactExchangeRate, FactInventory, FactSales, and FactSalesQuota.

5.   In the same dialog select the FactSales table and click on the "Preview & Filter" button. You will see the Preview Selected Table dialog for the FactSales table, as shown in Figure 2-4. This dialog provides you with a preview of the columns in the table (the first 50 rows). With the help of the drop-down arrows next to a column, you can apply a specific filter (such as seeing the sales for a specific date). This dialog shows the 50 rows for a filter chosen. In addition to applying filters to imported data, you can also de-select columns that you do not want to bring into PowerPivot. This dialog provides a preview of the data first and enables you to avoid importing data that is not needed for your analysis.

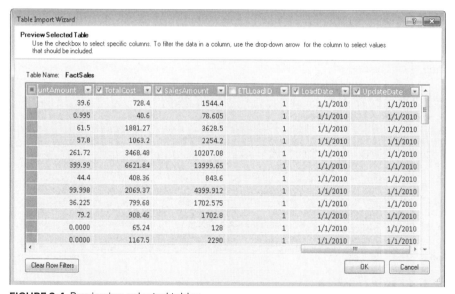

FIGURE 2-4 Previewing selected tables

6.   Uncheck the box next to ETLLoadID, which will not be used for analysis during this tutorial. Click OK.

7.   You will see the Filter Details column in the "Select Table and Views" dialog next to the FactSales row, which shows "Applied Filters." If you click on this, you will see the filters you have applied.

8. Click the Finish button.

After you click the Finish button, PowerPivot for Excel sends a command to the VertiPaq engine to create the PowerPivot data store (Analysis Services database), and to retrieve the data from the relational backend. The PowerPivot data will be used for further operations initiated by you in the PowerPivot Window, as well as from the PowerPivot tab in Excel.

You will see the progress of the import in the summary dialog. You will be able to see the total number of rows imported from each table. In addition to importing the tables, PowerPivot for Excel will also attempt to import the relationships between tables that are specified in the backend relational database. These relationships are also re-created within the Analysis Services in-memory database along with the import operation. You can see the relationships created by clicking on the Details link in the Data Preparation row of the summary dialog. In some cases, PowerPivot will not be able to import the relationship, and, in those cases, the dialog will indicate which relationships were not able to be successfully imported.

9. Click Close in the Import summary dialog.

You will see the PowerPivot Window now populated with all the tables that have been imported, as shown in Figure 2-5. Each table is shown in a separate tab, similar to Excel. Notice that the background color for all the tables is green.

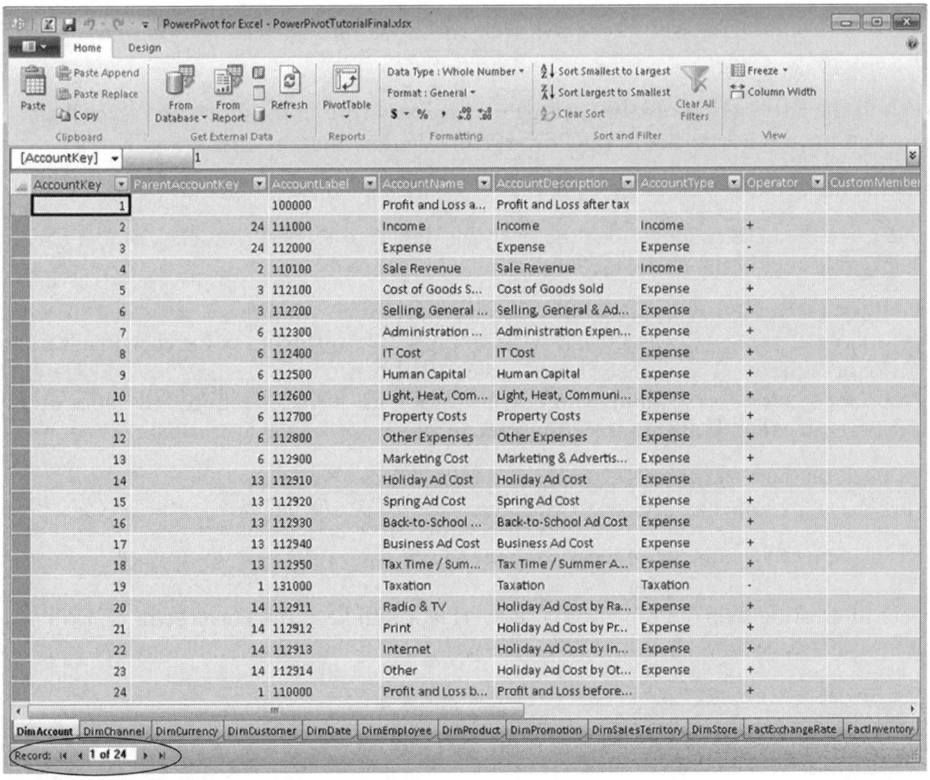

Selected row and total Rows in Table

FIGURE 2-5 PowerPivot Window with imported tables

Don't worry if you do not like the green background; you can change it. PowerPivot follows Excel's theme to choose an appropriate color scheme. You can change the color in the PowerPivot Window by changing the theme in the Page Layout tab in Excel. However, remember to close and re-launch your PowerPivot Window, since PowerPivot will update its colors on load.

Once you choose a specific table, you will see the various columns of the table. You can see the total number of rows in the table just beneath the table next to the word "Record," as shown in Figure 2-5. You will also see on which record the cursor is currently positioned. You can scroll through the various records of a table by using the vertical scroll bars, or by clicking the arrows next to Record, which can take you to the previous or next pages or to the top or end of the table, or by entering a specific row number.

Switch to the `FactSales` table that contains close to 4 million records and scroll to various rows. When you perform operations such as filtering or scrolling in the PowerPivot Window, PowerPivot for Excel sends special SQL-style queries to the VertiPaq engine. These queries are referred to as *tabular queries*. These queries were specifically designed to retrieve data efficiently from the VertiPaq engine to achieve results in seconds, even while operating on millions of rows of data. You will learn more about the queries sent from the PowerPivot Window in Chapter 4.

From a Linked Table

Let's bring the data from the two sheets in the Excel workbook into PowerPivot for analysis. To do so, follow these steps:

1. Switch to the Excel workbook by clicking on the Excel icon in the quick access toolbar, located on the top-left corner of the PowerPivot Window (next to the PowerPivot icon).

2. Select the `DimProductSubCategory` sheet.

3. To integrate the `DimProductSubCategory` table data into PowerPivot, click on the Create Linked Table icon in the PowerPivot tab.

   PowerPivot creates a new linked table with the source data from the `DimProductSubCategory` worksheet. After doing so, PowerPivot for Excel switches to the PowerPivot Window. You will see a new table called `Table_localhost_ContosoRetailDW_DimProductSubcategory`, along with a link symbol, as shown in Figure 2-6. Notice a new contextual tab called Linked Table now appears at the top of the PowerPivot Window.

4. Right-click on the table name `Table_localhost_ContosoRetailDW_DimProductSubcategory` and select Rename.

5. Enter the new table name **DimProductSubcategory**.

The key benefit of creating a linked table is that PowerPivot will keep the PowerPivot table in sync with the source Excel table automatically. You will learn more about linked tables in Chapter 3.

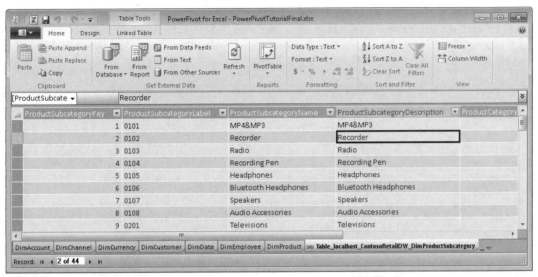

FIGURE 2-6 Linked table

Pasting from the Clipboard

Now, let's explore a way to create a PowerPivot table from data that has been pasted into the Windows clipboard. Follow these steps:

1. Switch to the Excel workbook by clicking on the Excel icon in the top-left corner of the PowerPivot Window.

2. Click on the `DimProductCategory` sheet.

3. Select the contents of the entire table. Right-click and select Copy to copy the contents to the clipboard.

4. Switch to the PowerPivot Window and click on the Paste button in the Home tab to create a new table.

5. In the Paste Preview dialog, enter the name of the table as **DimProductCategory** (as shown in Figure 2-7) and click OK.

The Paste button allows you to paste data from the clipboard into a new table. The data in the clipboard must be in table format, but can come from any application (such as the contents of a Web page). The Paste Preview dialog allows you to view the contents of the data to be imported as a new table, and you have the option to choose the first row as column header. Once you have copied and pasted the data into PowerPivot, PowerPivot will allow you to append data in an existing table that originally was created using the Paste operation.

You have now successfully assembled all the data to create a self-service BI application for Contoso into PowerPivot using three ways of bringing data into the PowerPivot data store — importing from a relational database, creating a linked Excel table, and using Paste from the clipboard. You are now ready to enrich the data in the PowerPivot Window.

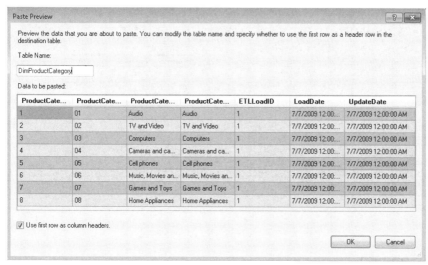

FIGURE 2-7 Pasting data in PowerPivot

Analyzing and Enriching Data

Let's explore some basic operations on tables using PowerPivot. Specifically, let's learn more about the following:

➤ Filtering and sorting

➤ Relationships

➤ Hide/Unhide

➤ Calculations

Filtering and Sorting

You were able to filter and analyze data while importing data from a relational database back-end. Once you have imported data into PowerPivot, you can filter and sort data in a table in the PowerPivot Window. This will help you to perform some analysis on your data.

For example, you can analyze the sales data by following these steps:

1. Switch to the `FactSales` table in the PowerPivot Window.

2. Click on the drop-down next to the `DateKey` column.

3. Click on the checkbox next to "Select All" item to deselect all dates.

4. Click the checkbox next to the date 9/27/2009 item, as shown in Figure 2-8, and then click the OK button.

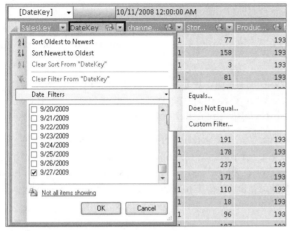

FIGURE 2-8 Filtering in PowerPivot

From Figure 2-8, you can see that the filter drop-down in the PowerPivot Window for a specific column allows you to invoke various filters. Since the DateKey is represented as a date column type, you see the options available for filtering dates — Equals and Does Not Equal — along with a Custom Filter option. Clicking on one of the options will launch the Custom Filter dialog, where you can choose the right filter option and enter the date value.

If you had a column represented as a whole number, you would see options for number filters similar to filter operations in Excel. If you had a string column, you would see Text Filters in the filter drop-down.

Once you have selected the 9/27/2009 item, you will immediately see that the table containing sales data has been filtered to 2,428 rows, and the operation occurred within a second. You can now view the maximum and minimum sales on that date by sorting the Sales Amount column. Follow these steps:

1. Select the column SalesAmount in FactSales table.

2. Click on the "Sort Largest to Smallest" button, as shown in Figure 2-9.

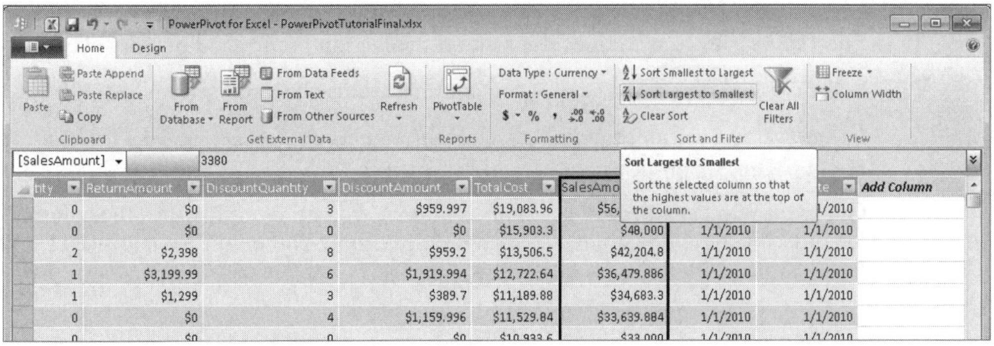

FIGURE 2-9 Sorting in PowerPivot

By scrolling through the rows in `FactSales` table, you can see that the maximum sales on the date 9/27/2009 was $56,639.82, while the minimum sales order was $19. The filtering and sorting operations you have just done are similar to what you would do in Excel. You didn't have to write a SQL query to your backend to perform these sorting/filtering operations. You can see that you are able to filter and sort a large table (such as `FactSales`) that contains close to 4 million rows of data, which cannot be accomplished in Excel. Additionally, you also saw that PowerPivot provides you the response within seconds.

You can move columns to a new position by simply dragging and dropping the column to the new location. Also, you can select a column (or a few columns) and click on Freeze to allow you to hold those columns in place while you scroll through the other columns.

After importing the data into PowerPivot, you can change the data type and formatting you want to view in the PowerPivot Window using the formatting options available in the Home tab. The Design tab allows additional operations that can be performed on a table, such as refreshing the data in the table, hiding, adding columns, or deleting columns. You can also establish relationships between various tables you have imported into PowerPivot.

Relationships

Creating the right relationships between tables helps you to analyze data between tables more accurately. PowerPivot for Excel supports *one-to-many* relationships. This essentially means that a column value in a specific table has multiple instances of the value in another table's related column.

For example, if you had a `Customer` table with `Country Name` as a column, and you had a `Country` table with `Country Name` as a column that is unique, then you would establish a one-to-many relationship between the two `Country Name` columns, where the country name in the `Customer` table forms the "many" side in the one-to-many relationship. Once the relationship is established, you could perform analysis such as counting the number of customers in a specific country.

Earlier, you learned that PowerPivot imports the relationships defined between tables in the relational backend at the time of the import. However, if there are no relationships in the relational backend, or if you have imported tables from different data sources, you should establish the right relationships between tables.

Earlier, you imported into PowerPivot data from the `DimProductSubCategory` and `DimProductCategory` tables from the Excel worksheets. Let's now establish the relationships in the PowerPivot Window. Follow these steps:

1. Select the `DimProduct` table and click on the Design tab in the PowerPivot Window ribbon.

2. Select the `ProductSubcategoryKey` column. Right-click and select Create Relationship.

3. In the Create Relationship dialog, select the `DimProductSubCategory` table in the Related Lookup Table drop-down, as shown in Figure 2-10.

   Once you select the `DimProductSubCategory`, PowerPivot identifies the column within the lookup table based on a name-matching algorithm. You might have noticed that PowerPivot automatically populated the `Related Lookup` column with `ProductSubCategoryKey`, which is the right column to be used for establishing the relationship.

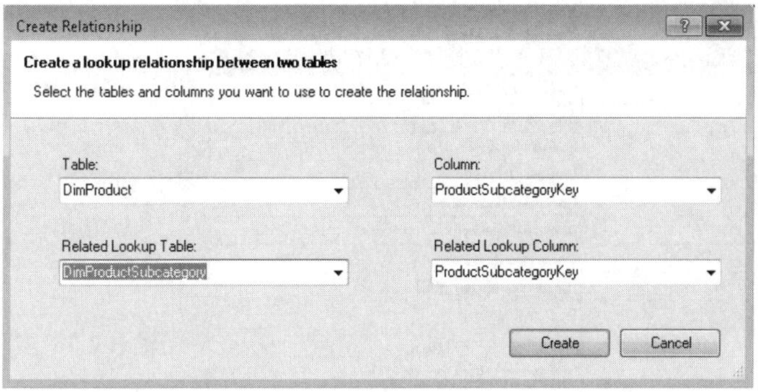

FIGURE 2-10 Create Relationship dialog

4. Click Create.

You can now see an icon next to the `ProductSubCategoryKey` column in the `DimProduct` table, indicating that a relationship has been established. In this release of PowerPivot for Excel, you can only use a column to participate in a single relationship, as well as only a single column in a relationship. Hence, if you must use multiple columns to establish a relationship, you must concatenate multiple columns using DAX. You will learn more about using multiple columns for relationships in Chapter 4.

If you right-click on the `ProductSubCategoryKey` column, you will see an option called "Navigate to Related Table." You will also notice that you cannot create any more relationships using the same column. If you select the "Navigate to Related Table" option, PowerPivot will switch the view to the related table, `DimProductSubCategory`, and the related table lookup column is selected.

Similar to creating the relationship between the `DimProduct` and `DimProductSubCategory` tables, you must create a relationship between the `DimProductSubCategory` and `DimProductCategory` tables. To do so, follow these steps:

1. Select `ProductCategoryKey` in the `DimProductSubCategory` table, right-click and select Create Relationship.

2. Select `DimProductCategory` as Related Lookup Table in the Create Relationship dialog and click Create.

3. Click on the Manage Relationships icon in the Design tab.

You can see the two relationships you created, along with all the relationships that have been imported in the Manage Relationships dialog, as shown in Figure 2-11. In this dialog, you can also create, modify, or delete relationships.

FIGURE 2-11 Manage Relationships dialog

4.   Click Close.

Let's move on to the hiding and unhiding of columns.

Hide/UnHide

Some of the columns that have been imported are not needed for analysis. For example, in the DimProduct table, the columns ImageURL, ProductURL, and ETLLoadID will not be used for analysis.

You can delete such columns from PowerPivot. However, if you have certain columns that you do not need at the present time, but might need for analysis in the future, you can hide them. Let's hide these columns by following these steps:

1.   Switch to the DimProduct table.

2.   Select the columns ImageURL, ProductURL, and ETLLoadID. You can select all the columns at the same time by holding the Shift key and selecting the three columns.

3.   Right-click and select Hide Columns ➪ "From PowerPivot and PivotTable."

You would typically build a PivotTable or PivotChart for analyzing data in an Excel spreadsheet, which you will learn about later in this chapter. Hence, you have the option of hiding columns in

PowerPivot, PivotTable, or both. Once you hide the columns, you will notice that the three columns are removed from view in the PowerPivot Window. You can click on the Hide and Unhide button to view columns that have been hidden or to modify the hidden state for any column in the current table.

Calculations

Similar to performing calculations within an Excel workbook, PowerPivot for Excel allows you to create calculated columns within the PowerPivot Window with the help of DAX. DAX provides you with a set of functions and operators that aid you in writing expressions for calculations on your PowerPivot data. DAX functions are grouped into seven major categories:

- ➤ Date and Time
- ➤ Math and Trig
- ➤ Statistical
- ➤ Text
- ➤ Logical
- ➤ Filter
- ➤ Time Intelligence

You will learn DAX in detail in Chapter 4. You will create a few DAX calculations in this section just to help you understand basic use of DAX.

In the `FactSales` table of the `Contoso` database, you have `SalesAmount` and `TotalCost` columns. If you want to calculate the profit, you would create an expression `Profit = SalesAmount - TotalCost`.

In Excel you can create this expression using the cells for corresponding columns of `TotalCost` and `SalesAmount`, and then copying the expression to each row. In PowerPivot, you can perform this calculation using a DAX expression, and the calculation is automatically applied to each row.

Follow these steps to create a calculated column called `Profit`:

1. In the PowerPivot Window, select the `FactSales` table.

2. Move to the last column in the table and click on the column `Add Column`.

3. In the expression window, enter **=** and select the column `SalesAmount` by using your mouse. You will see that PowerPivot has added the column name `FactSales[SalesAmount]`.

4. Enter the subtraction symbol - and then select the column `TotalCost` using your mouse. Press the Enter key.

You will see the full DAX expression to calculate `Profit` in the expression window. After you press the Enter key, PowerPivot calculates the profit for each row, and you will see the results in the new column. You can see that the profit calculation on about 4 million rows was quite fast. This provides you with an indication of the response time, even while working on large data sets. The column would be called `CalculatedColumn1`, as shown in Figure 2-12.

5. Right-click on the `CalculatedColumn1` column and select Rename Column.

6. Enter **Profit** as the name of the column.

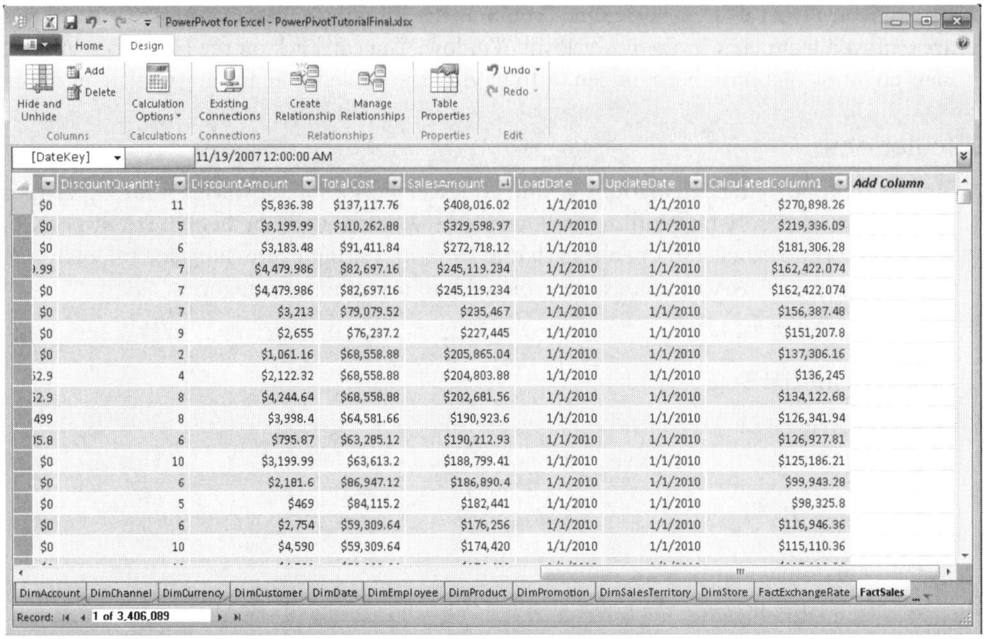

FIGURE 2-12 Calculated column

The next example using DAX performs calculations using columns from multiple tables that are related. Assume you want to understand the total sales of each product. Then, if you were a SQL expert, you would write a SQL query to join the tables and aggregate the data. In Excel, if you were to do this, you could use the VLOOKUP function. However, you would not be able to operate on a large dataset.

In PowerPivot, you can achieve this with a DAX expression, and then analyze which products are providing maximum revenue. Follow these steps:

1. Switch to the DimProduct table.

2. In the last column of the DimProduct table, enter the DAX expression **=SUMX(RELATEDTABLE (FACTSALES),FACTSALES[SALESAMOUNT])** and press Enter.

3. Right-click on the column and rename it to ProductTotalSales.

Now, let's take a closer look at the DAX expression you entered.

There is a one-to-many relationship between FactSales and DimProduct tables that was imported from the relational backend. You can view this relationship via the Manage Relationships dialog in the Design tab. The RELATEDTABLE function helps you get data from a table related to the current table that's being used. In this example, the DimProduct table is related to FactSales. Hence, the RELATEDTABLE function returns the data from the FactSales table.

Once all the data from FactSales data is returned, then the SUMX function is used to aggregate the data. The SUMX function needs a table as its first parameter and a column from that table for which the data needs to be aggregated. The SUMX function in this example aggregates the data in the SalesAmount column in the FactSales table for each row in the DimProduct table. Since each row corresponds to a specific product, PowerPivot (via the specified DAX expression) aggregates the SalesAmount for each product, based on the data in the FactSales table.

You can see the power of a DAX expression in this example, and how quickly you were able to get the sales data for each product. Now that you have the data, you can sort the column to identify the product that has the maximum sales and minimum sales. If you sort the column ProductTotalSales largest to smallest, you will see the product with product ID 552 has the maximum sales of $51,901,056.27, and the product with product ID 944 does not have any sales. From this, you can define a strategy on how to increase the sales of specific products.

Creating a PivotTable/PivotChart

So far, you have imported data, integrated data from Excel, defined relationships, created DAX calculations, and even analyzed some of the data in the PowerPivot Window. Now, if you want to share your analysis with your peers or key decision-makers, you probably want the information in a familiar form such as a PivotTable or PivotCharts.

Let's take a look at how to create a PivotTable/PivotChart for the sales and inventory of various products in an Excel sheet. PowerPivot provides you with various layout options to design your Excel worksheet for analysis. Follow these steps:

1. In the Home tab of the PowerPivot Window, click on PivotTable drop-down and select "Chart and Table (Horizontal)."

2. In the "Create PivotChart and PivotTable (Horizontal)" dialog that appears, select the radio button for the default New Worksheet and click OK.

You will now see a new worksheet called Sheet1 created with the layouts for a PivotTable and a PivotChart next to each other, as shown in Figure 2-13. If you were an information worker using Excel and analyzing data using PivotTables, you would notice that the field list is similar, with a few more drop zones.

In Figure 2-13, the areas called Slicer Vertical, Slicer Horizontal, Report Filter, Column Labels, Row Labels, and Values are called the *drop zones*. The PowerPivot field list resembles Excel's PivotTable field list and includes new drop zones called Slicer Vertical and Slicer Horizontal that enable you to add slicers to your report in Excel.

Slicers help you to filter and analyze the data effectively across PivotTables and PivotCharts connected to them. The tables from your PowerPivot Window are shown in the PowerPivot field list, with the first table in the list being expanded. In addition to this, the PowerPivot field list has a Search tab that enables you to quickly locate columns.

Let's try this out by following these steps:

1. Click on the PivotTable in Sheet1.

2. In the PowerPivot field list, locate the FactSales table. Drag and drop the SalesAmount column to the Values drop zone.

3. Add the `SalesAmountQuota` column from `FactSalesQuota` table to the Values drop zone.

4. Drag and drop the `CalendarYear` and `CalendarYearMonthLabel` columns from `DimDate` table to `RowLabels`.

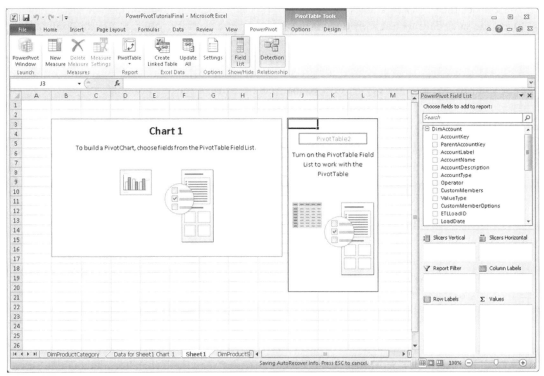

FIGURE 2-13 PivotTable and PivotChart

You will now see the `SalesAmount` and `SalesAmountQuota` for each year and month in the PivotTable. You might notice that the months are ordered alphabetically, rather than by the order of month within a year. This is a limitation in the current version of PowerPivot. However, you can use the manual sort option in the PivotTable by right-clicking in one of the months, and selecting Sort ⇨ More Sort Options ⇨ Manual. After the manual sort order option, you must drag and drop the months in the right order to achieve the desired result. This helps you to analyze which months you were able to meet the specified sales target and provides the capability to drill down to each month.

You will notice that Excel names the value fields "Sum of SalesAmount" and "Sum of SalesAmountQuota," since, by default, Excel aggregates the data of the column as a sum. Let's change these names.

A column added to the Values drop zone is called as a *measure*, which means that you have the capability to aggregate the contents of this column. If you must change the aggregation type of the measure (for example, you need to get the count of sales), you can change it via editing the measure.

Follow these steps:

1. Right-click on the `Sum of SalesAmount` column in the Values drop zone and select Edit Measure.

2. In the Measure Settings dialog, change the Custom Name to `SalesAmount`, as shown in Figure 2-14. As you can see in Figure 2-14, you have the option to change the aggregation type for the values of this column to Sum, Count, Min, Max, or Average.

3. Right-click on the `Sum of SalesAmountQuota` field in Values drop zone and select Edit Measure.

4. Set the Custom Name to `SalesAmountQuota` in the Measure Settings dialog for the `SalesAmountQuota` column.

FIGURE 2-14 Changing a measure name

You will now see the updated measure names, along with data for each calendar year and month, as shown in Figure 2-15. You can see the months under each year. You can collapse the months by clicking on the + symbol next to each year. Alternately, you can collapse all the months.

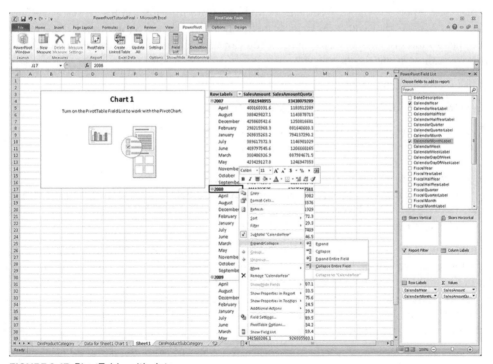

FIGURE 2-15 PivotTable with data

Now, let's make use of slicers by following these steps:

1. Select one of the years in the Row Labels column.

2. Right-click and select Expand/Collapse ➪ Collapse Entire Field.

3. Select the PivotChart.

4. Drag and drop `OnHandQuantity`, `OnOrderQuantity`, and `SafetyStockQuantity` columns from `FactInventory` table in the PowerPivot field list to the Values drop zone.

5. Drag and drop `ProductSubCategoryName` column from `DimSubProductCategory` table to the Row Labels drop zone.

6. Drag and drop the `ProductCategoryName` column from `DimProductCategory` table to the Slicers Horizontal drop zone.

7. Drag and drop the columns `RegionCountryName` and `StateProvinceName` from `DimGeography` table to the Slicers Vertical drop zone.

You have now created a sheet with data on sales and inventory that you can analyze. Slicers provide the capability to view all the values in the column. Also, when you select a specific column, and there is a relationship between the column in the slicer and the data in PivotTable or PivotChart, you will see those values reflected appropriately.

For example, your report in `Sheet1` has the sales and inventory information for all stores and products of Contoso. Assume that you want to look at the sales and inventory for stores in the United States, and the products of category `Computers`. You can very easily analyze the data by selecting the appropriate values in the slicers.

1. Click on the product category `Computers`.

2. In the `RegionCountryName` slicer, click on the `United States` value.

3. In the PivotTable, click on the plus symbol (+) next to year 2007 to compare the `SalesAmount` and `SalesAmount Quota` for each month of 2007.

Your PivotChart and PivotTable would now change to reflect the data for the chosen slicers, as shown in Figure 2-16. Since you have relationships established between the columns in the slicers and the data in PivotTable and PivotCharts, you will now only see the `Inventory` information for the product subcategories for the category `Computers`.

Also, note that the value `Computers` is highlighted in a specific background color, indicating the selection, while all other values do not have a background (white background). Similarly you can see `United States` highlighted for `RegionCountryName`. Also, notice that `StateProvincename` vertical slicer has `Alaska` as the first member. As soon as you select `United States`, the slicer is able to identify the states within United States that are of importance, and, hence, all the states not part of United States are automatically moved down.

If you scroll through the values in the StateProvinceName slicer, you can see that, after all the states in the United States, the remaining states in other countries appear in alphabetical order with a lighter background. The light background indicates that there is no data for those specific states.

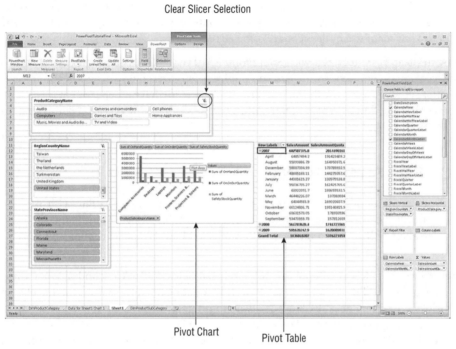

FIGURE 2-16 Sales and inventory data for Computer category products in United States

This visual representation helps you to analyze the data effectively. The x symbol in the slicer helps you to clear the slicer selection, and you can select multiple values in the slicer by using Ctrl key and the value selection. Analyze the data from various categories and countries or states in this report.

Select File in Excel and click Save to save the workbook as PowerPivotTutorialFinal.

When you save the Excel workbook, you are saving the report you have created, along with all the PowerPivot metadata, data, and calculations you have applied. Since the PowerPivot data is stored in memory, at the time of the save, the data is stored in Analysis Services backup format within the Excel workbook as a custom data part, along with metadata information within the Excel file, as you learned in Chapter 1.

Sharing Your Data

You have now built a self-service application that Contoso executives can use to analyze the sales and inventory information. This is referred to as an application rather than an Excel workbook, since you have actually integrated data from various sources, established relationships, and then created a report, all within an Excel worksheet. Now that you have built a report in Excel, you want to be able to share this information.

There are several ways to share the Excel workbook with the key decision-makers of the organization. SharePoint 2010 allows you to share and collaborate on documents within the organization. Hence, similar to sharing your other documents, you can publish your PowerPivot workbook with PowerPivot data to your team site built on SharePoint 2010.

PowerPivot provides features integrated with SharePoint 2010 that allow you to effectively share and manage PowerPivot data in workbooks. Before you publish the PowerPivot workbook you have created, you must first set up PowerPivot for SharePoint. If you already have a departmental SharePoint Server 2010 server running PowerPivot for SharePoint, you can skip to the section "Publishing Your Workbook," later in this chapter.

POWERPIVOT FOR SHAREPOINT

You have seen the capabilities of PowerPivot for Excel. Once you have created a PowerPivot workbook, you most likely will want to share this workbook with others via SharePoint 2010. PowerPivot for SharePoint helps you to interact with published PowerPivot workbooks on SharePoint 2010.

Excel Calculation Services (ECS) is an application server that helps you to view and interact with Excel workbooks from your Web browser. Since PowerPivot data embedded within the Excel workbook is seen by ECS as external data, ECS needs a way to interact with the data by connecting to a server. Chapter 1 included an overview of PowerPivot for SharePoint architecture, and how it integrates with SharePoint 2010 and ECS as an application server. You will learn more about SharePoint 2010, ECS, and PowerPivot for SharePoint architecture in Chapters 8 and 10.

The steps in the next section walk you through setting up PowerPivot for SharePoint.

Single-Machine New Farm Install

PowerPivot for SharePoint provides you with two setup options — a New Farm install and an Existing Farm install. The *New Farm install* is typically expected to be used in a single-machine install where PowerPivot will take care of installing and configuring all the relevant services effectively for you. This chapter takes you through the New Farm install.

> *SharePoint 2010 is only supported on Windows Server 2008 Service Pack 2 or higher, and Window Server 2008 R2, and only on 64-bit.*

Follow these steps to install your PowerPivot service:

1. Log in to Windows Server 2008 R2 server as an administrator.

2. From your Office Server installation DVD, run the `PrerequisiteInstaller.exe` in the administrator mode.

3. You will see all the prerequisites to be installed listed in the welcome screen of the Microsoft SharePoint 2010 Product Preparation Tool dialog. Proceed through the pages of this dialog, accepting the license agreements, and click Finish.

4. Restart your computer for the prerequisites to take effect, and log in as an administrator.

5. Run Office Server's setup.exe as an administrator.

6. Accept the license agreements and click Continue.

7. In the "Choose the installation you want" dialog, click the Server Farm button. PowerPivot for SharePoint is only supported in the Server Farm mode.

8. In the Server Type dialog, click the radio button next to "Complete — Install all components." Click the Install Now button.

9. In the "Welcome to SharePoint Products" dialog, you now have the option to configure your SharePoint 2010 server or cancel the configuration. To configure your SharePoint 2010 server, you need a database server, a database name, and login credentials. You will use the PowerPivot for SharePoint setup to configure the SharePoint 2010 server. Hence, click the Cancel button.

 PowerPivot for SharePoint configures your SharePoint 2010 as part of the New Farm install option. Hence, you do not invoke the option to run the SharePoint 2010 Configuration Wizard.

For a PowerPivot for SharePoint install, you must use the SQL Server 2008 R2 enterprise edition. Follow these steps:

1. Launch SQL Server 2008 R2 setup.exe in administrator mode.

2. Click Installation ⇨ "New installation or add features to an existing installation" in the SQL Server Installation center.

3. Click OK after passing the Setup Support rules.

4. In the Product Key page, select the "Enter the product key" radio button. Specify your product key and click Next.

5. Review the license terms and then click the "I accept the license terms" checkbox to accept the license terms. Click Next.

6. In the Setup Support Files dialog, click Install.

7. In the Setup Support Rules dialog, Click Next.

8. In the Setup Role page, select "SQL Server PowerPivot for SharePoint," as shown in Figure 2-17. Click Next.

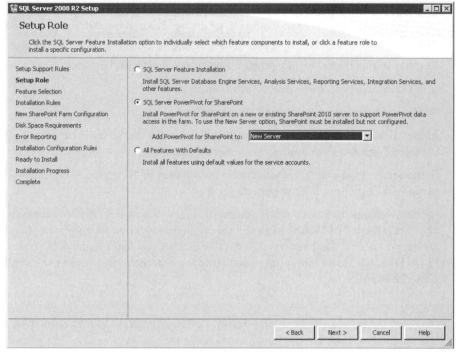

FIGURE 2-17 Setup Role page

9. In Feature Selection page, click Next.

10. Click Next in the Installation Rules pages after the Install Rules Check has been completed and passed.

As part of PowerPivot for SharePoint new farm setup, SQL Server 2008 R2 will set up an instance of SQL Server Engine and SQL Server Analysis Services. By default, the instance name is called POWERPIVOT, and the default installation path is displayed to the user, as shown in Figure 2-18. You are welcome to change the instance ID and the path based on your system configurations.

11. Select the default values for instance configuration and click Next.

12. In the New SharePoint Farm Configuration page, enter your credentials (username and password), as shown in Figure 2-19. The credentials specified in this dialog represent the account under which the SharePoint farm will be running. This must be a domain account. You have the option to change this account from the SharePoint Central Administration page after installation.

13. Enter the secure text "Password@1" in the "Pass phrase" field and confirm it. The "Pass phrase" is needed for a secure farm configuration, and this phrase must be specified when you want to add additional servers to this SharePoint farm.

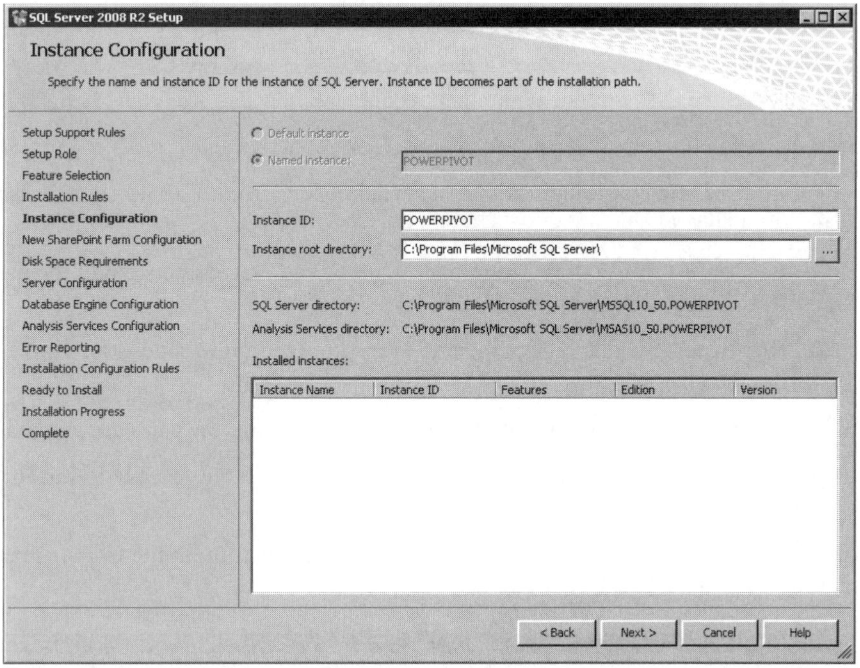

FIGURE 2-18 Instance Configuration dialog

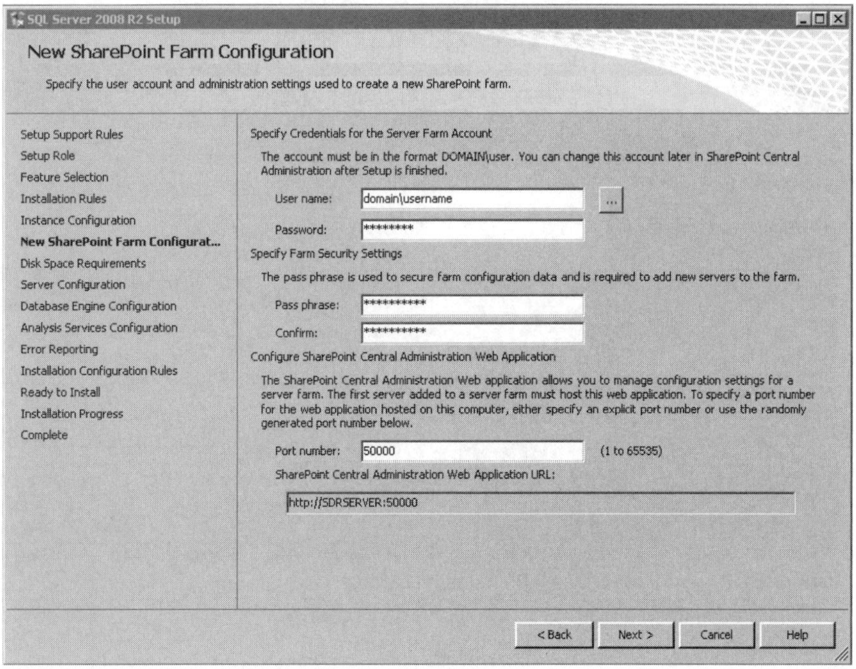

FIGURE 2-19 New SharePoint Farm Configuration page

14. The port number specified will be the port number at which the SharePoint Central administration page will be hosted. Change the port number to 50000 and click Next.

15. Click Next in the Disk Space Requirements page.

16. Enter the account names and passwords for the services in the Server Configuration page.

17. In the Database Engine Configuration page, click Add Current User to add the user as administrator, and click Next.

18. In the Analysis Services Configuration page, click Add Current User to add the user as administrator, and click Next.

19. In the Error Reporting page, select the error reporting option to send error reports to Microsoft, and click Next.

20. Click Next in the Installation Configuration Rules page after the rules are verified.

21. Review the summary information of the install selections in the "Ready to Install page," and click Install.

22. After a successful installation, review the summary information in the Complete page, as shown in Figure 2-20. Click Close.

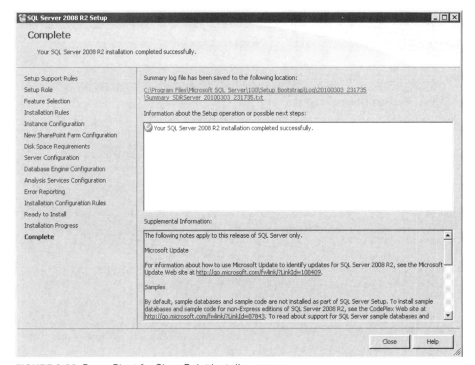

FIGURE 2-20 PowerPivot for SharePoint install summary

After successful installation of PowerPivot for SharePoint, you should verify the installation. Open your Web browser under administrator's privilege mode and enter **http://<machinename>** with

<machinename> being the name of the server machine where you performed the PowerPivot for SharePoint install.

You should see a link to the PowerPivot Gallery on the left side of the page, as shown in Figure 2-21. PowerPivot users will publish their workbooks to the PowerPivot Gallery, which is a special type of SharePoint document library that can display PowerPivot workbooks in different views.

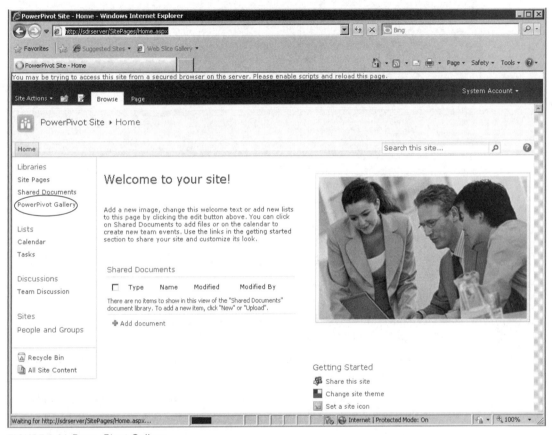

FIGURE 2-21 PowerPivot Gallery

To view PowerPivot workbooks published to the PowerPivot Gallery, you need Silverlight. Because Silverlight is not available in a 64-bit version, you must use the 32-bit Web browser to see PowerPivot workbooks using the PowerPivot Gallery's special views. Also, PowerPivot workbooks may be quite large, since they do include PowerPivot data. SharePoint 2010 has a default maximum limit for file size, and you would need to change this setting to be able to publish/upload large PowerPivot workbooks.

Follow these steps to configure specific properties to complete PowerPivot New Farm installation:

1. Launch the SharePoint Central Administration page from Start ➪ All Programs ➪ Microsoft SharePoint 2010 Products ➪ SharePoint 2010 Central Administration.

2. Click on the "Manage web applications" link under the heading Application Management.

3. Select the item "SharePoint - 80" and click on General Settings ➪ General Settings in the SharePoint ribbon, as shown in Figure 2-22.

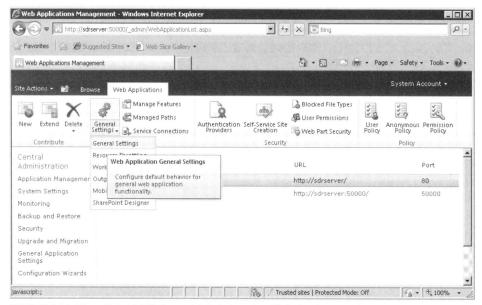

FIGURE 2-22 SharePoint 2010 Central Administration Web Application General Settings

4. In the Web Applications General Settings dialog, navigate to the value "Maximum upload size" and change the value from 200 MB to 2047 MB. Click OK.

5. Navigate to SharePoint Central Administration ➪ Application Management ➪ Manage Service Applications.

6. Select ExcelServiceApp1 (Excel Services Application Web Service Application) and click Manage, as shown in Figure 2-23.

7. Click on Trusted File Locations.

8. Click on http:// to change the Excel Services settings.

9. Navigate to Workbook Properties sections and change Maximum Workbook Size to 2,047 MB and Maximum Chart or Image Size to 100 MB. Click OK.

10. For these settings to take effect, open a command prompt in administrator mode, type the command **iisreset** and press Enter to reset the Internet Information Services (IIS) applications.

You have now successfully completed PowerPivot for SharePoint installation. You are ready to publish and share your PowerPivot tutorial workbook.

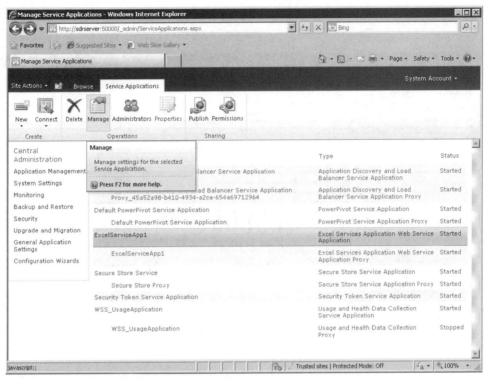

FIGURE 2-23 Manage Excel Service Applications

Publishing Your Workbook

To publish your `Contoso` workbook, follow these steps:

1. Switch to your machine with Excel and PowerPivot for Excel.

2. Open your `PowerPivotTutorialFinal.xlsx` workbook.

3. Click on File ➪ Save and Send ➪ Save to SharePoint ➪ Save As.

4. Enter `http://<yourPowerPivotserver>/PowerPivot Gallery` in the folder path of the Save As dialog, and click Save.

Viewing PowerPivot Workbooks

Excel publishes the PowerPivot workbook to your SharePoint 2010 server and opens the workbook in your Web browser. At this point, Excel Services renders your workbook on your Web browser, as shown in Figure 2-24. You interact with the workbook (for example, apply filtering or slicers) to analyze the data similar to what you would do in Excel.

Once you have published this workbook, you can provide appropriate permissions to the site or sub-site so that collaborators or key decision-makers can view and analyze the data.

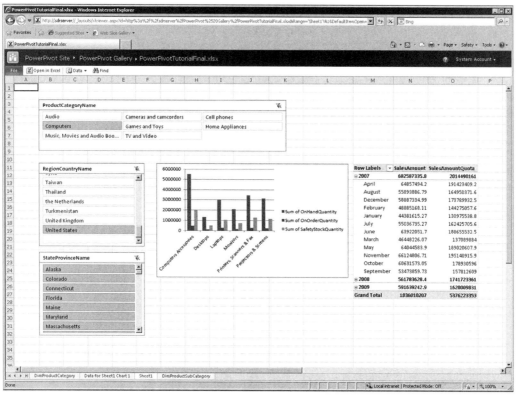

FIGURE 2-24 PowerPivot workbook rendered by ECS

Viewing the PowerPivot Gallery

When you publish your PowerPivot workbooks to the PowerPivot Gallery, PowerPivot can display your workbooks using different views. These views provide an interactive way to view the content in the workbook. PowerPivot Gallery also allows you to create Reporting Services or Excel reports, as well as set up the refreshing of your PowerPivot data on a periodic basis.

You will learn more about the PowerPivot Gallery in Chapter 6.

For a quick view of the PowerPivot Gallery, follow these steps:

1. Open your Web browser and enter the address **http://<yourmachinename>** where you have installed PowerPivot for SharePoint.

2. Click on PowerPivot Gallery.

3. If your machine does not have Silverlight, you will be prompted to install Silverlight. Click on the Install Silverlight icon to install Silverlight on your machine.

4. Refresh your Web browser once Silverlight is installed.

You will see the various sheets in the `PowerPivotTutorialFinal.xlsx` file within the PowerPivot Gallery, as shown in Figure 2-25. You can hover over each sheet to see the larger view of the sheet on the left side. This visual effect of the document helps you to quickly view the sheet content. The two icons on the top right help with creating reports off of the current PowerPivot workbook, and to manage scheduled data refresh.

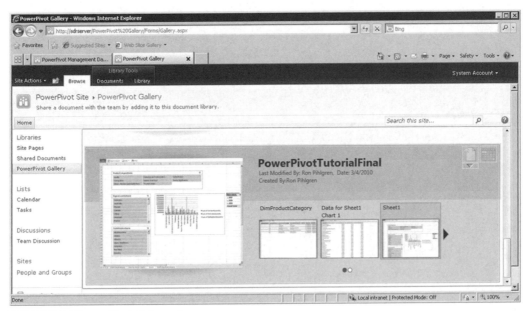

FIGURE 2-25 PowerPivot Gallery view

SUMMARY

This chapter introduced you to Microsoft PowerPivot. Using PowerPivot for Excel, you learned how to integrate data from several data sources, establish relevant relationships between the tables, analyze data within the PowerPivot Window, and create custom calculations using DAX. You then created an Excel report on Sales and Inventory data to help analyze data effectively using the PowerPivot field list and slicers, a new feature in Excel 2010.

You learned how to set up PowerPivot for SharePoint by installing Office Server 2010 and SQL Server 2008 R2 in the New Farm install mode. PowerPivot for SharePoint helps you share PowerPivot workbooks with end users who are making decisions and allows you to help people build additional reports. You published the sample `PowerPivotTuorialFinal.xlsx` built using PowerPivot for Excel to the PowerPivot Gallery, and were able to view the workbook in the PowerPivot Gallery, as well as interact with the workbook that was rendered using Excel Services.

In Chapter 3, you will learn about importing data from various data sources into PowerPivot for Excel and begin building a more in-depth PowerPivot application.

PART II
Creating Self-Service BI Applications Using PowerPivot

3

Assembling Data

WHAT'S IN THIS CHAPTER?

➤ Importing data into PowerPivot

➤ Understanding other ways of bringing data into PowerPivot

➤ Introducing the healthcare audit application

➤ Assembling data for the healthcare audit application

BI applications (including self-service BI applications) are all about making sense of data. In order to make sense of it, you must start with the data. This chapter is about this aspect of building PowerPivot applications — assembling the data you will analyze and/or report on.

Unlike the common corporate BI approach, where you assemble all your data into a data warehouse and then import it into your online analytical processing (OLAP) database, PowerPivot strives to make it easy to bring data into the application directly from many different data sources without bringing it first into an intermediate staging area. This allows a more interactive, exploratory approach to BI that is one of the hallmarks of self-service BI.

Keep in mind that self-service BI is an alternative to, not a replacement for, corporate BI. There are contexts where the traditional corporate BI approach is the right one. Two examples are analyzing massive quantities of data or using the full power of Multidimensional Expressions (MDX) if the calculation requirements of your application require it.

This doesn't mean that the data that lives in data warehouses or in corporate BI databases can't be used in self-service BI applications. Data from these types of applications is included in the diverse types of data that can be brought into your self-service BI applications with PowerPivot. This chapter looks at how to bring data into PowerPivot applications from those and other data sources.

IMPORTING DATA

The primary way of bringing data into your PowerPivot application is by importing it. PowerPivot for Excel includes a tool for doing this called the Table Import Wizard. The Table Import Wizard is started from the Get External Data section of the Home tab of the ribbon in the PowerPivot Window. Figure 3-1 shows this section of the PowerPivot ribbon.

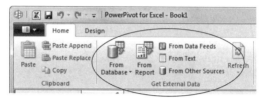

FIGURE 3-1: The Get External Data section of the PowerPivot Window ribbon

As you can see, there are multiple drop-downs and buttons corresponding to the multiple data source types that PowerPivot supports:

➤ The From Database drop-down enables you to import data from various Microsoft database types — SQL Server, Access, and Analysis Services/PowerPivot.

➤ The From Report button enables you to import data from Microsoft SQL Server 2008 R2 and later Reporting Services reports.

➤ The From Data Feeds button helps you to import data from data feeds (a new technology for making available updatable data sources that will be described later in this chapter).

➤ The From Text button enables you to import data from text files.

➤ The From Other Sources button enables you to import data from every type of data source that PowerPivot supports, including those that aren't available from the other buttons.

The following sections describe the different types of data sources from which you can import data into PowerPivot.

Relational Databases

In Chapter 2, you learned about importing data from Microsoft SQL Server. But, using PowerPivot, you can import data from a variety of different relational databases in addition to Microsoft SQL Server. Figure 3-2 shows a list of the supported relational data sources from PowerPivot's Table Import Wizard.

You can see that, in addition to Microsoft SQL Server, PowerPivot supports importing data from the following:

➤ *Microsoft SQL Azure* — This is a cloud-based relational database service built on Microsoft SQL Server technologies.

➤ *Microsoft SQL Server Parallel Data Warehouse* — This is a highly scalable system for data warehousing that employs massively parallel processing.

➤ *Microsoft Access* — This is the desktop database component of Microsoft Office.

➤ *Oracle* — This is the relational database management system (RDBMS) product from Oracle Corporation.

➤ *Teradata* — This is the RDBMS product from Teradata Corporation.

➤ *Sybase* — This is the RDBMS product from Sybase, Inc.

➤ *Informix* — This is an RDBMS product owned by IBM.

➤ *IBM DB2* — This is another RDBMS product from IBM.

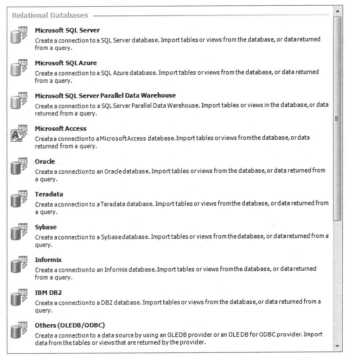

FIGURE 3-2: The variety of relational data sources supported by PowerPivot

If you click one of these relational data sources in the PowerPivot ribbon (or if you click the From Other Data Sources button and select one of the data sources in the resulting dialog) and click the Next button, you will be presented with the first page of the Table Import Wizard for that data source. From there, you can provide information, set properties, choose the data you want to import, and import the data into PowerPivot.

Like other data source clients, PowerPivot requires database providers and, in some cases, client libraries in order to be able to import data from these sources. You can view the providers that are supported for a particular data source by clicking on the Advanced button in the data source's Import Wizard page. The provider is shown in the Providers drop-down at the top of the resulting Set Advanced Properties dialog, as shown in Figure 3-3. In some cases, multiple providers will be supported by PowerPivot for the same database back end. For example, Figure 3-3 shows the three different SQL Server providers supported by PowerPivot.

When multiple providers are supported, but not all are installed on the machine, PowerPivot will select one that is available. For example, in Figure 3-3, the machine didn't have the SQL Server Native Client 10.0 provider, so PowerPivot selected the Microsoft OLE DB Provider for SQL Server as the default. If the SQL Server Native Client 10.0 provider were present, PowerPivot would choose it as the default provider because of its better performance.

In most cases, the database providers and client libraries are not provided by PowerPivot for Excel and must be acquired and installed separately. PowerPivot will not prohibit you from attempting to import data when the required drivers are not installed. If you attempt to import from a data source where an appropriate driver is not available, PowerPivot will display an error, as shown at the bottom of Figure 3-4. This is your cue to install the provider from that data source and retry your import.

The Table Import Wizard page for each relational database type has controls that let you specify the most common properties in order to connect to the data source and import data. If there are properties that you must specify for your particular data source that aren't available on its initial page, you can access them by clicking the Advanced button. This will bring up a dialog (Figure 3-3) that allows you to specify any connection string property available for that data source type.

PowerPivot was built and tested with certain relational database types in mind, and those are the ones that you saw in Figure 3-2. If you want to bring in data from a data source that isn't among those in that list, PowerPivot provides a generic option that allows you to import data from any OLE DB or ODBC data source. This is the "Others (OLEDB/ODBC)" item in this list.

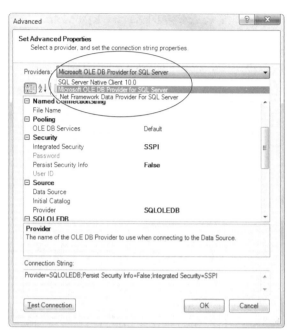

FIGURE 3-3: The different SQL Server providers supported by PowerPivot

FIGURE 3-4: Attempting to use an unavailable database provider

If you choose that option, a dialog will appear that allows you to enter in a simple text box the connection string needed to access your particular data source. There is also a dialog that can help you build the needed connection string based on any OLE DB provider installed on the machine, as shown in Figure 3-5. This Data Link Properties dialog can be seen by clicking on the Build button in the Import Wizard page for "Others (OLEDB/ODBC)."

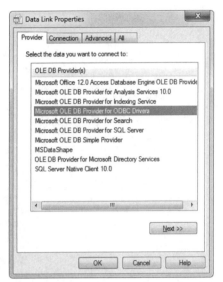

Specifying the Data to Import

Once you've specified how to connect to a relational database as just described, you can then select which data in the database you want to import. There are two methods you can use:

FIGURE 3-5: The Data Link Properties dialog

➤ Select (and optionally filter) specific tables and views

➤ Specify a SQL query

Selecting tables and views is the easiest method, but specifying a SQL query gives you the most control over the data you will bring in. You select which method of specifying data on the second page of the Table Import Wizard, as shown in Figure 3-6.

Selecting Tables and Views

If you choose to select data by selecting tables and/or views, the Table Import Wizard will show you all the available tables and views in a page and allow you to select them. It also provides a dialog that lets you preview the data of the selected table, as well as filter out columns and rows from the data that will be imported. Column filtering can be done by unchecking the checkbox at the top of a column.

FIGURE 3-6: "Choose How to Import the Data" dialog

Row Filtering

This filtering enables you to cut down the amount of data you will import, which may be helpful for very large data sets. Figure 3-7 shows the AddressLine2 column unchecked (the whole column will be filtered out on import) and the "0-1 miles" value of the `CommuteDistance` column unchecked (rows with that value will be filtered out on import).

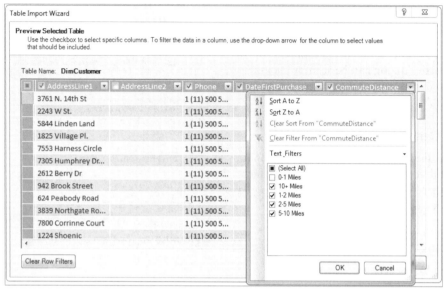

FIGURE 3-7: Table Import Wizard Preview Selected Table dialog

It's important to filter out data that's not needed if you are working with very large data sets. Although PowerPivot's in-memory technology includes patented compression technology, memory is less plentiful than disk space, and importing data will fail if there is not enough memory in the system.

Specifying a SQL Query

For ultimate control over the data you are importing, PowerPivot provides the option to specify a SQL query whose result will be the data that gets imported into a PowerPivot table. This option enables you to use the full power of the SQL language to tailor the data. If you choose "Write a query that will specify the data to import" in the "Choose How to Import the Data" page (see Figure 3-6), you will be presented with the dialog shown in Figure 3-8.

FIGURE 3-8: "Specify a SQL Query" page of Table Import Wizard

This dialog is sparse and unhelpful — just a text box where you can type in the SQL query, and another text box that allows you to give a name to the table that will be imported. It will work if you know the exact SQL query you want to specify for the data import. This dialog doesn't seem to be aligned with the exploratory and agile nature of self-service BI. Luckily, you can click the Design button to gain access to a much better tool — a query designer, as shown in Figure 3-9.

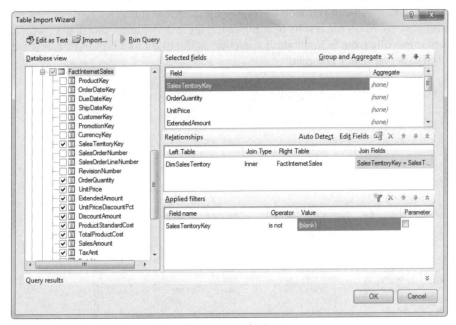

FIGURE 3-9: The SQL Server PowerPivot query designer

The SQL query designer is much more helpful than just a plain text box. You can view all the tables and views from the database you selected in the pane at the right. You can check checkboxes to include tables and columns within tables in your query. You can create or auto-detect relationships between the tables that you select and also apply filters.

INSIDE POWERPIVOT

In the Applied filters section of the dialog, notice that there is a checkbox where you can indicate that an item is a query parameter. This functionality (the capability to specify a query parameter) does not work in the current version of PowerPivot.

If you are familiar with the Microsoft SQL Server 2008 R2 Report Builder 3.0 application, you may recognize the query designer as the same component used to create data sets in that application. PowerPivot for Excel uses that component as its SQL query designer (and also as its MDX query designer, as described later in this chapter in the section, "Multi-Dimensional Data Sources"), but didn't implement parameterized queries, and couldn't disable the checkbox.

Once you have specified the data that you want in your query, you can click the Run Query button at the top of the query designer to bring back the actual data that your query will return. Note that this query designer functionality is available only if SQL Server is your database.

For non-SQL Server data sources, you can still click the Design button and you will get a dialog that won't be quite as useful as the one in Figure 3-9. It still has an advantage over the plain text box that you saw in Figure 3-8 in that you can run your query, see the data that the query returns, and be able to adjust your query based on the results of running it. Figure 3-10 shows this dialog, which is also available when importing from SQL Server if you click on the "Edit as Text" button at the top of the PowerPivot SQL Server query designer.

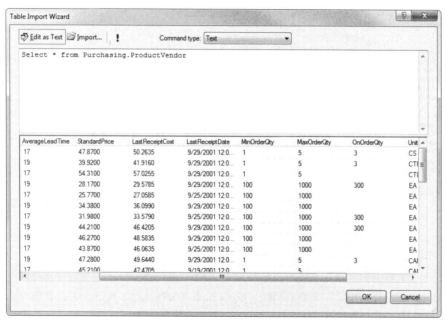

FIGURE 3-10: "Edit as Text" dialog in the PowerPivot Table Import Wizard

After you specify your query in the query designer or "Edit as Text" dialog and click on the OK button, the "Specify a SQL Query" page is filled in with the query you have built. You can give the query a friendly name that will be used as the name of the PowerPivot table that will be created from the imported data. Click the Finish button to do the actual data import.

Before examining what happens when data is imported, let's look at some of the other data sources that can be used to import data into PowerPivot.

Multi-Dimensional Data Sources

The PowerPivot Table Import Wizard will also let you import data from Microsoft Analysis Services cubes, as well as other PowerPivot workbooks. In order to do that, you would click on the From Database button in the PowerPivot Window and choose "From Analysis Services or PowerPivot."

This will bring up the Microsoft SQL Server Analysis Services page in the Table Import Wizard, as shown in Figure 3-11.

Microsoft SQL Server Analysis Services

To import from an Analysis Services cube, type the name of your Analysis Services Server in the "Server or File Name" field of the Analysis Services page of the Table Import Wizard shown in Figure 3-11. This will bring up a dialog similar to the one shown in Figure 3-8, except that, instead of prompting you for a SQL query, it asks you for an MDX query. Also, similar to importing data from SQL Server, there is a Design button that will bring up a more useful query designer, as shown in Figure 3-12.

FIGURE 3-11: Analysis Services page of the Table Import Wizard

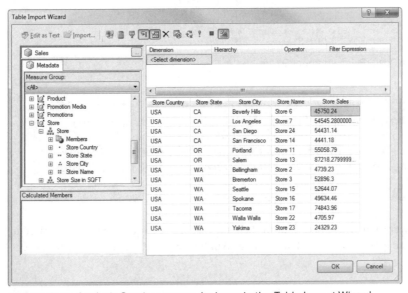

FIGURE 3-12: Analysis Services query designer in the Table Import Wizard

If you are familiar with Analysis Services you may be aware that the result of an Analysis Services query is called a `CellSet` object. A `CellSet` is a multi-dimensional object (rather than a tabular object) and contains properties like a collection of axes, a collection of cells, and so on that allows Analysis Services clients to expose OLAP operations on the returned `CellSet` data.

Data imported into PowerPivot, however, must be in the form of tables. Hence, when you import from Analysis Services, the Import Wizard will bring the results of the Analysis Services query into PowerPivot in a "flattened" tabular form called a *rowset*. The Import Wizard's Analysis Services query designer will display the results of your underlying query in this flattened form.

When you import data from Analysis Services you won't have the interactivity of slicing and dicing that data that you will have when using corporate BI client tools, such as Excel connected to an Analysis Services Unified Dimension Model (UDM) cube. Once the data is brought in as a table, though, you will be able to work with it in the same manner as any other PowerPivot data (such as filtering, creating relationships with other PowerPivot tables, and adding DAX calculations to the table).

Published PowerPivot Workbooks

Since PowerPivot knows how to connect to data in an Analysis Services database, it can connect to data in published PowerPivot workbooks, which contain, under the hood, Analysis Services databases. To do that, type a URL to a published PowerPivot workbook in the "Server or File Name" field of the Analysis Services page in the Table Import Wizard (shown in Figure 3-11). The URL should be in the following form:

```
http://<PowerPivot for SharePoint server>/<document library>/<workbook name>
```

Figure 3-13 shows an example.

FIGURE 3-13: Specifying a PowerPivot workbook in the Table Import Wizard

 If you are running PowerPivot for Excel on a Server operating system like Windows Server 2008 or Windows Server 2008 R2, you should install the Desktop Experience feature. Installing this feature will prevent a problem when importing data from a published PowerPivot workbook that will cause Excel to crash.

The contents of the PowerPivot workbook data in the Analysis Services query will look different from what you would see if you imported data from an Analysis Services cube. This is because

PowerPivot workbook data uses the same format as a traditional Analysis Services cube, but the Analysis Services engine organizes and queries the data in a somewhat different way when it is in VertiPaq mode. Figure 3-14 shows this organization.

Note the following differences:

➤ Every PowerPivot table has both a measure group and a dimension.

➤ Every measure group has a `_Count <table name>` measure. These are there to force a measure group on every table, and should not be considered useful when querying and reporting.

➤ You will not see key performance indicators (KPIs), as they are not supported in VertiPaq mode for this version of PowerPivot.

Also note that you can import data from PowerPivot workbooks only if they are published to PowerPivot for SharePoint. You cannot import data from PowerPivot workbooks if they are `.xlsx` files on a local disk drive.

FIGURE 3-14: PowerPivot workbook metadata in the Analysis Service query designer

---

INSIDE POWERPIVOT

The reason that PowerPivot data appears as it does in the Analysis Services query designer is because, when the Analysis Services team implemented PowerPivot, they wanted to reuse as much existing implementation as possible. This led to using the existing Analysis Services Unified Dimension Model (UDM) format as the underlying storage mechanism for PowerPivot data and modifying its organization to support the design of PowerPivot (which was to be much more user-friendly and Excel-like than Analysis Services cubes and the MDX query language). This implementation decision has both pluses and minuses.

On the plus side, existing tools that know how to retrieve and interpret data from Analysis Services servers can work with PowerPivot data without modification. This is a big advantage for a version 1 product like PowerPivot. This allowed PowerPivot to be implemented as an Excel add-in without having to disrupt its own development plans and shipping cycle too much. To Excel, PowerPivot data looks just like an Analysis Services data source, data provider, and Excel communicates with it exactly that way. On the PowerPivot side, it means that a lot of existing code didn't need to be rewritten, especially on the server. This allowed the Analysis Services team to get the first version of PowerPivot developed and shipped much faster than if they built everything from scratch with a clean sheet of paper.

continues

continued

On the minus side, it means that sometimes implementation details will leak through like they do with the Analysis Services query designer in the Table Import Wizard. Another minus that was felt by the part of the Analysis Services team was building the Excel add-in. Add-ins are restricted in what they can do, as well as the information they can get through the add-in interface. That led to a lot of time figuring out how to do some of the things they had to do and circumventing those limitations.

The PowerPivot team felt that the pluses outweighed the minuses, especially considering the goal they had with shipping alongside Office 2010.

Data Feeds

Data feeds are a new technology that aims to provide tabular data in a format that users can subscribe to in order to receive updated data as the source changes. Data feeds are based on the Open Data Protocol, which uses the Atom Publishing Protocol and its Data Services URI and Payload Extensions. Data feeds are supported in ADO.NET Data Services and also are being adopted more broadly across the industry.

 For more information on the Open Data Protocol, see `http://odata.org`*. For more information on the Atom Publishing Protocol and its Data Services URI and Payload Extensions, see* `http://msdn.microsoft.com/en-us/library/dd541188.aspx`*.*

In SQL Server 2008 R2, data feeds are supported by both PowerPivot for Excel (as a consumer) and SQL Server Reporting Services (as a provider). PowerPivot for Excel has the capability to import data from data feeds. PowerPivot for Excel and PowerPivot for SharePoint have the capability to refresh PowerPivot data whose source is from one or more data feeds.

PowerPivot for Excel allows you to specify the import of data from data feeds from either the Table Import Wizard or from the producer side of the data feed. The following sections describe both of these methods.

Microsoft SQL Server Reporting Services Reports

In SQL Server 2008 R2, SQL Server Reporting Services are exposing their report data as data feeds that can be consumed by PowerPivot for Excel. To import data using a Reporting Services data feed, from the Table Import Wizard, click on the From Report button in the PowerPivot Window. This brings up the Reporting Services Report page of the Table Import Wizard, as shown in Figure 3-15.

If you click the Browse button in this dialog, you can navigate to a Reporting Services report server and view the different reports in the dialog to help you decide which report contains the data you will import into PowerPivot.

SQL Server Reporting Services 2008 R2 includes support for exporting report data as a data feed. If you navigate to a report in your Web browser, you will find a button on the report's toolbar that will allow this, as shown in Figure 3-16.

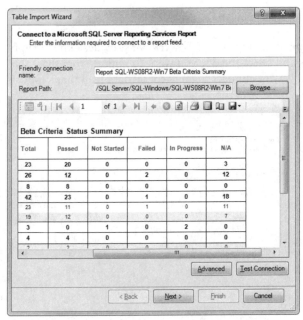

FIGURE 3-15: The Reporting Services Report page in the Table Import Wizard

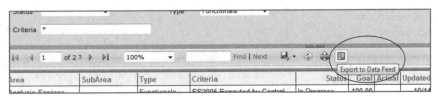

FIGURE 3-16: "Export to Data Feed" button in Reporting Services 2008 R2

PowerPivot for Excel includes an application called `Microsoft.AnalysisServices.AtomLauncher.exe` (or Atom Launcher for short) that will be set up as the default application for opening files of type `.atomsvc` (the extension of data feed definition files). This application will be invoked if you click on the "Export to Data Feed" button of a Reporting Services 2008 R2 report on a computer that has PowerPivot for Excel installed. Figure 3-17 shows the dialog that comes up when you do this.

This dialog allows you to import the data feed into any open PowerPivot workbook, or into a new workbook.

FIGURE 3-17: The Atom Launcher dialog

After you make your selection and click OK, the Atom Launcher will create a new workbook if you selected "Create a New Workbook," bring up the PowerPivot Window for that workbook, and start the Table Import Wizard at the generic data feeds page, which is described next.

Other Data Feeds

Reporting Services reports are only one type of data feed, and PowerPivot provides explicit support for them that allows you to browse reports and select the one you want to import from the Table Import Wizard. PowerPivot also provides a way to connect to any generic data feed that supports the OData protocol.

To import from those sources, you can use the From Data Feeds button in the PowerPivot Window. When you click on that button, you will see the "Connect to a Data Feed" page of the Table Import Wizard, as shown in Figure 3-18.

This Table Import Wizard page is really bare-bones, and assumes that you know the URL of the data feed from which you want to import. Data feeds are relatively new, and common practices have not yet emerged.

For an example of importing data from a data feed, let's use the data at the Open Government Data Initiative (`http://ogdisdk.cloudapp.net/DataCatalog.aspx`). Select the "District of Columbia" container and the "Environment" category on the left. Then, click on the "Recreation Parks" link in the list to open it in the Data Browser. In the Results section of the browser, copy the URL following Show Details and paste it into the Data Feed page of the Table Import Wizard. Click the Next button.

FIGURE 3-18: The "Connect to a Data Feed" page of the Table Import Wizard

You will see a single item in the Tables and Views list that you can view in the "Preview and Filter" dialog. From this point on, importing from a data feed is the same as from any other data source's table.

Text Files

Another important source of data is text files. Many applications provide a way to export their data in delimited files. Delimited text files are also popular formats for publicly available data on the Web.

PowerPivot provides support for importing data from text files with the From Text button on the PowerPivot tab of the Excel ribbon. When you click on that button, you get the dialog shown in Figure 3-19.

This page allows you to set various parameters that describe the type of text file you are importing. These parameters include the following:

➤ *The column separator* — You can choose among several column separators, including tab, comma, semicolon, space, colon, and vertical bar.

➤ *The encoding* — This is set from the Advanced dialog, which you can bring up by clicking on the Advanced button on the page. The choices for encoding are ANSI, UTF-8, and Unicode (UTF-16).

➤ *The locale* — This is also reachable in the Advanced Settings dialog.

➤ *Headers* — You can select whether or not to use the first row as column headers.

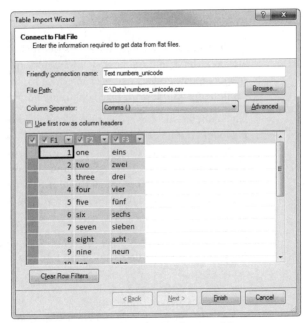

FIGURE 3-19: "Connect to Flat File" page of the Table Import Wizard

In addition, this page also includes a preview area that you can use to filter out rows and columns on import.

WHAT ABOUT FIXED-LENGTH-FIELD TEXT FILES?

Delimited text files are one kind of text file, possibly the most common type. But there is another category of text files that is also important — fixed-length-field text files. These are files that have their fields defined not by a delimiter, but rather by the positions in the line they occupy. For example, a fixed-length-field file may be constructed such that the first three positions in every line are the first field of that row, the second field may be the next six characters, and so on.

Suppose the contents of a text file named `numbers.txt` looked like this:

```
 1  one  eins
 2  two  zwei
 3three  drei
 4 four  vier
 5 five  fünf
 6  six sechs
 7sevensieben
 8eight  acht
 9 nine  neun
10  ten  zehn
```

continues

continued

In this file, the first three characters of every line are a number, the next five characters are a text field, and the next six characters are another text field. There is no explicit support in the PowerPivot user interface for importing a text file like this with the result being a table with three columns, but there is a way to do it.

Under the hood, PowerPivot for Excel uses a text file driver known as the *ACE provider* that has a mechanism that allows talking to fixed-width-field text files. To make use of this capability, you must provide a file that defines which positions correspond to which fields. The name of this file must be `schema.ini`, and it must exist in the same directory as the text file. The contents of the `schema.ini` file are described in the MSDN topic at `http://msdn.microsoft.com/en-us/library/ms709353(VS.85).aspx`.

Using the information from that article, you can define a `schema.ini` file for the file described previously that looks like this:

```
[numbers.txt]
Format=FixedLength
Col1=Number Short Width 3
Col2=English Text width 5
Col3=Deutsch Text Width 6
```

If you place this file in the same directory as `numbers.txt` and try importing from the text file into PowerPivot for Excel, the following figure shows what you get.

Note that the informative message at the bottom of the Table Import Wizard page lets you know that the schema.ini file was used and the currently specified import settings were overridden. (Settings in the Advanced Settings dialog are not overridden.)

Note also that the schema.ini file can also specify settings that can be applied when importing delimited files as well. The MSDN article talks about how to specify those settings, which include setting delimiter characters other than the ones selectable from the Import Wizard, specifying the data types of fields (including conversions), and specifying how data should be formatted.

Microsoft Excel Files

Although it's not accessible from the From Text button in the PowerPivot Window ribbon, you can import from Excel files. There is an entry for this in the dialog that comes up when you click the From Other Data Sources button in the ribbon, as shown in Figure 3-20.

Selecting this item and clicking the Next button brings up the "Connect to a Microsoft Excel File" page of the Table Import Wizard. You can specify three properties on this page — the friendly name, the path to the Excel file from which you want to import, and whether to use the first row as column headers. Clicking Next on this page brings you to the familiar "Select Tables and Views" page, where you can select tables to import and filter and preview the table.

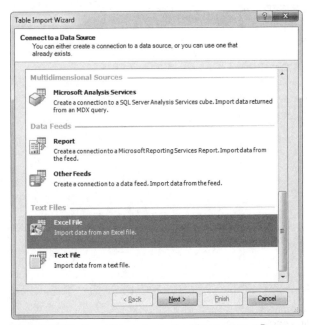

FIGURE 3-20: Excel File entry in the "Connect to a Data Source" dialog

Note that, when importing data from Excel workbooks, PowerPivot considers each worksheet a table. If you have multiple Excel tables in a single worksheet, PowerPivot will choose the smallest rectangle of cells on the worksheet that includes all cells that have data in them.

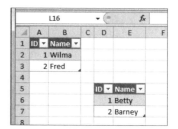

FIGURE 3-21: An Excel worksheet with two tables

For example, if you have an Excel worksheet that has data on it that looks like Figure 3-21, when you import that worksheet into PowerPivot, you will get a table that looks like Figure 3-22. Also note that only data within cells will be included in the imported data. Objects on an Excel worksheet (such as charts and slicers) will not be included in the imported data.

Importing the data

Once you've specified all the properties needed to import the data from any of the data sources supported by PowerPivot, you start the import process by clicking on the Finish button. PowerPivot for Excel will then import the data into its local PowerPivot data store. This can take a while if you are bringing in a lot of data. The progress will be displayed in the Importing page of the wizard, shown in Figure 3-23.

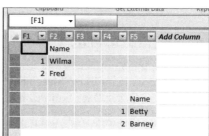

FIGURE 3-22: PowerPivot table imported from the worksheet in Figure 3-21

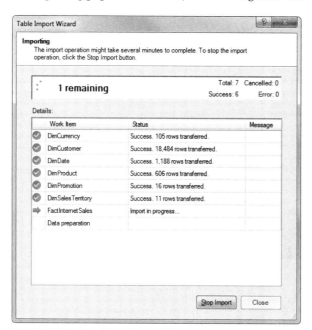

FIGURE 3-23: The Table Import Wizard Importing page

Note that the last item in the list of tables to import is not a table, but rather an item called "Data preparation." For relational data sources where you have specified more than one table to be imported, the Table Import Wizard will attempt to discover relationships between the tables based on the relationships defined in the source data and will create relationships between the imported PowerPivot tables based on them. In some cases, the relationships will not be able to be created. For example, PowerPivot doesn't allow a single related table to participate in more than one relationship to columns in one base table.

 In Analysis Services UDM terms, PowerPivot doesn't support role-playing dimensions.

The results of the relationship-detection part of the import process can be seen by clicking on the Details link in the message column on the Importing page once the import is completed. Figure 3-24 shows the Details dialog you get when clicking on that link. This figure also shows the errors you get for the case described previously.

Once you have imported your data into PowerPivot for Excel, you can use it to build Excel PivotTable reports and charts. That will be the subject of Chapter 5. Next, this chapter shows two other ways to bring external data into PowerPivot.

FIGURE 3-24: Details dialog

DATA TYPES AND IMPORTING

PowerPivot can import data from many diverse data sources. Each of these data sources has its own set of supported data types that may or may not be the same as any other data source. PowerPivot also has its own set of supported data types. As data is imported, PowerPivot will convert the data types of the source data's columns into data types that it supports.

PowerPivot supports the following data types:

➤   `Boolean`

➤   `Currency`

➤   `Datetime`

➤   `Double`

continues

continued

➤ Long

➤ String

➤ Timespan

Note that PowerPivot, unlike some source data providers (such as SQL Server), supports only one integer type, one floating-point type, one datetime type, and so on. Back-end databases that support more than one of these types will have them all mapped to the single PowerPivot types listed previously. For example, when importing from SQL Server, all of the following types will be mapped to PowerPivot's Long type:

➤ integer

➤ bigint

➤ int

➤ smallint

➤ tinyint

Some source data types are not supported by PowerPivot. Columns whose data types are unsupported by PowerPivot will not be shown, and will not be imported by PowerPivot. In general, data types designed to hold large binary values (such as blob or binary data types) are not supported by PowerPivot.

In some cases, PowerPivot cannot get catalog information from the source data provider. In those cases, PowerPivot will import all columns as the String data type, even numeric columns. An example of this provider type is Analysis Services. If you are in this situation, you can change the data type after importing using the Formatting section of the Home ribbon tab in the PowerPivot Window.

Another point to be aware of with respect to data types and importing relates to importing currency values. PowerPivot will import currency types as general currency types. This means that PowerPivot will assume that currency values should be interpreted as currency in the regional format settings of the machine on which you are running PowerPivot. This can lead to unexpected results. For example, if you import a currency column from the source data that you know is in French francs, and your machine has its regional settings set to Japanese, PowerPivot will import the currency values and format them as Japanese yen. As in the situation described earlier, you can use the PowerPivot formatting tools to adjust the columns' data type, and format after the import is completed.

OTHER WAYS TO BRING DATA INTO POWERPIVOT

Importing is one way to bring data into PowerPivot workbooks. There are two other ways: pasting data from the Windows clipboard and linked Excel tables.

Pasting From the Clipboard

PowerPivot will allow you create a new table in the PowerPivot data store by pasting data copied in from the Windows clipboard (as you saw in Chapter 2). If the content of the clipboard is in a tabular format that PowerPivot recognizes, you can use the Paste button on the Home ribbon tab of the PowerPivot Window (shown in Figure 3-25) to create a PowerPivot table from the contents of the clipboard. This can be useful if you have data you would like to use in

FIGURE 3-25: PowerPivot ribbon clipboard commands

PowerPivot that comes from a data source from which you can't import. One example would be a table on a Web page.

When you click any of the Paste buttons in PowerPivot, you will get a preview dialog that lets you view the data that is about to be pasted into the PowerPivot table. This dialog is shown in Figure 3-26. Here you can ensure that the data you are about to paste is what you expect. You can also name the table and decide if you want the first row to be treated as column headers.

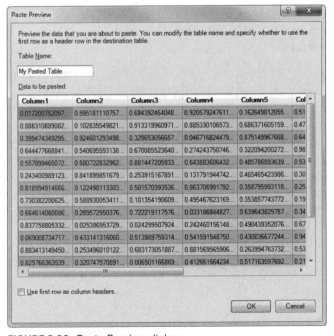

FIGURE 3-26: Paste Preview dialog

When you click the OK button, PowerPivot will create a new table based on the contents of the clipboard.

Once you have a pasted a table in PowerPivot, you can update the data in that table in two ways: appending and replacing. In both cases, the number of columns in the pasted table must be the same as the number of columns of the data you are pasting. In addition, the data types of the data you are pasting must match the data types of the columns in the table you are appending to or replacing. Also, when doing a replace, all the previous data in the table will be replaced by the data you are pasting. You cannot replace selected rows in a pasted table.

Linked Excel Tables

Another way of bringing data into a PowerPivot application is through a PowerPivot feature called *linked Excel tables*. The advantage of linked Excel tables over pasting from the clipboard is that PowerPivot for Excel will keep the tables in sync automatically. If you change the data in the Excel table, the next time the PowerPivot Window has focus on the data, the PowerPivot table will be updated.

To create a linked Excel table (or linked table, for short), you must have an Excel table in your workbook. Select the Excel table and, in the PowerPivot tab in the ribbon, click the Create Linked Table button. If your selection in Excel is not formatted as an Excel table, PowerPivot will pop up a dialog prompting you to create an Excel table for the current selection in the Excel worksheet. This dialog also allows you to specify whether or not your table includes values that should be used as column headers.

Once the Excel table is created, PowerPivot creates a PowerPivot table from the contents of the Excel table. In the PowerPivot Window, you can tell if a table is a linked table by the presence of the link glyph on the table's tab as you saw in Chapter 2.

Linked tables have their own ribbon tab in the PowerPivot Window, which will show up when you select linked table data. Figure 3-27 shows this ribbon tab and the commands that are available for linked tables.

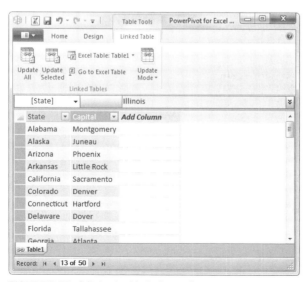

FIGURE 3-27: A linked table in PowerPivot

The commands on the ribbon allow the following:

➤ Setting the linked table update mode between manual and automatic

➤ Updating either all or the currently selected linked table

➤ Navigating to the Excel table that is the source of the currently selected linked table

➤ Selecting the Excel table that will be linked to this PowerPivot table

When something happens that breaks the link between the Excel table and the PowerPivot table (such as when you delete or rename the Excel table), PowerPivot notices this, and displays the error dialog shown in Figure 3-28.

When this happens, you can click on the Options button to get a list of choices for how to deal with this problem, as shown in Figure 3-29.

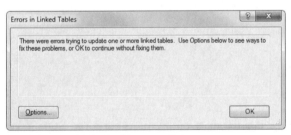

FIGURE 3-28: Linked table error dialog

FIGURE 3-29: Options for dealing with a linked table error

Following are the available options:

➤ *Do Nothing* — This option will not do anything to fix the situation. The error dialog will continue to appear every time you do an action that would attempt to refresh the linked table data.

➤ *Change Excel Table Name* — This option allows you to change the Excel table that is linked to this PowerPivot table. This is the appropriate option to choose when the Excel table has been renamed.

➤ *Remove Link to Excel Table* — This option will change the linked table to, in essence, a pasted table. It will not be linked to an Excel table, but will retain all its current data values.

➤ *Delete PowerPivot Table* — This option will remove the table from the PowerPivot data store.

Both pasted tables and linked tables have a disadvantage relative to imported tables: They cannot be updated by PowerPivot for SharePoint. If you want to update these types of tables after they have been published to the server, you must open them up in PowerPivot for Excel, do the updates, and then save them back on the server. This limitation argues for using pasted tables and linked tables only for data that isn't expected to change, or would rarely need to be updated.

Now that you've learned about all the different ways that data can be brought in to PowerPivot, let's take a look at the application you will be building in the next few chapters and use PowerPivot for Excel to assemble its data.

THE HEALTHCARE AUDIT APPLICATION

To proactively protect patient data and comply with the 1996 Health Insurance Portability and Accountability Act (HIPAA), SDR Healthcare (a fictional company) would like to create an application that can help clarify how physicians, nurses, and other medical staff are using and accessing patient data. SDR would like to understand trends in data usage by department, database, and class dimensions. It would like to look at monthly trends of this data.

Let's use the knowledge you have gained from looking at how to bring data into PowerPivot applications to assemble the initial data for the SDR Healthcare Audit application using PowerPivot for Excel.

ASSEMBLING DATA FOR THE HEALTHCARE AUDIT APPLICATION

To assemble the necessary data for SDR, you must tackle three tasks:

> ➤ Import the main audit data

> ➤ Import related tables

> ➤ Add data from other sources

Let's explore each of these in a bit more detail.

Importing the Main Data Table

The main audit data for SDR Healthcare is stored in a database on one of its corporate SQL Servers. To begin, let's import the view that contains the audit event information that will be the basis of the healthcare application.

> *The following steps assume that you have access to the SDR Healthcare Audit sample database. Information on setting up this database, as well as the other data sources needed for the SDR Healthcare application, can be found in Appendix A.*

1. Launch Excel (with PowerPivot for Excel installed) and open the `SDR_Healthcare.xlsx` file that can be found on this book's companion Web site (`www.wrox.com`). The workbook will contain an Excel table that will be used in a later step.

2. Start PowerPivot for Excel. Select the PowerPivot tab in the ribbon, and click on the PowerPivot Window button to bring up the PowerPivot Window.

3. In the PowerPivot Window, click on the From Database button and, in the drop-down, select From SQL Server. The Table Import Wizard appears.

4. Enter the information as shown in Figure 3-30 to connect to the SDR Healthcare SQL Server database (your SQL Server name may be different) and click the Next button.

5. In the "Choose How to Import the Data" page, choose the option to select from a list of tables and click the Next button.

6. In the next "Select Tables and Views" page, navigate to the `vAuditLog_ServerActions` source table and check it.

FIGURE 3-30: Connection information for the SDR Healthcare database

7. Click on the "Preview and Filter" button to bring up the Preview Selected Table dialog. This is a huge table, and cutting down the amount of data per row will really help performance. So, let's filter out the columns you don't need. Click on the checkbox at the far left of the dialog to deselect all columns, and then check the following columns:

➤ `EventDate`

➤ `audited_action_id`

➤ `audited_class_type_id`

➤ `server_principal_name_id`

➤ `database_principal_name_id`

➤ `audited_object_id`

➤ `session_id`

➤ `client_address_id`

➤ `event_count`

8. Click OK to close the "Preview and Filter" dialog. If you click the Applied Filters link in the Filter Details column of the grid, you should see the columns listed, as shown in Figure 3-31.

FIGURE 3-31: Applied filters for the `v_AuditLog_ServerActions` table

9. Click the Finish button to begin the import.

Importing will take a while, as more than 45 million rows are in the table. Once the import is completed, save the workbook. This is the main data for the sample application. Assuming all went well, the PowerPivot Window should look like Figure 3-32.

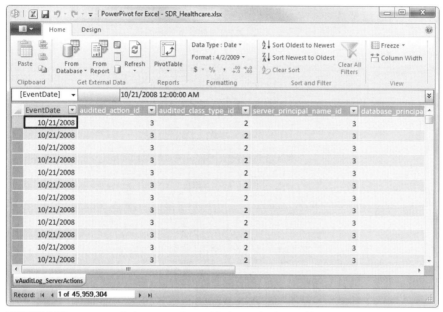

FIGURE 3-32: `SDR_Healthcare.xlsx` with the main data table imported

Importing the Related Tables

Now you are ready to import the related tables that you will need to analyze the main table data and create the reports for the sample application. The following steps show how to do this:

1. In the PowerPivot Window, click the Design tab in the ribbon and click on the Existing Connections button to bring up the Existing Connections dialog. Since the related tables are in the same SQL Server database, there is no need to create a new connection to do the import, which is what would happen if you started the Import Wizard from scratch again.

2. In the Existing Connections dialog, select the SDR Healthcare Database connection in the PowerPivot Data Connections section of the list. Then click the Open button. The Table Import Wizard opens at the "Choose How to Import the Data" page.

3. Choose the option to select from a list of tables, and click the Next button.

4. In the "Select Tables and Views" page, check the following tables:

> ➤ `auditedAction`

> ➤ `AuditedClassType`

> ➤ `AuditedObject`

➤ ClientAddress

➤ DatabasePrincipalName

➤ ServerPrincipalName

5. Click the Finish button to import the related tables. This should take much less time than importing the main data table. Assuming the import succeeded, the Table Import Wizard Importing page should look like Figure 3-33.

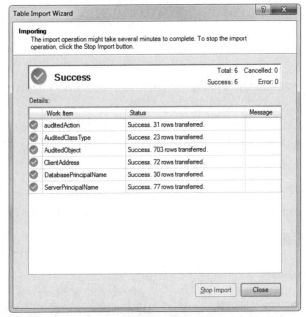

FIGURE 3-33: Successful Import of the related tables for SDR_Healthcare.xlsx

6. Click the Close button and save the workbook.

Adding Data from Other Sources

You're almost finished with bringing the initial data into the SDR_Healthcare.xlsx PowerPivot application. You just need to add some data to Excel that you need for analysis and reporting, but this data isn't available in any of the databases from which you can import.

Creating a Linked Excel Table

The ServerGroupName worksheet in the SDR_Healthcare.xlsx workbook contains data that maps servers to server groups. *Server groups* are an organizational concept that is not reflected in any database at SDR Healthcare, but was asked for by the users of the healthcare application. This data is not expected to change very often, but at some point, it may have to be updated. For example, when new servers are added, they will have to be added to this table. When servers are retired, they will have to be removed.

For this reason, you should bring this data in as a linked table. The following steps show how to do this:

1. Select the `ServerGroupName` worksheet and select all the cells that have data in them.

2. In the PowerPivot tab of the ribbon, click on the "Create Linked Table" button. The Create Table dialog appears. Click the OK button.

3. The PowerPivot Window comes up, and PowerPivot adds a linked table from the data in the Excel table. Right-click the linked table's tab and rename it to `ServerGroupName`.

4. Save the workbook.

Importing from SharePoint

SDR Healthcare has a SharePoint list that maps database names to groups. Let's import this SharePoint list into your PowerPivot workbook. Follow these steps:

1. With the `SDR_Healthcare.xlsx` workbook open, navigate to the SharePoint list that contains the database name mapping. (See Appendix A for information on how to set this up.)

2. In the SharePoint Ribbon, under List Tools, click on the List tab.

3. Click on the "Export as Data Feed" button, as shown in Figure 3-34.

4. The Atom Launcher dialog comes up. Select `SDR_Healthcare.xlsx` and click the OK button.

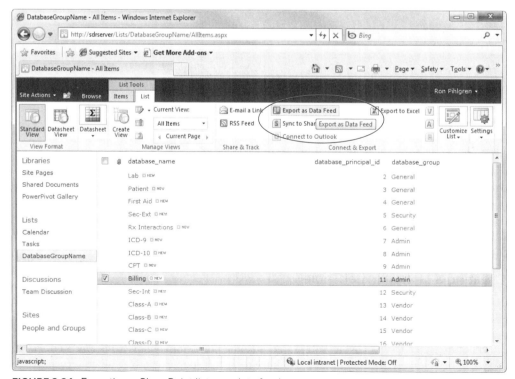

FIGURE 3-34: Exporting a SharePoint list as a data feed

5. The PowerPivot Window appears, followed by the Table Import Wizard's Data Feed page. Click the Next button.

6. In the "Select Tables and Views" page, ensure that the `DatabaseGroupName` item is checked. Click on the "Preview & Filter" button and clear the checkbox on the upper-left corner of the data grid to deselect all columns. Then, select only the following columns for importing:

➤ `Database_principal_id`

➤ `Database_name`

➤ `Database_group`

7. Click the OK button.

8. Back in the "Select Tables and Views" page, click the Finish button to do the import.

You now have the `DatabaseGroupName` table imported from a SharePoint list in your workbook.

Importing from Reporting Services 2008 R2

The last data source to import data from in this chapter is a SQL Server Reporting Services 2008 R2 report. Follow these steps:

1. Ensure that the `SDR_Healthcare.xlsx` workbook is opened.

2. Navigate to the `ClientAddressToState` report. (Appendix A contains instructions for setting this up.) If you set up your report server on a machine named `sdrserver` and created your report in the `Shared Documents` folder, the URL would be as follows:

```
http://sdrserver/ReportServer/Pages/ReportViewer.aspx?http://sdrserver/
    Shared%20Documents/ClientAddressToState.rdl
```

3. Click on the report's "Export to Data Feed" button, as shown in Figure 3-35. Select to open the file.

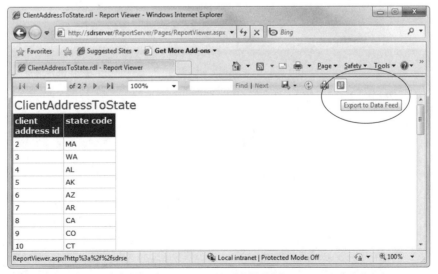

FIGURE 3-35: Exporting a Reporting Services 2008 R2 Report as a data feed

4. In the Atom Launcher dialog, select the `SDR_Healthcare.xlsx` workbook and click the OK button. The "Connect to a Data Feed" dialog appears.

5. Click the Next button and then the Finish button to import the data from the data feed.

6. Once the import completes, click the Close button.

7. Rename the table to `ClientAddressToState`.

Congratulations! You have successfully brought in all the initial data into the SDR Healthcare application.

SUMMARY

This chapter explained all about bringing data into PowerPivot from various external data sources. It talked about importing data and touched on all the different data sources that could be imported into PowerPivot workbooks. It also described how to create linked Excel tables. The SDR Healthcare application, which you will progressively build through the following chapters of the book, was introduced, and you brought in the initial data that you'll use to start building the application.

Chapter 4 focuses on taking the data that was brought into PowerPivot and working with it to build an analytical application. You'll learn how to enrich the data you brought in to PowerPivot by creating relationships between tables, adding calculated columns to your tables, and adding calculated measures to your PowerPivot data using the power of the DAX expression language. You'll see how to use filtering and sorting in the PowerPivot Window to do some initial analysis of your data. You'll also learn how to update your PowerPivot data when the data changes or the analysis you want to do requires it. Those capabilities are key aspects of creating a self-service BI application.

Enriching Data

In Chapter 3, you learned how to import data into PowerPivot for Excel. After importing data from multiple sources, the most natural thing to do is to integrate and enrich your data. The PowerPivot Window helps you to integrate data from multiple sources by setting up relationships. In addition, you can enrich your model and data within the PowerPivot Window.

You performed both integration and enrichment of data in Chapter 2. In this chapter, you will learn these in depth. After enriching your data, you can perform preliminary analysis of your data within the PowerPivot Window with operations such as filtering and sorting. In addition, you also have the capability to refresh your data within the PowerPivot Window. You'll learn about these operations in this chapter, along with internal details.

EXPLORING THE POWERPIVOT WINDOW

As a refresher to what you learned in Chapter 2 and Chapter 3, Figure 4-1 shows various tabs in the PowerPivot Window. In the top and middle of Figure 4-1, you can see the tabs Home and Design. The common operations expected to be performed by customers appear in the Home tab. As the name suggests, the Design tab has operations that help in enhancing the data. You also have a context-sensitive tab called Linked Table shown in the bottom portion of Figure 4-1. This tab is enabled only when a linked Excel table is selected in the PowerPivot Window.

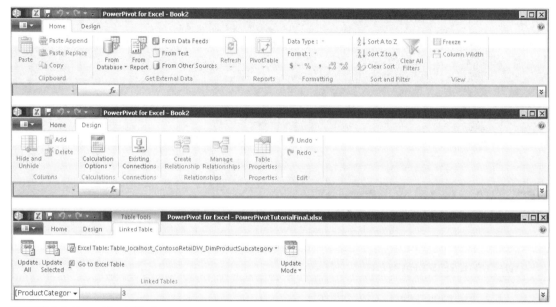

FIGURE 4-1: PowerPivot Window

You have learned about using the Home tab to import data from external data sources, including relational databases, flat files, Reporting Services reports, and Atom data feeds. All these can be accomplished by launching the import wizard for the appropriate data source, as you learned in Chapter 3.

Data Refresh

Since the time you imported data into PowerPivot, more data may have been imported into your back-end data source, or the data on your backend might have been updated or changed. To get the updated data (which can be either updates to existing data within PowerPivot, or new rows), PowerPivot provides you with the option to refresh the data.

To refresh data within a specific table, or refresh data from all the tables that have been retrieved from an external data source, PowerPivot provides the Refresh and Refresh All options that you can access by clicking the Refresh button, as shown in Figure 4-2. The Refresh option refreshes data from the currently selected table. The Refresh All option refreshes data on all the tables.

FIGURE 4-2: Refreshing imported data

You might recall from Chapters 2 and 3 that PowerPivot for Excel loads an in-memory engine called the VertiPaq engine that aids in storing imported data efficiently, as well as enabling efficient execution time on any operations on the model and data stored within the VertiPaq engine. Once you click Refresh, PowerPivot sends a command to the VertiPaq engine to update any metadata changes that you might have done in the PowerPivot modeling window and then retrieves the most recent content from external data sources.

PowerPivot sends two commands to the VertiPaq engine when you click Refresh:

➤ `Alter` — The first command, `Alter`, makes any metadata changes you might have made in the PowerPivot Window.

➤ `Process` — The `Process` command refreshes the data from external data sources and any calculations that depend on the refreshed data. A `Process` command with the `ProcessData` processing type option refreshes the data in the selected table. A `Process` command with the processing option `ProcessRecalc` helps in evaluating all calculations that have been defined in the PowerPivot Window, based on the data in the current table.

 You'll learn more about the various types of calculations in PowerPivot later in this chapter, and in Chapter 6.

If you select the Refresh All option, PowerPivot first sends the `Alter` command to update the metadata and then sends a command that contains only a single `Process` command with the processing option `ProcessFull`. When there are multiple tables that need to be updated, `ProcessFull` is an efficient way to retrieve data for all the tables in parallel, as compared to sending `Process` commands for each table. The Analysis Services VertiPaq engine determines the most efficient parallelization of data retrieval for each table, based on the dependencies, and then completes an evaluation of any calculations in the tables.

After you click the Refresh or Refresh All option, you will see a Data Refresh Progress dialog, as shown in Figure 4-3. You will periodically see the progress of your refresh based on the number of tables selected. If there are any issues during data refresh, you will be able to see these in the Message column. You can stop the refresh at any time by clicking the Stop Refresh button. Any data that was imported up to that time will be ignored, and the previous data within PowerPivot will be restored.

Formatting Data

After you have imported data into PowerPivot, you may need to change the type of the data, or format the data to help in your analysis. In the Home tab of the PowerPivot Window, you can see a group called Formatting (located to the right of the Refresh button in Figure 4-1) that helps you to perform formatting on the columns imported into PowerPivot. PowerPivot provides ways to change the data type, as well as apply formatting on the data.

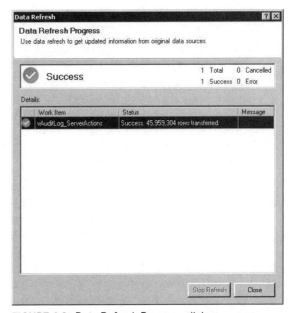

FIGURE 4-3: Data Refresh Progress dialog

PowerPivot supports the data types Text, Decimal Number, Whole Number, Currency, True/False, and Date. While importing the data from a data source, PowerPivot maps the columns in a table to one of the six data types that are supported. As mentioned in Chapter 3, PowerPivot Window behavior is such that, if a data type is not supported, it will not be shown or imported.

After data is imported into PowerPivot, you have the capability to change the data type of each column of the data. For example, let's say that you imported a column from Decimal Number or Whole Number to a Currency data type, just in case the actual data in the column represents currency. Similarly, if a specific column containing integer data was imported as Text, then you might consider changing the data type to Whole Number.

PowerPivot for Excel provides the flexibility to change the underlying storage data type for a column. To change the data type of a column, first select the column, and then click the Data Type drop-down button, as shown in Figure 4-4. Then select the desired data type. PowerPivot sends an Alter command to change the underlying data type of the column chosen. Updated results for the column will be reflected in the PowerPivot Window after the operation has successfully completed.

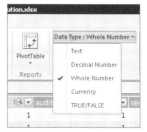

FIGURE 4-4: Changing column data type

For specific data types such as Date, you will not see all six data type formatting options in the Data Type drop-down. Instead, you will only see the data type conversions that are feasible, such as Text, Decimal Number, and Date. In certain cases, changing the data type can result in loss of precision for the underlying data. PowerPivot for Excel recognizes this, and will provide you a warning dialog if you still want to continue. Some data type conversions are not feasible, such as changing a column of data type Text to True/False. You will get an error in the PowerPivot Window.

Changing the data type changes the underlying storage of the column. However, for efficient viewing, and in order to not lose precision, you might just want to simply see the data formatted, rather than changing the underlying data type. PowerPivot provides the Format button that helps in changing the format of a column within the PowerPivot Window. This helps in analysis of data within the PowerPivot Window.

Figure 4-5 shows the formatting options for columns that have the data types Whole Number (on the left) and Date (on the right). For the Whole Number data type column, you can see formatting types General, Decimal Number, Whole Number, Currency, Accounting, Percentage, and Scientific. Changing the formatting results in the column data reflecting the change based on chosen format. On the right of Figure 4-5, you can see a wide range of formatting options for a column of data type Date.

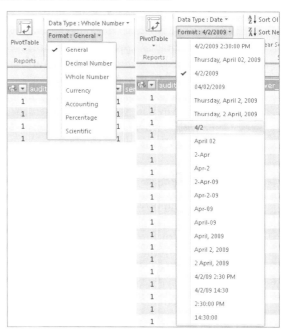

FIGURE 4-5: Formatting column data

In addition to the Format drop-down button in the Formatting group of the Home tab, PowerPivot for Excel provides a set of buttons that help you with formatting numbers efficiently, similar to the formatting available in Excel. Figure 4-6 shows the formatting buttons. You can see that you can change the formatting of a number to a specific currency such as Dollar, Pound, Euro, and so on. You can choose the More Formats option to gain the capability to change the currency symbol for any country in a Currency Format dialog.

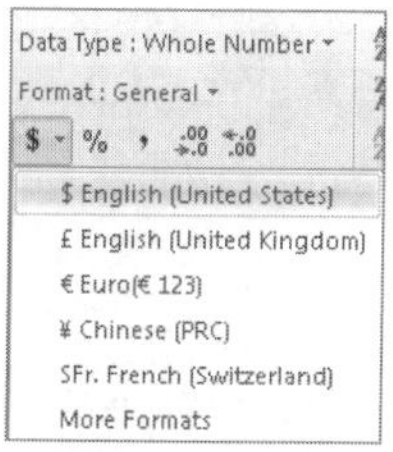

Other buttons include (with icons shown from left to right in Figure 4-6) percentage formatter, thousands separator (comma), decrease decimal format-

FIGURE 4-6:
Formatting columns

ting, and increase decimal formatting. These also allow you to change the specific formatting for the column. If you perform a similar formatting operation in Excel, the formatting is only applied to a specific cell. However, in PowerPivot, the formatting is applied to the entire column.

Column Operations

PowerPivot allows you to view the data in the tabular format of rows and columns. Conceptually, everyone who has performed an analysis of data is familiar with rows and columns, since they have viewed or analyzed data in Excel, or managed data in a relational database system. PowerPivot allows you to view the data in the form of tables that contain rows and columns.

PowerPivot allows you to perform operations such as sorting or filtering that help in data analysis. You can also perform operations on the columns, such as freezing or changing a column width for efficiently viewing data in the PowerPivot Window. Finally, the PowerPivot Window allows you to hide or unhide columns, as well as to add or delete columns.

Sorting and Filtering

One of the key operations performed in Excel or other tools used for analyzing data is the capability to sort or filter data. Sorting and filtering data allows you to analyze the data, such as finding the maximum or minimum and/or unique values in a column. You can perform sorting in two ways within the PowerPivot Window.

After you select a column, you can use the "Sort Smallest to Largest" or "Sort Largest to Smallest" buttons in the "Sort and Filter" group of the Home tab, as shown in Figure 4-7. The second way to sort a column is to choose these options from the drop-down selection for the column, which is also shown in Figure 4-7. The sort option you see in the Home tab or in the drop-down depends on the data type of the column selected. For a column of Date data type, you will see "Sort Oldest to Newest" and "Sort Newest to Oldest." For a column of Text data type you will see "Sort A to Z" and "Sort Z to A."

Filtering of values within a specific column is accomplished by choosing the right filter from the drop-down list after you select a specific column. When you choose a specific column drop-down, PowerPivot sends a query to the VertiPaq engine to retrieve the data to be shown in a list of unique values for that column. The VertiPaq engine supports a style of SQL queries called *tabular queries*. Support for these queries was added as part of PowerPivot development to ensure fast execution time on millions of rows of data.

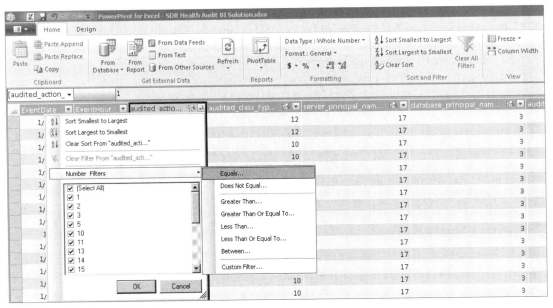

FIGURE 4-7: Sorting and filtering

The tabular queries are similar to the SELECT statements in SQL. The syntax of a tabular query is as follows:

```
SELECT
[SKIP <integer argument>]
[TOP <integer argument>]
<list_of_columns> | COUNT(*)
FROM <object>
[NATURAL JOIN <object>][NATURAL JOIN <object>...]
[WHERE <search_condition>]
ORDER BY [<column> [ASC | DESC],] <$Row_Num> [ASC]
```

The tabular query syntax provides the option to skip certain rows, or retrieve the first N rows, along with the option to order the queries in ascending or descending order. When a table is imported into PowerPivot, a column called RowNumber is added to it, which is not visible in the PowerPivot Window. This RowNumber column is utilized to retrieve appropriate data when you scroll through the pages of data in the PowerPivot Window for a specific table so that data is retrieved efficiently by the VertiPaq engine. You can specify the appropriate RowNumber in the tabular query.

PowerPivot retrieves the first 1,001 distinct values of the chosen column when you select the drop-down for a specific column. The first 1,001 values are shown as values that you can filter. There are two ways to filter data in PowerPivot. The first option is to select the specific values in the column shown in the drop-down to apply the filter. The second option is to select the filter via filters allowed for the data type.

For example, if you have a column with a Number, you can specify a filter of equals, not equals, in between, and so on. When you select one of the Number filter options shown in Figure 4-7, you can specify the filter condition in the Custom Filter dialog shown in Figure 4-8.

You have the option to specify two filter conditions using the And operator. Unlike Excel, which allows you to specify both And and Or operators, PowerPivot currently only supports the And operator. If you have a column of Text or Date data type, PowerPivot currently only supports Equals and Does Not Equal operators, while Excel sup-

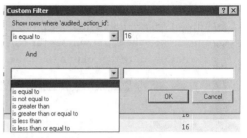

FIGURE 4-8: Custom Filter dialog

ports a rich set of filters. You can perform a few custom filter operations such as "begins with" for a text column using a calculated column with appropriate DAX expression. You should look forward to enhancements in custom filters in future releases of PowerPivot. The filter and sort only help to view and analyze the data efficiently in the PowerPivot Window. These operations do not change the underlying PowerPivot data stored in the VertiPaq database.

View, Move, and Edit

PowerPivot allows you to adjust the column width, as well as freeze certain columns, for more efficient viewing of the columns in a table. PowerPivot provides a default column width for each column after importing the data. You can change the width of the column by selecting the column and clicking the Column Width button shown in Figure 4-9 in the Home tab of the PowerPivot Window. You can enter the new column width in the Column Width dialog.

FIGURE 4-9: Freeze and Column Width buttons

However, the most intuitive way to change the column width is to select the right end of the column and double-click or drag to the desired length. Double-clicking on the right edge of the column adjusts the column to the maximum width needed for displaying the values and title of the column.

When a table contains columns that do not fit within the PowerPivot Window, then you must use the scroll bar at the bottom of the window to navigate to the columns not visible in the PowerPivot Window. However, while navigating to those columns on the right, the columns on the left are not seen within the PowerPivot Window. If you want specific columns to be visible while navigating to other columns, one of the ways is to freeze the columns using the Freeze button shown in Figure 4-9.

For example, for a Customer table, you may have the columns social security number, name, salary, address, city, state, country, age, occupation, education, and marital status. Assume that some of the columns such as city, state, country, age, occupation, and education do not fit within the PowerPivot Window. To view the values in those columns, and associate them with a specific customer, you must be able to see them together within the PowerPivot Window. Freezing the columns social security number and name helps you to view the values corresponding to a specific customer as you scroll right to view the columns in the PowerPivot Window.

In order to freeze a column, select the column and click the Freeze button. You will immediately see this column moved to the far left (the first column) of the table. If you want to choose multiple columns, and then select Freeze, those columns must be adjacent to each other. You can select the columns by pressing the Shift key and selecting the columns, or by multi-selecting the columns using your mouse. If you want to freeze columns that are not adjacent to each other, then you must first move the columns next to each other, and then select Freeze.

Moving columns from one location to another is as simple as selecting a column and then dragging and dropping it to the desired location. First, select the column, and move the mouse cursor to the column name, where you will see the cursor change to a "four arrows" shape. While clicking the left mouse button, drag the column to the desired location, as shown in Figure 4-10.

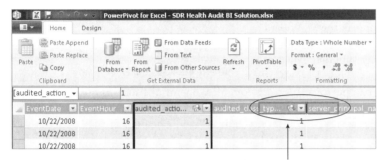

New location for the column

FIGURE 4-10: Moving a column

Other operations you can perform on a column include Rename, Copy, Delete, Hide, or Unhide, and creating relationships between columns. You can perform these operations (as well as the Filter, Freeze Columns, and Column Width operations) from the context menu of a column. Right-click on a column to reveal the operations or actions that can be performed on a column, as shown in Figure 4-11.

To rename a column, in the PowerPivot Window, either double-click on the column name, or choose Rename Column from the context menu of the column. Then, enter the new name for the column.

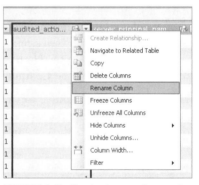

FIGURE 4-11: Context menu for a column

To delete a column of a table that was imported into PowerPivot, right-click on the column, and click Delete Columns, or click the Delete button in the Columns group of the Design tab, as shown in Figure 4-12.

PowerPivot allows you to hide or unhide columns from the PowerPivot Window, or from the PowerPivot field list when you create PivotTables or PivotCharts. Chapter 2 discussed how to hide or unhide columns in the PowerPivot Window using the Hide and Unhide button in the Columns tab, or using the context menu of the column shown in Figure 4-11. Typically,

FIGURE 4-12: Column operations in the Design tab

you would hide a column from the PowerPivot Window or PivotTable (or both) when you use the column for calculations to derive a value, and the actual column is not beneficial in analysis.

An example of such a column would be when you have a `Date` column from source data that is then used to create calculated columns for `Year`, `Month`, and `Date` using DAX expressions. While you need the original `Date` column, it would be more meaningful to just show the `Year`, `Month`, and `Date` columns for analysis and reports.

Relationships

So far, you have learned about most of the operations to analyze and update the data that can be accomplished in the Home tab of the PowerPivot Window, as well as operations on columns in the Home and Design tabs. There are two key aspects to enriching your data and model in PowerPivot:

➤ Establishing relationships between tables

➤ Creating custom calculations that help you with business analysis of your data

This section focuses on creating and managing relationships.

A *relationship* is essentially a link between two tables. When you define a relationship between two tables, you are connecting a single record in one table to one or more records in another table. For example, assume you have `Customer` and `Geography` tables, as shown in Figure 4-13.

The `Customer` table has `CustomerID` as the *primary key* (PK) that is unique to each customer, and has the columns `LastName`, `FirstName`, `Address`, `GeographyID`, `Salary`, `Age`, and `Marital Status`.

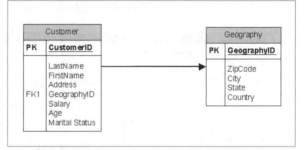

FIGURE 4-13: Relationship between Customer and Geography tables

The `Geography` table has `GeographyID` as the primary key (PK), and has the additional columns `ZipCode`, `City`, `State`, and `Country`.

Essentially, the `GeographyID` has a unique entry for each `ZipCode`. The `GeographyID` in the `Customer` table is linked to as a `GeographyID` in the `Geography` table. The `GeographyID` in `Customer` table is also referred to as a *foreign key* (FK1), as it is linked to the primary key in another table. This link forms a *one-to-many relationship* between the two tables.

There are obviously many customers living in a `ZipCode`. Hence, the `GeographyID` in the `Customer` table forms the "many" side of the relationship, while the `GeographyID` in the `Geography` table forms the "one" side of the relationship. Once you establish this relationship, you can perform data analysis such as counting the number of customers in a specific city or the number of customers in a specific income range in a specific city or state. These types of analysis are only feasible because there is a one-to-many relationship between the `Customer` and `Geography` tables.

When you import data into PowerPivot from a specific data source, PowerPivot looks for relationships defined between tables in that data source at the time of import. As discussed in Chapter 3, if PowerPivot identifies the relationships, PowerPivot will import all the relationships between the tables being imported, and create those relationships between the tables imported into PowerPivot. However, if there is no relationship, or if you import data from multiple data sources, and if you know there are one-to-many relationships between the tables in PowerPivot, you can define the relationships in the PowerPivot Window, as discussed in Chapter 2.

You define relationships between the two tables by selecting the column in the table that contains the "many" side, right-click, and select Create Relationship from the context menu. Alternately, you can select the column to be used to define the relationship, and click on the Create Relationship button in the Relationships group in the Design tab of the PowerPivot Window.

In the Create Relationship dialog shown in Figure 4-14, the Related Lookup Table is the table that contains the data on the "one" side of the one-to-many relationship. The Related Lookup Column should be a column with unique values only. You must specify the Related Lookup Table and the Related Lookup Column from the drop-down lists, and then click the Create button. When you click Create, PowerPivot sends a command to verify, and then marks the Related Lookup Column unique. PowerPivot then creates the relationship between the tables so that you can query the aggregated data via the Related Lookup Column values.

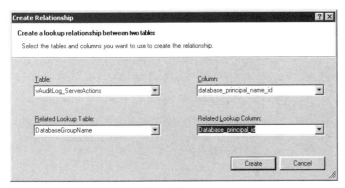

FIGURE 4-14: Creating a relationship

You should be aware of two important factors concerning relationships between tables in this version of PowerPivot:

➤ Relationships between two tables can only be accomplished via a single column.

➤ You can only have a single relationship between any two tables.

As shown in Figure 4-14, the dialog only allows you to create a relationship using a single column. Hence, if you have two tables where you need to utilize a combination of columns to define relationships, then you must create a calculated column that combines one or more columns using DAX before creating the relationship.

For example, let's say that you have a Sales table containing product sales information for each day, and a Date table that contains information from only a week. If you must establish relationships between the tables to view and analyze the product sales for each month, you need a way to define a calculated column called SalesWeekYear that maps to the correct week based on the date of transaction, and then you would need to create a relationship with the appropriate week column in the Date table. While importing data from the data source, if PowerPivot detects multiple columns utilized for relationships between any two tables, it does not import the relationship.

PowerPivot only allows a single relationship between any two tables. This means that if you want to establish two distinct relationships between two tables, you must import another instance of the table. For example, say you had `Sales` and `Customer` tables. You might have `ShippedToCustomerID` and `BilledToCustomerID` as two columns in the `Sales` table. All the customers are in the `Customer` table. However, since PowerPivot only allows a single relationship to be established, you can only define one relationship. If you want to aggregate and analyze data of `ShippedToCustomers` and `BilledToCustomers`, then you should import another instance of the `Customer` table.

Once all the relationships have been created, you can then use the Manage Relationships button in the Design tab to see all the relationships between the tables in PowerPivot, as shown in Figure 4-15. Using the Manage Relationships dialog, you can create, modify, or delete relationships using the Create, Edit, and Delete buttons, respectively.

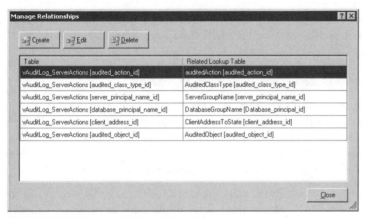

FIGURE 4-15: Manage Relationships dialog

You can create cascading relationships between tables by creating relationships between two tables at a time. For example, if you have the tables `Sales`, `Product`, `ProductSubCategory`, and `ProductCategory`, then you would create relationships between the table pairs `Sales-Product`, `Product-ProductSubCategory`, and `ProductSubCategory-ProductCategory`. After establishing these relationships, you can calculate aggregated sales for each product category. After creating the relationships between tables (which is a very important task for data analysis via PowerPivot), you next can enrich your data by creating calculated columns using DAX expressions.

Data Analysis Expressions (DAX)

Excel provides a variety of functions that help in analysis of the data in Excel workbooks typically within a single sheet. In order to perform analysis on business data, corporations typically build a data warehouse and multi-dimensional databases. Excel workbooks with PivotTables and PivotCharts connect and retrieve data from the multi-dimensional database for analysis.

The creation of a multi-dimensional database typically requires specialized knowledge of dimensional modeling and multi-dimensional expressions (MDX) used for defining calculations and querying from multi-dimensional databases. It is not an easy transition for an Excel end-user to learn and create multi-dimensional databases. Also, accomplishing data analysis operations in Excel (such as time intelligence calculations) are either limited or extremely challenging.

PowerPivot for Excel helps to bridge the gap between Excel users and multi-dimensional database specialists. Excel users can make an easy transition from Excel knowledge to PowerPivot to enjoy the richness of analysis that can be accomplished with PowerPivot, without having to learn multi-dimensional concepts or MDX. With the help of Data Analysis Expressions (DAX), PowerPivot enables the Excel user to use capabilities that are not available in Excel and, at the same time, make a smoother transition with Excel-style functions that help in more advanced analytics.

DAX has been created primarily with two key goals in mind:

➤ To ensure ease of use for an Excel user, it has relational database concepts of tables and columns, which a majority of users understand.

➤ Once the PowerPivot user defines the DAX calculations, then the user can create PivotTables or PivotCharts for analysis, similar to what the user would have done while working with data in Excel.

DAX calculations fall into two broad categories in PowerPivot for Excel:

➤ *Creating calculated columns in the PowerPivot Window* — This helps you to create new columns with DAX calculations that range from simple calculations (such as a sum or con-catenation of two columns within a table) to more complex ones that involve multiple tables and aggregating information (such as calculating a sum of revenue for each product, where the actual sales are in a different table). You have seen these examples in Chapter 2.

➤ *Using measures* — Measures are aggregated values that are added to the Values area in the PivotTable field list. While the DAX calculations to create calculated columns are calculated and stored after creating the calculations, measures are evaluated dynamically, based on the filters chosen in the PivotTables.

 Chapter 5 provides more detail on creating measures and PivotTables. This chapter focuses on a DAX overview, and on how calculations are evaluated and applied, along with the wide range of DAX functions available to you for your calculations.

Understanding DAX Expressions

Similar to Excel expressions, DAX calculations are quite simple, and are typically written as an expression that evaluates to a value with the help of tables, columns, DAX functions, and operators. Even in instances where you have complex DAX calculations, the expressions themselves are reason-ably easy to understand, since the expressions use the tables and columns elements. However, while Excel expressions include a range of cells, DAX expressions operate primarily on tables and columns.

Chapter 2 introduced you to the following two DAX expressions:.

```
=FactSales[SalesAmount]-FactSales[TotalCost]                          (1)

=SUMX(RELATEDTABLE(FactSales),FactSales[SalesAmount]))                (2)
```

The first expression (1) is a simple subtraction of two columns within a table that yields the profit. PowerPivot evaluates the DAX expression for each row in the table, and populates the column `FactsSales[Profit]` with the value.

The second DAX expression (2) is defined in the `DimProduct` table. A one-to-many relationship was defined between `FactSales` and `DimProduct` tables. The DAX function `RELATEDTABLE` takes a table as an argument, follows the direction of relationship, and returns all the rows in the table `FactSales`. The `SUMX` aggregation function takes a table and a DAX expression, and evaluates the value for each row in the table. In this DAX expression, DAX takes the `FactSales` table and evaluates the expression `FactSales[SalesAmount]` to calculate the sum of `SalesAmount` for each product in the `DimProduct` table.

DAX supports the basic arithmetic operators for addition (+), subtraction (-), multiplication (*), division (/), and power (^). In addition to the arithmetic operators, DAX supports the comparison operators greater than (>), less than (<), greater than or equal to (>=), less than or equal to (<=), equal to (=), and not equal to (<>). It supports the logical operators || (for OR operations) and && (for AND operations). DAX does not support the logical operators OR or AND that are supported in Excel. DAX supports the "&" as a concatenation operator to concatenate two strings. In addition, DAX supports logical constants, TRUE and FALSE, in DAX expressions.

Following are a few examples of DAX expressions using some of the DAX operators:

```
=FactSales[SalesAmount]*FactSales[CurrencyInUS]
=Customer[FirstName] & Customer[MI] & Customer[LastName]
=(Employee[Salary] > 100000 ) && Employee[DaysInService] = 60)
```

The DAX sample expressions in this chapter include the format `TableName[ColumnName]`. This is the recommended way to avoid any conflicts of column name clashes between two tables. However, you can include just the column name in the DAX expressions as shown in the following examples. If you include the format `TableName[ColumnName]`, those expressions are referred to as *fully qualified names*.

```
= [SalesAmount]* [CurrencyInUS]
= [FirstName] & [MI] & [LastName]
=( [Salary] > 100000 ) && [DaysInService] = 60)
```

To understand how DAX expressions get evaluated, you should understand the key concepts of row context and filter context.

When a DAX expression is specified for a calculated column, the value for each row is calculated in the context of the row. This is referred to as *row context* in DAX. In a simple DAX expression such as `"= [SalesAmount]-[TotalCost]"`, the `TotalCost` value for a specific row is subtracted from the `SalesAmount` column for the corresponding row. This is very similar to what you would do with expressions in Excel where you specify an operation between two cells.

In a more complex DAX expression in the `DimProduct` table such as `=SUMX(RELATEDTABLE(FactSales), FactSales[SalesAmount]))`, the value of the DAX expression for each row (each row consists of a product) is calculated by scanning the rows in the `FactSales` table for the current row. This means filtering the `FactSales` table that corresponds to the product of the current row, and aggregating the `SalesAmount` value.

When you create a measure with a DAX expression, then the measure is evaluated dynamically based on the filters applied. This is referred to as *filter context*. As discussed earlier, measures are used to create aggregate values, and can only be specified in the context of the PowerPivot field list in the Excel worksheet. If you are familiar with the Excel field list, you will be aware that you can apply filters to view the data in the PivotTable. Similarly, you can apply filters in the PowerPivot field list. The specified measure(s) get evaluated with the filter conditions. There are several DAX functions that are typically (or only) used in the filter context.

 Chapter 5 provides more information and examples of filter context, measures, and related DAX functions.

Understanding DAX Functions

In addition to the previously described operators, DAX provides many functions that help with efficient data analysis. As part of PowerPivot for Excel, DAX has a total of 135 functions. Of these, about 80 functions are supported by Excel. Supporting the Excel functions that Excel users are familiar with helps facilitate a smooth transition to PowerPivot and DAX.

In addition to supporting the Excel functions, DAX provides functions that operate on tables, as well as the capability to navigate between tables via relationships. Even though this appears to be similar to the VLOOKUP Excel function, the DAX functions provide a more powerful functionality required for advanced analytics.

DAX also provides a set of functions that help in identifying the current context of a calculation where certain filters might have been applied, and time-manipulation functions that help in calculations such as efficiently calculating year-over-year revenue growth.

The DAX functions can be categorized into eight broad categories:

➤   Date and Time

➤   Information

➤   Logical

➤   Math and Trigonometric

➤   Statistical

➤   Text

➤   Filter

➤   Time Intelligence

The following discussions provide a brief overview of the class of functions with sample DAX expressions that utilize the functions. Detailed information on all DAX functions is available in Appendix B, which is available for download from this book's accompanying Web site (www.wrox.com).

Date and Time Functions

The 17 *date and time* functions supported in DAX are similar to Excel functions with regard to arguments taken, and the results from the functions. For example, if your table contains a column that stores a date, and if you want to have separate columns for year, month, and day of the date, then you can use DAX expressions to define the respective calculated columns that utilize the DAX functions Year, Month, and Day.

In the following DAX expressions, FactSales is a table, and SaleDate is a column of data type Date, containing a date value. The function TODAY() returns today's date, which can then be utilized to calculate values such as elapsed days from the date a shipment was made to a customer. If you utilize the NOW() function, you get current date and time values. However, you would need to ensure that you chose the right date format in order to see the time.

```
=Year(FactSales[SaleDate])
=Month(FactSales[SaleDate])
=Day(FactSales[SaleDate])
```

Information Functions

Information functions help in evaluating a scalar value, or a DAX expression resulting in a scalar value, and return TRUE or FALSE. For example, you can identify if a value is a number, text, or blank using the information DAX functions. These functions are similar to functions in Excel but operate on columns or DAX expressions that evaluate to a value.

Following are some examples of DAX expressions using information functions:

```
=ISNUMBER(SalesFact[SalesAmount])
=ISTEXT(DimCustomer[LastName])
```

Logical Functions

There are seven *logical* functions supported by DAX that are similar to Excel. The functions AND, OR, and NOT help in evaluating expressions passed as parameters, based on the logical operation, and return the value TRUE or FALSE. These functions are an alternative to the logical operators supported by DAX.

The functions FALSE() and TRUE() return the logical value, and are typically expected to be used in a function or a DAX expression that returns multiple values. For example, IF() is also a logical function that, based on the result of an evaluation of first value, can result in either the second argument or the third argument.

Following are examples of logical DAX functions. The first expression evaluates if the SalesAmount of a transaction is between 50000 and 100000, and returns TRUE or FALSE. The second DAX expression "bucketizes" the customers based on their age as 60, 40, or 20. The IF function returns one of the two values provided as a parameter based on the result of the expression being evaluated.

```
=AND(FactSales[SalesAmount]>50000, FactSales[SalesAmount]< 100000)
=IF(DimCustomer[Age]>60, 60, IF(DimCustomer[Age]>40, 40,20))
```

Math and Trigonometric Functions

DAX supports 25 *math and trigonometric* functions. While Excel supports a larger set of math and trigonometric functions, PowerPivot for Excel currently supports the most important functions in this release. Some examples of the functions are ABS (which returns the absolute value of a number), INT (which converts a number to integer), SQRT (which calculates the square root of a number), RAND (which generates a random number greater than or equal to 0, and less than 1), and LOG10 (which calculates the logarithm of a number).

Most of the functions are self-explanatory and help in creating DAX expressions for calculated columns, as well as measures.

 For a complete list of math and trigonometric functions, as well as examples, see Appendix B (downloadable from www.wrox.com*).*

Statistical Functions

Similar to math and trigonometric functions, only a subset of Excel's *statistical* functions is supported by DAX in this release. The parameters for the statistical functions supported by DAX are column or table, or DAX expressions, while these functions in Excel take numbers or cell ranges.

Some of the statistical functions supported by DAX are COUNT (which returns the number of cells in a column that contain values), COUNTBLANK (which returns the number of blank cells in a column), and MAX and MIN (which returns the largest and smallest numeric values in a column).

Following are examples of DAX expressions using the statistical functions. The first expression uses a MAX function and returns the maximum SalesAmount value in the column by evaluating the value for each row. The second expression uses a COUNTROWS function as a DAX expression in the DimProduct table that takes the table SalesFact as an argument, and counts the number of rows where a relationship between FactSales and DimProduct has been established. You will see the calculated column be evaluated with the count of rows in the FactSales table.

```
=MAX(SalesFact[SalesAmount])
=COUNTROWS(SalesFact)
```

Text Functions

DAX supports 18 *text* functions for string manipulations (such as getting the length of the string, concatenating strings, and searching or replacing substrings). Similar to previous categories of DAX functions, Excel supports a large category of text functions.

Following are some examples of text functions used in DAX expressions. The first DAX expression is a simple concatenation operation of FirstName and LastName of a customer. The second expression is a calculated column that indicates whether a product contains the word "MILK." If the

SEARCH() function is unable to find a product that contains "MILK" then it returns an error. In order to capture this error and return a value, the IFERROR() function is used. The value returned from the IFERROR() function (-1 if unable to find "MILK," or the starting position where a product that contained "MILK" was found) is then compared against value -1 to determine the value to be returned from IF function. If yes, the calculated column will evaluate to ProductName; if not, the value will be blank with the help of a function called BLANK(). You can then easily sort this column or apply a count of rows to identify the number of products that contain "MILK" in the product name.

```
=CONCATENATE(DimCustomers[FirstName],DimCustomer[LastName])
=IF(IFERROR(SEARCH("MILK",DimProduct[ProductName]),-1)>0,DimProduct
     [ProductName], BLANK())
```

Filter Functions

Filter DAX functions are functions that specifically help in certain advanced analyses. These 14 functions help in navigating tables and iterating over columns to evaluate the DAX expressions. These functions are not supported by Excel. This examination only looks at three functions with examples.

Chapter 2 discusses the DAX expression using RELATEDTABLE. Consider the following three examples:

```
=SUMX(RELATEDTABLE(FactSales),FactSales[SalesAmount]))

=RELATED(DimProduct[ColorName])

=CALCULATE(COUNTROWS(FactSales))
```

In the first example, the expression is specified in the DimProduct table to evaluate the sum of SalesAmount for each Product. While RELATEDTABLE helps in navigating from the DimProduct table to the SalesFact table, the RELATED DAX function helps in navigating from the "many" side of the relationship to the "one" side.

The second DAX expression with the RELATED function retrieves the color name of the product involved in the sales transaction.

The third DAX expression is a variation of the COUNTROWS expression reviewed earlier that is specified in the DimProduct table. The CALCULATE function helps in evaluating the expression in the context of the current filter. Hence, creating a calculated column with CALCULATE will result in being able to identify the number of transactions for a specific product, while the expression without CALCULATE will simply provide the total number of rows in the FactSales table.

Time-Intelligence Functions

In order to perform business analysis, time is a key factor, and most analytics are based on an evaluation of sales, revenue, or inventory for a quarter, month, year, or year-over-year. DAX provides 34 *time-intelligence* functions (such as PARALLELPERIOD, TOTALMTD, TOTALQTD, and so on) that help in time-intelligence calculations based on the specific filters applied. Almost all the time-intelligence functions are primarily used to create measures.

Appendix B (available at www.wrox.com*) provides examples of the time-intelligence functions.*

Most of the sample DAX examples you've seen here included fully qualified column names, even though most DAX functions will accept just the column name. In addition to the set of time-intelligence functions, certain DAX functions only take fully qualified names as arguments. They are `Values`, `All`, `Distinct`, `Calculate`, `CalculateTable`, and `Related`. Let's now take a look at how to specify DAX expressions in the PowerPivot Window.

Creating DAX Calculations in the PowerPivot Window

Once you import data into PowerPivot, one of the key ways to enrich your data is to create calculated columns using DAX expressions. You can add a new calculated column to an existing table in the PowerPivot Window by going to the last column titled Add Column and entering a DAX expression in the formula bar.

Alternately, you can click the Add Column button in the Columns group of the Design tab, which will take you to the first Add Column column and position the cursor in the formula bar. Figure 4-16 shows a DAX expression using the RELATED DAX function specified in the formula bar.

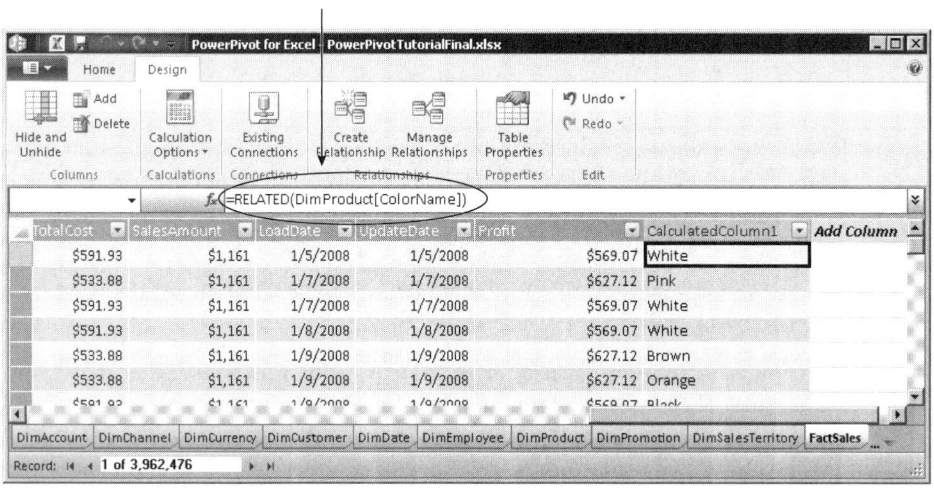

FIGURE 4-16: Adding a calculated column

The formula bar is where you enter DAX expressions. You can either type the entire DAX expression or do a combination of typing and selecting specific columns to be included in the DAX expression. Utilizing a combination of typing the DAX expression and selecting columns (by using a mouse and clicking), is a feature called *semi-select*. This essentially means that you do not have to type the entire table/column name or fully qualified names, and you have the capability to select columns.

In addition to the semi-select feature, the formula bar also supports *autocomplete,* which is an extremely useful feature, especially when you are learning new syntax of a language or expressions. The autocomplete feature provides hints to you that indicate the parameters to be provided to the function. This feature also helps in identifying closing parenthesis, as well as highlighting the list of table or column options available as you enter text.

Figure 4-17 shows the autocomplete feature available in the PowerPivot Window. You can see that a DAX expression with the IF function is being typed. Notice the parameter or arguments that must be passed for the IF function. As you type **dimpro**, PowerPivot shows all the table or column names starting with those characters. If you know a specific column name to be included, you can traverse through the drop-down list and press the Tab key to make the selection.

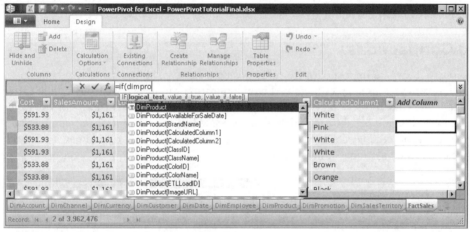

FIGURE 4-17: DAX formula editor and autocomplete

The autocomplete feature helps you to efficiently enter DAX calculations. If you have a semantic error or syntax error, then PowerPivot displays a warning symbol, and the new calculated column will be populated with #ERROR. Along with the warning, you will see a drop-down that provides more information on the type of error that occurred.

The PowerPivot Window supports two calculation modes. The default mode is the *automatic calculation mode,* where the DAX expression is evaluated immediately after the expression is entered for a calculated column or a measure.

In some cases, when you have millions of rows of data, you might want to defer the calculation evaluation until you have entered all the DAX expressions. In such a case, you can switch to the *manual calculation mode* using the Calculation Options drop-down, as shown in Figure 4-18. Once you switch to Manual Calculation Mode, you will see the Calculate Now option enabled, which, when pressed, will perform the evaluation of the DAX calculations.

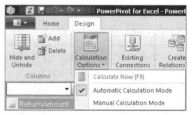

FIGURE 4-18: DAX calculation modes

When the calculation must be evaluated, the PowerPivot Window sends a `Process` command with the processing option `ProcessRecalc`, which is done for all the tables (since there can be calculated columns that are dependent on other calculated columns). The VertiPaq engine identifies the dependencies and only evaluates the calculated columns that need to be evaluated. Once the DAX expression is evaluated for a calculated column, the values are materialized (stored) within the table.

In the context of globalization and localization, there is one key thing about PowerPivot that you should be aware of. By default, PowerPivot for Excel matches the Excel language. If a specific language is not supported, then it falls back to English. When a PowerPivot workbook is created, PowerPivot stores the locale information in which the workbook was created. Because of this persistence, some of the formatting information might not change when you change the locale information in Excel. One such example is the `Currency` data type. Once you change the locale information in Excel, you should close and re-open PowerPivot Window to see most of the formatting changes take effect.

Managing Connections

Chapter 3 discussed ways to import data from various data sources. Since PowerPivot helps in integrating data from various sources, a PowerPivot application can have data from a wide variety of data sources. The PowerPivot Window only shows the tables and columns view, and you do not know which tables were imported from which data source. Also, your definitions or connection strings to your data sources may change, and you may need to refresh data or add new tables. This is when you can use the Existing Connections button.

If you click on the Existing Connections button, you will see the Existing Connections dialog shown in Figure 4-19. Here you will see the list of data sources being used in your PowerPivot application. You have the capability to open an existing data source and import more tables into PowerPivot.

You also have the option to edit the connection string to point to a different source by clicking the Edit button. For example, if you built your PowerPivot application on a sample data set to create the model and your official corporate data is on a different back-end system that has large volumes of data, you can update the connection string and click on the Refresh button to refresh the data in PowerPivot. You can only change one connection at a time. If you click Refresh, you will see the data being refreshed for all the tables that were imported from the chosen connection.

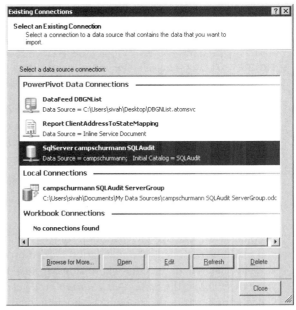

FIGURE 4-19: Existing Connections dialog

The Existing Connections dialog also allows you to delete connections by clicking the Delete button.

Update Import Definition

As just described, the Existing Connections button helps you import data from new tables, manage connections, and refresh all the tables that have been imported from a data source. However, it does not provide fine-grain control of a specific table to add additional columns from an imported table that you might have filtered during initial data import. It also does not allow you to filter some data that you have analyzed as not important within the PowerPivot Window.

The Table Properties button in the Design tab allows you to view and update imported data for a specific table. When you click on the Table Properties button, you will see the Edit Table Properties dialog shown in Figure 4-20. With the help of this dialog, you can see the data from the data source, or from PowerPivot, by clicking the appropriate radio button.

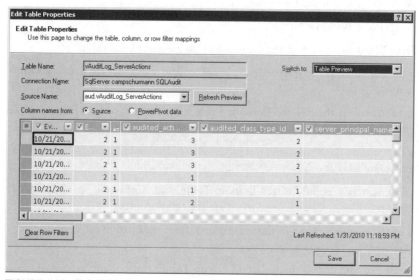

FIGURE 4-20: Edit Table Properties dialog

Also, you can select or de-select columns that were involved in the initial import from this specific table. The Edit Table Properties dialog allows you to switch between Table Preview and the Query editor, where you can provide your custom query to import specific columns, or merge columns via appropriate statements while interacting with the data source. Once you have updated all the query definitions and filters and clicked the Save button, PowerPivot imports the data as per the new query definition. Once all the data has been imported successfully, the old data is deleted, and the new columns and data are displayed in the PowerPivot Window.

ENRICHING DATA FOR THE HEALTHCARE AUDIT APPLICATION

In Chapter 3, you imported data for the SDR Healthcare Audit sample application from a relational data source, Reporting Services report, SharePoint 2010 list, and a linked table in Excel. Let's now enhance the SDR Healthcare Audit application to include the right relationships and calculated columns that will serve as the basis for building PivotTables and PivotCharts that will be used in analysis of the SDR Healthcare Audit data.

Establishing Relationships

The relationships between the tables imported from the relational data source have been established, as the relational back-end has these defined. However, you must establish the relationship between the vAuditLog_ServerActions table and the remaining tables that were imported into PowerPivot.

To do so, follow these steps:

1. Open the SDR_Healthcare.xlsx file at the end of Chapter 3 using Excel 2010.

2. Click on the PowerPivot tab in the Excel ribbon.

3. Click on the PowerPivot Window button.

4. In the PowerPivot Window, switch to the vAuditLog_ServerActions table.

5. Right-click on the column server_principal_name_id and select Create Relationship from the context menu.

6. Select ServerGroupName as the Related Lookup Table, and server_principal_name_id as the Related Lookup Column. Click Create to create the relationship.

7. Right-click on the column database_principal_name in the vAuditLog_ServerActions table and select Create Relationship.

8. Select DatabaseGroupName as the Related Lookup Table, and Database_principal_id as the Related Lookup Column. Click Create to create the relationship.

9. Right-click on client_address_id in the vAuditLog_ServerActions table, and select Create Relationship.

10. Select ClientAddressToState as the Related Lookup Table, and client_address_id as the Related Lookup Column. Click Create to create the relationship.

11. Right-click on audited_action_id in the vAuditLog_ServerActions table and select Create Relationship.

12. Select auditedAction as the Related Loop Table and audited_action_id as the Related Lookup Column. Click Create to create the relationship.

13. Right-click on audited_class_type_id in the vAuditLog_ServerActions table and select Create Relationship.

14. Select AuditedClassType as the Related Loop Table and audited_class_type_id as the Related Lookup Column. Click Create to create the relationship.

15. Right-click on audited_object_id in the vAuditLog_ServerActions table and select Create Relationship.

16. Select AuditedObject as the Related Loop Table and audited_object_id as the Related Lookup Column. Click Create to create the relationship.

17. Save the PowerPivot workbook to ensure that your relationships and DAX calculations are saved within the workbook.

You have now successfully created the relationships between all the tables in the SDR Healthcare Audit application. This will enable you to provide auditing data such as the number of users from a specific state, or a specific group such as Emergency Room, and be able to slice data based on various factors. Once all the relationships have been created, you should see the relationships in the Manage Relationships dialog, as shown in Figure 4-21.

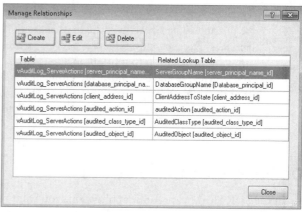

FIGURE 4-21: Relationships between tables in the SDR Healthcare Audit application

---

INSIDE POWERPIVOT

Data in a PowerPivot workbook is made up of two parts:

➤ Excel data, which contains things like definitions of PivotTables, PivotCharts, and other Excel objects

➤ PowerPivot data, which includes the VertiPaq database that contains the actual PowerPivot data.

When the Analysis Services team was implementing the storage model for PowerPivot, they considered two approaches. One approach was to save the Excel data and the PowerPivot database in separate files, and the other approach was to save everything — Excel data and PowerPivot data — together in one file. There were pros and cons to each approach.

If all the content were saved in a single file, Excel still needed to be able to open the file and read all relevant Excel data; PowerPivot needed to be able read the relevant PowerPivot data and load it into the in-memory VertiPaq engine. Also, when the PowerPivot workbook was stored in a SharePoint document library, Excel Calculation Services needed to understand that the workbook contained an in-memory data source that needed to be extracted from the workbook and loaded into the Analysis Services server in VertiPaq mode.

The behavior of extracting PowerPivot data would be challenging to implement; much more difficult than if the data were stored in separate files. However, from the customer perspective, the single-file approach would be easier to understand. If the workbook content were saved in separate files, there would be the added burden of having to keep multiple files together, and in sync.

continues

continued

Early on, there was some question as to whether the single-file solution would even
be possible. There were significant discussions involving members of the Analysis
Services, Excel client, and Excel Services teams. Long hours were spent coming
up with the solution that finally made it into Office 2010 and the first version of
PowerPivot. In the end, both the Office team and the Analysis Services team agreed
that the single-file approach was worth the effort, and provided the right model of
simplicity and ease of use for PowerPivot customers.

Defining DAX Calculations

In the SDR Healthcare Audit application, you want to perform analysis to help understand the activity for a specific year, month, or date. You do have a date column in the vAuditLog_ServerActions table. However, for analysis purposes, you must separate the Year, Month, and Date into separate columns.

Follow these steps to enrich the data in the vAuditLog_ServerActions table using DAX expressions:

1. Create a calculated column called EventYear with the following DAX expression:

   ```
   =YEAR([EventDate])
   ```

2. Create a calculated column called EventMonth with the following DAX expression:

   ```
   =MONTH([EventDate])
   ```

3. Create a calculated column called EventDay with the following DAX expression:

   ```
   =DAY([EventDate])
   ```

4. Create a calculated column called UserSessionID to uniquely identify a specific user's session with the following DAX expression:

   ```
   =CONCATENATE(CONCATENATE([session_id],100+[server_principal_name_id]),
       100+[client_address_id])
   ```

You have now successfully established required relationships to navigate between the various tables imported for the SDR Healthcare Audit application, and have created DAX expressions that will prepare you for creating PivotTables and PivotCharts for analysis.

SUMMARY

This chapter provided an in-depth examination of enriching data by using the PowerPivot Window. You first learned about how to refresh data from the data source, and then about formatting the columns in the PowerPivot Window with various column operations such as sorting, filtering, hiding, and freezing.

You learned about the two key ways to enrich data in the PowerPivot Window, namely, establishing relationships and creating custom calculations using DAX. This chapter provided an overview of DAX, with some examples of DAX expressions that involved various DAX functions. You learned about how DAX helps in data analysis by navigating between tables and iterating over rows in tables.

Finally, you enriched the SDR Healthcare Audit application by establishing appropriate relationships and using DAX expressions.

Chapter 5 focuses on how to create PivotTables and PivotCharts to build reports that help you to analyze the data effectively. Chapter 5 also discusses how to create measures using DAX, as well as the concept of filter context. It will introduce you to the PowerPivot field list and slicers (a new feature in Excel 2010), and how PowerPivot leverages slicers to make it easy to build your self-service BI application.

5

Self-Service Analysis

Up until now, you have seen how to assemble and enrich your self-service BI data using PowerPivot. This has all been preparation for what you will see in this chapter — using Excel to do self-service BI analysis. In the Microsoft BI world, and outside of Microsoft as well, Microsoft Excel is *the* BI analysis tool of choice. PowerPivot is an acknowledgment and acceptance of that fact. This chapter shows how to take your PowerPivot data and use Excel to analyze that data.

PIVOTTABLES AND PIVOTCHARTS

Two features that make Excel an ideal BI client tool are PivotTables and PivotCharts. These features allow you to analyze large quantities of data quickly and easily. This discussion won't go into much detail about how PivotTables and PivotCharts work (entire books have been written on the subject) but will instead focus on how PivotTables and PivotCharts work in the context of PowerPivot workbooks.

For a good look at several books on PivotTables and PivotCharts, see `http://www.amazon.com/s/ref=nb_sb_noss?url=search-alias%3D stripbooks&field-keywords=Excel+PivotTables+and+PivotCharts.`

PowerPivot provides commands that allow you to insert various combinations of PivotTables and PivotCharts into a workbook. These commands can be invoked from the PowerPivot Window (Figure 5-1) or from the PowerPivot tab in the Excel ribbon (Figure 5-2).

FIGURE 5-1: PivotTables and PivotCharts in the PowerPivot Window

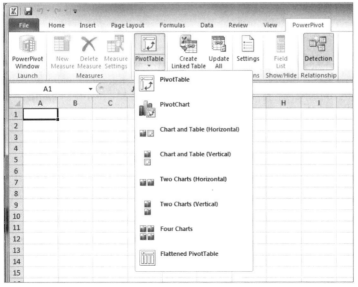

FIGURE 5-2: PivotTables and PivotCharts in the PowerPivot tab of the Excel ribbon

The selections on this menu are the ticket to creating PivotTables and PivotCharts using PowerPivot data. They provide a convenient way to insert a single PivotTable, a single PivotChart, or a combination of PivotTables and PivotCharts into a worksheet.

One reason for having these combinations is convenience — for example, if you know you will want to have four charts on your worksheet, you can insert them all with a single command. There is another reason you will want to choose one of the multi-PivotTable/PivotChart commands over adding them one by one to your workbook that will be discussed in the "Slicers" section later in this chapter. The following sections discuss different PivotTable/PivotChart configurations.

Single PivotTable

This is the most basic configuration. A single PivotTable will be created. Figure 5-3 shows a new PowerPivot PivotTable without any fields added. Note that, for PowerPivot PivotTables (and PivotCharts), the PowerPivot field list is shown, rather than the normal Excel field list. The PowerPivot field list will be described later in this chapter.

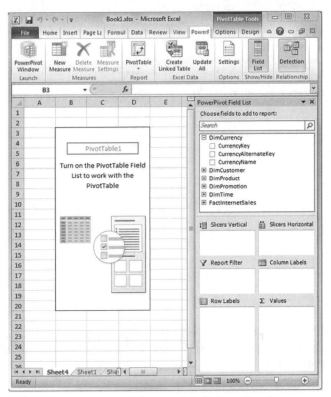

FIGURE 5-3: An empty PowerPivot PivotTable in Excel

Single PivotChart

This configuration creates a single PivotChart. Note that PowerPivot will also create a PivotTable on a separate sheet that contains the data the PivotChart will use. The sheet that is created for the backing PivotTable will be named "Data for Sheet<x> Chart<y>." This naming scheme can help you navigate from the backing PivotTable back to the PivotChart, as long as you don't rename the PivotChart's sheet or move the PivotChart to a different sheet.

There usually won't be a need to refer to the backing PivotTable and you may want to hide that sheet to lessen the number of visible worksheets in the workbook. PowerPivot doesn't do this automatically in order to make you aware that there is a PivotTable behind the PivotChart. Figure 5-4 shows a new PowerPivot PivotChart. Note the tab for the backing PivotTable, "Data for Sheet4 Chart 1."

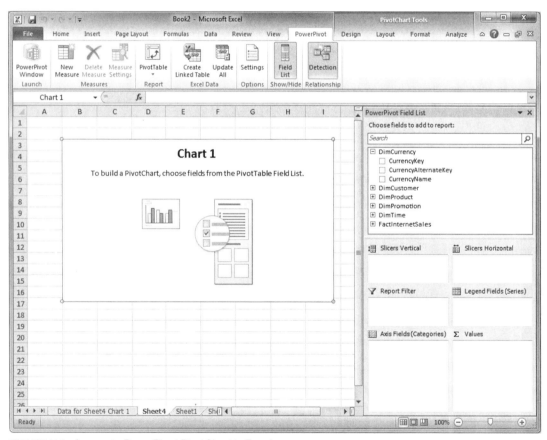

FIGURE 5-4: An empty PowerPivot PivotChart in Excel

The following five configurations will create various combinations of PivotTables and/or PivotCharts:

➤ PivotChart and PivotTable Horizontal

➤ PivotChart and PivotTable Vertical

➤ Two PivotCharts Horizontal

➤ Two PivotCharts Vertical

➤ Four PivotCharts

 Note that for each PivotChart created, there will be a backing PivotTable created on a separate sheet.

Flattened PivotTable

This configuration will create a Flattened PivotTable. When PowerPivot creates a Flattened PivotTable, it will set some PivotTable properties that will show the PivotTable in a more printer-friendly way. Figure 5-5 shows a side-by-side comparison between a PivotTable and a Flattened PivotTable.

	A	B	C	D	E	F	G	H	I
1		PivotTable:			Flattened PivotTable:				
2									
3		Row Labels	Sum of SalesAmount		CalendarYear	Color	Sum of SalesAmount		
4		⊟2003	$9,791,060.30		2003	Black	$3,851,090.66		
5		Black	$3,851,090.66		2003	Blue	$860,380.78		
6		Blue	$860,380.78		2003	Multi	$42,099.32		
7		Multi	$42,099.32		2003	NA	$184,354.22		
8		NA	$184,354.22		2003	Red	$953,203.05		
9		Red	$953,203.05		2003	Silver	$2,044,406.89		
10		Silver	$2,044,406.89		2003	White	$2,229.52		
11		White	$2,229.52		2003	Yellow	$1,853,295.85		
12		Yellow	$1,853,295.85		2003 Total		$9,791,060.30		
13		⊟2004	$9,770,899.74		2004	Black	$2,913,254.25		
14		Black	$2,913,254.25		2004	Blue	$1,418,715.50		
15		Blue	$1,418,715.50		2004	Multi	$64,371.42		
16		Multi	$64,371.42		2004	NA	$250,762.47		
17		NA	$250,762.47		2004	Red	$200,537.73		
18		Red	$200,537.73		2004	Silver	$2,062,985.67		
19		Silver	$2,062,985.67		2004	White	$2,876.80		
20		White	$2,876.80		2004	Yellow	$2,857,395.90		
21		Yellow	$2,857,395.90		2004 Total		$9,770,899.74		
22		**Grand Total**	**$19,561,960.04**						
23									
24									

FIGURE 5-5: Regular and Flattened PivotTables

WHY DOES EXCEL THINK THE FIELD LIST IS NOT CURRENTLY ON?

If you take a look at Figure 5-3, you will see that the graphic for the empty PivotTable says, "Turn on the PivotTable Field List to work with the PivotTable," even though the field list is shown. This is one side-effect of the implementation of PowerPivot. PowerPivot is implemented as an Excel add-in, and there are some aspects of Excel that add-ins cannot control in a seamless way.

In this particular case, the PowerPivot team wanted to create a replacement for the Excel field list that would show when PowerPivot PivotTables and PivotCharts are selected, and provide functionality specific to PowerPivot tables and charts. However, they didn't want the PowerPivot field list to be shown for non-PowerPivot tables and charts. So, for PowerPivot tables and charts, PowerPivot will turn off the Excel field list and display the PowerPivot field list.

Note, however, that the Excel field list is still available. You can go into the PivotTable Tools/Options tab in the Excel ribbon and click on the Field List button to show the Excel field list. The PowerPivot data that will show up in the Excel field list will not make as much sense as the same data shown in the PowerPivot field list, as described in this chapter in the section "The New PowerPivot Data Model."

THE POWERPIVOT FIELD LIST

As mentioned earlier in this chapter, PowerPivot includes a new field list that was built specifically for working with PowerPivot data. This section drills into the details of the PowerPivot field list.

Figure 5-6 shows the PowerPivot field list side by side with Excel's PivotTable field list.

You can immediately see several differences:

➤ The PowerPivot field list doesn't have a drop-down menu that enables you to pick how and what the field list will display.

➤ The PowerPivot field list doesn't have a drop-down list for filtering based on measure groups.

➤ The PowerPivot field list does have a search box that allows you to search based on table and column names.

➤ The list of available fields differs between the two field lists. Excel's PivotTable field list shows fields based on the traditional OLAP model of measures, dimensions, and key performance indicators (KPIs), whereas the PowerPivot field list shows fields as tables and columns.

➤ The PowerPivot field list has two additional drop zones, Slicers Vertical and Slicers Horizontal.

➤ The PowerPivot field list doesn't have support for deferring layout updates.

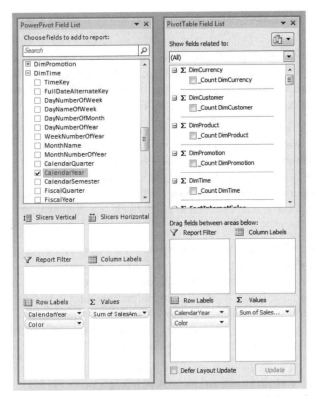

FIGURE 5-6: The PowerPivot and Excel field lists side by side

The two most significant differences are showing the fields as tables and columns (which is a different model than traditional OLAP) and the additional drop zones for slicers. The next section talks about the difference between the PowerPivot data model that is surfaced in the design of the PowerPivot field list. Slicers and support for them in the field list will be discussed later in this chapter.

The New PowerPivot Data Model

One of the design goals of PowerPivot was to simplify the data model used for business intelligence. The existing Analysis Services model, the Unified Dimensional Model (UDM), introduced in SQL Server Analysis Services 2005, provides great power at the cost of complexity. Cubes, dimensions, measures, hierarchies, and so on, and how they relate to each other, require a non-trivial effort to understand and use effectively.

The UDM's companion query language, Multidimensional Expressions (MDX), has these same attributes. When the creators of PowerPivot were designing the product, they wanted to bring BI capabilities to a larger group of people. They knew that one of the barriers to this was the complexity of the UDM and the MDX language.

To help with these issues, they came up with a simplified data model that is made up of just tables and relationships. This new, simplified data model was implemented under the hood, starting with much of the existing Analysis Services database engine. This allows PowerPivot to leverage Excel's capability to talk to Analysis Services.

For example, when you create a PowerPivot PivotTable or PivotChart, Excel thinks it's talking to a traditional OLAP data source. Under the hood, the new VertiPaq engine in PowerPivot is receiving the MDX queries that Excel is sending. It translates those queries into queries to the new data model, and returns appropriate results back to Excel for display in the PivotTable.

The structure of the underlying UDM that the VertiPaq engine works with is different from the traditional Analysis Services UDM, and doesn't correlate to the external data model in the same way that the traditional UDM does. This is why, for example, you see what you see in the Excel field list when you open it for a PowerPivot PivotTable or PivotChart, as shown on the right side of Figure 5-6. That figure shows the measures which, in the new PowerPivot data model, are present for every table, including dimension tables. Conversely, every table is also seen as a dimension when using traditional UDM tools.

In comparison, the PowerPivot field list doesn't make a distinction between measures and dimensions. Every table is just a table. The PowerPivot field list, on the left in Figure 5-6, simply shows every table as a node in a tree view, with sub-nodes for each table column. Tables are related by relationships between the tables that you learned about in Chapter 3, which described how relationships were created in the act of importing data, and Chapter 4, which showed how to manually create relationships between tables. There is another way in PowerPivot that relationships can be created that will be described in the following section, "Automatic Relationship Detection."

Working in this new data model can be a challenge for those who are used to working with the traditional UDM. Many of the features that were available in the UDM are not present in the PowerPivot data model. Things like parent-child dimensions, and even user hierarchies, are not available in the table/relationship model used by the first version of PowerPivot.

 These features may be added in future PowerPivot versions.

Automatic Relationship Detection

In the new PowerPivot self-service BI model, relationships between tables may not be predefined. PowerPivot will recognize and attempt to create relationships in imported relational data by reading the relational metadata, but one of the great features of PowerPivot is the capability to bring data in from many disparate data sources. One aspect of the power of PowerPivot and self-service BI is the capability to relate data from those multiple, disparate data sources into a single model and use that model for analysis. One PowerPivot feature that helps in this area is *automatic relationship detection*.

As you work with data in multiple tables, PowerPivot notices when a relationship is not present but might be needed. One indicator that a relationship may be needed in a PivotTable is when you are slicing data by some attribute — for example, in Row Labels — and the values showing for each row are exactly the same when you expect them to be different, as shown in Figure 5-7.

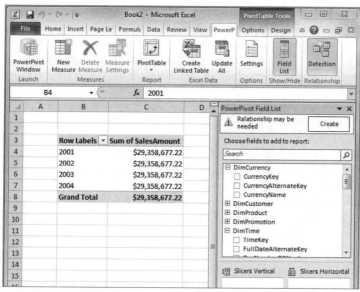

FIGURE 5-7: "Relationship may be needed" prompt

When this happens, you will see a prompt in the PowerPivot field list suggesting that you create a relationship, as shown in Figure 5-7. When you click on the Create button in this prompt, PowerPivot will analyze the data in your PowerPivot model. If it can, PowerPivot determines the relationship that is needed, and then creates the relationship. Figure 5-8 shows the dialog that will show the progress and results of this relationship detection.

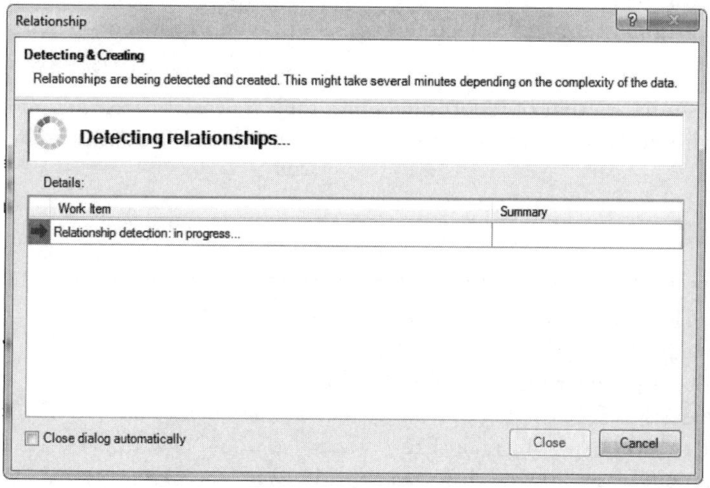

FIGURE 5-8: The Relationship Detection dialog

Automatic relationship detection uses a set of heuristics to determine which columns should have a relationship between them. It is not foolproof, however, and may not detect relationships that are needed for your data. When that happens, you can always go back to the PowerPivot Window and manually define relationships, as described in Chapter 4. If you prefer to not have automatic relationship detection active, there is a toggle button labeled Detection on the PowerPivot ribbon in Excel that allows you to turn it off.

Metadata Refresh

PowerPivot PivotTables and PivotCharts in Excel are based on the state of the PowerPivot data at the time the tables and/or charts are created. Because of the interactive nature of self-service BI analysis, you may be changing the underlying PowerPivot data such that the data model is now out of sync with the state of the data at the time the tables and charts were created. One example of when this happens is when you create a DAX-calculated column in the PowerPivot Window, such as what was discussed in Chapter 4.

If you do something that causes the PowerPivot data's metadata to update, and there is a PivotTable or PivotChart that uses that data, PowerPivot notices and displays a prompt (Figure 5-9), similar to the one shown by the automatic relationship detection feature.

FIGURE 5-9: Metadata refresh prompt

When that prompt appears, you can click the Refresh button to refresh the PowerPivot field list and its related PivotTable or PivotChart.

SLICERS

Slicers are one of the major new features of Excel for 2010. The idea for slicers grew out of a request from the PowerPivot team and a willingness to try something non-traditional (for Microsoft) in order to make it happen.

Slicers have functionality that is similar to that of report filters, but they are easier to use and more interactive. They are available without PowerPivot for Excel installed, but PowerPivot adds additional functionality.

> **INSIDE POWERPIVOT**
>
> In the early days of PowerPivot, ideas were swirling around in the heads of the architects and program managers about how to make BI analysis and reporting significantly easier. These product planners knew that a self-service BI product would require a reporting and analysis tool, but were not in agreement about whether the team should build its own, or use an existing one. (The existing one would be Excel.) There were two competing concerns: the suitability of existing tools for their vision of self-service BI, versus the cost of implementing a completely new tool from scratch.
>
> The proponents of building from scratch felt that Excel, while being a great general-purpose anaiytical application, was missing some things that were needed for the rapid analysis that was a part of what was envisioned for a self-service BI tool.

The proponents of using an existing tool felt that implementing a completely new tool would be extremely expensive, given the timeframe of the product release, and also that it would not be in line with the goal of a common Microsoft-wide approach to business intelligence.

The main proponents of the two different approaches got together to come up with a list of what was lacking in Excel that would prevent it from being the self-service BI client for PowerPivot. When all was said and done, the only critical missing piece was a friendly, graphical filtering tool. The main proponent of using Excel, Rob Collie (also known as the PowerPivot Pro, with a Web site at http://PowerPivotPro.com), was in agreement on this point. Before joining the Analysis Services team, he had worked on a BI project for another team, the football stats project, whose participants in a focus group identified this as a big sticking point for using that application.

With the issue clarified, the PowerPivot team brought the idea to the Excel team. Although it was late in the product cycle, the Excel team agreed to allow the addition of this new functionality into the product, but they didn't have the development and test resources needed to implement it. The Analysis Services team then made the decision to fund the effort, and sent a group of developers and testers on loan to the Excel team to implement what became slicers. Although the effort wasn't easy, this collaboration produced a feature that became an important part of Excel 2010 and an important part of PowerPivot for Excel.

Excel Slicers

Slicers are controls that can be placed on Excel worksheets and used to filter data in PivotTables. Figure 5-10 shows a slicer. By clicking one or more buttons, you can filter the data in the PivotTables (and corresponding PivotCharts) that are attached to the slicer.

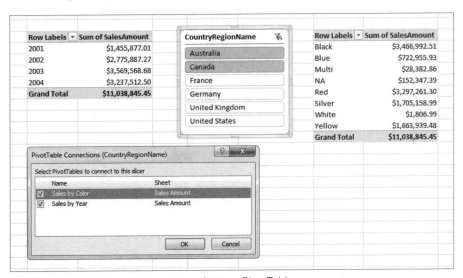

FIGURE 5-10: An Excel slicer connected to two PivotTables

Slicers are attached to Excel data at the data-connection level. This allows a single slicer to control multiple PivotTables and PivotCharts simultaneously. Figure 5-10 shows a single Excel slicer controlling two different PivotTables: one showing sales amount by year and one showing sales amount by product color.

Selecting one or more buttons in the slicer will cause the data in the PivotTables connected to the slicer to update to show only the data for the selected slicer button items. Clicking on the funnel with the red "X" button on the top right of the slicer will remove all filtering from the slicer, and select all items.

Slicers can also filter each other through a feature called *cross-filtering*. What that means is that, if multiple slicers are attached to a single PivotTable, and you click on one item in a slicer, the other slicers attached to the PivotTable will be aware of the selection, and will disable any slicer items that don't have data in the currently filtered PivotTable contents.

Figure 5-11 shows this cross-filtering. Notice that the `CountryRegionName` slicer has only `Australia` selected. The `StateProvinceName` slicer's only active items are provinces in Australia. All other items in the `StateProvinceName` slicer are shown grayed out and below the active items.

FIGURE 5-11: Slicer cross-filtering

There is one thing you should note about cross-filtering and working with PowerPivot data. Slicers do not behave as you would expect if you are used to the behavior of OLAP hierarchies — they merely reflect the state of other slicers connected to the PivotTable. This is a result of the fact that the initial version of PowerPivot doesn't support user hierarchies, and, hence, slicers filtering PowerPivot data can't be as intelligent about selecting items in related slicers.

For example, if you select a value of `Canada` in the `CountryRegionName` slicer, and then select `Texas` in the `StateProvinceName` slicer, the `CountryRegionName` slicer will not automatically select `United States`, and all data will disappear from the PivotTable. In contrast, if you had multiple slicers hooked up to a similar OLAP PivotTable with an appropriate hierarchy defined, clicking on `Texas` would select `United States` in the `CountryRegionName` slicer, and the PivotTable would be updated to show the data for `Texas`.

Slicers are designed to be controls that will appear on reports. They have multiple settings that can be used to change their appearance to be more appealing and fit the context of the report of which they are a part. You can select from a number of existing slicer styles and define new ones if you wish. You can also use the Slicer Tools ribbon controls to align multiple slicers with each other, change the size and orientation of the slicer buttons, and change the size of the entire slicer.

You can also group slicers and hide them. Figure 5-12 shows the slicers from Figure 5-11 with some of their properties changed to show some of the possibilities of slicer formatting.

Slicers are also supported in Excel workbooks rendered by Excel Services 2010. This allows slicers to be a part of the interactive thin client view of Excel and PowerPivot workbooks.

PowerPivot-Enhanced Slicers

Slicers by themselves are an exciting feature of Excel 2010, but the PowerPivot team had a more ambitious vision of what slicers could be in PowerPivot applications. They added functionality in PowerPivot for Excel to make slicers easier and faster to work with than plain-vanilla slicers.

Note that you can still use Excel slicers in PowerPivot PivotTables and PivotCharts without making use of the PowerPivot enhancements. There may be a good reason for doing that — PowerPivot will manage many aspects of slicers for you, and you may want to do something in a different way. You have the flexibility to opt for ease of use (using PowerPivot enhanced slicers), or maximum control (using regular slicers).

To make use of the additional slicer functionality that the PowerPivot team implemented, work with slicers through the slicers area sections of the PowerPivot field list as shown in Figure 5-13. These sections are called Slicers Vertical and Slicers Horizontal.

You can add fields from the field list into these slicer areas by dragging and dropping, or by using the context menus of the items in the field list. In either case, once you place a field into the slicer area of the PowerPivot field list, PowerPivot will control the display and position of the slicer.

PowerPivot manages the position of slicers by implementing two different *slicer zones* that are visually indicated by a rectangle around the slicers, and correspond to the two slicer areas in the PowerPivot field list. If you place a field in the Slicers Vertical area of the PowerPivot field list, you will see the position of the PivotTable automatically adjust and a slicer appear to the left of the PivotTable. Actually, the slicer doesn't just appear; it moves from the field list to its location in the vertical slicer zone. This is one way the PowerPivot team wanted to ensure that working with PowerPivot data and analysis would be easy and fun.

In Figure 5-14, you can see two slicers in each of the two slicer zones. Note the rectangle around each group of two slicers. By using this rectangle, you can change the size and position of the slicers in that zone.

FIGURE 5-12: Formatted slicers

FIGURE 5-13: Slicers area sections

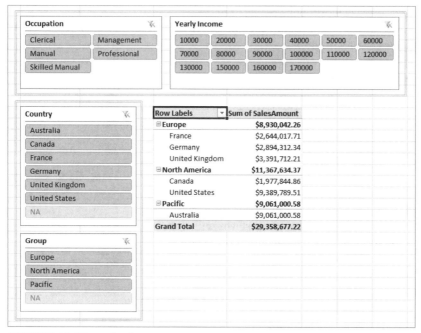

FIGURE 5-14: Slicers in slicer zones

Following are some of the things you can do with slicer zones:

➤ *Move the entire slicer zone to a different location* — By selecting the bounding rectangle and dragging it to a different location, you can move all the slicers in the zone to a different location on the worksheet. When you do this, the PivotTable position will not be adjusted as it is when you add the first slicer to the zone.

➤ *Resize the slicer zone* — By resizing the bounding rectangle, you can change the size of the slicer zone. PowerPivot will resize the slicers in the zone based on the new size of the bounding rectangle.

➤ *Move slicers around within the slicer zone* — You can change the order of the slicers in the zone by dragging and dropping them at different positions within the zone. You can also do this by changing the order of the slicer fields in the field list.

The bounding rectangle around each slicer zone will only appear when you are working with the corresponding PivotTable. If you click on a cell in the worksheet that isn't part of the PivotTable, the rectangle around the slicer zones will disappear. This rectangle is considered a part of the report's design mode and is not intended to be a part of the report in presentation mode.

You won't be able to totally control slicers that are in slicer zones. If you attempt to change their sizes, for example, PowerPivot will resize them back to what PowerPivot thinks they should be. If you need total control of the size and position of slicers, you can drag them out of the slicer zone, and then you can totally control their size and position. If you want to bring an independent slicer under the control of PowerPivot, you can drag and drop it onto the desired slicer zone, and PowerPivot will take control of it. You will see the slicer snap into position, and the field will show up in the corresponding slicer area of the PowerPivot field list.

> Note that, for these drag-and-drop actions, the upper-left corner of the slicer is what PowerPivot considers the control point.

Another PowerPivot feature that may be needed for building your PivotTables and PivotCharts is calculated measures.

DAX MEASURES

At their most basic level, DAX *measures* are DAX expressions that return a value. When you place a field into the Values area of the PowerPivot field list, you are creating a DAX measure. Measures created in this way are referred to as *implicit measures* — you aren't entering a measure formula; you are just dropping a field into the Values area.

What happens behind the scenes is that PowerPivot is creating a measure expression, and, when the PivotTable needs to display the value for a PivotTable cell based on that field, the expression is evaluated and a value is returned. You can see the expression that is generated if you right-click on a field in the Values area of the field list, and select Edit Measure to bring up the Measure Settings dialog. Figure 5-15 shows this dialog, which includes the DAX formula for the implicit measure.

FIGURE 5-15: Measure Settings dialog for an implicit measure

As you might have guessed by now, if you have implicit measures — measures created implicitly — you must also have *explicit measures* — measures created explicitly. As with implicit measures, explicit measures can be placed in the Values area of a PivotTable or PivotChart. However, unlike implicit measures, you explicitly specify the DAX expression used for that measure's calculations.

Explicit measures (which will be referred to as just "measures" in the rest of this discussion) are attached to a particular table in the PowerPivot data model.

To begin creating a measure, right-click on a table name in the PowerPivot field list and select Add New Measure. This will bring up the dialog shown in Figure 5-16. As you can see in the figure, AutoComplete is available when editing a formula in the dialog, similar to the formula bar of the PowerPivot Window when editing calculated columns, as discussed in Chapter 4.

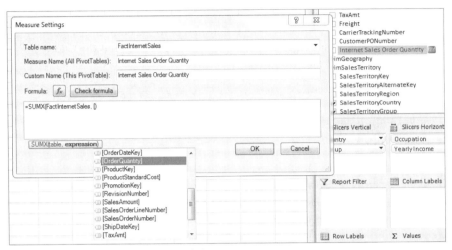

FIGURE 5-16: The Measure Settings dialog

The dialog also includes access to help, the capability to check the syntax of a formula before you commit it, and the capability to name the measure, as well as provide a separate custom name that will be used for this measure in the current PivotTable only. Measures in the field list are indicated by a calculator icon after the measure name, which you can see in Figure 5-16.

DAX measures use the same formula language that was used for calculated columns (as described in Chapter 4), but measures are used in a different way. Whereas calculated columns apply a DAX formula to each row in a PowerPivot table to form a new table column (referred to as "row context"), measures are calculated at query time (when the PivotTable/PivotChart asks the PowerPivot VertiPaq engine for data to be displayed). This context is referred to as "filter context." To effectively use DAX, you must understand this difference.

Conceptually, here is what happens when you create a calculated column:

1. A formula is entered into the formula bar in the PowerPivot Window.

2. For each row of the table:

   ➤ The formula is calculated in the context of the row (row context). For example, if you refer to another column of the table, the row value of that column is used at that point in the calculation.

   ➤ The calculated value is stored as that row's value in the calculated column.

In contrast, here's what happens when a DAX measure is created:

1. A formula is entered into the formula field of the Add Measure dialog.

2. When the measure is placed on the PivotTable, and the PivotTable needs to display the values of that measure in the PivotTable cells, Excel formulates a query that includes the context of each PivotTable cell (for example, any row labels, column labels, report filters, or slicer filters that apply to the cell), and sends it to the embedded VertiPaq engine to calculate and return the measure's value for that cell. This context that the measure calculation is run in is DAX filter context.

Note the difference. Calculated column values are materialized and stored into the workbook's PowerPivot data when you enter the formula. Measure values are materialized when they need to be displayed. Measure values are not stored in the PowerPivot data for the workbook (although they are cached in the workbook's PivotTable cache).

Since there is no row context when measure values are calculated, you cannot include a raw table column reference in your measure formula. Without a row context to indicate which column value to return, the VertiPaq engine doesn't know what value to use in the calculation for that column reference. Hence, when referring to a PowerPivot table column, you must wrap the column reference with some sort of aggregation function (sum, average, and so on) that will return a single value.

Conceptually, here is how measures in a PivotTable are calculated. They always start with data from the source table. Then, the context sent for each PivotTable cell is applied to the calculation. This means that the measure expression is recalculated for every cell using that cell's context.

It is important to note, though, that the VertiPaq engine has access to all the source table data. In the absence of any other filters, it will filter the source data based on the context for each cell that Excel sends. However, that context can be overridden by explicit measure formulas.

Looking at Some Examples

To see how measures work, let's walk through a series of simple examples and see how measures are calculated in different contexts. Let's use a workbook that contains data imported from the `Contoso` database that you used for the walk-through in Chapter 2.

First, let's place the `SalesAmount` field from the `FactOnlineSales` table into the Values area. PowerPivot will create an implicit measure whose formula looks like this:

```
=SUM('FactOnlineSales'[SalesAmount])
```

Because you haven't placed any values in any of the places in the PivotTable that Excel will use to ask for calculations in different contexts, Excel just requests the single value that is the sum of all the `SalesAmount` fields. This PivotTable will look like Figure 5-17.

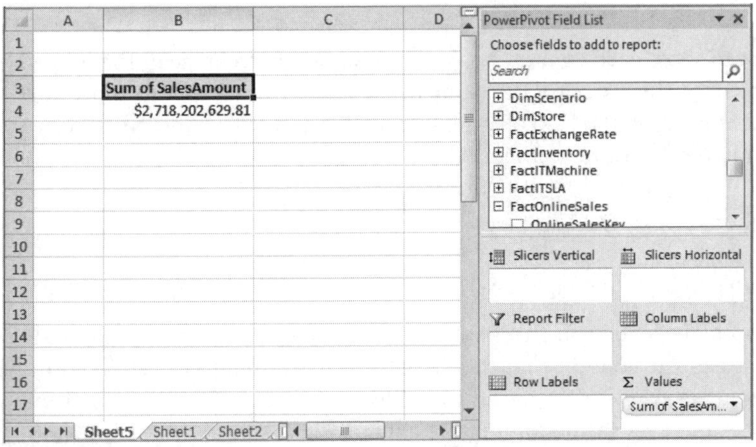

FIGURE 5-17: An Implicit sum measure with no filtering

If you then place the RegionCountryName field from the DimGeography table on Row Labels (and assuming relationships are correctly created), Excel will send a query to the VertiPaq engine with the context of each value in the Row Labels column, and the engine evaluates the implicit measure once in the context of each Row Labels value. The resulting PivotTable is shown in Figure 5-18.

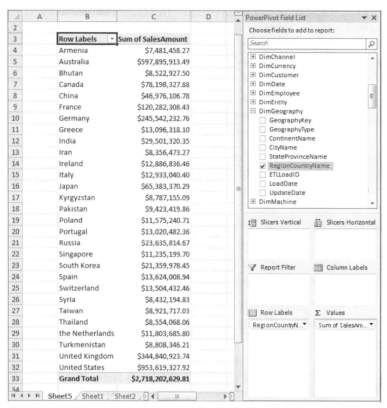

FIGURE 5-18: An Implicit sum measure filtered by Row Labels

Now, suppose that you want to show each country's sales amount as a percentage of the total sales amount. (Let's ignore the fact that this can easily be done in the Excel UI, in order to show how explicit measures work.) Right-click on the FactOnlineSales table and select Add New Measure. Enter the following formula in the Measure Setting dialog:

```
[Sum of SalesAmount] / CALCULATE([Sum of SalesAmount],
    ALL(DimGeography[RegionCountryName]))
```

This will update the PivotTable to look like Figure 5-19.

This measure expression calculates each country's sales amount as a percentage of the total sales amount. To do that, it uses the context that the PivotTable is passing to the engine for evaluating the numerator, [Sum of SalesAmount], and overrides the context that the PivotTable is passing to the engine when evaluating the denominator, CALCULATE([Sum of SalesAmount], ALL(DimGeography[RegionCountryName])). The All() function is what is used to do this.

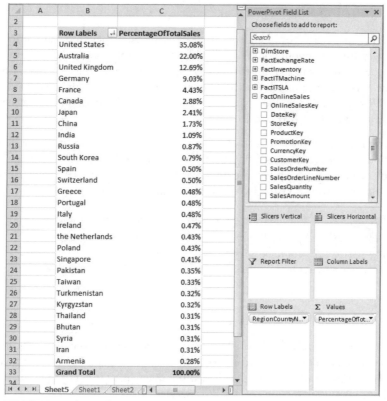

FIGURE 5-19: An explicit measure using the Row Labels filter and overriding the Row Labels filter

This measure expression demonstrates that the entire source table and related tables are available to a measure expression, and the measure expression can reach beyond the context passed to it by the PivotTable if needed. When it comes to using PowerPivot for self-service BI analysis, DAX measures give you a lot of power.

In this first version of PowerPivot, most of what is needed for sophisticated analysis is possible, although not necessarily convenient. You can expect that future versions of PowerPivot will provide more power and convenience than what is available in this initial version. Appendix B of this book (available online at www.wrox.com) contains more detailed reference information on DAX functions.

POWERPIVOT AND OTHER EXCEL FEATURES

One of the strengths of having PowerPivot inside of Excel is that PowerPivot PivotTables and PivotCharts can take advantage of all the features of Excel when analyzing and reporting on your PowerPivot data.

Cube Formulas

Although PivotTables and PivotCharts are powerful ways to work with data, there are some situations where they don't do everything that you would like in order to perform your analysis. Another technique to be aware of is the capability to use cube formulas to put values into cells in Excel. Cube formulas were built with the MDX user in mind, but they can also be used without detailed knowledge of MDX by creating a PivotTable that includes the data you want to work with and using the Excel feature of converting a PivotTable to formulas.

One thing to be aware of when converting a PivotTable to formulas is that the resultant data will not grow and shrink based on changes to data as a PivotTable will. You are, in essence, freezing the cell layout of your PivotTable data. You can update the underlying source data and have the changes reflected in your cube formula cells, and you can also use slicers to filter the data.

 For a more detailed look at cube formulas and PowerPivot, refer to Rob Collie's PowerPivot Pro blog post on the topic at `http://bit.ly/7olQb3`.

Named Sets

Named set support in Excel is a new feature for 2010. This feature was designed to make working with MDX named sets easier and more interactive from inside of Excel. Although PowerPivot was designed to be a different model than traditional OLAP, it is still implemented (under the hood) using the same data model as in previous versions of Analysis Services.

Since PowerPivot can speak MDX, it can make use of the named set feature of Excel, although making use of named sets does require MDX. Since one of the goals of PowerPivot is to provide a way to do self-service analytics without having to learn MDX, this discussion will not dive into how to use this feature with PowerPivot. But the feature is there for those who know and can use MDX.

ANALYSIS IN THE HEALTHCARE AUDIT APPLICATION

Let's now return to the sample SDR Healthcare Audit application introduced in previous chapters. In Chapter 3, you imported data, and in Chapter 4, you enriched it. Now, let's start to build useful analytical reports using the PowerPivot data in the workbook.

The Server Group PivotTable Report

Let's start building the SDR Healthcare application's analytical reports with a PivotTable report that can be used to analyze audit events by server group.

Open the SDR Health Audit BI Solution workbook that you saved from Chapter 4, or open the in-progress workbook from the book's download location at `www.wrox.com`.

Creating the Initial Report

For this report, let's use the PowerPivot "Chart and Table (Vertical)" report type. Follow these steps:

1. In the PowerPivot tab of the Excel ribbon, click on the drop-down arrow of the PivotTable button, and, from the drop-down list, select "Chart and Table (Vertical)."

2. In the "Create PivotChart and PivotTable (Vertical)" dialog, ensure that New Worksheet is selected and click OK.

A new worksheet is created with a PivotChart and a PivotTable on it, as shown in Figure 5-20.

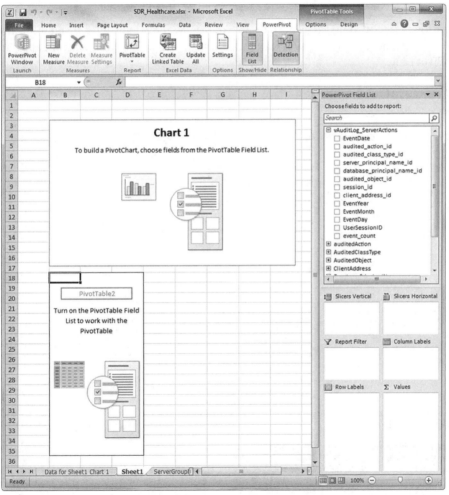

FIGURE 5-20: A new PivotChart and PivotTable report

Adding Data to the PivotTable

You want to perform analysis using the PivotTable. The following steps show how to add the fields you want to analyze to the PivotTable:

1. The quantity you want to analyze is the count of audit events. Add the event_count field in the vAuditLog_ServerActions table to the Values area of the PowerPivot field list.

2. This report will analyze audit events by the server group name. Add the server_group_name field in the ServerGroupName table to the Row Values area of the field list.

3. You also want to slice the data by year. Add the EventYear field in the vAuditLog_ServerActions table to the Report Filter area of the field list.

4. In order to see trends, you also want to be able to display the event counts by month. Add the EventMonth field from the vAuditLog_ServerActions table to the Column Labels area of the PivotTable.

At this point, if you set the Report Filter to show the year 2008, the report will look like Figure 5-21.

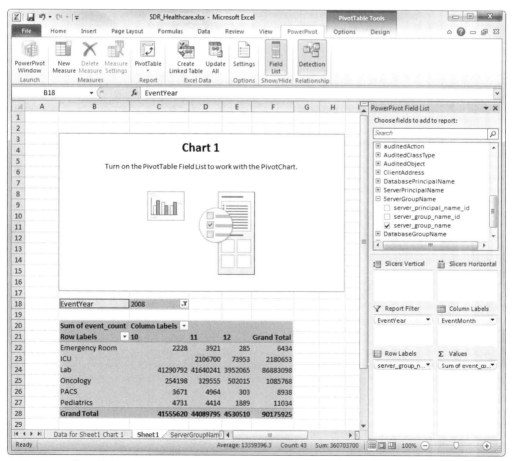

FIGURE 5-21: PivotTable data added to the server group report

Adding Data to the Pivot Chart

Now, add the same data to the PivotChart. The graphical display will help you see the relationship between the data items. Select Chart 1 and add the same fields you added to the PivotTable. The report now looks like Figure 5-22.

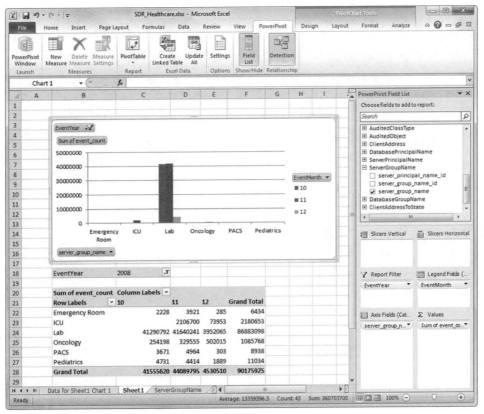

FIGURE 5-22: PivotChart data added to the server group report

Adding Slicers

As you perform analysis using this report, you will notice that you would like the PivotTable and PivotChart data to be in sync as you change the Report Filter settings. To have to change the year in two places is a tedious task. This is a job for slicers, especially since multi-object PowerPivot reports like the PivotTable and PivotChart report you are using are created in a way that adding slicers to the report will affect all the PivotTables and PivotCharts in the report.

Follow these steps to replace the Report Filters with a slicer:

1. Select the PivotChart and remove the EventYear field from the Report Filter area of the PowerPivot field list.

2. Select the PivotTable, and drag the EventYear field from the Report Filter area of the field list to the Slicers Vertical area.

3. To make the report look nicer, and to make better use of space, select the vertical slicer area's bounding rectangle and drag it down so that the top of the vertical slicers rectangle aligns with the top of the PivotTable. Move the PivotChart to the left so that it aligns left with the vertical slicer zone and fills the space you made by moving the vertical slicers zone down, as shown in Figure 5-23.

4. You can add other fields to the vertical slicer zone to help with your analysis. In Figure 5-23, you can see the `Database_group` field from the `DatabaseGroupName` table and the `class_type_desc` field from the `AuditedClassType` table added.

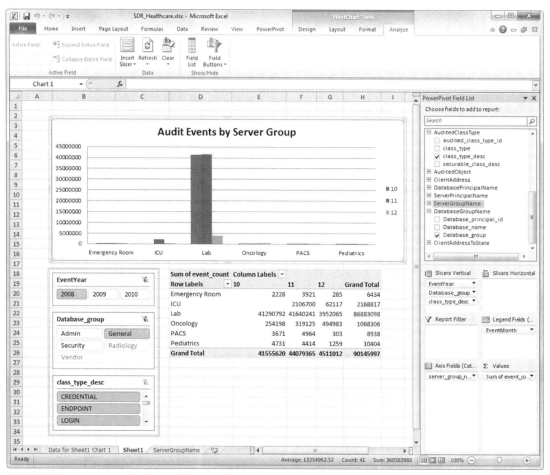

FIGURE 5-23: Replacing the Report Filters with a slicer

A chart title has also been added and field buttons on the chart have been turned off. This particular report was created to help analyze a particular aspect of audit data. The next report will be used to look at various aspects of the audit system, and also keep in mind that it will eventually be used for reporting as well.

The Dashboard Page

The next analytical report you will add to the workbook is a dashboard page that will allow you to analyze various aspects of the auditing system.

Creating the Initial Dashboard

Let's start building a dashboard by creating a new worksheet with four PivotCharts. Follow these steps:

1. In the PowerPivot tab of the Excel ribbon, click on the drop-down arrow of the PivotTable button, and, in the drop-down, select Four Charts.

2. In the "Create Four PivotCharts" dialog, ensure that New Worksheet is selected and click OK.

A new worksheet named Sheet3 that contains four PivotCharts appears in the workbook, as shown in Figure 5-24. Four additional worksheets are also created, with each containing a PivotTable that backs each PivotChart.

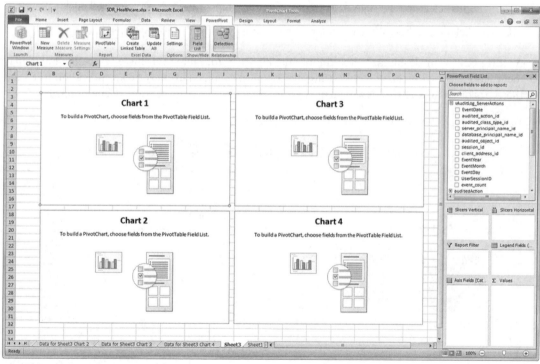

FIGURE 5-24: A Four-PivotChart report

Chart 1: Audit Events by Department

The first chart that you will create will show audit events by department. SDR management wants to know which departments are generating the most audit events in order to focus on reviewing the processes of those departments and performing risk analysis. You will show this data using a "Bar of Pie" chart.

Follow these steps:

1. Click on `Chart 1` to select it.

2. In the PowerPivot field list, open the `ServerGroupName` table node and click on the `server_group_name` checkbox. The `server_group_name` field gets added to the Axis Fields area of the field list.

3. Similarly, add the `event_count` field in the `vAuditLog_ServerActions` table to the Values area of the field list. This adds a Sum of `event_count` implicit measure to the chart and its backing PivotTable, as you can see if you look at the `Data for Sheet3 Chart 1` worksheet.

4. Click on the PivotChartTools\Design tab in the Excel Ribbon and click on the "Change Chart Type" button.

5. In the Change Chart Type dialog, click on Pie on the left to select the pie chart row on the right. Select the far right item in this row, the "Bar of Pie" chart type, and click OK.

6. Click on the title of the chart and rename it to "Audit Events by Department."

At this point, your dashboard should look like Figure 5-25. Note that, historically, the Lab department has generated by far the largest number of audit events. This may be an indication to review the types of events the Lab department is generating, and to perform some deeper analysis.

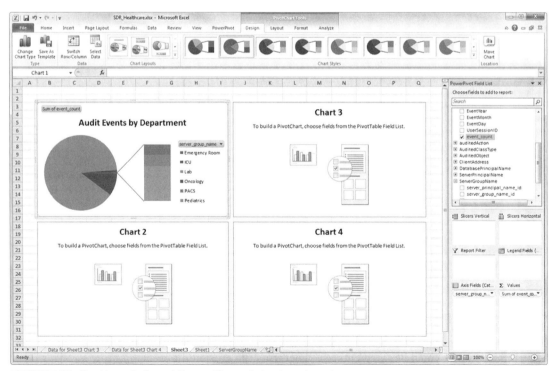

FIGURE 5-25: Dashboard after adding audit events by department

Chart 2: Audit Events By Database

The second chart that you'll add to the dashboard will show audit events by database. The IT department wants to be aware of which databases are generating the most audit events, to ensure that those databases are provisioned on appropriate hardware for capturing the audit logs (which can be quite verbose). On the other side of the scale, they want to know which databases (if any) generate the least number of audit events. These databases are candidates for hardware consolidation.

At SDR, databases belong to groups for easier administration. You want to show the databases whose audit events you are analyzing organized by group. You'll use a Clustered Bar chart type for this.

Follow these steps:

1. Click on `Chart 3` to select it.

2. In the PowerPivot field list, open the `DatabaseGroupName` table and add `Database_group` and `Database_name` to the Axis Fields area of the field list.

3. Add the `event_count` field from the `vAuditLog_ServerActions` table to the Values area of the field list.

4. In the PivotChart Tools\Design tab of the Excel Ribbon click on the Change Chart Type button and select the leftmost Bar item, Clustered Bar, and click OK.

5. Rename the title of the chart to "Audit Events by Database."

Figure 5-26 shows the dashboard after adding `Chart 3`. After looking at the data, you discover that the `Patient` and `Lab` databases generate most of the audit events. Every other database is quite small by comparison. SDR management will pass this information to the IT department to take appropriate action.

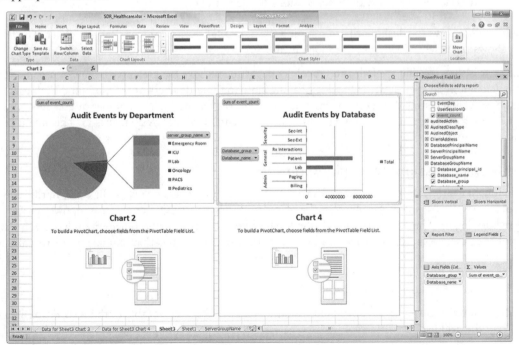

FIGURE 5-26: Dashboard after adding audit events by database

Chart 3: User Sessions by Department

Another chart that would be helpful in managing the audit system at SDR would show the number of user sessions that generate audit data by department. This information isn't directly available in the data you've assembled so far, but you can generate it using a DAX measure.

The server actions table (vAuditLog_ServerActions) has a field that contains the user session ID number for each audit entry. If you create a distinct count measure using that field, you can get the data you need. Here's how to do it:

1. Click on Chart 2 to select it.

2. In the PowerPivot field list, select the vAuditLog_ServerActions table node and, in the PowerPivot tab of the Excel ribbon, click on the New Measure button.

3. In the Measure Settings dialog, enter **UserSessions** for the Measure Name.

4. Enter the following formula for the measure and click OK:

   ```
   =CountRows(Distinct('vAuditLog_ServerActions'[UserSessionID]))
   ```

   This formula uses the DAX Distinct() function to return a table that contains the values of the UserSessionID field with all the duplicates removed for the current context. This is then passed to the CountRows function, which will count the number of entries in that generated table. When you click the OK button, the measure is created, added to the field list, and placed in the Values area.

5. As in Chart 1, you are analyzing the data by department, so add the server_group_name field from the ServerGroupName table to the Axis Fields area of the field list.

6. Rename the chart title to "User Sessions by Department."

Figure 5-27 shows the dashboard after adding the User Sessions by Department chart. The field list shows the newly added UserSessions measure.

Chart 2 is showing that the Lab and Oncology departments have the greatest amount of user sessions that generate audit events, with Oncology having close to three-quarters of the amount of Lab user sessions. An interesting data point is that Oncology has the second highest number of user sessions, but, looking at Chart 1, its percentage of total audit events is smaller by comparison. This might be something to investigate.

Chart 4: User Sessions by Login Audit Class

The fourth chart in the dashboard will show the number of user sessions by audit class. In this particular case, management is trying to move teams from relying on SQL logins to Windows Active Directory logins. They want to track this in the dashboard. This chart will help in understanding the number of user sessions that generate audit events in two audit classes that management cares about.

Follow these steps:

1. Click on Chart 4 to select it.

2. Add the class_type_desc field from the AuditedClassType table to the Axis Fields area of the field list.

3. Add the `UserSessions` measure from the `vAuditLog_ServerActions` table to the Values area of the field list.

4. Rename the chart title to "User Sessions by Login Audit Class."

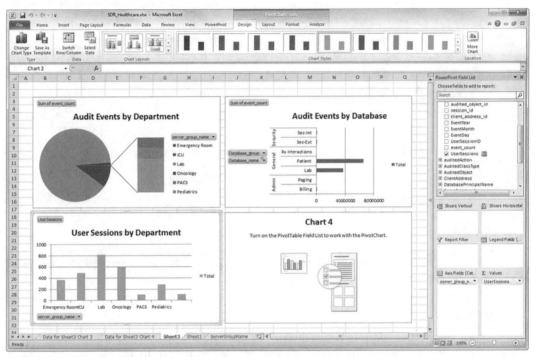

FIGURE 5-27: Dashboard after adding User Sessions by Department

At this point, the chart shows all the audit classes, but management is really only interested in two: WINDOWS LOGIN and SQL LOGIN. So, let's modify the backing PivotTable to only show audit classes that meet the desired criteria. To do so, follow these steps:

1. Click on the "Data for Sheet3 Chart 4" tab in the workbook to show the backing PivotTable for `Chart 4`.

2. Right-click on the down arrow button on the Row Labels header cell to show the sort and filter drop-down. Click on the "(Select All)" item in the tree view at the bottom of the drop-down to clear all checkboxes. Then, click on the Windows Login and SQL Login items to check them.

3. Return to the dashboard sheet. In the PivotChart Tools area of the ribbon, select the Design tab and click on the Change Chart Type button. Change the chart type to Clustered Bar as you did with `Chart 3`.

The dashboard sheet now appears as shown in Figure 5-28.

The dashboard so far has yielded insights that have been helpful, but what if you wanted to view this data for different time periods? Let's add that capability to the report.

FIGURE 5-28: Dashboard after all charts are added

Adding Slicers

The charts that you've added to the dashboard up until now have included all the audit data you've collected to date. However, it is also useful to look at slices of data. In most BI situations, one of the most popular ways to slice data is by time.

You already created calculated columns for year and date in Chapter 4, so let's use those columns to slice the charts by date. Follow these steps:

1. Select any chart in the dashboard.

2. Add the `EventYear` field from the `vAuditLog_ServerActions` table to the Slicers Vertical area in the field list.

3. Add the `EventMonth` field from the same table to the Slicers Vertical area below the `EventYear` field.

If you go to the PowerPivot tab of the Excel ribbon and hide the field list, you will see the dashboard. Note the `EventYear` and `EventMonth` slicers on the left side of the report. You can select different combinations of buttons to select different time periods, and all four charts will update to show the data for only the selected time periods.

Cleaning Up

Follow these steps to make the dashboard look nicer, and to facilitate better maintenance:

1. At this point, you have renamed the charts. So, if you want to use the backing PivotTables to make changes in the data the charts display, you must know which sheet corresponds to which chart. You can probably remember right now which ones correspond to which chart, but you may forget if you have to come back a month later to update something. Rename the backing PivotTable sheets as follows:

➤ Data for `Sheet3 Chart 1` — "Dashboard Events by Department"

➤ Data for `Sheet3 Chart 2` — "Dashboard Sessions by Department"

➤ Data for `Sheet3 Chart 3` — "Dashboard Events by Database"

➤ Data for `Sheet3 Chart 4` — "Dashboard Sessions by Class"

➤ Rename Sheet3 (the dashboard sheet) to "Dashboard."

2. All the charts except "Audit Events by Department" don't have data that need a legend (that is, the item that says "Total" on the right side of the chart.) Delete the legends from those three charts.

3. If you look at the charts in Figure 5-29, you can see the various field buttons on all the charts. In a dashboard situation, these buttons clutter the charts, and use screen real estate that could be better used to present the data. Let's delete these field buttons. For each chart, select it and go to the PivotChart Tools\Analyze tab in the Excel ribbon and click on the Field Buttons drop-down button and select Hide All.

Figure 5-29 shows the completed and cleaned-up dashboard.

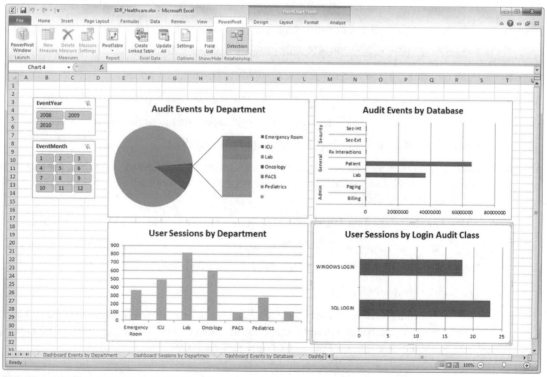

FIGURE 5-29: The completed dashboard

The "Top 5" Report

Another report that would be helpful to management is a report that shows the top five sources of audit events based on different slices of the data — for example, by department, by database, by server actions, or by location. For this report, you are requested to show time granularity by the day, unlike the dashboard report, where monthly was sufficient. It's also important that these charts show actual numbers of audit events, so you'll have to include that in your chart. This section will walk through building this "Top 5" report.

Like the dashboard report, let's use the PowerPivot report type that contains four charts. Create the basic four-chart report as you did previously. Choose to create the report on a new sheet, and rename that worksheet to `Top5`. In this report, all the charts will be of the same type — only the dimension on which you slice the data will be different.

Complete the following steps to create all four charts:

1. Click on `Chart 1` and add the following fields to the following areas in the PowerPivot field list:

   ➤ `server_group_name` field of the `ServerGroupName` table to the Axis Fields area

   ➤ `event_count` field of the `vAuditLog_ServerActions` table to the Values area

   Rename the chart title to "Top 5 Audit Events by Department."

2. Click on `Chart 2` and add the following fields to the following areas in the field list:

   ➤ `action_name` field of the `auditedAction` table to the Axis Fields area

   ➤ `event_count` field of the `vAuditLog_ServerActions` table to the Values area

   Rename the chart title to "Top 5 Audit Events by Server Action."

3. Click on `Chart 3` and add the following fields to the field list areas:

   ➤ `DatabaseName` field of the `DatabaseGroupName` table to the Axis Fields area

   ➤ `event_count` field of the `vAuditLog_ServerActions` table to the Values area

   Rename the chart title to "Top 5 Audit Events by Database."

4. Click on `Chart 4` and add the following fields to the field list areas (note that, for this chart, you are using the `UserSessions` measure rather than the `event_count` field that you used in the other three charts):

   ➤ `state_code` field of the `ClientAddressToState` table to the Axis Fields area

   ➤ `UserSessions` measure of the `vAuditLog_ServerActions` table to the Values area

   Rename the chart title to "Top 5 User Sessions by Location."

5. For each of the four charts:

   ➤ Go to its backing PivotTable and click on the drop-down button of the Row Labels header cell. Select Value Filters, and then select "Top 10…." In the Top 10 Filter dialog, change it from Top 10 to Top 5 and click OK.

➤ Still in the backing PivotTable, click on a cell in the values column of the PivotTable (the one whose header starts with "Sum of..."). Right-click and select Sort. Then, select "Sort Smallest to Largest."

➤ Go back to the chart and, in the PivotChartTools\Layout tab on the Excel ribbon, click on the Data Labels drop-down button, and select Outside End.

6. Add the `EventYear`, `EventMonth`, and `EventDay` fields from the `vAuditLog_ServerActions` table to the Slicers Vertical area in the PowerPivot field list. Expand the bounding rectangle around the vertical slicer zone until all slicers don't have scroll bars.

7. At this point, the Top 5 report is completed. You may want to do the cleanup actions that you performed on the dashboard report earlier in this chapter in the section, "Cleaning Up."

Figure 5-30 shows the completed Top 5 report. Notice that for three of the charts, the horizontal axis has been formatted to display numbers in the thousands (Select the Axis, right-click, and select Format Axis. Under Axis Options, set Display Units to Thousands). This makes the report a bit more readable. Also, note that, because you have a slicer for days, you can look at the top five audit events/user sessions at the granularity of a single day. This meets the requirements you were given for this report.

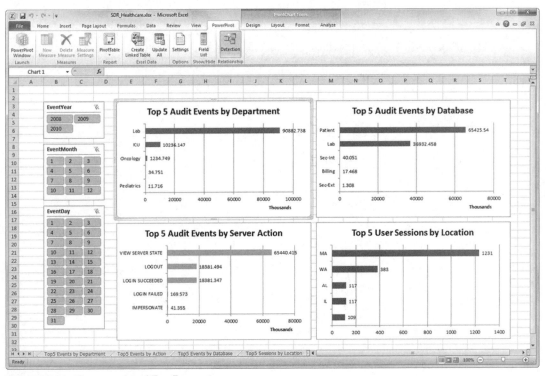

FIGURE 5-30: The completed Top 5 report

SUMMARY

PivotTables and PivotCharts are the primary ways to analyze and present the large volumes of BI data in Excel. With self-service BI using PowerPivot, this is still true. PowerPivot includes its own PivotTable field list that is customized to effectively work with the new PowerPivot data model, which is built around tables and relationships, rather than dimensions and cubes, as is found in traditional corporate BI.

Slicers are an exciting new feature in Excel 2010 that PowerPivot makes even better. At the PivotTable level of a workbook, DAX measures provide the capability to create powerful analytic calculations beyond what is possible in Excel. Because PowerPivot workbooks are also Excel workbooks, most Excel features used for data analysis are also available when working with PowerPivot data.

You have now added analytical charts and reports to the SDR Healthcare application using the features described in this chapter, and have already discovered some useful issues. But you have only done this at your desktop. The rest of the organization can't fully benefit from the analysis work you've done so far. You should share the reports you've created in this chapter with the rest of the organization. That is the subject of Chapter 6.

Self-Service Reporting

WHAT'S IN THIS CHAPTER?

➤ Publishing PowerPivot workbooks

➤ Using PowerPivot for SharePoint

➤ Using the PowerPivot Gallery

➤ Using automatic data refresh

➤ Building ad hoc reports

➤ Adding reporting to the SDR Healthcare application

In Chapters 3 through 5, you worked inside PowerPivot for Excel to create a PowerPivot workbook, starting with the importing of data from different external data sources. You saw how to enrich your imported data, and create PivotTables and PivotCharts in order to do analysis. In this chapter you will learn how to take a PowerPivot workbook beyond PowerPivot for Excel on the desktop, and use PowerPivot for SharePoint, along with Excel Services, to do self-service reporting using Report Builder or Excel.

In Chapter 2, you learned how to set up PowerPivot for SharePoint — that is, the server side of PowerPivot. This chapter assumes that you have PowerPivot for SharePoint available.

PUBLISHING POWERPIVOT WORKBOOKS

PowerPivot for Excel is a powerful tool for performing personal self-service BI. However, once you have a useful PowerPivot workbook that contains your self-service BI analysis reports, the natural next step is to share those reports with others. Your report becomes much more useful for many more people in your department or organization, as well as the entire business, if you can share it.

As mentioned in Chapter 1, sharing by copying or sending around your reports in an email has many problems, the chief one being the proliferation of multiple copies that aren't in sync. When using your PowerPivot workbook as a report, what you would really like is for there to be a single version of it containing up-to-date data that anyone who needs the information in your report can access as a single version of the truth. This is exactly what PowerPivot for SharePoint provides.

Publishing your workbook to SharePoint as a report implies that you won't be changing the data model — or at least you won't be changing it as much as you would if you were doing analysis rather than reporting. You can definitely make changes to your model and report, and re-publish the workbook. You should turn on document versioning in SharePoint 2010 to help you monitor the versions of your PowerPivot workbook. You should also consider how your workbook will look as a report once it is published to SharePoint and prepare the report for that usage.

Following are some things to consider doing:

➤ Remove empty worksheets and hide worksheets that aren't part of the real report. One example of this is the backing PivotTable worksheets that PowerPivot creates whenever you create a PowerPivot report that contains one or more charts, as you did in Chapter 5.

➤ Consider the placement and appearance of your worksheets. When you are using them for analysis, you may not have paid much attention to this aspect of your worksheets. However, once they are published and have an audience, you want them to look good.

➤ Take into account some of the limitations of published workbooks compared to workbooks in PowerPivot for Excel. Think about how you will update linked table data if needed. If you need your external data to be refreshed, ensure that the appropriate providers are installed on the server.

➤ Turn off gridlines in Excel using View ➪ Gridlines and unchecking the checkbox. This will provide a more professional appearance for your published PowerPivot workbook.

Assuming that your workbook is ready for publishing, here's how you publish it to PowerPivot for SharePoint:

1. In Excel, click on the File tab of the Excel Ribbon.

2. In the resulting page, click on "Save & Send," as shown in Figure 6-1.

3. In the "Save & Send" section, click the "Save to SharePoint" button.

In the "Save & Send" section, when you click on the Publish Options button, you will see a dialog that lets you choose whether to publish the entire workbook, just selected sheets, or just selected items (such as particular PivotTables or charts).

 If you are using Windows Server 2008 or Windows Server 2008 R2 servers, you must enable the "Desktop experience" feature on the server to be able to view and publish to a SharePoint 2010 site.

You will also see a list of known SharePoint locations in the dialog. If you click on one of those locations and then click the Save As button, a save dialog will open with the SharePoint site populated. Alternately, you can select Save As and enter your SharePoint site. In that dialog, you can navigate to the desired location and save your report there. You do have the option of just publishing the sheets that you want to publish as part of the options in the Save As dialog's Publish Options.

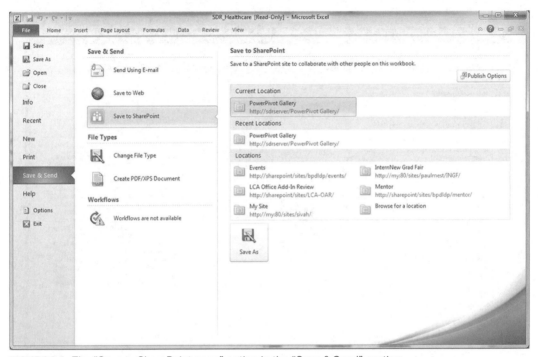

FIGURE 6-1: The "Save to SharePoint page" option in the "Save & Send" section

If you are publishing to a SharePoint site that has PowerPivot for SharePoint installed, you should publish to the PowerPivot Gallery. As you have seen throughout this book, this is a special PowerPivot-enabled document library that understands PowerPivot workbooks, and provides additional functionality above what is available in standard SharePoint 2010 document libraries. Although you can perform the core operations (such as scheduling data refresh) for your PowerPivot workbook, when it is saved in any document library, there are some PowerPivot for SharePoint features that are only available to workbooks stored in PowerPivot Gallery. You will learn about some of these features throughout this chapter.

Once you click OK in the Save As dialog, Excel publishes your workbook to the SharePoint site at the location you specified. This process can take some time, especially for large workbooks. If the "Open with Excel in the browser" checkbox is enabled, Excel will open your workbook from the SharePoint site in the browser once the publishing process has completed, as shown in Figure 6-2.

You can interact with the published Excel workbook on the server side only if PowerPivot for SharePoint is installed on your SharePoint farm. Excel Web Access (EWA), Excel Calculation Services (ECS), PowerPivot System Services, and SQL Server Analysis Services (SSAS) get involved when you interact with the published workbook (such as clicking on slicers, as well as sorting or filtering in PivotTables or PivotCharts). Later in this chapter, you'll take another look at the PowerPivot for SharePoint architecture and see how this is accomplished.

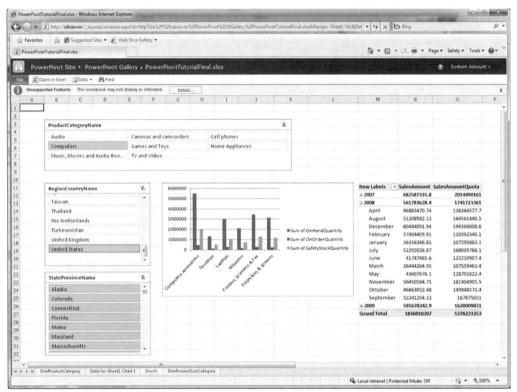

FIGURE 6-2: Published workbook opened in the browser

POWERPIVOT FOR SHAREPOINT

Once you have published your workbook to SharePoint, you can use the features of PowerPivot for SharePoint and other server-side components that enhance the value of the PowerPivot experience (such as taking advantage of PowerPivot Gallery views, creating Excel and Report Builder reports, refreshing data from the data sources periodically, and analyzing the use of workbooks for the IT department that manages your departmental SharePoint site).

PowerPivot for SharePoint administration features such as installing on an existing SharePoint 2010 farm, analyzing the use of PowerPivot workbooks by end users, and troubleshooting issues with PowerPivot are discussed in Chapters 7 through 11.

Now, let's take a look at the features of PowerPivot and other server-side components that relate to end-user reporting.

PowerPivot Gallery

Typically, when you publish a workbook to your departmental SharePoint site, you will publish to a site containing documents. You get a list of documents or some of the default views provided by SharePoint. However, these default views do not provide a visual representation of the content within the documents.

With PowerPivot Gallery, the end user will be able to use a self-service BI application created using PowerPivot. This visual presentation helps the end user to better interpret the data in each sheet of the PowerPivot workbook. You then click on a specific sheet in the PowerPivot workbook to open the workbook in Excel Services and further analyze the data.

There are three views provided by PowerPivot Gallery in addition to the default All Documents view provided by SharePoint in standard document libraries:

➤ Gallery view

➤ Theatre view

➤ Carousel view

Gallery View

The Gallery view is the default view in the PowerPivot Gallery. After you publish your PowerPivot application (that is, PowerPivot workbook) to the PowerPivot Gallery folder, you connect to your organization site and click on PowerPivot Gallery, as shown in Figure 6-3. You will see the documents published on the site, along with a visual representation of each sheet of the PowerPivot workbook (in this case, the sample SDR_Healthcare application) as thumbnails. By pressing the right arrow key, you can move over the thumbnails for each sheet of the Excel workbook.

As you move your mouse over each sheet, you will see a larger image of the current sheet that is in focus. When your application has a visual representation of data (such as charts), it's very helpful to use PowerPivot Gallery to get an overview of trends. If you click on a thumbnail, it will open the sheet in your browser using Excel Services.

In addition to the PowerPivot application published to the PowerPivot Gallery, you can also see a visual representation of any reports that are created on top of the PowerPivot model. For example, in Figure 6-3, you can see a partial image of a report called SDR_Healthcare Report 1, which is a Reporting Services report created from the PowerPivot model. You'll learn how to create this report later in this chapter.

Within the PowerPivot Gallery, you will be able to see a visual representation of PowerPivot workbooks and Excel (or Reporting Services) reports that import data from PowerPivot. PowerPivot for SharePoint deploys a SharePoint solution as part of the installation. This solution contains several components that integrate with SharePoint for managing PowerPivot.

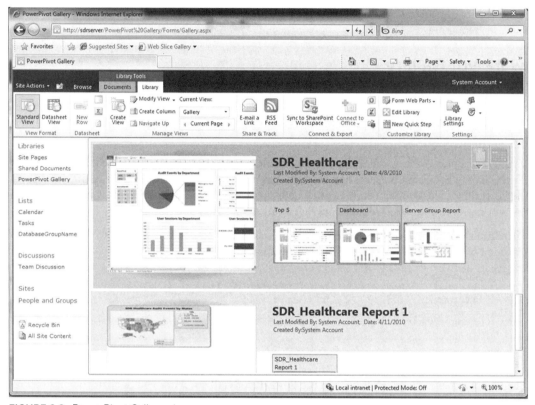

FIGURE 6-3: PowerPivot Gallery view

One of the components, `Microsoft.AnalysisServices.SharePoint.Integration.DLL`, helps in PowerPivot Gallery. This component helps in obtaining snapshots of each sheet of the PowerPivot workbook published, as well as the Reporting Services report. When a document is uploaded or updated on the PowerPivot Gallery site, SharePoint notifies the `PowerPivotGallery` component with appropriate events that a document in the PowerPivot Gallery has changed. This component then retrieves the name of the document, loads the PowerPivot workbook (or Reporting Services report) and gets an image snapshot of the document using the program `GetSnapshot.exe` (which is installed as part of the PowerPivot for SharePoint installation). If you view the document in the `PowerPivotGallery` site before the snapshot is created, you will see an hourglass indicator, as shown in Figure 6-4.

These snapshots are the ones that help you with the visual representation of the document in the PowerPivot Gallery site. Documents in the PowerPivot Gallery whose types are not supported by PowerPivot (for example, Word documents or PowerPoint presentations) will not get snapshots generated for them by PowerPivot. Instead, you see an image, along with an indicator that the snapshot is not supported, as shown in Figure 6-5. If Excel workbooks and Reporting Services reports contain data sources other than PowerPivot embedded within them, then PowerPivot will show a locked icon (as shown in Figure 6-5).

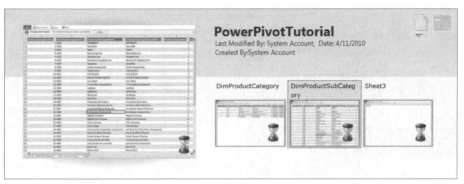

FIGURE 6-4: PowerPivot Gallery when a snapshot is being obtained

FIGURE 6-5: Non-PowerPivot documents in PowerPivot Gallery site

PowerPivot Gallery relies upon Excel Services and Reporting Services to render the documents whose snapshots are taken to be shown as thumbnails. If any kind of error occurs while generating the snapshot, then PowerPivot Gallery will display a different graphic, as shown in Figure 6-6. This can be caused by several things that might occur while the snapshot is being created, including a PowerPivot workbook upload that didn't complete, or unavailability of system resources needed for rendering the document in Excel Services or Reporting Services.

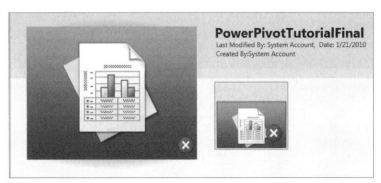

FIGURE 6-6: PowerPivot document that has encountered an error

 Chapter 9 provides more information about troubleshooting issues in PowerPivot for SharePoint.

One of the ways to identify the cause of the problem for a PowerPivot document is to click on the icon to see if you are able to open the document. If you are able to open the document in Excel Services or Reporting Services, then you should update the document so that the PowerPivot Gallery component can initiate a snapshot recapture. You can do this by updating the document, or by changing the description of the document.

Theatre View

You can change the default view of the PowerPivot Gallery by clicking on the Library tab in the SharePoint ribbon and changing the Current View drop-down selection to Theatre, as shown in Figure 6-7. Once you change the view, you will see the thumbnails for each sheet or document below a larger image of the document item that is currently in focus. You will see the name of the document and additional attributes of the document in the lower view.

The Theatre view helps in viewing the content as a larger image, and provides you with the flexibility to select the item to view by hovering the mouse over the desired thumbnail.

Carousel View

You can also change the Current View selection to Carousel view in the PowerPivot Gallery, as shown in Figure 6-8. Similar to an actual carousel, the thumbnails viewed in Carousel view rotate along as you traverse over the thumbnails clockwise or counterclockwise using the arrows. The name of the current document or sheet in focus is shown in the top-left corner, along with attributes such as last updated time.

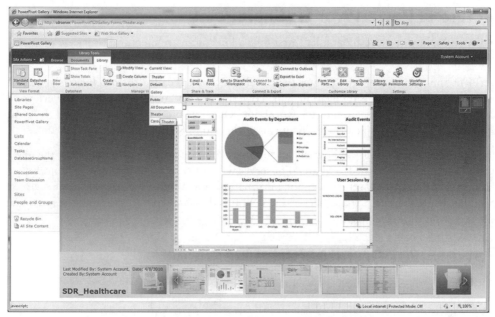

FIGURE 6-7: PowerPivot Gallery Theatre view

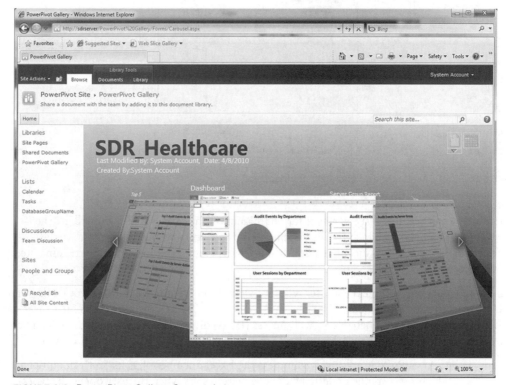

FIGURE 6-8: PowerPivot Gallery Carousel view

Architecture of PowerPivot for SharePoint

Before discussing how to refresh data, let's first take a look at an architectural overview of PowerPivot for SharePoint.

A PowerPivot application user who creates the Excel workbook is called the *producer*, since he or she first creates the self-service application. This PowerPivot workbook contains the PowerPivot data in a custom data part (CDP) section of the workbook. Once the producer has completed the creation of an application, he or she uploads the document to the team's SharePoint site.

Chapter 2 discussed how to install PowerPivot for SharePoint on a single machine using the new farm install. As you have learned, a SharePoint server will typically contain the Web Front End (WFE), a content database server to store the information, and a set of services such as Excel Services. Figure 6-9 shows a physical server that contains the SharePoint Server and the relational database server on the same machine.

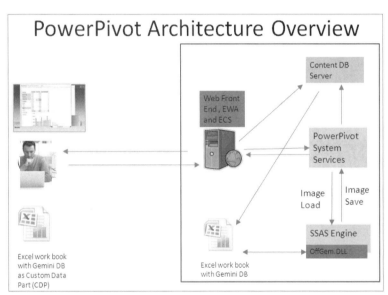

FIGURE 6-9: PowerPivot for SharePoint 2010 architecture

Additionally, when you install PowerPivot for SharePoint on the same server, you will get the PowerPivot System Service (which is a shared SharePoint service) and the SQL Server Analysis Services engine. Once the producer has published a PowerPivot workbook to the SharePoint site, it can then be consumed by the end user.

As shown in Figure 6-9, a typical end user will first view the content in the PowerPivot Gallery, and then click on the thumbnail to open the sheet in Excel Services. When the user clicks on a sheet, the request is sent to the WFE, where Excel Web Access (EWA) directs the request to ECS, which performs all the calculations in the workbook and sends the data to EWA to render in a browser.

Up to this point, PowerPivot is not involved, unless the Excel document has its "refresh on open property" set, which requests the underlying data to be refreshed when the user opens the workbook. Then, when the user interacts with the content in the Excel sheet in a way that requires interaction with the workbook's PowerPivot data (such as clicking on slicers, filtering, or sorting operations in a PivotTable), ECS sends the request to the PowerPivot System Service.

The PowerPivot data is stored as an Analysis Services database within the Excel workbook. The PowerPivot System Service first checks if the Analysis Services database corresponding to the requested PowerPivot workbook is already loaded on the SSAS engine. If it is, the request is sent to the Analysis Services engine, and the results are returned back to ECS. However, if the database is not there, then it extracts the Excel workbook from the content database server, and stores this in a location where the Analysis Services engine has access. It then sends a command called ImageLoad to the SQL Server Analysis Services engine.

The Analysis Services engine extracts the PowerPivot data from the workbook using OffGem.DLL, which helps in operations connected with retrieving or storing the PowerPivot data stored in the workbook. The PowerPivot data stored within the workbook is actually an Analysis Services database backup. Once the PowerPivot data is extracted, it is restored on the Analysis Services engine in read-only mode so that queries against this database can be executed.

In addition, the end-users interacting with the workbook, administrators, or the producers can update the content, or schedule a data refresh at a specific time. In this case, the PowerPivot System Service sends an ImageLoad request to the Analysis Service engine so that the corresponding database is restored in a read-write mode. After the database is restored in a read-write mode, the PowerPivot System Service sends a Process command with the Processing option of ProcessFull (process the entire database) to the Analysis Services engine, with the appropriate credentials information provided by the administrator or author of the document, to refresh the data.

The Analysis Service engine then processes the database with the latest data from the data sources involved in the data refresh. Finally, the PowerPivot System Service sends an ImageSave command to the Analysis Services engine to store a backup of the database within the PowerPivot workbook. Once the ImageSave operation is successful, PowerPivot System Service uploads the updated PowerPivot workbook to the content database, which then triggers PowerPivot Gallery to get new snapshots.

 Chapter 10 provides more detail on the PowerPivot architecture.

Now that you understand the overall architecture of PowerPivot for SharePoint, let's see how PowerPivot data refresh works.

PowerPivot Data Refresh

Once you publish your PowerPivot application to the PowerPivot Gallery site, your end users can view and interact with your application. Chapter 4 discusses how to refresh data in PowerPivot for Excel. However, to update the content in your PowerPivot application, you definitely do not want to download your document, refresh, and then upload back to PowerPivot for SharePoint. Hence, PowerPivot for SharePoint provides a way for you to refresh the data from underlying data sources used in your PowerPivot application.

When you view a specific PowerPivot workbook in the PowerPivot Gallery default view, you will see two icons for each document in the top-right corner, as shown in Figure 6-10. When you hover over the icons you will see the tool tip icons for New Report and Manage Data Refresh. You'll learn how to create new reports on a published PowerPivot workbook later in this chapter. Click on the Manage Data Refresh icon to schedule a data refresh.

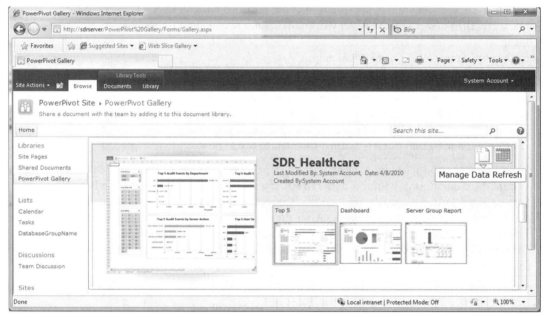

FIGURE 6-10: Manage Data Refresh icons from PowerPivot Gallery

When you click on the Manage Data Refresh icon for a PowerPivot workbook, you see the Manage Data Refresh page, as shown in Figure 6-11. You must click on the Enable checkbox to enable the capability to schedule a data refresh.

The PowerPivot data refresh feature allows you to schedule a data refresh at specific time intervals. In the Schedule Details section of the page, you can specify Daily, Weekly, Monthly, or simply Once. In this section of the dialog, you can also specify a daily interval, a weekday interval, or specific days of the week.

The PowerPivot data refresh feature currently does not support data refresh within a day's granularity. For example, you cannot schedule a refresh every 6 hours or 12 hours each day. However, you can perform an immediate data refresh, which allows you to initiate a data refresh immediately. To do this, you must enable the checkbox "Also refresh as soon as possible" to get an immediate refresh, and specify the time in the Earliest Start Time section of the screen.

If you have configured email notifications on your SharePoint server, Manage Data Refresh also allows you to send automated email to a user after the completion of the data refresh. In the E-mail Notification area of the dialog, you may specify the email address where the message should be sent.

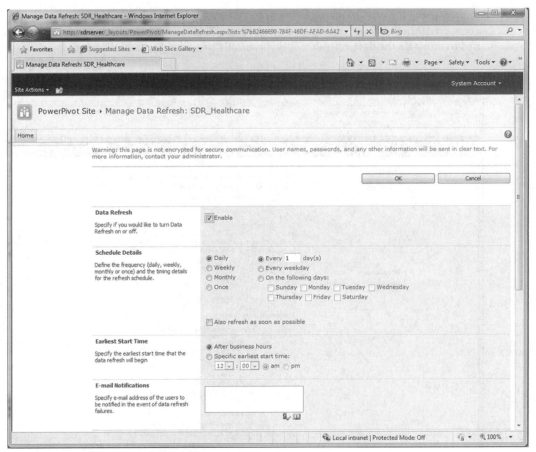

FIGURE 6-11: Data Refresh configuration (Part 1)

If you scroll further down on the dialog page, you will see the Credentials section that contains options to specify credentials for data refresh, as well as the Data Sources section where you can choose which data sources to refresh, as shown in Figure 6-12.

As you can see, you have three options to specify credentials for data refresh:

➤ *Use the data refresh account configured by the administrator* — If you select this option, the PowerPivot System Service will schedule the data refresh using the unattended service account (called the *PowerPivot Unattended Data Refresh account*) under which it's running (which is usually a low-privilege account, and one that doesn't have access to the data sources). The SQL logins specified in the connection string for the data sources are used.

➤ *Connect using the following Windows user credentials* — If you select this option, the data refresh is scheduled at the specified time using the credentials specified, which are stored and retrieved within SharePoint. Typically, these Windows credentials have trusted access to the data sources.

➤ *Connect using the credentials stored in Secure Store Services* — You select this option when a secure credential is stored in Secure Store Services. The Secure Store ID for that credential is used to schedule the data refresh. (This is typically provided by administrators.)

FIGURE 6-12 Data Refresh configuration (Part 2)

For all three of these options, PowerPivot for SharePoint stores the account credentials specified in the options in Secure Store Services. When data refresh for a PowerPivot workbook is scheduled, then the PowerPivot System Service impersonates using the account credentials specified, and then schedules the data refresh to the SSAS engine.

You can select the list of data sources from which you want to refresh the data in the Data Sources section. Here you can specify that data is refreshed for all data sources, or you have the option of specifying custom data refresh schedules for each data source.

If you choose to specify refreshes for each data source, you can either use the credentials you supplied for the entire workbook if the connection uses Windows credentials or specify a username and password (typically the SQL login and non-Windows credential) for that specific data source. You can also use a credential stored in the Secure Store Services application. If you do not want a specific data source to be updated, uncheck the box corresponding to that data source.

> *If you have a linked table established within the PowerPivot workbook, that connection will not show up in the Data Source list for the workbook, and the data cannot be refreshed using PowerPivot data refresh.*

Once you have supplied all the needed properties for data refresh, click OK.

PowerPivot for SharePoint uses the Timer Job available in SharePoint, and schedules a data refresh for a specific PowerPivot workbook based on the configuration/credentials specified by the user. The PowerPivot System Service will send the `ImageLoad` and `Process` commands with the right data source credentials for data refresh to be executed by the SQL Server Analysis Services engine, and the updated PowerPivot data (Analysis Services database backup) is stored back in the PowerPivot workbook. Any new users connecting to the workbook will then see the new data.

If you click on the Manage Data Refresh icon after a successful, failed, or in-progress data refresh, you will see a screen similar to Figure 6-13 that shows the results of the data refresh. You can configure or change the refresh schedule by clicking the Configure Schedule link near the middle of the page.

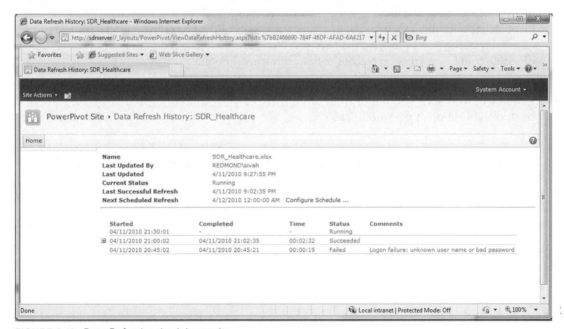

FIGURE 6-13: Data Refresh schedule results

The PowerPivot data refresh feature performs an automatic update of the data at the scheduled time. Typically, a data refresh is scheduled as a nightly process, and this can be done by the end-user who has published the PowerPivot workbook. This feature is primarily targeted for the information producer (author) of the PowerPivot workbook. Some of the features that are typically needed by the administrators (such as real-time updates or frequent updates within a day) are not available in this release of PowerPivot for SharePoint.

Chapter 10 provides additional information on the PowerPivot data refresh feature.

Now that you have learned how to successfully perform a data refresh for a published workbook, let's see how to create reports from the published PowerPivot workbook's data. This PowerPivot workbook data essentially exposes the information as a model for end users to build reports, and, hence, is referred to as a *PowerPivot model* in this chapter.

Building Ad Hoc Reports

After you have published a PowerPivot workbook and shared it with end users and colleagues (with appropriate permissions), those users can create their own ad hoc reports based on the PowerPivot model. In this case, the PowerPivot data can be used as a data source.

Typically, end users first interact with the published workbooks using Excel Services. They might find that they would like to build a slightly different workbook with appropriate PivotTable and PivotCharts catering to their needs, or create reports off of the PowerPivot model. Instead of the end users coming to you and making the requests, PowerPivot for SharePoint provides the functionality of building ad hoc reports on top of the PowerPivot workbook.

End users can build their own ad hoc reports within Excel using PivotTables without help from the PowerPivot workbook's author or from administrators. As an author or administrator, you can then track the utilization of the workbooks.

You will learn more about the administrative operations and enterprise considerations in Chapters 7 through 11.

If you hover over the first icon in the upper-right corner of a PowerPivot workbook, you will see New Report. As shown in the drop-down in Figure 6-14, there are two kinds of reports that can be created from PowerPivot data:

➤ Open New Excel Workbook

➤ Create Report Builder Report

Let's begin by looking at the Open New Excel Workbook option.

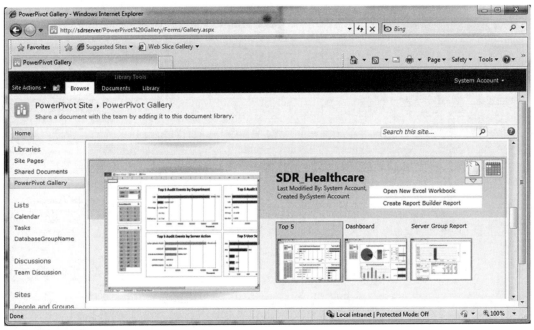

FIGURE 6-14: Reports from PowerPivot data

Excel Workbook Connected to PowerPivot Data

The PowerPivot Gallery provides a template of an Excel file. As soon as you request to open a new Excel workbook, it creates a connection to the chosen PowerPivot workbook and initiates a download of the Excel workbook onto the client. You will then be asked if you want to download a file and Open. Click on Open.

A workbook is opened in Excel, and you will be asked if you want to enable data connections. Click on Enable. At this point, you should see an Excel PivotTable with the field list populated, as shown in Figure 6-15. The PowerPivot data stored within the PowerPivot workbook is seen by Excel as an Analysis Services database, since the PowerPivot model is essentially an Analysis Services Vertipaq database. When the Excel workbook is created, PowerPivot Gallery establishes a connection to the Analysis Services database with the full path of the PowerPivot workbook. Hence, the data seen in the field list is the PowerPivot model with measure groups and dimensions, as with a traditional Analysis Services database.

Each table in the workbook's PowerPivot data (as seen in the PowerPivot Window) has a corresponding measure group and a dimension created. By default, measures are created for each measure group. If you drag and drop a column from a table to the values area, any new measure created from a table using DAX (explicitly or implicitly) can be seen within the measure group.

You can build an Excel report as you would against an Analysis Services database. You can also publish this workbook to the PowerPivot Gallery site. When a data refresh is done on the PowerPivot workbook, you can now see the data updated on this workbook using Excel Services by clicking on the Refresh Data option.

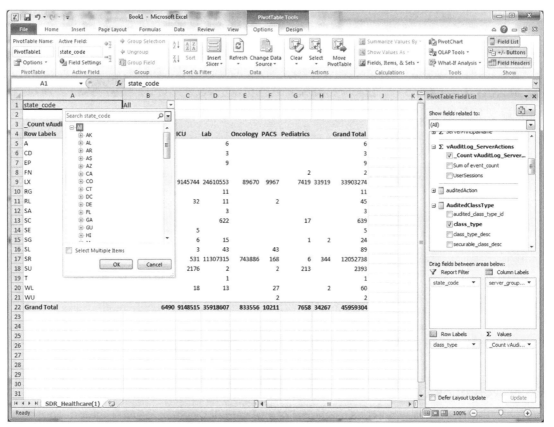

FIGURE 6-15: Excel workbook connected to PowerPivot data

Report Builder Report from PowerPivot Data

Report Builder is an end-user tool that is part of SQL Server Reporting Services. Report Builder enables you to build ad-hoc end user reports and publish them to SQL Server Reporting Services. Once published to Reporting Services, you can utilize the server-side features of Reporting Services to automate the report delivery when needed.

PowerPivot for SharePoint has a tight integration with Report Builder to enable end users to build these ad hoc reports. If you have used earlier versions of Report Builder or Report Designer (both of which are part of SQL Server Reporting Services), you might be familiar with creating reports using tables or a matrix, and these were done as separate data regions. Report Builder allows you to create reports from a wide range of data sources, as well as providing the flexibility to create interactive reports such as document maps, drilling through to reports, and providing report parameters for filtering and customized views. You can also export the reports in a wide range of presentation formats such as HTML, Word, Excel, and PDF.

However, one of the important features in Report Builder 3.0 (the version shipped with SQL Server 2008 R2) is the capability to create reports with maps, where data is aggregated and presented in a map

(Reports with maps are discussed later in this chapter.) After you publish your reports to SQL Server Reporting Services in the SharePoint integrated mode, you can configure the reports to be executed at a specific time (similar to PowerPivot data refresh) and set up email subscriptions to end users.

So, let's take a look at how to get started with Report Builder. Click on the New Report icon drop-down for a PowerPivot workbook (Figure 6-14) and select Create Report Builder Report. PowerPivot Gallery will send the appropriate commands to launch Report Builder with a connection established to the PowerPivot workbook. You will now be asked to download and run the Report Builder 3.0 on your machine.

Click Yes to start Report Builder 3.0 on your machine. If you followed the instructions in Appendix A before importing the main data table for the SDR Healthcare application in Chapter 3, you should now see Report Builder 3.0 launch on your machine, as shown in Figure 6-16. You can see that a data set based on the PowerPivot workbook has already been established. Similar to what happens with an Excel report, Report Builder 3.0 also establishes an Analysis Services connection to the workbook. Hence, you will see measure groups and dimensions when you add data from this connection.

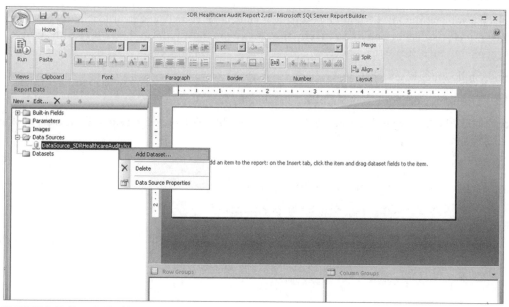

FIGURE 6-16 Report Builder connected to PowerPivot workbook

You can add a data set from this connection by selecting Add Dataset. In the Add Dataset dialog, you can use the query designer to select the measures and dimension attributes to be included in the report, or you can use an MDX query. Since the connection is an Analysis Services connection, you will see the MDX query designer in the Add Dataset dialog. You use Home and Insert tabs to design the report, and the View tab lets you preview the report in Report Builder.

Once a report is created, you can save the report to the PowerPivot Gallery so that you can see snapshots of the report.

ADDING REPORTING TO THE SDR HEALTHCARE APPLICATION

In Chapters 3 through 5, you created the SDR Healthcare Audit application using PowerPivot for Excel. In Chapter 2, you set up PowerPivot for SharePoint and, in preparation for creating the SDR Healthcare Audit application in Chapter 3, you set up Reporting Services in integrated mode as part of following the instructions found in Appendix A. To continue with the SDR Healthcare Audit application development, let's use the same SharePoint server with PowerPivot to publish the application created up to Chapter 5. In this chapter, you will enhance it by creating a Report Builder 3.0 report with a map.

There is a lot of interesting information within the SDR Healthcare PowerPivot workbook. And, as powerful as PowerPivot for Excel is, sometimes all you want is to create an eye-catching report. What would be even better is if you could create an eye-catching Reporting Services report using the data within your PowerPivot workbook. After all, you have taken the time to import data from different sources, added in your business logic, and created your metrics and key performance indicators (KPIs). If IW consumers wanted to create a custom report based on your Excel workbook, it would be nice if they could simply use your PowerPivot workbook as their data source.

By placing your workbook within the PowerPivot Gallery of your PowerPivot for SharePoint environment, it is possible for you to do exactly this. First, you must publish the SDR Healthcare Excel workbook and then create the report.

Begin by following these steps:

1. Open the workbook you completed in Chapter 5.

2. Hide the following sheets in the PowerPivot workbook by selecting each sheet, right-clicking the sheet, and selecting Hide:

   - ➤ `Data for Server Group Report`
   - ➤ `Dashboard Events by Department`
   - ➤ `Dashboard Sessions by Department`
   - ➤ `Dashboard Events by Database`
   - ➤ `Dashboard Sessions by Class`
   - ➤ `Top 5 Events by Department`
   - ➤ `Top 5 Events by Action`
   - ➤ `Top 5 Events by Database`
   - ➤ `Top 5 Sessions by Location`
   - ➤ `ServerGroup Name`

   After you have done this, you should have the three sheets `Top 5`, `Dashboard`, and `Server Group Report` visible in your workbook.

3. Click on the View tab in Excel and uncheck the checkbox next to Gridlines in the "Show group" option for each of the sheets `Top 5`, `Dashboard`, and `Server Group Report`.

4. Select File ⇨ Save and Send ⇨ Save to SharePoint ⇨ Save As button.

5. In the Save As dialog, enter the SharePoint server set up in Chapters 2 and 3 (or another SharePoint server with PowerPivot for SharePoint installed) and select the PowerPivot Gallery site to publish the workbook.

6. Open a Web browser and navigate to the PowerPivot Gallery site where you published the SDR Healthcare workbook.

7. Click on the New Report icon drop-down, and select Create Report Builder Report, as shown in Figure 6-17.

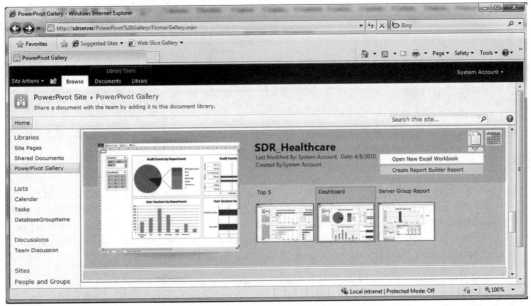

FIGURE 6-17: Creating a Report Builder report

A new Report Definition Language (RDL) report will be added to the PowerPivot Gallery with the naming convention of `<Workbook Name> Report 1`, as shown in Figure 6-18. The RDL format/file type is the standard format in which Reporting Services stores and executes reports. A snapshot is captured after the report file is created in PowerPivot Gallery. You will see a blank snapshot, since there is no report in the file. When you save the report to the PowerPivot Gallery, an updated snapshot will be created.

If you do not have Report Builder 3.0 on your machine, then you will be prompted to install and run Report Builder, since Report Builder is a Windows ClickOnce application. What is advantageous about this process is that, as new versions of Report Builder become available, updates can be deployed to the SharePoint/Reporting Services integration from the SharePoint UI, so that the newer versions are made immediately available to everyone without having to find the correct installation bits. When prompted to download and run Report Builder 3.0, accept by clicking Yes.

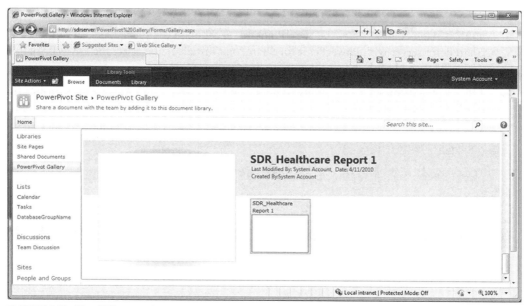

FIGURE 6-18: The RDL report has been created within the PowerPivot Gallery

As noted earlier, the benefit of creating Reporting Services reports within the context of the PowerPivot Gallery is that you can create Reporting Services reports by using PowerPivot workbooks as a data source. Now that you've opened up your PowerPivot Gallery generated report in Report Builder, expand the `Data Sources` folder and double-click on the data source (which will be a reference to your PowerPivot workbook) to see the data source properties.

The key thing to observe is that your connection string is `Data Source=http://$servername$/PowerPivot%20Gallery/SDR_Healthcare.xlsx`, as shown in Figure 6-19. That is, the data source is the PowerPivot workbook you uploaded to PowerPivot Gallery.

One of the great things about the SDR Healthcare data source is that, if you have been following along with the building of the application, you have already imported in the Client Address to State Mapping from a separate Reporting Services data source. This mapping provides a translation from the `client_address_id` column to a mapping of the states within the continental United States where the audit event had occurred.

With Report Builder using the SDR Healthcare PowerPivot workbook data source as its source, you can now build a bubble map showing the audits by geographic location. Follow these steps to create your bubble map:

1. Click on the Insert tab in Report Builder ribbon.

2. Click Map ⇨ Map Wizard in the menu bar, as shown in Figure 6-20.

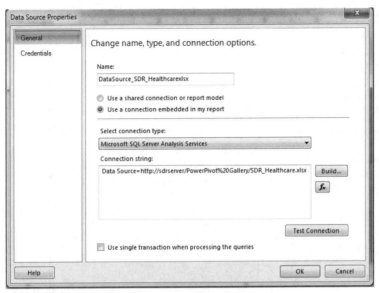

FIGURE 6-19: Data source for your Report Builder report

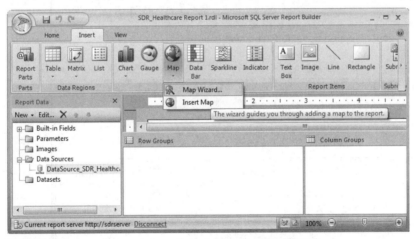

FIGURE 6-20: Insert a map to your report using the Map Wizard

3. The New Map dialog shown in Figure 6-21 appears and provides you with the option to choose the map area definitions. In this case, keep the default "Map gallery," as it contains the spatial data for the United States.

4. Choose the "USA by State Exploded" option under the map gallery so that you can emulate the bubble map you're about to create. Click Next.

5. In the "Choose spatial data and map view options" dialog (Figure 6-22) that appears next, you will be able to configure the map, including the size and location (left of the map), map resolution (right of the map), and add a Bing Maps layer (by checking the Add a Bing Maps layer checkbox). For the purpose of this demonstration, let's not include the Bing Maps layer, since the image does not translate very well in the book. Select the defaults and click Next.

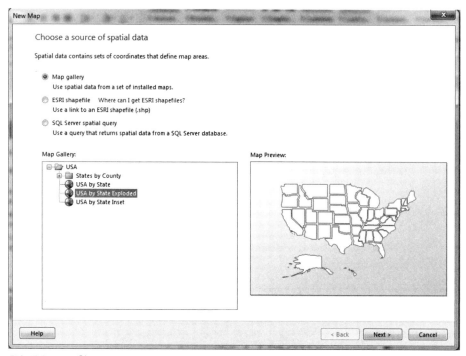

FIGURE 6-21: Choose your map area definitions and map gallery

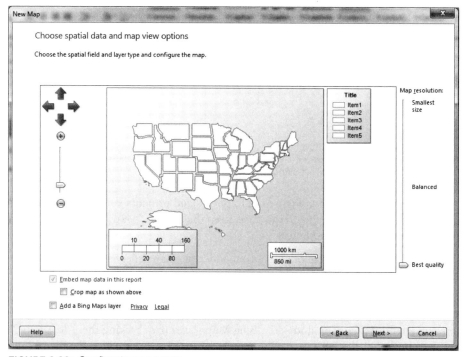

FIGURE 6-22: Configuring your map

If you do like working with road, aerial, and hybrid maps, you should try additional reports later.

6. In the next "Choose map visualization" page shown in Figure 6-23, you are provided three different options for your map visualizations. The first option is Basic Map where the data is used to shade the states or regions using a theme or color gradient. The second option, Color Analytical Map, helps with representing data in varying colors. The third option, Bubble Map, shows the maps along with size of a bubble indicating the data chosen. Choose the Bubble Map option and click Next.

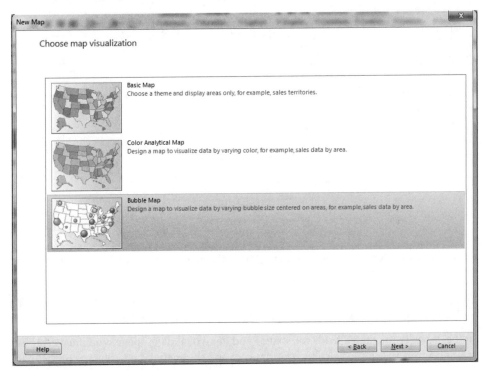

FIGURE 6-23: Choosing your map visualization

7. Since this is a brand new report, you have not yet created a new dataset that is to be used for the map. In the "Choose the analytical dataset" page, select the option "Add a dataset that includes fields that relate to the spatial data that you chose earlier" and click Next.

8. In the "Choose a connection to a data source" dialog, you will see the data source connection to the PowerPivot workbook. Click Next.

9. If you are familiar with Report Builder or Analysis Services in general, you will then be familiar with the MDX query designer. From here, you will want to choose the measures and dimensions (which are really columns from available tables) you will want to use for your bubble map. In the "Design a query" page of the Map Wizard, drag and drop Measures ➪ vAuditLog_ServerActions ➪ "Sum of event_count" to the data area, as shown in Figure 6-24. The Sum of event_count measure indicates the number of audit events that will be used to create the bubble map.

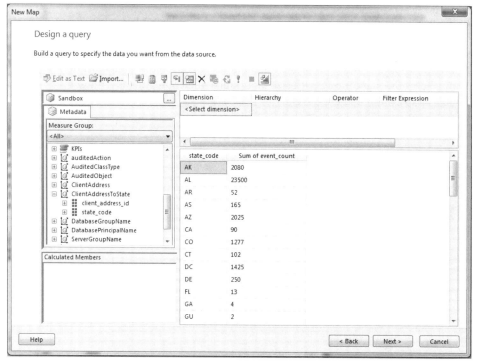

FIGURE 6-24: Query Designer choosing the state_code column and sum of event_count measure

10. Drag and drop the ClientAddressToState ➪ state_code column to the data area. You will see the aggregated event_count for each state, as shown in Figure 6-24.

11. In the "Specify the match fields for spatial and analytical data" page, you must establish the relationship between the fields in your data set and the spatial data columns of the map. The *spatial data* is the data defined by the map gallery itself, while the *analytical data* is the data defined by the state_code column. The state_code is a two digit state-code that happens to also match the spatial dataset values in the STUSPS column. Click the Match Fields checkbox next to STUSPS and ensure that you have chosen the state_code column within the analytical dataset fields column, as shown in Figure 6-25. Click Next.

12. In the "Choose the color theme and data visualization" page shown in Figure 6-26, you will be able to choose your color theme and data visualization. You should choose the right color scheme based on the end-user audience being targeted for this report. So, for the purposes of this sample, choose the default Ocean theme.

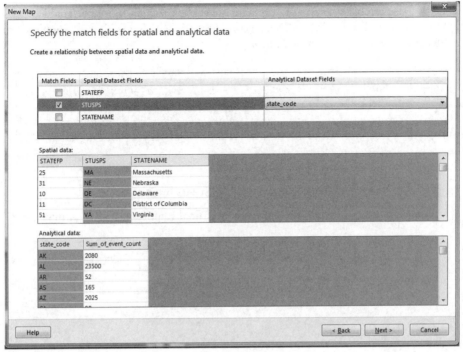

FIGURE 6-25: Matching the spatial and analytical dataset fields

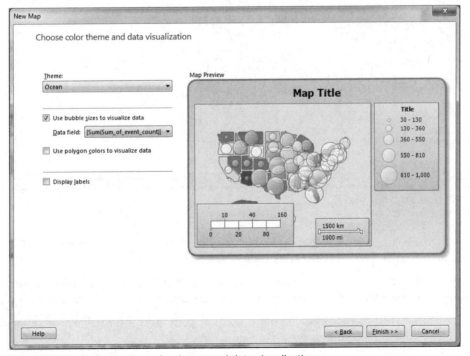

FIGURE 6-26: Choosing the color theme and data visualization

13. Under the "Use bubble sizes to visualize data" checkbox (which should be enabled), ensure that you have the "Data field" specified as the measure, which, in this case, should be the `Sum(Sum_of_event_count)`. Click Finish.

> *You can also choose to use polygon colors to visualize data — that is, different shades of color visually representing the range of values (for example, darker colors for a larger number of events, and lighter colors for smaller number of events). Also, you have the option to display labels by checking the checkbox.*

14. Change the map title to "SDR Healthcare Audit Events by States."

15. Click the Run button in the Home tab to see your final Report, as shown in Figure 6-27.

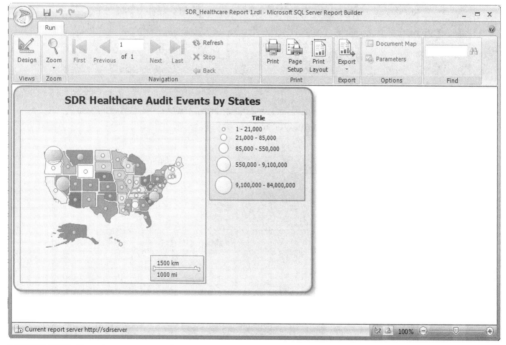

FIGURE 6-27: Running your report

16. Switch to the Design mode in Report Builder, and click the Save button (or press Ctrl + S) to save the report on to your PowerPivot Gallery site.

17. Now, go back to your PowerPivot Gallery site in your Web browser. You will notice that the report is now available, and the report thumbnail can also be seen, as shown in Figure 6-28.

18. Click on the SDR Healthcare Audit report, and now your users will be able to view your eye-catching bubble map report, as shown in Figure 6-29.

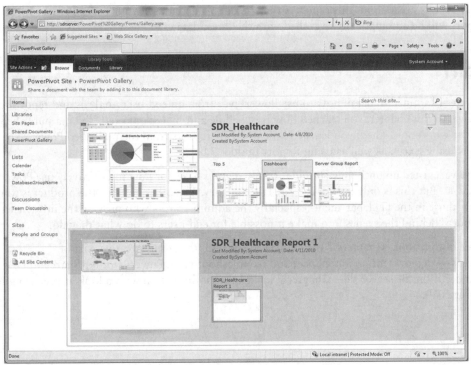

FIGURE 6-28: SDR Healthcare PowerPivot and Bubble Map report in the PowerPivot Gallery

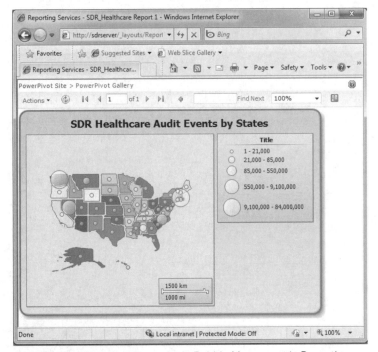

FIGURE 6-29: SDR Healthcare Audit Bubble Map report in Reporting Services (SharePoint Integrated mode)

As noted, what is great about this report is that, as data is updated in your PowerPivot workbook, your report will be automatically refreshed with the latest data.

SUMMARY

This chapter examined in detail how to use PowerPivot from an end-user analysis and reporting perspective. In this chapter, you learned how to schedule automated data refresh on a published PowerPivot workbook. Then, you learned how to create reports from the published PowerPivot workbook using Excel, as well as using Report Builder 3.0.

What you've learned up until now should give you a good basis for how to effectively use PowerPivot as an analyst. But this is only half of the PowerPivot story. The other goal for the product is to make it easy for those in the IT department (especially the administrators who provide the infrastructure and support "behind the scenes") to make it possible for end-users to do what they do.

Part three of this book, Chapters 7 through 11, deals with the administrative part of PowerPivot — deployment, maintenance, and troubleshooting of PowerPivot for SharePoint — all of which occur on the server side. Chapter 7 kicks off that discussion with a look at preparing for SharePoint 2010.

PART III
IT PROFESSIONAL

7

Preparing for SharePoint 2010

WHAT'S IN THIS CHAPTER?

➤ Taking a look at SharePoint 2010

➤ Taking a look at Excel Services

➤ Taking a look at SharePoint Server components for PowerPivot for SharePoint

➤ Taking a look at key services for PowerPivot for SharePoint

➤ Understanding the PowerPivot for SharePoint services architecture workflow scenarios

This chapter provides information on SharePoint services and servers so that you can do the setup and configuration described in Chapter 8. Chapter 9 will provide you with the operational "how-to" for monitoring, securing, and troubleshooting. Chapter 10 dives even deeper than this chapter into the PowerPivot for SharePoint services and component architecture. Understanding this will provide you with the background and context for the Enterprise Considerations described in Chapter 11.

SHAREPOINT 2010

One of the key concerns for IT administrators regarding Excel in general is the continuing dissemination of "spreadmarts" throughout the organization. What's great about these Excel spreadmarts is that they help solve business problems, and can be created and calculated rather quickly by business analysts.

With the addition of PowerPivot for Excel, these same analysts or Information Workers (IWs) can now harness even larger volumes of data, and are provided an even more powerful toolset to augment the already powerful set of Excel functions. This, in turn, could lead to even more spreadmarts being emailed or shared throughout the organization with no control, security, or even recording of the necessary domain knowledge or business logic.

So, how do IT administrators control the flow of this data while ensuring everyone who needs to have easy access to the data can still do so? The answer to this question is Microsoft SharePoint 2010. SharePoint is an Office Server product that allows you to organize and secure all of your content. It also helps you develop process management and collaboration (within the context of this content) from your Web browser. Organizations benefit from SharePoint because of their capability to find all of their important information all in one location (documents, lists, and so on) and share this information securely.

Yet, content management is just the beginning, since SharePoint includes many services. It also allows users to quickly create wikis, blogs, and lists that contain their own custom content from their browsers. With Word Services, Visio Services, and Excel Services, you can view Office documents in the browser directly — that is, without needing to install the application software. With a large library of Web parts ranging from custom templates to PerformancePoint services, you can integrate and create mashups of Web content (for example, from RSS feeds or atom feed sources) or data (for example, SQL or Analysis Services data) into your SharePoint dashboard.

With all of this information, you can develop workflow processes (for example, users read a document, fill out a list, review PowerPoint for instructions, all before proceeding to a dashboard to view data) to help your organization be more productive. For those on the go, you can make use of the improved mobile services (for example, improved rendering to multiple mobile browsers, or the capability to take SharePoint content to your Windows Mobile device) included within SharePoint 2010 as well.

 Because SharePoint 2010 is a powerful business collaboration platform, this chapter does little justice to describing it all. For more information, review the Microsoft SharePoint 2010 Web site at `http://sharepoint2010.microsoft.com/Pages/default.aspx`. *Also, there is an excellent blog by Jeff Teper (Corporate Vice President of SharePoint Server at Microsoft) about what's new in SharePoint at* `http://bit.ly/4GcGRm`.

WHY NOT SHAREPOINT "LITE" BI EDITION?

This was a common question asked by many database administrators (DBAs) and IT administrators — especially ones with background or familiarity with the existing Corporate BI Analysis Services. The question has been asked because, as you will see in this chapter and Chapter 8, there is a degree of complexity in the architecture, configuration, and maintenance of PowerPivot for SharePoint. Instead of having to learn SharePoint, why not just provide an edition of SharePoint specifically for BI users only?

To some extent, this has already been provided to you with the installation instructions for a single-server PowerPivot for SharePoint setup, which you learned about in Chapter 2.

For the technophile focused on BI and used to working within the complexities of database design and Multidimensional Expressions (MDX), you may initially only be concerned with Excel Services and PowerPivot services. So, the thought is, why not have a simplified system that contains only those services and nothing else? Regardless of your technical background, your analytics persona is using PowerPivot, because it is all about self-service BI — providing you with the capability to quickly perform BI calculations on large volumes of data, and to discover patterns in the data without needing to build the data warehousing infrastructure first.

But, as an analyst, powerful analytics is only one piece of the "Self-Service Understanding" puzzle. You also have other Excel workbooks that contain business logic and domain data, Word documents that contain specifications, PowerPoint presentations, Visio diagrams, information lists, and so on. How do you keep all of this organized? Well, *this* is the reason for using SharePoint as the base framework for PowerPivot. It is about keeping *all* of your information organized, easily accessible, and secure.

 Over the years, SharePoint has had a number of different names associated with it, from Windows SharePoint Services to Microsoft Office SharePoint Services (MOSS). The quick take on this is that Windows SharePoint Services (WSS) is still being worked on, and there is a version 4 planned as of publication. On the other hand, the official name MOSS is now SharePoint 2010 — that is, no "Office."

While SharePoint is still very much part of the Office infrastructure, the name change was done to help differentiate the client tools (for example, Excel, Word, and so on) that Office is commonly associated with from SharePoint itself. Oh, and don't use the acronym MSS, since this represents Microsoft Search Server. It's now just SharePoint.

For more information, refer to a handy blog from the SharePoint Team at http://bit.ly/6S1I.

EXCEL SERVICES

Excel Services is one of the services available within SharePoint. It is the service that allows users to view Excel workbooks within SharePoint using their Web browsers. As noted earlier (and throughout this book), one of the key concerns for Excel workbook users is the prevalent habit of creating spreadmarts that are disseminated throughout an organization with lack of control or security. By having the creators of these workbooks upload them to SharePoint, you can utilize SharePoint's security model to restrict or enable access to these workbooks. You can also utilize SharePoint to share the Excel workbook with users who only have thin clients (that is, Web browsers) readily available.

Comparing Excel and Excel Services

Figure 7-1 shows a simple table within Excel (with the ribbon minimized). Figure 7-2 shows the same simple table rendered by Excel Services within SharePoint 2010.

As you can see, the screenshots depicting the Excel client (Figure 7-1) and Excel Services (Figure 7-2) are quite similar. Keeping in mind the IW who is consuming data within Excel Services, you can utilize many of the functionalities within the Excel client to read and understand the data, such as filtering and slicing. Figure 7-3 shows the same simple table within Excel Services filtered to the `DatabaseGroup` called `Vendor`.

Because many functions have been designed with the IW producer (that is, the analyst who regularly creates reports, compared to the even more users who read the reports — the IW consumers) in mind, this means that the user must go back to Excel. To do this, as noted in Figure 7-3, you only need to click on the "Open in Excel" button, and the Excel client will open up with the same report.

Excel Services and PowerPivot

The reason this chapter spotlights Excel Services (as opposed to the many other services within SharePoint) is because of PowerPivot's strong dependency on Excel in general. As noted earlier in this book, PowerPivot for Excel (the client component of PowerPivot) is an add-in to the Excel 2010 client. PowerPivot for Excel augments and provides additional functionality to what already exists within Excel.

Going back to personas, the IW producer is able to make use of a familiar tool that is made even more powerful. For example, Figure 7-4 shows an Excel workbook that presents Healthcare Audit information. The IW producer has imported data from many disparate data sources (including server audit logs totaling more than 44 million rows) and joined them together to create this report.

FIGURE 7-1: Simple table within Excel 2010 client

FIGURE 7-2: Simple table within Excel Services of SharePoint 2010

database_principal_id	DatabaseName	DatabaseGroup
13	Class-A	Vendor
14	Class-B	Vendor
15	Class-C	Vendor
16	Class-D	Vendor
17	Class-E	Vendor
18	Class-F	Vendor
19	Class-G	Vendor

FIGURE 7-3: Simple table filtered within Excel Services of SharePoint 2010

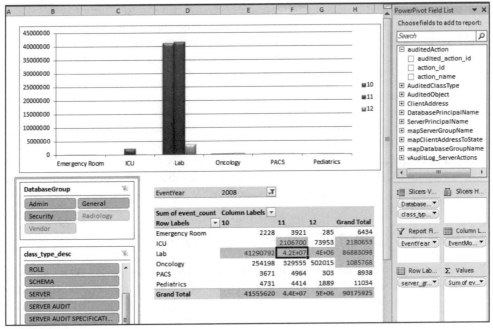

FIGURE 7-4: Healthcare Audit report in Excel client

But as an IW consumer, the analyst typically reads reports and does little data manipulation. Figure 7-5 shows the same report rendered by Excel Services.

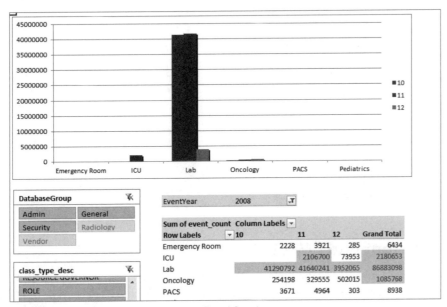

FIGURE 7-5: Healthcare Audit report in Excel Services

There are some notable similarities and differences between the two views. Within Excel Services, IW consumers are able to make use of slicers and filtering to customize their views of data. Formatting between client and server is kept the same, including the conditional formatting of the numeric values. But an important function that is lacking in Excel Services (shown in Figure 7-5) is the PowerPivot Field List (shown on the right side of Figure 7-4).

This is an important difference, because the IW producer, the one who created the reports, needs the PowerPivot Field List. This provides the capability to add different attributes such as slicers, labels, or values, and, ultimately, the capability to alter the entire look, feel, and, most important, meaning of the report. The IW consumer, on the other hand, is provided with the capability to slice and filter as per the functionality available in Excel Services (Figure 7-5). But while the IW consumer can customize the view of the report, the underlying meaning of the report cannot be altered, which ensures report consistency throughout the organization.

KEY SERVERS IN POWERPIVOT FOR SHAREPOINT

Now that you are familiar with the functionality and a few of the features of SharePoint Services, let's dive into the more technical details, starting with the SharePoint Services servers, and, in particular, the ones PowerPivot relies on. Figure 7-6 shows the SharePoint Services server architecture. The following discussion examines the details depicted in this figure.

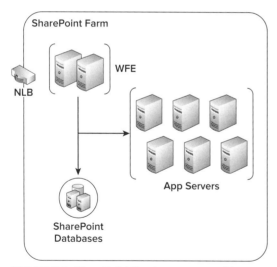

FIGURE 7-6: SharePoint Services server architecture

SharePoint Web Front End (WFE)

The SharePoint Web Front End (WFE) represents the Web server that the users access from their browsers. In addition to rendering Web pages, it will also utilize Excel Web Access (EWA) to render the Excel workbooks calculated by Excel Calculation Services (ECS). For large deployments, there typically will be multiple SharePoint WFEs.

To load balance between these servers, you should make use of a load balancer, whether it be hardware (for example, F5, Big IP, and so on) or software (for example, Windows Load Balancing Service).

Since load balancing is a common scenario, you should also be familiar with SharePoint Alternate Access Mapping (AAM). The basic principle of AAM is that you tell SharePoint how to map Web requests (for example, a PowerPivot Gallery for the HR Department) to the correct Web application and site (for example, the correct URL for the application). Within load-balancing scenarios, the URL that a user types in the browser window (for example, `http://contoso.com/HR/Power%20 Pivot%Gallery/default.aspx`) is not the URL that the Internet Information Server (IIS) will receive (for example, `http://192.168.0.1/HR/PP`). Hence, the purpose of AAM is to ensure that SharePoint can map the IIS-received URL to the correct site (that is, HR) and application (that is, Power Pivot Gallery).

EXPLORING AAM

For more information on AAM, take a look at Troy Starr's excellent blog series on the topic. While the blog posts were written for SharePoint 2007, the information is very applicable to SharePoint 2010.

➤ "What every SharePoint administrator needs to know about Alternate Access Mappings (Part 1 of 3)": `http://bit.ly/LxnDF`

➤ "What every SharePoint administrator needs to know about Alternate Access Mappings (Part 2 of 3)": `http://bit.ly/4vnHW5`

➤ "What every SharePoint administrator needs to know about Alternate Access Mappings (Part 3 of 3)": `http://bit.ly/xbg2c`

SharePoint Application Servers (App Servers)

When performing a complete SharePoint installation, all available services from Web Access to Excel Services are installed. In large-scale environments, it is beneficial to have one set of servers act as WFEs (that is, turn off most services except for Web Access) and another set of servers act as App Servers (that run various SharePoint services). Therefore, the only real difference between a SharePoint WFE and a SharePoint App Server is that the latter does not have the Web services (Microsoft SharePoint Foundation Web Application) enabled.

 Chapter 11 dives into more detail on recommended topologies.

While this seems like a minor distinction, this is important in order to load balance the entire SharePoint farm. Web servers typically perform the task of rendering Web pages, so enterprise-commodity IIS servers (which you scale out) will be sufficient to perform these tasks. But, SharePoint App Servers will typically require more resources, whether they are the calculations performed by Excel Services, the search indexing by SharePoint Search Service, or the Analysis Services VertiPaq Engine Service. In these situations, it is important to scale up each App Server — that is, have more memory, processors, and a powerful disk — as well as scaling out the servers.

Another important aspect within SharePoint is its capability to load balance services within the farm. In the case of Excel Services and PowerPivot services, they have their own health-monitoring services to determine the server instance that is "healthiest" when it assigns which user request goes to which server instance.

SharePoint Databases

All the information stored within SharePoint (from the lists to Excel workbooks) is stored within a set of SQL Server databases known as the SharePoint *content databases*. By default, documents such as Word documents and Excel workbooks are stored as a Binary Large Object (BLOB) within the SQL database. As is typical with any SharePoint service, you can scale out the content databases to multiple physical databases placed on multiple servers in order to handle the load.

The profile of a SharePoint content database is similar to that of an online transaction processing (OLTP) environment, where there are a lot of transactions. With PowerPivot, these are large transactions because of the size of a PowerPivot workbook and the VertiPaq database stored within it. So, some standard database optimization techniques do come into play, including file group configuration and having fast I/O for the underlying disk.

In addition to the content databases, most SharePoint environments include the SharePoint configuration and administration databases, as well as other databases to store metadata. Examples include the PowerPivot application database (to store PowerPivot metadata) and the Secure Store Service database (to encrypt and store user authentication details). While there are exceptions (for example, Microsoft Search Service databases), in general, these databases are relatively small in size.

KEY SERVICES IN POWERPIVOT FOR SHAREPOINT

As noted in the previous discussions, Excel Services is a key service dependency for PowerPivot for SharePoint. Additionally, by default, the WFE (or Microsoft SharePoint Foundation Web Application) is another key service to render the Excel Services workbooks (via EWA). Other key services for PowerPivot for SharePoint include the following:

➤ PowerPivot Web Service

➤ Analysis Services in VertiPaq mode

➤ PowerPivot System Service

Let's take a look at the last two in more detail; we will discuss the PowerPivot Web Service in Chapter 10.

The Analysis Services Service in PowerPivot

Within the SharePoint farm, to access a VertiPaq instance you connect to the Analysis Services Service. This is a version of the Analysis Services Engine that is running in VertiPaq mode, as opposed to the traditional Multidimensional Online Analytical Processing (MOLAP), Hybrid Online Analytical Processing (HOLAP), or Relational Online Analytical Processing (ROLAP) engines. For the self-service BI scenario that is being delivered as part of PowerPivot in SQL Server 2008 R2, the only supported way of accessing the Analysis Services in VertiPaq mode is by way of it being a SharePoint service. Traditional Analysis Services development tools such as Visual Studio 2008 Business Intelligence Development Studio (BIDS) will not be able to interact with this engine in an understandable way.

However, you will be able to use tools such as SQL Server Profiler to debug the interactions against the service (more on this in Chapter 9). More importantly, this version of the Analysis Services engine within SharePoint can be queried via MDX like any other client that can generate MDX. For example, Figure 7-7 shows a Report Builder dashboard including charts and a bubble map that notes a Healthcare Server audit based on source location against a state map.

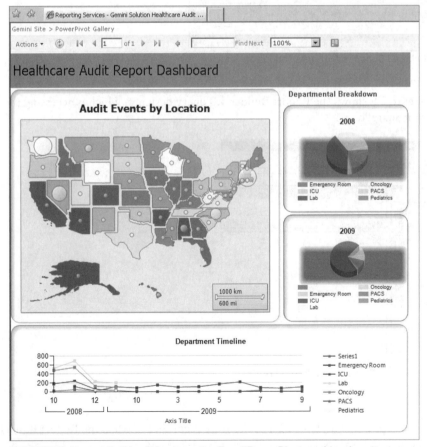

FIGURE 7-7: Report Builder 3.0 map using Excel PowerPivot workbook as its source

To show that this report from Report Builder is using the Excel workbook as its data source, Figure 7-8 shows the data source connection of this report. Note how the data source provider isn't a traditional source server and database but rather a URL to an Excel workbook within SharePoint.

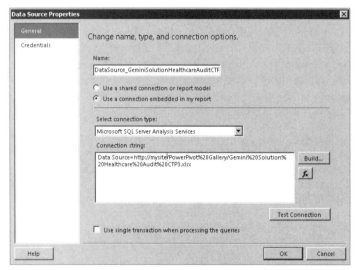

FIGURE 7-8: Report Builder 3.0 map report data source

To come full circle, Figure 7-9 shows the Report Builder 3.0 query designer, which is accessing the Excel workbook within SharePoint.

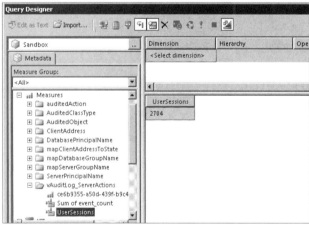

FIGURE 7-9: Report Builder 3.0 query designer querying the PowerPivot sandbox

Figure 7-10 shows an excerpt of the SQL Server Profiler trace recording of when the Report Builder 3.0 Map report is accessing the Analysis Services Server in VertiPaq mode.

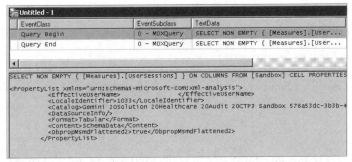

FIGURE 7-10: Excerpt of Profiler trace recording Report Builder 3.0 access of the sandbox

For those who are familiar with SQL Profiler (for Analysis Services), you will see the familiar `EventClass = Query Begin` with the `TextData` noting the familiar look of MDX.

```
SELECT NON EMPTY {
        [Measures].[UserSessions]
    } ON COLUMNS
    FROM [SandBox]
    CELL PROPERTIES…
```

> *Any client that is able to query a traditional Analysis Services Server by way of* MDX *will have the same capability against the Analysis Services Server in VertiPaq mode within the SharePoint farm without any modifications.*

PowerPivot System Service

This service was also known as SQL Server Analysis Services Mid-Tier Service. This name still shows up within the Windows event log and SharePoint Unified Logging Services (ULS) logs (more on this in Chapter 9). To better understand this service, let's take a look at the following key features of this service: connectivity and data refresh.

Connectivity

All communication from the SharePoint WFE to the Analysis Services Service within the SharePoint farm is facilitated by this service. It is automatically installed on every App Server on which the Analysis Services Service is installed.

Whenever Excel Services must connect to a PowerPivot data source, the System Service will determine if that data source is already loaded on a PowerPivot App Server in the SharePoint farm. If the data source is loaded, the System Service will connect the WFE to it (that is, EWA on a WFE to Excel Services on an App Server to Analysis Services Service on an App Server). If the PowerPivot data source is not already loaded, the System Service will perform the following tasks:

1. Open the Excel workbook.

2. Extract the PowerPivot data from the workbook.

   3. Use the PowerPivot health-monitoring service to determine which server is the healthiest.

   4. Copy the PowerPivot data to that server.

   5. Attach the database to that Analysis Service Server.

Finally, it will provide a pointer to the SharePoint WFE so that it can connect to the server where the data is loaded.

Data Refresh

The PowerPivot System Service is also responsible for performing data refresh. As you will recall, data refresh is the feature that allows users to configure PowerPivot to automatically connect to and refresh their PowerPivot for Excel workbooks with the latest source data. Figure 7-11 shows an example of data refresh being enabled.

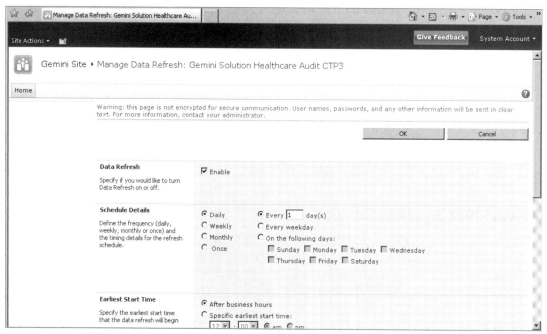

FIGURE 7-11: Enabling data refresh for the workbook

The information recorded on the data refresh page includes the user credentials needed to execute the data refresh. This is important, because the service accounts within the SharePoint farm most likely will not have access rights to the data sources used to populate the workbook. Therefore, the PowerPivot System Service will impersonate the user with the credentials provided.

 Note that these credentials are stored within the SharePoint Secure Store Service (SSS), which, as its name describes, stores the credentials in a secure manner.

For the PowerPivot System Service to perform the task of data refresh, the following must happen:

1. The Windows SharePoint 2010 Timer Service runs a PowerPivot timer job called the PowerPivot Data Refresh Timer Job every minute (by default).

2. The PowerPivot Data Refresh Timer Job calls the PowerPivot Service Application, which is a configurable, independent instance of the PowerPivot System Service, to read predefined schedules stored in the PowerPivot System Service Database.

3. If the Timer Job finds a schedule in the PowerPivot System Service database, then the Timer Job hands the request to the PowerPivot System Service.

4. The PowerPivot System Service then impersonates the PowerPivot Unattended account or specified user to open the workbook from the content database.

5. The PowerPivot System Service will perform the automatic data refresh task to update the database within the PowerPivot for Excel workbook using the credentials within the Secure Store.

SERVICES ARCHITECTURE WORKFLOW SCENARIOS

Now that you understand the servers and services that are involved with PowerPivot for SharePoint, let's put this all into context. Let's take a look at the interactions of all the servers and services in three common PowerPivot for SharePoint workflow scenarios.

Excel Client Upload to SharePoint

Let's first take a look at one of the more common scenarios concerning the upload of a PowerPivot workbook to your SharePoint site. Take a look at Figure 7-12.

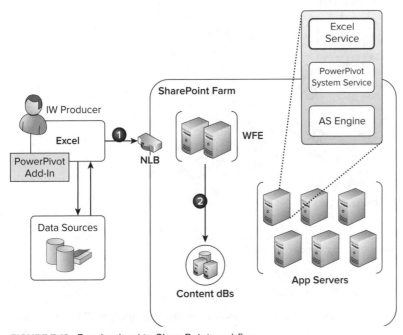

FIGURE 7-12: Excel upload to SharePoint workflow

There is no difference between a SharePoint and PowerPivot for SharePoint workflow in this particular case. Following are the steps in the workflow:

1. The IW producer uploads a workbook to SharePoint using Excel Save-As or SharePoint Upload functionality. The workbook is uploaded to the SharePoint WFE.

2. In turn, the SharePoint WFE then stores the workbook within the SharePoint content database. By default, this is stored as a BLOB within the database.

 Note that there is a 2 GB maximum size limitation for your PowerPivot workbook because this is the maximum size SharePoint 2010 can store. By default, the maximum size is 50 MB, so you will need to configure it to this upper limit if desired.

Excel Services Rendering

Now that the workbook is uploaded to the SharePoint content database, your IW consumers will want to open up the workbook within SharePoint. This is reflected in Figure 7-13, with the numbered steps indicated in the diagram.

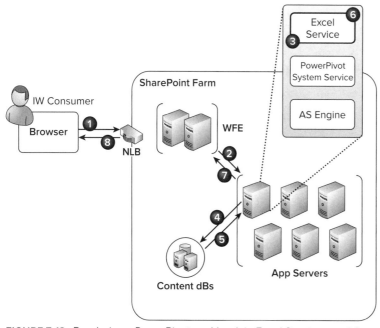

FIGURE 7-13: Rendering a PowerPivot workbook in Excel Services workflow

As you can see, there are a number of steps needed to make this happen:

1. The IW consumer requests a PowerPivot workbook from the SharePoint WFE via his or her browser.

2. Because it is an Excel Services request, the EWA component on the SharePoint WFE will now make the request to Excel Calculation Services (ECS) on the App Server.

3. Excel Services has its own load balancer within the SharePoint farm, so the EWA request will be load-balanced (by default) to the healthiest App Server.

4. Excel Services requests the originally requested workbook (from Step 1) from SharePoint.

5. Excel Services obtains the workbook from the SharePoint content database and brings it back to the App Server.

6. ECS performs any calculations required from the workbook.

7. Excel Services pushes the data to the originating EWA component on the SharePoint WFE. EWA will then render the workbook to the browser.

8. The IW consumer is now able to view and work with this workbook.

It is important to recognize here that, at no point, has PowerPivot Services (PowerPivot System Service, Analysis Services in VertiPaq mode) been called. These actions are strictly Excel Services interacting with the SharePoint databases.

Excel Services Server Action

After Step 8 in the preceding scenario, the IW consumer may click on a slicer or perform some other action that will result in interacting with the data stored within the workbook. Figure 7-14 shows this process, again with the numbered steps indicated in the diagram.

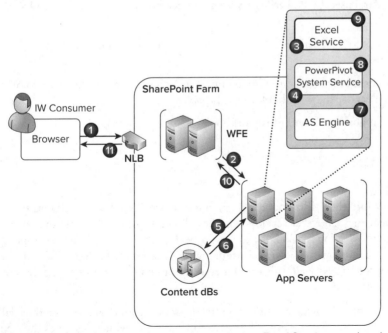

FIGURE 7-14: Performing a server action against an Excel Services rendered PowerPivot Workbook scenario

Following are the steps to make this happen:

1. The IW consumer makes a server action request (such as clicking on a slicer). That this is a server action is transparent to the user.

2. Because it is an Excel Services request, the EWA component on the SharePoint WFE now makes the request to Excel Services on the App Server.

3. Excel Services has its own load balancer within the SharePoint farm, so the EWA request will be load-balanced (by default) to the healthiest App Server. Because it is a server action, Excel Services connects to the Analysis Services OLEDB Provider.

4. This is your standard Analysis Services OLEDB provider request, except that the call from Excel Services enables the `IsHosted` flag. In this case, the OLEDB provider will know to engage with the PowerPivot System Service. Similar to Excel Services, PowerPivot System Service has its own load-balancing service to help it determine the healthiest App Server. The purpose of this is to determine which App Server should host the PowerPivot data.

5. The PowerPivot System Service makes a request for the PowerPivot workbook from the SharePoint content database if Excel Services doesn't already have a workbook.

6. The PowerPivot System Service obtains the workbook and/or obtains any necessary metadata from the `DefaultPowerPivotServiceApplicationDB` database.

7. The PowerPivot System Service extracts the PowerPivot data from the workbook, and makes the request to attach the database to the Analysis Services Server. This attach command is the same as a traditional Analysis Services Engine attach statement.

8. Upon attaching the database, the PowerPivot System Service provides the location to Excel Services.

9. Excel Services connects to the Analysis Services Service to perform its query and its calculations.

10. Excel Services then pushes the data to the originating EWA component on the SharePoint WFE. EWA will then render the workbook to the browser.

11. The IW consumer can now work with this workbook.

SUMMARY

This chapter provided a peek into the infrastructure surrounding PowerPivot for SharePoint. It discussed PowerPivot's dependency on Excel Services, and how PowerPivot is itself a set of services that works on top of the SharePoint foundation. It provided a peek at the SharePoint server topology (more on this in Chapter 11), as well as the services installed with PowerPivot for SharePoint (more details will be found in Chapter 10). As well, this chapter also examined the workflow of three common PowerPivot for SharePoint actions.

The goal of this chapter has been to provide a foundation for the services and components that will be installed as part of PowerPivot for SharePoint. This leads to Chapter 8, which describes the steps needed to set up and configure PowerPivot for SharePoint.

8

PowerPivot for SharePoint Setup and Configuration

WHAT'S IN THIS CHAPTER?

➤ Understanding hardware and software requirements

➤ Setting up and configuring a multi-server PowerPivot for SharePoint environment

➤ Understanding optional (but important) configurations for a PowerPivot for SharePoint environment

The installation for a single-server PowerPivot for SharePoint farm as described in Chapter 2 is a full installation of SharePoint 2010. Hidden from view within those installation steps are also scripts that preconfigure various dependent services (for example, IIS, Excel Services, PowerPivot System Service, Analysis Services in VertiPaq mode, and so on). Not only does this SharePoint environment provide all PowerPivot services, but (once enabled) it also allows you to work with other SharePoint services, including (but not limited to) Access Database Service, PerformancePoint service, Microsoft Search Service, and Visio Graphics Services. As more users utilize PowerPivot and other SharePoint services, it will be necessary to scale out your SharePoint farm.

This chapter focuses on the setup and configuration of PowerPivot for SharePoint multi-server farms. It is important to note that many of the preconfiguration scripts that were available in the single-server farm setup are not available for the multi-server farm setup. Therefore, you will need to do these steps yourself as described in this chapter.

The discussion begins with an examination of hardware and software required for both single-machine and multi-machine PowerPivot for SharePoint deployments, with a focus on the multi-machine side.

REQUIRED HARDWARE AND SOFTWARE

Standard SharePoint Web Front End (WFE) servers typically utilize commodity Web servers with 4GB RAM, dual processors, and local disk storage. With PowerPivot for SharePoint, you will require more powerful hardware to support more resource-intense services such as Excel Services, Analysis Services in VertiPaq mode, and other SharePoint services utilized to support PowerPivot.

Single-Server Hardware Requirements

For test or evaluation purposes, Table 8-1 shows the minimum requirements for a single-box setup (where all SharePoint, SQL, IIS, Excel Services, and PowerPivot components are installed on the same server).

TABLE 8-1: Minimum Hardware Requirements (Single-Box Setup)

RESOURCE MINIMUM REQUIREMENT	EXPLANATION
16 GB RAM	Recall that PowerPivot makes use of Analysis Services in VertiPaq mode, which is an in-memory engine (that is, the database fully resides in memory). You will need more memory than your standard Web server because it will need to support all concurrent online database instances. For example, if you have 20 users who are accessing 8 different databases, each 1 GB in size, then at least 8 GB of memory will be used to support the 8 different databases. Even though there are 20 users, there is relatively low overhead for concurrent users querying the same VertiPaq database.
64-bit	This is required because, from SharePoint 2010 onward, SharePoint will only be available in 64-bit. Utilizing 64-bit is optimal for the PowerPivot environment, since it utilizes so much memory.
Four core processors	There are a lot of operations that occur between the various components and services that are running under PowerPivot for SharePoint. Therefore, you should utilize a minimum of four cores to support the large number of processes that are being executed.
Fast disk	If you're working in a test environment, utilizing a local disk should be sufficient to support your workloads. But, for any enterprise systems, it is highly suggested that you have fast disk. The concern here is higher RPMs, not just large capacity (for example, greater than or equal to 10,000 RPM SATA or SAS drives, Direct Attach Storage, SAN, and so on). Chapter 11 dives deeper into issues surrounding fast disk I/O.

Multi-Server Hardware Requirements

The previous recommendations are applicable to both your single-server farm as well as your multi-server environment. The reason for going to a multi-server environment is to support more concurrent users and more PowerPivot workbooks.

Chapter 11 examines configuration and topology recommendations for your multi-server environment. For now, here are some key design points:

➤ Handling large numbers of concurrent users may require more than one SharePoint WFE server. This will require a Network Load Balancer (NLB) to balance traffic between the WFEs. While NLBs have different configurations, the general rule is to route user traffic round-robin initially and then utilize cookie persistence so that subsequent queries make use of the cache from the initial set of queries.

➤ The size of your PowerPivot workbooks impacts the amount of memory you will need for the SharePoint App Servers running PowerPivot. You can estimate the amount of memory required based on the number of online concurrent workbooks. If you have a multi-server SharePoint farm, the amount of memory required can be spread across multiple SharePoint App Servers running PowerPivot.

➤ As you add more SharePoint WFEs and App servers, there will be more requests to your SharePoint databases. The ones most impacted will be the SharePoint Content database and the PowerPivot Service Application database (`DefaultPowerPivotServiceApplicationDB`). While the content database stores the PowerPivot workbooks, all operational data is stored and accessed from the PowerPivot Service Application database. You will need to optimize the resources (processor, memory, network, and disk) for your SharePoint database server(s). Fortunately, many standard transactional SQL optimization techniques can be beneficial to improving performance (for example, disk file group layout strategies).

Software Requirements

The following is the software required for PowerPivot for SharePoint:

➤ *SharePoint 2010 Enterprise* — This will include Excel Services, Secure Store Service, and other services necessary for PowerPivot. Note that SharePoint 2010 is available only in 64-bit.

➤ *SQL Server 2008 R2* — This version of SQL Server includes the PowerPivot server components that will be integrated within SharePoint.

The prerequisites include the following:

➤ *Windows Server 2008 (64-bit) or Windows Server 2008 R2* — If you are using Windows Server 2008 (64-bit), the SharePoint Prerequisite Installer will install Windows Server 2008 SP2. However, you may want to perform this install beforehand to reduce installation duration.

➤ *.NET 3.5 SP1* — If you have not already done so, ensure that you have .NET 3.5 SP1 installed on your server.

SETUP AND CONFIGURATION

To familiarize yourself with the different SharePoint 2010 topologies, a very good series of technical diagram poster board references can be found at `http://bit.ly/4oa8pi`. While these poster board references are helpful, the figures presented in Chapter 7 should provide the context for the setup and configuration.

While not absolutely necessary, experience has proven that you should heed the following tips:

➤ You should first run the PowerPivot for SharePoint single-server installation. This way, you can work out the kinks and more easily resolve issues such as account, operating system, and firewall policies that may prevent a smooth installation. Once you work out those issues, then you can proceed with the multi-server farm installation.

➤ If possible, perform your initial set of installations using Hyper-V or some other virtualization mechanism. The authors could have saved countless hours in testing and at customer sites if they could have easily reverted to a working snapshot and continued testing the installation, rather than flattening and rebuilding the entire box. Don't forget to snapshot all of the machines involved, including the SharePoint databases. Otherwise, when you revert, your databases are out of sync with the farm.

➤ Use the same domain service account to perform the installation and to specify the SharePoint farm account *initially*. Different components require different security rights (for example, Excel Services needs access to the content database, and so on). So, at least when you initially test this, use the same account to minimize the likelihood that your installation fails because of access rights. Once you get this up and running, it will make sense to use different user accounts with the appropriate minimum necessary security rights.

INSIDE POWERPIVOT

The setup instructions included in this chapter were originally created by Leon Cyril (Microsoft Tester, and a member of the PowerPivot development team) in order to better understand how to set up SharePoint environments that more closely looked like standard customer scenarios. Over time, the instructions were improved based on early customer feedback by a team of secondary authors that included the following:

➤ Denny Lee (Microsoft Program Manager, SQLCAT team)

➤ Dave Wickert (Microsoft Program Manager, PowerPivot development team)

➤ Kathy Macdonald (Microsoft Program Manager, PowerPivot development team)

Additionally, the following technical reviewers and contributors also chipped in:

➤ Jim Howey (Microsoft Program Manager, PowerPivot development team)

➤ Jennifer Chu (Microsoft Service Engineer, SQL IT Support)

➤ Heidi Steen (Microsoft Technical Writer, SQL UE Team)

➤ Ed Campbell (Consultant, Murphy & Associates)

In the end, four separate whitepapers were developed that provided the basic steps of how to get a PowerPivot for SharePoint environment up and running.

Because of the many components of PowerPivot and SharePoint, the instructions were revised on a regular basis — hence the need to post draft versions of the documents at `http://powerpivotgeek.com/server-installation/`.

The final instructions called out in this chapter are derived from all of this hard work. So, thanks to Cyril and all the contributors for providing the authors with these instructions! As well, in this chapter, additional material provides context and background information so that you can more easily troubleshoot, in case issues occur with your installation.

Note that, by the time this book hits the shelves, the SQL Server 2008 R2 Books Online should have been updated to contain a very complete set of installation instructions as well.

MULTI-SERVER FARM SETUP

With the single-server install as described in Chapter 2, many configuration steps were performed by scripts embedded within the setup. However, for a multi-server farm setup, many of these steps will require user interaction. While it is a more complex task to install and configure a multi-server SharePoint farm, it provides you with a scale-out SharePoint environment to better handle disaster recovery and availability scenarios. This is especially important for enterprise PowerPivot for SharePoint environments that must handle hundreds or thousands of concurrent users accessing a large number of PowerPivot workbooks.

Chapters 10 and 11 provide more information about capacity planning and the various SharePoint topologies. Meanwhile, the installation steps outlined here describe how to set up a three-server configuration involving one WFE, one App Server, and one separate SQL database, as shown in Figure 8-1.

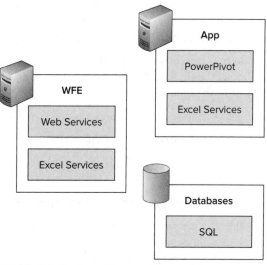

FIGURE 8-1: Basic multi-server SharePoint farm configuration

There are many variations of the multi-server farm configuration, and more of these are examined in Chapter 11. But these are all variations or additions to the basic setup explored here. Hence, understanding this will provide you with the context and knowledge to expand your farm when you decide it is necessary.

Install SQL Server on the SharePoint Database Server

It is important to have at least one separate server designated as your SharePoint database server because this server will be the gatekeeper (positively) or bottleneck (negatively) for your entire SharePoint farm. Following are some examples:

➤ All operational transactions (for example, usage and error logging) for the PowerPivot System Service interact with the `DefaultPowerPivotServiceApplicationDB` database.

➤ All the documents (including PowerPivot workbooks) are stored in the `SharePoint_Content` database(s).

➤ For the PowerPivot for SharePoint environment, all user rights delegation interactions (for example, data refresh) must interact with the `[Secure Store Service]` database.

Your PowerPivot for SharePoint environment includes a number of databases. The key thing to remember is that within any SharePoint farm (and especially one that is PowerPivot enabled), there will be a lot of transactions with the SharePoint databases. Therefore, to minimize resource contention, it is important to separate those resources (for example, put your farm's database on a separate server) to provide the dedicated resources for different SharePoint functions such as SharePoint database transactions.

Let's break down the required steps to set up your farm's database.

Step 1: Database Engine Installation

Go to the SQL Server installation folder and run `setup.exe`. If you're not familiar with the SQL Server database installation setup, follow all of the default install steps. At a minimum, you should install the following:

➤ Database Engine Services

➤ SQL Server Books Online

➤ Management Tools (Basic and Complete)

Step 2: Database Engine Configuration

Once the installation completes, go to the SQL Server Configuration Manager and ensure that Named Pipes and TCP/IP are both enabled. To do this, go to All Programs ➪ Microsoft SQL Server 2008 R2 ➪ Configuration Tools ➪ SQL Server Configuration Manager. Follow these steps:

1. Ensure the SQL Server Native 10.0 Configuration ➪ Client Protocols (both 32-bit and 64-bit) have enabled both Named Pipes and TCP/IP, as shown in Figure 8-2.

2. Ensure the SQL Server Network Configuration ➪ Protocols for MSSQLSERVER have both Named Pipes and TCP/IP enabled, as shown in Figure 8-2.

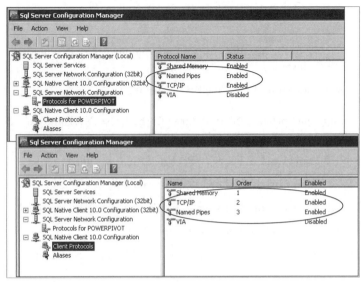

FIGURE 8-2: Database engine configuration

Step 3: Firewall Ports

Additionally, you must open up the server's firewall ports for TCP/IP port 1433 to allow SQL Server access. To do this, click Start ➪ Run, type **firewall.cpl**, and click "Allow a program through Windows Firewall." You will be given the option to add a port here. For Windows 2008 R2, you will need to create a new inbound rule in the advanced settings to "Allow the connection" for the appropriate domain.

Install SharePoint 2010 on the SharePoint WFE

As you may recall from Chapter 7, the SharePoint WFE is the Web Front End server. Referring to Figure 8-1, this is the server that has Web services (Microsoft SharePoint Foundation Web Application) and Excel Services installed. SharePoint users will point their browser or applications to this server to interact with the farm.

Step 1: Execute the SharePoint Prerequisite Installer

The SharePoint Prerequisite installer installs required software and components, as well as configures the Web and application server roles with minimal manual intervention.

 Note that you may want to download the prerequisite files manually and run the Prerequisite installer from the command line for a faster install. In the past, it would have been necessary for an administrator to perform each of these tasks separately.

First, the Prerequisite installer will ensure that you have the latest service packs and PowerShell version.

➤ If you are on Windows Server 2008, the installer ensures that you have at least Windows Server 2008 Service Pack 2 (SP2) installed

➤ The installer ensures that Windows Server PowerShell V2 is installed

The installation of the next five components provides SharePoint with the latest .NET and SQL connectivity, as well as the latest .NET Chart Controls. The following tasks are performed:

➤ Ensuring that Microsoft .NET Framework 3.5 Service Pack 1 (SP1) is installed

➤ Ensuring that Microsoft Sync Framework Run-time v1.0 is installed

➤ Ensuring that Microsoft Chart Controls for Microsoft .NET Framework 3.5 is installed

➤ Ensuring that Microsoft SQL Server 2008 Native Client is installed

➤ Ensuring that Microsoft SQL Server 2008 Analysis Services ADOMD.NET is installed

The installer also installs a number of components that enhance SharePoint's Search capabilities, including the following:

➤ *Microsoft Filter Pack 2.0* — Installs and registers IFilters with the Microsoft Windows Indexing Service (ultimately to help Search).

➤ *Microsoft Server Speech Platform Run-time and Recognition Language* — Enables phonetic name-matching to work correctly within Search service.

The next few tasks revolve around the installation and configuration of IIS Web service, since the SharePoint WFE service heavily leverages IIS:

➤ Install Application Role IIS (if not already installed)

➤ Configure IIS to utilize the latest ASP.NET framework (in this case, this is ASP.NET v2.0.50727)

➤ Configure IIS, including (but not limited to) the creation of the SharePoint site, SharePoint Central Admin, and SharePoint Web Services sites

A very important component new to SharePoint 2010 is the inclusion of the Windows Identity Foundation (formerly known as the Microsoft Geneva Framework), which the prerequisite installer installs and configures.

 For more information on how to determine hardware and software require- ments, including the installation of the software prerequisites, see the TechNet article "Determine hardware and software requirements (SharePoint 2010)" at `http://bit.ly/QzdQC.`

ABOUT WINDOWS IDENTITY FOUNDATION

While outside of the scope of this chapter (or book), from a high level, the Windows Identity Foundation (formerly known as the Microsoft Geneva Framework) allows you to avoid the "double-hop issue." Typically, a SharePoint farm involves multiple servers where a user communicates from the client to the SharePoint WFE to the SharePoint App Server to the data source and back. PowerPivot is a good example of this type of communication, or "hopping."

The idea of a "double hop" is that there is more than one hop for the communication between the client and the target server component. In the case of the following figure, for the client to perform a server action against Excel Services and Analysis Services in VertiPaq mode, there are four "hop" occurrences:

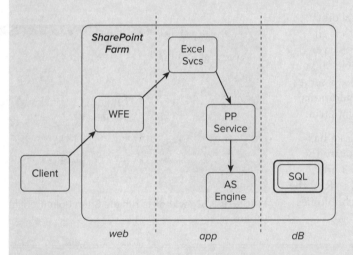

Traditionally, to solve this multi-hop problem, you would need to set up Kerberos authentication. This is quite prevalent throughout many SharePoint farms today. But, with Windows Identity Foundation, SharePoint makes use of claims authentication tokens that contain the attributes identifying the user without actually being the actual user authentication rights. This way, it is possible for services within SharePoint (for example, Excel Services) to obtain data or documents on behalf of that user without actually being that user.

By utilizing the Windows Identity Foundation, it is possible for communication to occur between many server components within SharePoint without needing to utilize Kerberos. The key here is that PowerPivot does not require Kerberos. Chapter 10 provides more information about Windows Identity Foundation and SharePoint, as well as claims authentication.

Step 2: Install Data Services Update for .NET 3.5 SP1 (Optional)

One of the great features of SharePoint 2010 is the capability to use SharePoint lists as an Atom data feed. With this feature, you can have a SharePoint list as a data source for your PowerPivot workbook. To do this, you will also want to install the Data Services Update for .NET 3.5 SP1. For more information about what and where to download, see the WCF Data Services Team blog posting at: `http://bit.ly/b08Joq`.

Step 3: Run Setup.exe

When you execute SharePoint `setup.exe`, ensure that you enable the following options:

➤ *Installation Type* — Server Farm (as opposed to Stand-alone)

➤ *Server Type* — Complete (as opposed to Stand-alone)

For your PowerPivot for SharePoint environment, it is important that all components and services for a server farm configuration are available on your server. By choosing the `Complete` server type, you will be able to add additional servers to form your SharePoint farm.

Once the SharePoint `setup.exe` has completed the installation, locate the checkbox shown in Figure 8-3 and enable the checkbox that says "Run the SharePoint Products and Technologies Configuration Wizard now."

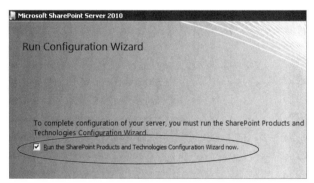

FIGURE 8-3: Checkbox to run the SharePoint Configuration Wizard

 Recall that, in the PowerPivot for SharePoint single-server farm installation instructions provided in Chapter 2, it was very important that you unchecked the checkbox indicating that you did not want to run the SharePoint Configuration Wizard. In the PowerPivot for SharePoint existing farm or multi-server farm installation, you will need to run the SharePoint Configuration Wizard (that is, check the checkbox, indicating that you do want to run the SharePoint Configuration Wizard).

Configuring the SharePoint WFE

Because you checked the checkbox in the Run Configuration Wizard dialog, the script will now execute the SharePoint Configuration Wizard.

Step 1: SharePoint Configuration Wizard Services Restart Warning

When the configuration wizard opens up, it will provide a SharePoint Products Configuration Wizard dialog. When you click Next, you will be told that the IIS, SharePoint Administration

Service, and SharePoint Timer Service will be restarted, if required. Click Yes when prompted, because this is the only way to configure SharePoint.

Step 2: Create a New Server Farm

Because this is the first SharePoint server instance for your multi-server SharePoint farm, choose "Create a new server farm" within the SharePoint Configuration Wizard (as opposed to connecting to one) when prompted from the "Connect to a server farm" dialog, as shown in Figure 8-4.

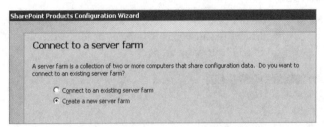

FIGURE 8-4: Create a new server farm option

Step 3: Specify Configuration Database Settings

At this point, you see the Specify Configuration Database Settings dialog, where you specify the name of the database server and the Windows domain account that you will use to access the database, as shown in Figure 8-5. This is the account that you used to install the SQL database described in the earlier section, "Install SQL Server on the SharePoint Database Server."

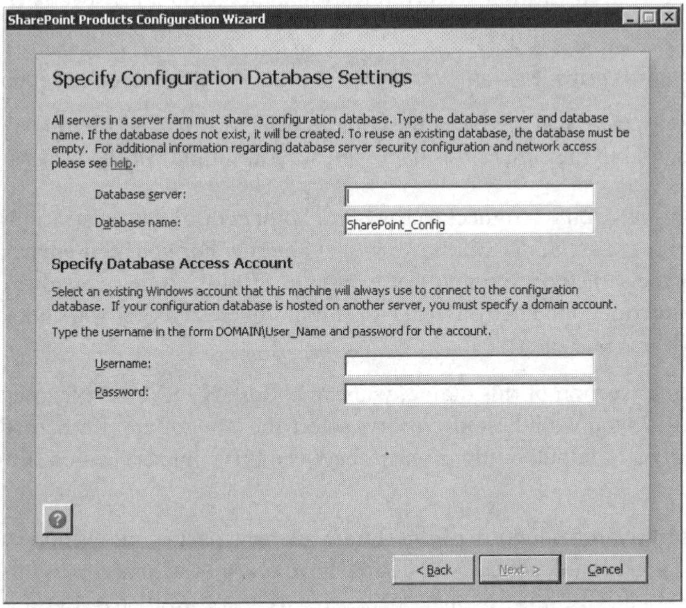

FIGURE 8-5: Specify Configuration Database Settings dialog

Note that, as shown in Figure 8-5, you specify the configuration database (`SharePoint_Config`), rather than the `SharePoint_Content` database. This is important to note because, although the `SharePoint_Content` database is where the PowerPivot workbooks reside, all of the metadata that controls what services are running on which server within your SharePoint farm reside in the `SharePoint_Config` database. The SharePoint configuration database *defines* your farm, so ensure that you back it up and protect it.

Step 4: Specify Farm Security Settings

On the next dialog shown in Figure 8-6 (Specify Farm Security Settings), you specify a pass phrase for your Farm Security Settings. Remember this phrase, because this is what is used to add more machines to your SharePoint farm (which you do in the following steps).

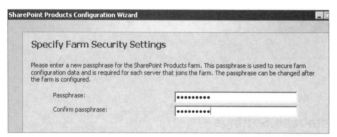

FIGURE 8-6: Specify Farm Security Settings dialog

Step 5: Configure SharePoint Central Administration Web Application

In the Configure SharePoint Central Administration Web Application dialog, you must specify the following:

➤ *Specify port number* — Here you provide a number between 1 to 65535 (for example, 55000).

➤ *Configure Security Settings* — Here you are given the choice of NTLM or "Negotiate (Kerberos)". In most cases, and in the case of this deployment, you should choose NTLM.

By specifying a port number, this allows you to connect to the SharePoint central administration with your browser via the URL: `http://$SharePointWFE$:[PortNumber]`. For your test environments, it may be helpful to specify the same port number (for example, 55000), so that you always know the value. However, for your production environment, it is highly suggested that you choose different port numbers to reduce the surface of attack.

Under the Configure Security Settings section of this dialog, you can choose NTLM or "Negotiate (Kerberos)." Prior to SharePoint 2010, you would almost always select the "Negotiate (Kerberos)" option, because there was almost always a double-hop problem between different services on different servers.

As noted earlier in this chapter, with the introduction of the claims token as part of the Windows Identity Foundation, there are no longer issues concerning double hops *within* the SharePoint farm. Hence, in many multi-server farm situations, it is no longer necessary to utilize Kerberos. In the case of the PowerPivot for SharePoint deployment described in this chapter, you should choose the default choice of NTLM, unless your environment specifically requires Kerberos. Remember that PowerPivot itself does *not* require Kerberos.

Step 6: Completing the SharePoint Products Configuration Wizard

At this point, you are provided with a summary dialog noting all of the configurations you have chosen. Once you have verified the information, click Next to start the configuration process.

Initial Farm Configuration Wizard on the WFE

As noted in the name of the wizard, the initial farm configuration wizard performs the task of initializing the SharePoint WFE. As opposed to the single-server setup, you will configure and provision the SharePoint services you want to use by following the steps outlined here.

Step 1: Configure Your SharePoint Farm

In the opening dialog shown in Figure 8-7, you see a question, "How do you want to configure your SharePoint farm?" Unless you are a SharePoint expert, it is highly recommended that you start configuration by selecting the option "Yes, walk me through the configuration of my farm using this wizard" and click "Start the Wizard."

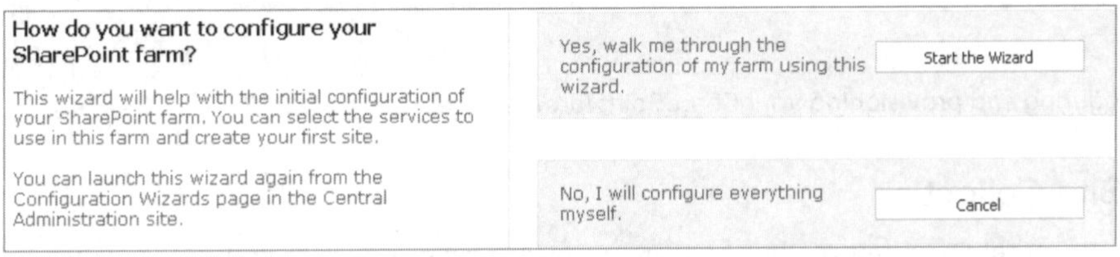

How do you want to configure your SharePoint farm?

This wizard will help with the initial configuration of your SharePoint farm. You can select the services to use in this farm and create your first site.

You can launch this wizard again from the Configuration Wizards page in the Central Administration site.

Yes, walk me through the configuration of my farm using this wizard. | Start the Wizard |

No, I will configure everything myself. | Cancel |

FIGURE 8-7: "How do you want to configure your SharePoint farm" wizard dialog

Step 2: Choose the SharePoint Service Account

In the next dialog, you see information related to the service account and the associated services, as shown in Figure 8-8. This service account may be different from the SharePoint Farm and/or Installation user account. This is the managed account used to run the various services that you are about to provision. (Chapter 9 provides more information on managed accounts.)

For example, you may want to have `MyDomain\SharePointFarmAcct` as your SharePoint Farm account, while `MyDomain\SharePointSvcsAcct` would be the managed account that runs the SharePoint services (such as Secure Store Service and Excel Services).

On this configuration page, you also specify the different SharePoint services to operate within your farm. Note that the more services you specify, the longer it will take the wizard to complete. As a general rule, it is a good practice to only specify the services you really need within your farm. At a minimum, for PowerPivot for SharePoint, you should enable the following services:

➤ Excel Services

➤ Secure Store Service

➤ Usage and health data collection

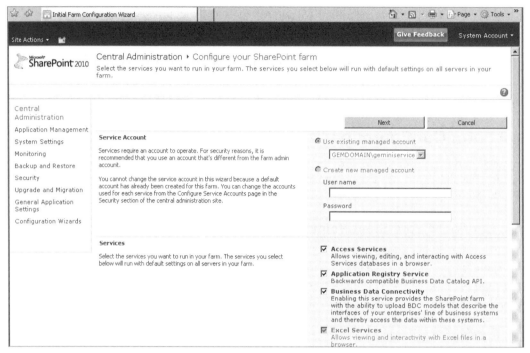

FIGURE 8-8: Configuring and provisioning your SharePoint farm services

Step 3: Create Site Collection

After clicking Next on the "Configure your SharePoint farm" page shown in Figure 8-8, you have the option to create a SharePoint site collection. Performing this task is highly recommended because to create other SharePoint sites and sub-sites (for example, your site that contains the PowerPivot Gallery), you will first need to create a site collection.

To create a SharePoint site collection, provide the following information:

➤ *Title and Description* — Enter the title for your SharePoint Site collection (for example, "My Site").

➤ *Web Site Address* — Enter a new URL name and path, or choose the default path provided for your site collection.

➤ *Template Selection* — By default, the site template chosen is the "Collaboration: Team Site" template.

Typically, you can simply enter the name (that is, the Title) of your default site collection, and then click OK to continue to the next step.

Step 4: Completing the Configuration

To complete this configuration, click Finish.

Once the configuration has finished its tasks, there are a couple of configurations that you will need to do outside of the SharePoint wizard.

Step 5: Open the Firewall Ports

Confirm the server's firewall ports for SharePoint Web access. In this case, you will need to open up TCP/IP port 80 (for regular HTTP access, which is also the port for your SharePoint default Web application) and the TCP/IP port specified earlier in the section, "Step 5: Configure SharePoint Central Administration Web Application," during the "Configuring SharePoint WFE" discussion (for example, 55000). To do this, click Start ⇨ Run. Type **firewall.cpl**, and click "Allow a program through Windows firewall." You will find an option to add a port there. For Windows 2008 R2, you will need to create new inbound and outbound rules in the Advanced settings to "Allow the connection" for the appropriate domain.

Step 6: Set a Key for the Secure Store Service Application

You must set a key for the Secure Store Service to ensure that the user access attributes (such as the ones required for the PowerPivot data refresh feature) stored in the Secure Store Service database are properly encrypted. To do this, go to the SharePoint Central Administration and click on Application Management ⇨ Manage Service Applications. From here, click on the Secure Store Service link to enable you to manage this service, as shown in Figure 8-9.

From here, click on Generate New Key, as shown in Figure 8-10. You will then be prompted for a pass phrase used to generate a new key. This key will then be used to encrypt all of the credentials stored within the Secure Store Service database. This pass phrase is any phrase of your choice, but it should not be the same phrase used to join your SharePoint farm.

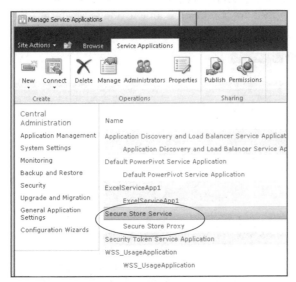

FIGURE 8-9: Selecting Secure Store Service within Manage Service Applications

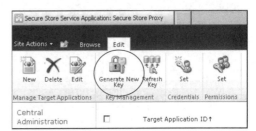

FIGURE 8-10: Generate New Key option

Install SharePoint 2010 on the SharePoint App Server

Referring back to Figure 8-1, the SharePoint Application Server (or App Server) is the server that is running Excel Services and PowerPivot Services. The component breakdown of these two services will be described more in detail in Chapter 10.

To install SharePoint 2010 on your SharePoint App Server, follow the steps outlined in the earlier section, "Install SharePoint 2010 on the SharePoint WFE" *only*. Once you have completed the installation, then proceed to the steps outlined in the following section, "Configuring the SharePoint App Server."

After the installation, the Microsoft SharePoint Server 2010 setup wizard will provide you the Run Configuration Wizard dialog. Ensure that the checkbox prompting you to run the SharePoint Configuration Wizard is checked, so that the install script will run the configuration wizard.

Configuring the SharePoint App Server

Configuring the SharePoint App Server is quite different (though simpler) than how you had configured the SharePoint WFE. This is because when you configured the SharePoint WFE, you were *defining* the initial SharePoint farm configuration. In the case of configuring your SharePoint App Server, you are simply attaching this SharePoint server to an existing farm (the one defined during the SharePoint WFE configuration steps).

Step 1: Connect to an Existing Farm

One of the key differences between the WFE and App Server setups is that, in the "Connect to a server farm" dialog, you will now choose the option to "Connect to an existing server farm," as shown in Figure 8-11.

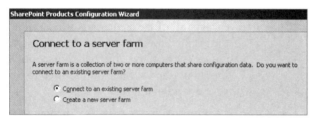

FIGURE 8-11: Connect to an existing server farm

 The terms "multi-server farm" setup and "existing server farm" setup are often used interchangeably. The reason for this is that, once you create a SharePoint farm that involves more than one server, as you can see from these install steps, you will have to first create and establish an existing SharePoint farm.

Step 2: Specify Configuration Database Settings

In the next dialog, Specify Configuration Database Settings, you specify the database server name that you used previously in the earlier section, "Install SQL Server on the SharePoint Database Server." To specify the configuration database settings, you must provide the following information:

➤ *Database Server* — First, fill out the database server name as noted earlier and then click Retrieve Database Names.

➤ *Database Name* — Following the steps within the "Install SQL Server on the SharePoint Database Server" section earlier in this chapter, the name should be SharePoint_Config.

Recall from the discussion in the "Configuring the SharePoint WFE" section earlier in this chapter, the SharePoint WFE originally connected to this server to create and configure the SharePoint_Config database. The metadata defining the SharePoint farm services and components are all stored in this database. Therefore, to join the SharePoint App Server to the farm, you must tie it to the same configuration database settings.

Step 3: Specify Farm Security Settings

In the next dialog, Specify Farm Security Settings, enter the pass phrase that you created when you were configuring the SharePoint WFE. (Refer back to the earlier steps outlined in the section, "Configuring the SharePoint WFE," specifically, "Step 4: Specify Farm Security Settings.") This pass phrase is the security mechanism to allow SharePoint servers to join a farm.

Step 4: Completing the SharePoint Products Configuration Wizard

In the next dialog, "Completing the SharePoint Products and Technologies Configuration Wizard," click Next to start the configuration process.

Once this wizard has completed, you will then get the "Configuring your SharePoint farm" Web page, just like Figure 8-7, when you had initially configured the SharePoint Farm. In this case, click "Start the Wizard," and SharePoint will complete the configuration to turn on the services. As you can see from Figure 8-12, the same services that were started on your SharePoint WFE are also enabled and activated on your SharePoint App Server.

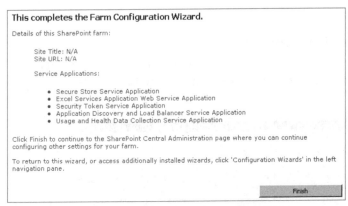

This completes the Farm Configuration Wizard.

Details of this SharePoint farm:

    Site Title: N/A
    Site URL: N/A

  Service Applications:

- Secure Store Service Application
- Excel Services Application Web Service Application
- Security Token Service Application
- Application Discovery and Load Balancer Service Application
- Usage and Health Data Collection Service Application

Click Finish to continue to the SharePoint Central Administration page where you can continue configuring other settings for your farm.

To return to this wizard, or access additionally installed wizards, click 'Configuration Wizards' in the left navigation pane.

                                      Finish

FIGURE 8-12: Farm Configuration Complete page on the SharePoint App Server

Confirm SharePoint Farm Setup

Now that you have installed and configured all three servers (SharePoint WFE, the SharePoint Database Server, and SharePoint App Server), you will want to validate and verify that the farm configuration is as designed. To do this, go to the SharePoint Central Administration ➪ System

Settings ➪ "Manage servers in this farm." You will see information displayed that shows the config-uration as it has been completed for the farm, similar to the "Servers in Farm" view in Figure 8-13.

Server	SharePoint Products Installed	Services Running
GEMAPP01R2	Microsoft SharePoint Server 2010	Excel Calculation Services Microsoft SharePoint Foundation Incoming E-Mail Microsoft SharePoint Foundation Web Application Microsoft SharePoint Foundation Workflow Timer Service Secure Store Service
GEMSQLR2		Microsoft SharePoint Foundation Database
GEMWFE01R2	Microsoft SharePoint Server 2010	Central Administration Excel Calculation Services Microsoft SharePoint Foundation Incoming E-Mail Microsoft SharePoint Foundation Web Application Microsoft SharePoint Foundation Workflow Timer Service Secure Store Service

FIGURE 8-13: Servers in Farm View

Install SQL Server 2008 R2 Analysis Services on the SharePoint App Server

The installation and configuration of SQL Server 2008 R2 Analysis Services in SharePoint Integrated mode is performed by this next series of steps.

Step 1: Execute SQL Server 2008 R2's Setup.exe

Similar to your standard SQL Server 2008 installation, the standard SQL Server Installation Center dialog box will show up. Click on Installation ➪ "New installation or add features to an existing installation."

Follow through with the product key dialogs, and licensing agreements, and install the setup sup-port files.

Step 2: Choose Existing Farm within the Setup Role

When you see the Setup Role dialog appear, choose the "SQL Server PowerPivot for SharePoint" radio button, as shown in Figure 8-14. In the "Add PowerPivot for SharePoint" drop-down, choose the Existing Farm selection.

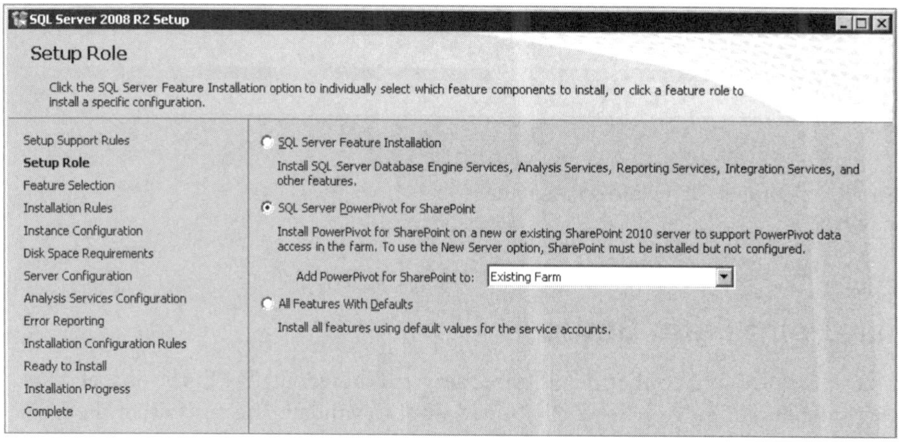

FIGURE 8-14: Choose Existing Farm for the Setup Role

This choice will now install the PowerPivot Services (component details can be found in Chapter 10). However, unlike "New Farm" role chosen in Chapter 2 where the subsequent configuration steps were included as part of the install script, you must perform the configuration of these services.

From this point forward, choose all of the default selections and click Next until the Server Configuration dialog appears.

Step 3: Server Configuration

In the Server Configuration dialog, specify the service accounts for SQL Server Analysis Services *only*. As noted in previous sections, this version of SQL Server Analysis Services installed is configured to run in VertiPaq mode.

Step 4: Complete the Installation

At this point, continue selecting the defaults as part of your installation.

 Ensure that, in the Analysis Services Engine dialog, you specify Add Current User so that the SharePoint Farm account/installation account has access rights to the SQL Server Analysis Services service.

You should be able to continue through the rest of the setup wizard using default options. When you reach the end of the wizard's dialog boxes, click Install.

Once installation has finished, if you go to the SharePoint Central Administration ⇨ System Settings ⇨ "Manage servers in this farm," you will see all of the services running on the WFE and both App Servers, as shown in Figure 8-15.

Server	SharePoint Products Installed	Services Running
GEMDAPP01	Microsoft SharePoint Server 2010	Excel Calculation Services Microsoft SharePoint Foundation Incoming E-Mail Microsoft SharePoint Foundation Web Application Microsoft SharePoint Foundation Workflow Timer Service Secure Store Service SQL Server Analysis Services SQL Server PowerPivot System Service
GEMDSQL		Microsoft SharePoint Foundation Database
GEMDWFE	Microsoft SharePoint Server 2010	Central Administration Excel Calculation Services Microsoft SharePoint Foundation Incoming E-Mail Microsoft SharePoint Foundation Web Application Microsoft SharePoint Foundation Workflow Timer Service Secure Store Service

FIGURE 8-15: Farm Information screen

Deploy, Configure, and Activate PowerPivot for SharePoint

The next steps will be performed on the SharePoint Central Administration application.

Step 1: Deploy PowerPivotWebApp Solution to Your Web Application(s)

Although the PowerPivot Services have been installed on your SharePoint App Server, specific PowerPivot Web application components have not been configured nor deployed to all of the servers running your Web applications (that is, it has not been deployed to the SharePoint WFE). To do this, you must go to SharePoint Central Administration ➪ System Settings ➪ Manage Farm Solutions page. From here, you will be able to choose the PowerPivotWebApp.wsp and choose to "Deploy solution."

Note the PowerPivotWebApp.wsp may have already been deployed to your Central Administration (for example, http://mysite:55000), but has not yet been deployed to your default Web application (for example, http://mysite). When you click the Deploy Solution link, you will notice that the Deploy To link has a drop-down indicating the Web application to deploy to, as shown in Figure 8-16. Ensure that this is your default Web application (for example, http://mysite).

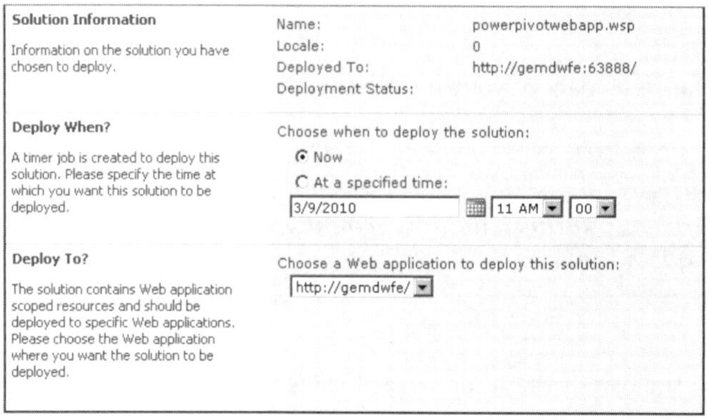

FIGURE 8-16: Deploying PowerPivotWebApp.wsp to the default Web application

If you are following the steps provided in this chapter, you should only have one default Web application, and will only need to apply this to the default solution. Once this has finished, you should see the deployment summary shown in Figure 8-17. Notice that the Deploy Solution link is no longer available (only Retract Solution and "Back to Solutions").

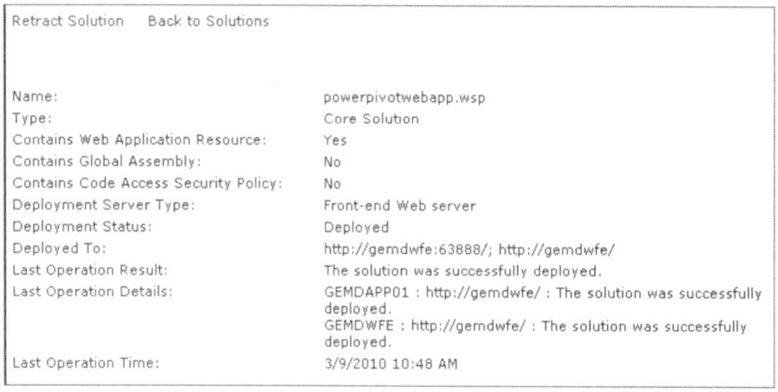

FIGURE 8-17: PowerPivotWebApp.wsp solution has been deployed to the default Web application

Step 2: Create the PowerPivot Service Application

This next step will allow you to create the PowerPivot Service Application. While you have already installed PowerPivot Services on the SharePoint App Server, and deployed the PowerPivot Web application (in the previous step), the PowerPivot Service Application has yet to be created. The PowerPivot Service Application is required so that the SharePoint WFE can communicate to the PowerPivot Services via the PowerPivot System Service proxy. You'll learn more about the PowerPivot System Service proxy in Chapter 10.

To do this, go to SharePoint Central Administration ⇨ Application Management ⇨ Manage Service Applications. From the ensuing dialog, click on New from the menu bar, and then choose SQL Server PowerPivot Service Application.

From here, you will be provided various configuration options for your new PowerPivot Service Application. For most of the configuration options, choose the default values. But there are two configurations that will require manual intervention, as shown in Figure 8-18:

➤ *Application Pool* — Choose "Use existing application pool" and choose `SharePoint Web Services Default`.

➤ *Default* — Ensure that you check the "Add the proxy for this PowerPivot service application to the default proxy group" checkbox at the bottom of the page.

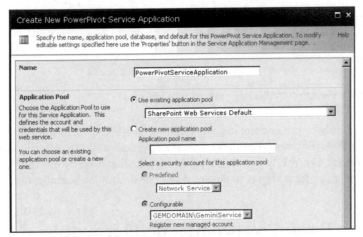

FIGURE 8-18: Creating a new PowerPivot Service Application

For your application pool choice, it is a common security best practice to create a new application pool running under different managed accounts. (You'll learn more about this in Chapter 10 and Chapter 11). To do this, follow these steps:

1. Click the "Create a new application pool" radio button.

2. Enter a new application pool name (for example, PowerPivot Service Application AppPool).

3. Select Configurable for the security account for this application pool.

4. Choose one of the security accounts available under the Configurable drop-down menu. or click on "Register new managed account" to use a new managed account.

While this may be a good security best practice, you may still want to use an application pool and/ or managed account that is tied to your SharePoint Farm account. As will be noted in Chapter 9, for the PowerPivot data refresh feature to work, the PowerPivot Service Application and PowerPivot System Service requires Farm account rights to access the Secure Store Service database.

Step 3: Activate the "PowerPivot Feature Integration for Site Collections"

In the previous step, you created the PowerPivot Service Application. In this step, you will ensure that the SharePoint WFE can actually work with the PowerPivot Service Application. To do this, open your default Web site on the WFE and click Site Actions ⇨ Site Settings ⇨ Site Collection Administration ⇨ "Site collection features." From here, click the Activate button next to the PowerPivot Feature Integration for Site Collections. Figure 8-19 shows the screen you should see after clicking the Activate button.

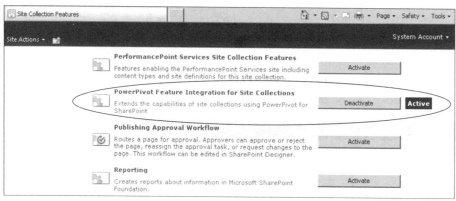

FIGURE 8-19: Configure PowerPivot System Service application

At this point, there should only be the one site collection. But if you had created more site collections, you should activate PowerPivot on your other site collections as well through this dialog. It is possible that the SharePoint Central Administration Web application already has this feature activated. Nevertheless, the important step is to ensure that your default Web application has this feature activated.

Configuration of the PowerPivotUnattendedAccount

The `PowerPivotUnattendedAccount` is an account that is stored within the Secure Store Service that is primarily used for data refresh when no user credentials are specified for the workbook. To configure the `PowerPivotUnattendedAccount`, you must access the Secure Store Service.

You will be configuring the following three sets of accounts:

➤ *Target Application Administrators* — This is the set of accounts that is allowed to manage the settings of the PowerPivot Service Application.

➤ *Credential Owner* — This is the account that is allowed to change the User Name/Password combination.

➤ *User Name/Password Combination* — This is the default account that is used for data refresh.

Step 1: Manage Secure Store Service

To access the Secure Store Service, go to SharePoint Central Administration and click on Application Management ➪ Manage Service Applications. From there, click on the Secure Store Service link (see Figure 8-9 earlier), which will allow you to manage this service.

Step 2: Add New PowerPivotUnattendedAccount

Click on New in the ribbon. In the next dialog, at a minimum, fill in the following values and then click Next:

➤ *Target Application ID* — Fill in this field with a unique identifier such as `PowerPivotUnattendedAccount`

➤ *Display Name* — For this field, fill in the following: **Unattended Account for Data Refresh.**

➤ *Contact Email* — This must be a valid email address of the primary contact for the PowerPivot application.

Step 3: Specify the Initial Credentials for the PowerPivotUnattendedAccount

On the "Specify the credential fields for your Secure Store Target Application" page, no actual entries are required. Accept all of the defaults and click Next.

Step 4: Configure Target Application Administrators for the PowerPivotUnattendedAccount

On the next page, "Specify the membership settings," enter a list of users who can manage the settings of the PowerPivot Service Application. You will need to enter at least one user. You can also enter the account that you are using to create the target application ID. Once you have completed this task, then click OK.

Step 5: Set the Credentials for the PowerPivotUnattendedAccount

At this point, you should be back on the Secure Store Service management page. Click on the checkbox next to the `PowerPivotUnattendedAccount` you just created, and click Set Credentials.

On the "Set Credentials for Secure Store Target Application" page shown in Figure 8-20, provide the following:

➤ *Credential Owner* — This is the *owner* of the credentials being used by the `PowerPivotUnattendedAccount`, not the actual credentials being used by the `PowerPivotUnattendedAccount`. This is typically the account you had specified as the Analysis Services administrator when you ran the Analysis Services setup.

➤ *User Name/Password Combination* — This is the username and password of the actual credentials being used by the `PowerPivotUnattendedAccount`.

The *User Name/Password Combination* is the set of credentials that the PowerPivotUnattendedAccount will use to perform its data refresh if user credentials are not specific. Using the example in Figure 8-20, the PowerPivot System Service will connect to the data source using PowerPivotTwins\siva when credentials are not specified.

Set Credentials for Secure Store Target Application (Individual)

Set values for the credential fields that are defined for this Secure Store Target Application.

Warning: this page is not encrypted for secure communication. User names, passwords, and any other information will be sent in clear text. Information, contact your administrator.

Target Application Name: PowerPivot Unattended Account for Data Refresh
Target Application ID: PowerPivotUnattendedAccount

Credential Owner: PowerPivotTwins\dennyl

Name	Value
User Name	PowerPivotTwins\siva
Password	••••••••••
Confirm Password	••••••••••

Note: Once the credentials are set, they cannot be retrieved by the administrator. Any existing credentials for this will be overwritten.

FIGURE 8-20: Set credentials for PowerPivotUnattendedAccount

The *Credential Owner* is the one who specifies that the PowerPivotUnattendedAccount will use the PowerPivotTwins\siva account. The credential owner is required because, once these credentials are assigned (that is, once PowerPivotTwins\siva is specified), there is no way to get these credentials back, and they will simply need to be overwritten.

These two accounts can be the same if the PowerPivot service account is also a target application administrator for you application ID.

Step 6: Set the PowerPivotUnattendedAccount for the Data Refresh Action

Finally, to set the PowerPivotUnattendedAccount to have the capability to perform the data refresh action, you must follow these steps:

1. Go to SharePoint Central Administration ➪ Application Management ➪ Manage Service Applications.

2. Select the Default PowerPivot Service Application. Click on the Manage icon shown in the ribbon.

3. The PowerPivot Management Dashboard will appear. On the right, click on "Configure service application settings" under Actions. At this point, you may get a refresh external data

warning dialog. At this point, click "Yes" so that the PowerPivot Management dashboard can continue working. You can turn off this warning dialog by following the "Turn off External Data Warning on Data Refresh" step outline in the section, "Optional Setup Steps," later in this chapter.

4.   Under the Data Refresh section, type **PowerPivotUnattendedAccount.**

Now, with all of these configurations completed, users are capable of having automatic data refresh for their PowerPivot workbooks without necessarily entering their own user credentials.

If a user does not specify his or her credentials when configuring the data refresh for their workbook, the data refresh may fail because the PowerPivotUnattendedAccount *may not have the necessary rights to access the source data. So, it is still recommended that users who want data refresh specify individual credentials.*

Enabling PowerPivot Management Dashboard Data Collection

The last major configuration in the farm is to enable monitoring of PowerPivot usage and health data to gain insight on usage within the PowerPivot Management Dashboard. To do this, follow these steps.

1.   Go to SharePoint Central Administration ⇨ Monitoring ⇨ "Configure usage and health data collection."

2.   Ensure that the "Enable usage data collection" checkbox is checked, as well as any events that you want to log (at a minimum, all four PowerPivot events), as shown in Figure 8-21.

3.   Do not forget to click the "Enable health data collection" checkbox if you want to generate health reports.

By doing this, PowerPivot will collect the data into its own set of workbooks which are then used in the PowerPivot Management Dashboard.

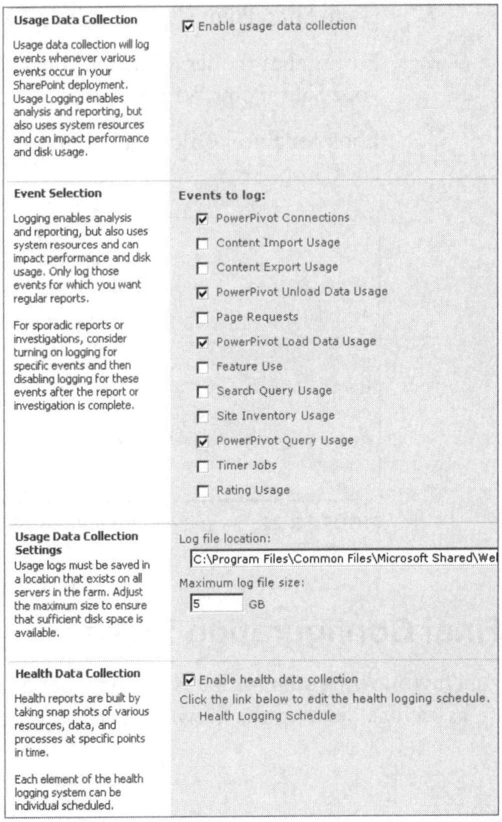

FIGURE 8-21: Enable PowerPivot Event Data Collection

Chapter 9 provides more information on the PowerPivot Management dashboard.

Turn off Excel Calculation Services on the SharePoint WFE

The details surrounding Excel Services (and, specifically, Excel Calculation Services) are described in Chapter 10 and Chapter 11. Quickly put, the reason to turn off Excel Calculation Services (ECS) from the SharePoint WFE is to allow the bulk of the calculations performed by Excel Services to be performed on the SharePoint App Server. This allows the SharePoint WFE to better handle the workload of rendering workbooks and other documents.

Since the SharePoint deployment examined in this chapter involves one WFE, one App Server, and one Database server, keeping ECS enabled on the SharePoint WFE may result in a failure when ECS attempts to connect to PowerPivot Services. The cause of the failure is because the SQL Server 2008 R2 Analysis Services OLE DB driver has not been installed on the SharePoint WFE. To avoid the failure, either install the SQL Server 2008 R2 Analysis Services OLE DB driver, or turn off ECS on the SharePoint WFE.

To turn off Excel Calculation Services on the SharePoint WFE, follow these steps:

1. Go to SharePoint Central Administration ➪ System Settings ➪ "Manage services on server."

2. Ensure that the server listing (near the top right, as shown in Figure 8-22) shows the name of your SharePoint WFE server.

3. Look for Excel Calculation Services under the Service heading and, under the Action heading, click Stop.

	Server:	GEMDWFE ▼	View:	Configurable ▼
Service		Status	Action	
Access Database Service		Stopped	Start	
Application Registry Service		Stopped	Start	
Business Data Connectivity Service		Stopped	Start	
Central Administration		Started	Stop	
Claims to Windows Token Service		Started	Stop	
Document Conversions Launcher Service		Stopped	Start	
Document Conversions Load Balancer Service		Stopped	Start	
Excel Calculation Services		Stopped	Start	

FIGURE 8-22: Stop Excel Calculation Services on the SharePoint WFE

Final Configuration Steps

The following steps will ensure that the services required for PowerPivot for SharePoint are started, as well as open up the firewall ports required for inter-farm communication.

Step 1: Ensure PowerPivot for SharePoint Dependent Services Are Started

If you have not already done so, ensure that, at a minimum, the following services have been started on the SharePoint WFE.

➤ Claims to Windows Token Service

➤ Microsoft SharePoint Foundation Web Application

➤ Microsoft SharePoint Foundation Workflow Timer Service

➤ Secure Store Service

On the SharePoint App Server, ensure, at a minimum, that the following services have been started:

➤ Claims to Windows Token Service

➤ Excel Calculation Services

➤ Microsoft SharePoint Foundation Web Application

➤ Microsoft SharePoint Foundation Workflow Timer Service

➤ SQL Server Analysis Services

➤ SQL Server PowerPivot System Service

To perform the service start verification, go to SharePoint Central Administration ➪ System Settings ➪ "Manage services on server."

Step 2: Firewall Ports

Additionally, you may need to open up the server's firewall ports for Excel Services and the Analysis Services Engine. To do this, click Start ➪ Run. Type **firewall.cpl**, and click "Allow a program through Windows Firewall." You will be given the option to add a port or a program here. For Windows 2008 R2, you will need to create new inbound and outbound rules in the Advanced settings to "Allow the connection" for the appropriate domain. Do the following:

➤ *32843* — This is the port Excel Services uses to communicate with itself, as well as with PowerPivot Services. Open the port on both the SharePoint WFE and SharePoint App Server.

➤ *Allow the Analysis Services Engine access* — To do this, ensure that the program `C:\Program Files\Microsoft SQL Server\MSAS10_50.POWERPIVOT\OLAP\bin\msmdsrv.exe` is allowed through the firewall.

 This last step needs only to be performed on the App Server.

At this point, you will want to verify that your PowerPivot installation is working. To do this, refer to the following section, "Verify the PowerPivot for SharePoint Setup." There are additional optional steps that you may want to perform, which are noted in the section, "Optional Setup Steps," later in this chapter, but they should be done after you have verified your PowerPivot for SharePoint environment is working.

VERIFY THE POWERPIVOT FOR SHAREPOINT SETUP

Now that you have completed the installation of PowerPivot for SharePoint, you should verify that this setup is working properly.

 You may want to perform some additional configuration steps such as increasing the file size limits, Reporting Services integration, and adding more servers to your PowerPivot for SharePoint farm. However, these steps should occur after verification, in case there are issues with your environment.

To verify your setup, you will perform three common tasks:

➤ Publish your Excel workbooks

➤ View workbooks in PowerPivot Gallery

➤ View workbooks in Excel Services

While these verification steps may not seem like much, each one of these steps tests the services and components required for your PowerPivot for SharePoint installation. By performing all three tasks, you will have verified the operation of most of your PowerPivot for SharePoint environment.

Publishing Your Excel Workbooks

After you have set up PowerPivot for SharePoint, you may already have the PowerPivot Gallery option, shown in Figure 8-23.

If you do not, don't fret! You can create a new PowerPivot Gallery by going to your SharePoint Web application ribbon, and then clicking on Site Actions ➪ More Options.

When the Create Web dialog box shown in Figure 8-24 appears, do the following:

1. Under the Filter By section, choose Library.

2. Choose PowerPivot Gallery.

FIGURE 8-23: PowerPivot Gallery

3. Within this dialog, on the right-hand side, type in the name of your new PowerPivot Gallery (for example, My PowerPivot Gallery).

4. Click Create.

From here, it's just a matter of uploading your PowerPivot workbook to SharePoint. As a quick reminder, to do this, follow these steps:

1. Click on your PowerPivot Gallery. Note that you may be asked to install the latest version of Silverlight, because

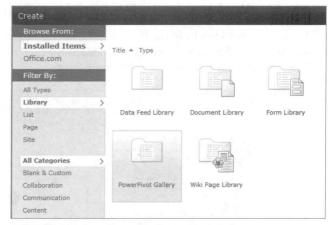

FIGURE 8-24: Creating a new PowerPivot Gallery

it is a dependency. You will be provided the guidance to install Silverlight, and then you can continue.

2. Within the ribbon, click on the Documents tab and then click on Upload Document ➪ Upload Document.

3. The "PowerPivot Gallery — Upload Document" dialog will appear, and from here, choose the file you want to upload.

4. Click OK to upload your file.

Upon initially uploading your workbook to the gallery, you may get the *hourglass* view, as shown in Figure 8-25. The reason you are seeing the hourglass is because PowerPivot is generating the thumbnails for the report preview that is part of the PowerPivot Gallery.

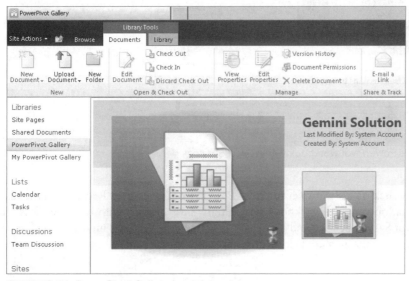

FIGURE 8-25: PowerPivot Gallery hourglass view

Viewing Workbooks in PowerPivot Gallery

To view the workbooks in the PowerPivot Gallery, wait a short while and simply refresh the browser screen. You will be able to see the thumbnails for each of the worksheets in your recently uploaded PowerPivot workbook, as shown in Figure 8-26.

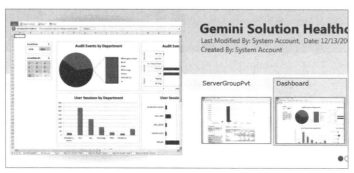

FIGURE 8-26: PowerPivot Gallery workbook thumbnail view

Viewing Workbooks in Excel Services

To view the workbook in Excel Services, all you must do is hover over the thumbnails and click on one of them. Excel Services will retrieve the workbook from the SharePoint content database and render it in your Web browser, as shown in Figure 8-27.

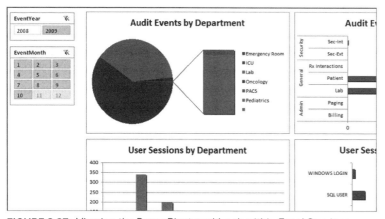

FIGURE 8-27: Viewing the PowerPivot workbook within Excel Services

Don't forget to actually click on a slicer to ensure that PowerPivot is working. Recall from the discussion in Chapter 7 that opening the workbook will initially only interact with Excel Services. To interact with PowerPivot System Service and the Analysis Services in VertiPaq mode, you will also need to perform a server action, such as clicking on a slicer.

Additional Verification Steps (Optional)

To be entirely sure that your environment is working, you may also want to do the following:

➤ *Run a Data Refresh* — After you have uploaded a workbook, enable data refresh for the workbook. You can view the PowerPivot Management dashboard to see if it has succeeded or failed.

➤ *PowerPivot Management Dashboard* — After you have uploaded your workbooks, it may take up to a day for the usage events to be processed. To view them, go to SharePoint Central Administration ➪ General Application Settings ➪ PowerPivot Management Dashboard. Chapter 9 provides more information on the PowerPivot Management dashboard.

OPTIONAL SETUP STEPS

While the steps outlined here are optional, many of them are quite important for your multi-server PowerPivot for SharePoint environment. This section examines the following:

➤ Configuring the file size limits

➤ Turning off the external data warning on data refresh

➤ Integrating Reporting Services

➤ Adding more servers to your PowerPivot for SharePoint farm

Configuring File Size Limits

You may want to configure the file size limits of your SharePoint farm because, by default, SharePoint will limit the upload size of your files to 50 MB, and Excel Services will limit the size of a workbook it can render to 10 MB. Remember, in the case of PowerPivot for Excel, the VertiPaq database resides within the workbook itself. While compressed in comparison to the original source data, this is still larger than your typical Excel workbook. So, while optional, it is recommended that you reconfigure SharePoint to handle much larger file sizes.

Figure 8-28 shows the SharePoint Central Administration page with the Application Management tab selected.

To increase Web application limits, follow these steps:

1. Go to SharePoint 2010 Central Administration ➪ Application Management ➪ Manage Web Applications (next to the triangle shown in Figure 8-28).

FIGURE 8-28: SharePoint Central Administration Application Management

2. Select SharePoint-80 (which is the default Web application) and then, on the ribbon, select General Settings ⇨ General Settings.

3. Near the bottom of the Web Application General Settings page, change the Maximum Upload Size setting to the limits (megabytes) you want. The maximum allowed by SharePoint is 2,047 MB.

To increase Excel Services limits, follow these steps:

1. Go to SharePoint Central Administration ⇨ Application Management ⇨ Manage Service Applications (next to the square in Figure 8-28).

2. Click your Excel Services application (for example, "Excel Services Application"). Click on the text link itself, which is equivalent to clicking the row containing the Excel Services Application, then, on the ribbon, selecting Manage.

3. On the Manage Excel Services Application page, click Trusted File Locations, and then click http:// (the default file).

4. Under Workbook Properties (approximately half way down the page), change the Maximum Workbook Size (the maximum is 2,000 MB) and the Maximum Chart or Image Size to 100 (because of the larger chart images typically embedded within PowerPivot for Excel workbooks).

With these settings, you and your users can now upload much larger files, which will be typical of your PowerPivot users.

Turning off the External Data Warning on Data Refresh

In your multi-server SharePoint farm, when you access your PowerPivot workbook within Excel Services, you will receive the Excel Web Access warning requesting that you enable queries to external data in this workbook (Figure 8-29). All PowerPivot workbooks result in Excel Services querying external data (as noted in Chapter 7, and described more in detail in Chapter 10) because Excel Services is connecting to an Analysis Services in VertiPaq mode instance.

To avoid having your users need to click "Yes" every time, you can change the configuration within Excel Services by following these steps:

1. Go to SharePoint Central Administration ⇨ Application Management ⇨ Manage Service Applications (next to the square in Figure 8-28).

2. Click your Excel Services application (for example, "Excel Services Application"). Click on the text link itself, which is equivalent to clicking the row containing the Excel Services Application. Then, on the ribbon, select Manage.

FIGURE 8-29: Excel Web Access enable queries to external data warning

3. On the Manage Excel Services Application page, click Trusted File Location, and then click http:// (the default file).

4. Under External data (near the bottom of the page), ensure the "Warn on Refresh" checkbox is *not* checked.

This configuration change does not need to occur with your single-server PowerPivot for SharePoint environment (as described in Chapter 2) because the SQL Server 2008 R2 Analysis Services (SharePoint Integrated Mode) install script automatically performs this task.

Integrating Reporting Services

Integrating Reporting Services for your PowerPivot for SharePoint environment allows you to create Reporting Services reports against your PowerPivot workbooks. For example, in the earlier section, "Verify the PowerPivot for SharePoint Setup," you uploaded a PowerPivot workbook to SharePoint and verified that it worked. However, the workbook itself also contained audit event data broken out by state. Instead of providing a list of states and a corresponding bar chart or pie chart, with Reporting Services integration, you can now use Report Builder 3.0 and its map functionality to create an interactive map, as shown in Figure 8-30.

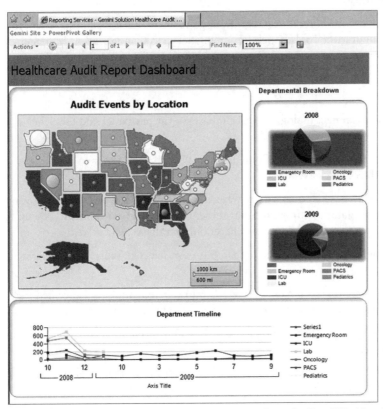

FIGURE 8-30: Report Builder 3.0 Map against PowerPivot for Excel Workbook

To enable Reporting Services Integration, follow the steps outlined in the next few sections.

Install Reporting Services

For this walkthrough, you will be installing a new instance of Reporting Services SharePoint integrated mode on your SharePoint WFE server. To do this, run the SQL Server 2008 R2 `setup.exe`:

1. Click Installation ➪ "New installation or add features to an existing installation."
2. Within the Setup Role dialog, choose the SQL Server Feature Installation.
3. Within the Feature Selection dialog, choose *only* Reporting Services.
4. Click on all of the default selections and then click on Install when prompted.

 You may want to use the same account specified for Analysis Services and SQL Service for easier manageability.

Configure Reporting Services

To configure Reporting Services for SharePoint integration, go to Start ➪ All Programs ➪ Microsoft SQL Server 2008 R2 ➪ Configuration Tools. Click Reporting Services Configuration Manager. The Reporting Services Configuration Connection will prompt you for the Server Name and Report Server Instance that you just installed. Enter this information and click Connect.

Follow these steps:

1. Select Database on the Connect dialog, select Database on the left pane, and then click Change Database in the main window.
2. Ensure that the Report Server Database Configuration Wizard has "Create a new report server database" enabled. Click Next.
3. In the Report Server Database Configuration Wizard, choose the database server you want to host your Report Server database. In your multi-server SharePoint environment, a common choice is the same server that is holding your SharePoint databases. Click Next.
4. Enter the name of your database, and ensure that you have selected SharePoint Integrated Mode. Click Next.
5. For the credentials, ensure that you have selected Windows Credentials and specified the account that will be used to connect to the Report Server database. Click Next.
6. A Summary Page will appear. Click Next and then click Finish (Figure 8-31) after the configuration wizard completes.
7. Within the left-hand dialog of the Report Services Configuration Manager, click Web Services URL and then click Apply.

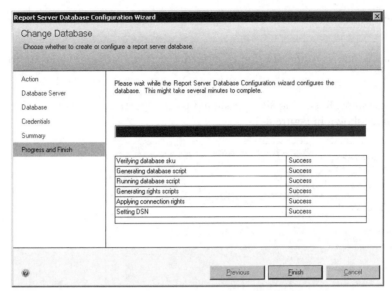

FIGURE 8-31: Report Server Database Configuration Wizard successfully completes

8. In the results section, you should see the message "The url was successfully reserved," as shown in Figure 8-32.

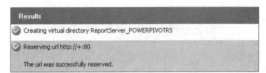

9. Do not close the Reporting Services Configuration Manager, because you will need the Report Server Web Service URLs in order to perform the Reporting Services SharePoint integration.

FIGURE 8-32: "The URL was successfully reserved" message

Integrate Reporting Services with SharePoint

To integrate Reporting Services with SharePoint, follow these steps:

1. From an administrator command window, go to the `1033` folder (for example, `1033_ENU_LP\x64\Setup`) where the SQL Server 2008 R2 `setup.exe` is located. Execute the following command and complete the wizard:

```
rsSharePoint.msi SKIPCA=1
```

2. From the same command window, go to your `temp` folder (`%systemdrive%\users\$username%\appdata\local\temp`) and execute the following command:

```
rsCustomAction.exe /i
```

3. Go to SharePoint Central Administration ➪ General Application Settings ➪ Reporting Services Integration.

4. In the Report Server Web Service URL field, enter the Web Service URL from the previous section.

5. Confirm that Windows Authentication is selected, specify the account you want to use, and then click OK.

After you follow these steps, Reporting Services should be configured in SharePoint Integrated Mode on your farm, as shown in Figure 8-33.

FIGURE 8-33: Reporting Services integration summary

LOG FILES

In case any issues arise when you are performing your installation, it is important to note that there are two sets of log files that you will need to read in order to debug why your installation has run into trouble.

The first is the SQL Server Setup Log Files. These are the standard set of log files that record information concerning the new setup of the SQL Server component. You can find the logs at `%programfiles%\Microsoft SQL Server\100\Setup Bootstrap\Log\`. For more information about these logs, refer to SQL Server Books Online ⇨ How to: View and Read SQL Server Setup Log Files at `http://msdn.microsoft.com/en-us/library/ms143702.aspx`.

Another very important set of log files is the SharePoint ULS log files. All SharePoint events are recorded in these log files. Chapter 9 discusses these logs in more detail.

Add More Servers to your PowerPivot for SharePoint Farm

The multi-server farm setup described in this chapter involved the most basic topology of one WFE, one App Server, and one SQL server. But, because of the workload that you are expecting, you may want to have more WFE and App Servers to handle the workload.

The following instructions are broken down in terms of adding more App Servers to your farm and adding more WFE servers to your farm.

Adding More App Servers

In the multi-server farm setup steps, the WFE installation occurred before the App Servers. But the reason for addressing the instructions for more App Servers first is because, in your PowerPivot for SharePoint environment, you will most likely need App Servers before you will need more WFE servers.

To install additional App Servers, follow these steps:

1. Follow the steps outlined in the earlier section, "Install SharePoint 2010 on the SharePoint App Server."

2. Follow the steps outlined in the earlier section, "Configuring the SharePoint App Server."

3. Follow the steps outlined in the earlier section, "Install SQL Server 2008 R2 Analysis Services on the SharePoint App Server."

4. Follow the steps outlined in the earlier section, "Final Configuration Steps."

Adding More WFE Servers

If you have a lot of concurrent users or a lot of concurrent workloads on your SharePoint WFE, you may want to add more SharePoint WFEs.

To install additional WFE servers, follow these steps:

1. Follow the steps outlined in the earlier section, "Install SharePoint 2010 on the SharePoint WFE."

2. Follow the steps outlined in the earlier section, "Configuring the SharePoint App Server." Note that, while the instructions say "App Server" here, this is applicable to your additional WFE in that you are adding this new SharePoint server to an existing farm.

3. Follow the steps outlined in the earlier section, "Turn off Excel Calculation Services on the SharePoint WFE."

4. Follow the steps outlined in the earlier section, "Final Configuration Steps."

Now you have an additional SharePoint WFE for your PowerPivot for SharePoint farm.

At this point, you will also want to place a network load balancer in front of the two (or more) SharePoint WFE servers so that users are not specifying the specific WFE URLs to access SharePoint. Instead, they can access an alias, which will direct the Web traffic to the WFE servers (for example, you type in the browser `http://myWFE`, which load balances traffic between the two WFEs: `http://WFE1` and `http://WFE2`).

You will also need to set up the SharePoint Alternate Access Mapping (AAM) so that Web traffic can be directed to the correct application. To do this, follow these steps:

1. Go to SharePoint Central Administration ⇨ System Settings. Select Configure Alternate Access Mappings under Farm Management.

2. Click the link Add Internal URLs. Select "SharePoint – 80" in the Alternate Access Mapping Collection drop-down. Enter the WFE server and port in the "URL protocol, host and port" text box (for example, `http://wfe2:80`).

3. Select the appropriate zone (most corporate SharePoint deployments will choose Intranet), then click Save.

 Chapter 7 provides more information on load balancing and SharePoint AAM. Additional hints and tips for capacity planning are provided in Chapter 11.

SUMMARY

This chapter provided necessary steps, as well as guidance, to build a multi-server PowerPivot for SharePoint farm. You also learned about the hardware and software requirements for your multi-server environment. While most of the instructions provided in this chapter focused on the basic topology (one WFE, one App Server, and one SQL Server), this chapter provides the foundation for all of the other PowerPivot for SharePoint topology scenarios discussed in Chapter 11.

Chapter 9 examines troubleshooting, monitoring, and securing PowerPivot Services. Now that you have a multi-server environment up and running, Chapter 9 will help you keep it that way.

Troubleshooting, Monitoring, and Securing PowerPivot Services

WHAT'S IN THIS CHAPTER?

➤ Getting to know the tools and tips to troubleshoot PowerPivot

➤ Resolving some common (and not so common) PowerPivot trouble-shooting issues

➤ Understanding how to monitor your PowerPivot environment

➤ Understanding SharePoint security issues surrounding PowerPivot users or administrators

At the end of Chapter 7, you learned about some of the services surrounding PowerPivot for SharePoint. In Chapter 2, you learned how to build a simpler Single-Server Install, while in Chapter 8 you learned how to build a more complex Multi-Server PowerPivot for SharePoint environment. But now that your environment is up and running, what are you going to do with it?

One of the first concerns with your environment is how to troubleshoot it when issues arise. As was shown in Chapter 7 (and will be explored more deeply in Chapter 10), there are a lot of moving parts for your PowerPivot for SharePoint environment. For example, a common issue will be that when users try to view their PowerPivot workbooks, they may get an Excel Services delegation error. And, if you've read this far into this book, there is a very good chance that the person who needs to fix this is you.

This chapter provides not only a review of the tools that you use to troubleshoot your environment, but also provides resolutions to common (and not so common) troubleshooting issues. Once you have ensured that the environment is up and running, you can then monitor and secure the environment, which you'll learn about in this chapter.

TROUBLESHOOTING TOOLS

Since PowerPivot Client is an add-in to Excel, and PowerPivot for SharePoint is a set of services added to SharePoint, the capability to analyze and troubleshoot problems is tied directly to the infrastructure of Excel and SharePoint, respectively. This section examines some of the tools that have been added to augment the capability to understand any issues that may be occurring

Tracing Tool in PowerPivot for Excel

The first tool that you should become most familiar with is the client-side tracing tool that is included with the PowerPivot add-in to the Excel client. To access it, you click the Settings button within the PowerPivot ribbon selection, as shown in Figure 9-1.

FIGURE 9-1: Accessing client-side tracing in PowerPivot for Excel by starting with the Settings

The "PowerPivot Options & Diagnostics" dialog then appears, and the first tab is the "Support & Diagnostics" tab, as shown in Figure 9-2. Check the "Client tracing is enabled" checkbox and a trace file will be created on your desktop, as noted in the Trace File Location box in Figure 9-2. Note that the trace does not actually start until you've opened the PowerPivot Window.

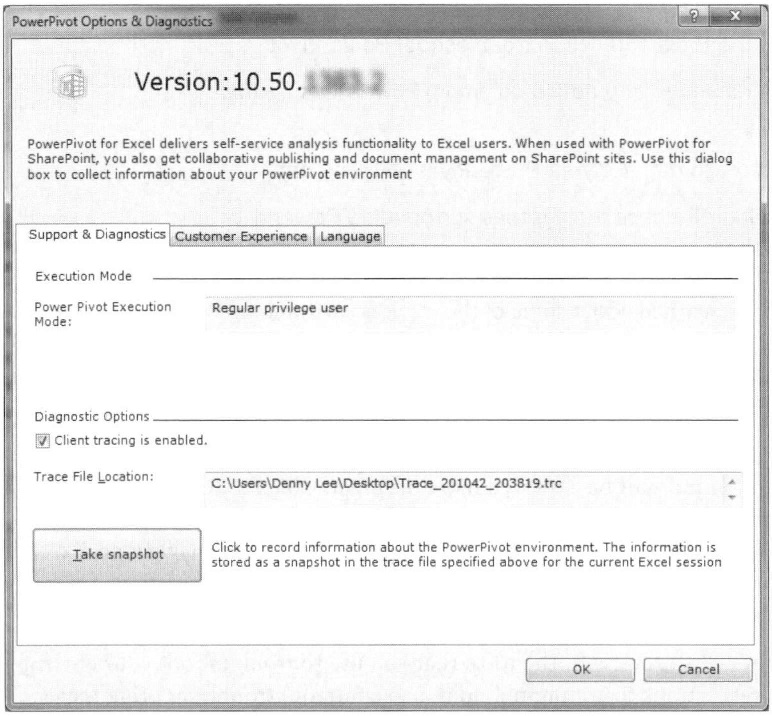

FIGURE 9-2: Enabling tracing PowerPivot for Excel by checking the "Client tracing is enabled" checkbox

The reason that the trace does not actually start until you open the PowerPivot Window is because the VertiPaq database isn't initialized. Once you click the PowerPivot Window button, the VertiPaq database is initialized, and is now in memory.

For debugging purposes, ensure that you click the "Take snapshot" button. The snapshot records the current state of your VertiPaq database. If you were to use the SQL Profiler to view the trace immediately after taking the snapshot (more on this later in this chapter), you would notice a lot of Server State Discover Data events. These events provide server state information such as currently open sessions, transactions, locks, and cube schema. This is the same event class information that you would find in traditional Analysis Services. This is possible because the PowerPivot Add-In initiates a local Analysis Services VertiPaq Engine to query the VertiPaq database. Understanding the state of the VertiPaq Engine is often helpful in determining why an error has occurred.

However, if you can access the Excel workbook experiencing issues, and if you have PowerPivot installed, you can also gain an understanding of the structure of the cube. Keep the following in mind:

➤   The VertiPaq database is actually stored within the Excel workbook itself.

➤   When you click the PowerPivot Window button, the VertiPaq database is working and in memory.

➤   The temporary file cache of this in-memory database is located in the `C:\Users\$Your Name$\AppData\Local\Temp` folder (defined by the `%TEMP%` variable).

➤   The latest `VertiPaq_$GUID$` folder is the VertiPaq temporary file cache.

➤   When you open up this folder, you will find a structure that looks remarkably like the Analysis Services traditional data folder structure — because it *is* Analysis Services.

The basic principle is that this information (that is, the structure of your VertiPaq database) is also recorded within the trace when you click on the "Take snapshot" button.

 For more information on the structure of the VertiPaq database within PowerPivot for Excel, see Chapter 10, or see the blog postings at `http://bit.ly/2odUpL`. *("For Excel PowerPivot, the database is IN the workbook") and* `bit.ly/8y4Fp4` *("Understanding why an Excel PowerPivot workbook is so large").*

SQL Server Profiler

So, how do you read the trace that you have just created on your desktop? You will notice that the file has a `.trc` file extension, which indicates that it is a SQL Server Profiler trace. However, you are not able to simply open up Profiler and read the trace. In order to read the file, you must ensure the following:

➤   You are using SQL Server 2008 R2 Profiler to read the trace.

➤   If you are using SQL Server 2008 Profiler, you must connect to a SQL Server 2008 R2 Analysis Services server first before opening the trace file.

> ➤ Or you can copy over the trace definition file defining these events from the `\Program Files (x86)\Microsoft SQL Server\100\Tools\Profiler\Tracedefinitions` location of SQL Server 2008 R2 Analysis Services server to the same location on your box.

You must use one of these options, because the trace definition for SQL Server 2008 R2 Analysis Services has changed from its predecessor, and requires a new trace definition.

> *For more information, see the blog posting, "Reading your PowerPivot Profiler Trace" at* `http://bit.ly/aTLkGV`.

> *It would be tempting to connect to your SQL Server 2008 R2 Analysis Services instance by using SQL Server Management Studio (SSMS). Be careful if you do this, because most of the tweaks or changes that you are used to doing with traditional Analysis Services are unsupported. Except for specific changes such as those associated with memory utilization, all other changes will not have the same effect as traditional Analysis Services and are unsupported.*

Reading the PowerPivot for Excel Trace

To help explain how to read and understand a PowerPivot for Excel trace, let's refer to the Table Import Wizard error shown in Figure 9-3.

If the business analyst who sees this error is technically knowledgeable, he or she may click the "Error details" link on the right side of the Table Import Wizard dialog. As shown in Figure 9-4, clicking that link shows that there was a network error (for example, database went offline, network connection offline, and so on) during the import; hence, the error.

But if the business analyst is not technical, he or she may rely on an IT professional or Database Administrator (DBA) like you to determine the cause of the problem. Errors like these (for example, network

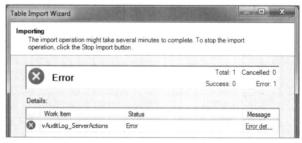

FIGURE 9-3: Table Import Wizard error

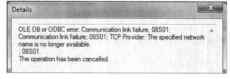

FIGURE 9-4: Message error details from the client

connectivity, access rights, and so on) are difficult to pinpoint, since it may be difficult to reproduce the same problem. Therefore, you can guide the analyst to turn on the client trace, repeat the same action, and send you the trace.

As you can see from Figure 9-5, when you scroll through the Profiler trace, you will quickly find the same error message as noted here:

```
OLE DB or ODBC error: Communication link failure; 08S01;
    Communication link failure; 08S01; TCP Provider:
    The specified network name is no longer available.; 08S01.
    The operation has been cancelled.
```

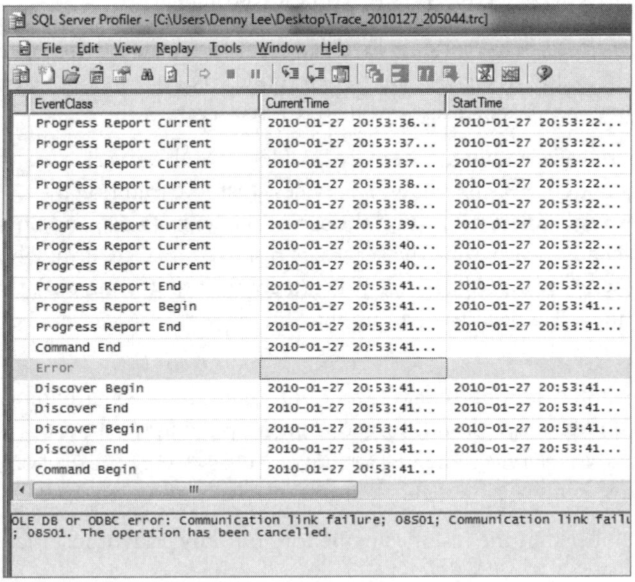

FIGURE 9-5: Table Import Wizard Profiler trace

While this scenario is not exactly enlightening, the point is that it is similar to how you would approach any other Analysis Services error.

For more information on how to use the SQL Server Profiler, you can also refer to "Using SQL Server Profiler" at http://bit.ly/9A6JZ and "Viewing and Analyzing Traces with SQL Server Profiler" at http://bit.ly/eIavq.

Reading the Analysis Services in VertiPaq Mode Trace

When it comes to understanding errors with PowerPivot for SharePoint, specifically the Analysis Services in VertiPaq mode instance, the actions are very similar to how you would analyze SQL Server Analysis Services. That is, you open up SQL Server Profiler and connect to your Analysis Services instance.

However, there are a few things worth noting. Note that, for a single-server installation, you most likely will not be running into the issues outlined here, because all of the SQL Server client tools (including Profiler) are already installed, and the various ports are already opened. Once you have connected Profiler to your Analysis Services (POWERPIVOT) instance, you will be able to track and record the events for further analysis.

➤ Unlike when you install Analysis Services, SQL Server Profiler is not automatically installed with an *existing* farm installation of SQL Server 2008 R2 Analysis Services SharePoint integrated mode. For your existing farm installation, this means that you must install SQL Server Profiler, or use a remote instance of SQL Server 2008 or 2008 R2 Profiler.

➤ If you have multiple Analysis Services Engine services installed on various SharePoint App Servers, you may need to connect to any or all of them to determine what is going on, since the VertiPaq database of issue may be attached to any one of those servers.

➤ Ensure that the SQL Browser Service is running, otherwise Profiler or SQL Server Management Studio (SSMS) cannot connect to Analysis Services. Just like traditional Analysis Services, you could always connect to it using the server name, instance, and port. But the latter port number will change every time the service is restarted. Hence, it may be easier to ensure SQL Server Browser is running so that you can connect to it using only the server name and instance. You may also need to open up the SQL Server Browser Service port, which is UDP 1434.

➤ You may need to open up ports 2382 (Inbound) and 2383 (Outbound) on the SharePoint App Server with PowerPivot installed. Also, do not forget to open up the firewall port (Inbound/Outbound) for the Analysis Services engine (%ProgramFiles%\Microsoft SQL Server\MSAS10_50.POWERPIVOT\OLAP\bin\msmdsrv.exe).

➤ When connecting Profiler, remember that the instance name for your PowerPivot instance is $Server Name$\POWERPIVOT.

Similar to the PowerPivot for Excel trace, let's present a slightly more complex error scenario. In this scenario, you have noticed that many analysts using PowerPivot for SharePoint are complaining that they will get an intermittent error message when they click on a slicer (after clicking on many slicers before). But when they click on another slicer, the Excel interaction will work again.

To understand what is going on, you turn on a Profiler trace, record the events, and start analyzing. Figure 9-6 shows the pertinent information you find in the trace.

Near the top of the Profiler trace window, you see the TextData entry of Either the user, SHAREPOINT\system.... The full text of this error message is as follows:

```
Either the user, SHAREPOINT\system, does not have access to the
    SDR Healthcare Audit Sandbox e87d1c95-c738-4676-b167-
    e322c8a473f7 database, or the database does not exist.
```

This error message indicates that, for some reason, the VertiPaq database for the SDR Healthcare Audit workbook is no longer available. Since analysts had been able to work with this workbook before, and this is an intermittent error, it appears that the VertiPaq database for this workbook has been removed from the Analysis Services Engine service for some reason. But how could the user continue working?

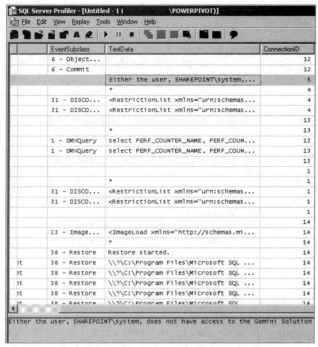

FIGURE 9-6: PowerPivot for SharePoint Profiler trace

Let's continue reading the Profiler trace. A few rows down in the trace shown in Figure 9-6, you notice the following:

➤ EventSubClass (23) — Image...

➤ TextData — <ImageLoad xmls="...

This is the ImageLoad command to load the VertiPaq database to the Analysis Services instance. The pertinent lines of the XMLA statement are as follows (with sections removed or modified for readability):

```
<ImageLoad xmlns="$" xmlns:ddl100="$"
    xmlns:ddl200_200="$" xmlns:ddl100_100="$">
    <ddl200_200:ImagePath>C:\Program Files\Microsoft SQL
        Server\MSAS10_50.POWERPIVOT\OLAP\Backup\Sandboxes\Default
        PowerPivot Service Application\ReadOnlyExclusive-2fa2510a-19f1-
        4489-add8-b0c15613c17b-SDR Healthcare Audit
        .xlsx</ddl200_200:ImagePath>
    <ddl200_200:ImageUniqueID>9fbba36c-a684-4a8d-9bb8-9a78d4b7af1b</
        ddl200_200:ImageUniqueID>
    <ddl200_200:ImageVersion>12/14/2009 19:57:33</ddl200_200:ImageVersion>
    <ddl200_200:ImageUrl>http://sqlcatgem12/PowerPivot Gallery/SDR
        Healthcare Audit.xlsx</ddl200_200:ImageUrl>
    <ddl100_100:DbStorageLocation>C:\Program Files\Microsoft
        SQL Server\MSAS10_50.POWERPIVOT\OLAP\Backup\Sandboxes\
```

```
              Default PowerPivot Service Application</
              ddl100_100:DbStorageLocation>
      <ddl100:ReadWriteMode>ReadOnlyExclusive</ddl100:ReadWriteMode>
          <DatabaseName>SDR Healthcare Audit Sandbox
              2fa2510a-19f1-4489-add8-b0c15613c17b</DatabaseName>
      <DatabaseID>2fa2510a-19f1-4489-add8-b0c15613c17b</DatabaseID>
  </ImageLoad>
```

Chapters 6 and 10 provide more details about `ImageLoad`, but you can see a lot from the XMLA command. Note the following:

➤ The `ddl200_200:ImagePath` node reveals that the workbook is also stored in the `C:\ Program Files\...\OLAP\Backup` folder.

➤ The `ddl200_200:ImageVersion` node reveals the last time this particular workbook was refreshed — that is, the current version of the workbook.

➤ The `ddl200_200:ImageUrl` notes the original URL location of your workbook within SharePoint.

➤ The `ddl100_100:DbStorageLocation` notes the location of the database itself.

➤ The `DatabaseName` denotes the name of VertiPaq database.

As discussed in other chapters, PowerPivot uses the `Backup` folder to keep a cache copy of the database. Thus, if it ever needs a copy of it, it can simply attach this database from this location. This step is much faster than restoring it (that is, obtaining the Excel workbook from the content database, extracting the database from the workbook, and then attaching it from there). In referencing the previous XMLA statement, Excel Services uses the `ddl200` nodes to obtain the workbook components it needs in order to render the workbook. Analysis Services uses the `ddl100` nodes to load the portion of the workbook it needs (that is, the database).

If you go a few rows down on the Profiler trace, you'll notice the `EventSubClass 38 - Restore` events. The restore process had a duration of 566 milliseconds — the time it took to attach the database from the `C:\Program Files\...\Olap\Backup` folder to the Analysis Services service instance. While not visible in the Profiler trace shown in Figure 9-6, immediately after the restore events, there were `EventSubClass 0–MDX Query` events indicating the database was responding to queries again.

In summary, the profiler trace states the following:

➤ A user query (from Excel Services, in this case) lost connectivity to the database for some yet-to-be-identified reason.

➤ Since the database was no longer available, the PowerPivot System Service retrieved the database from the OLAP `Backup` folder, and the Analysis Services Engine attached the database, as noted by the `ImageLoad` command and `Restore` events.

➤ Once restored, the database was able to continue returning queries to the user without any issues.

INSIDE POWERPIVOT

Because the SQL Server Profiler trace actually recorded the connection attempt to the database from the SHAREPOINT\System account, it is safe to say that issues surrounding SQL Browser or Claims to Windows token service are not involved here. The SHAREPOINT\System account in this particular instance represents the PowerPivot System Service logging into Analysis Services Engine using Windows NT authentication. (You'll learn more about this in Chapter 10.) So, unless the Windows account that is running the underlying services was revoked, or a password changed in mid-query, most likely this problem does not involve the actual service account. Also, password changes involve many moving parts within SharePoint, so, typically, a password change issue would involve much more complex connectivity issues (see the "Troubleshooting Problems" section of this chapter for more information).

So, how would you lose database connectivity in mid-query? Well, databases that are not used often will be removed after a set time period, but this most likely is not the case, since an Excel Services session timeout period is measured in seconds or minutes, while the removal of the database is measured in days. Under high memory-pressure situations, where there are a lot of user queries hitting a lot of databases concurrently (recall, memory usage by PowerPivot is a product of the number of databases in use concurrently with some overhead caused by the number of users), the PowerPivot System Service will detach unused databases (when under the health-based, load-balancing allocation method). It may be possible that the system is under such high memory pressure that it would detach a database within the session timeout period described by Excel Services. But this would have to be a pretty extreme case and is rare within customer scenarios.

So, while this is not a common issue, it is an actual issue that had occurred. To create this error scenario, the IT Administrator had logged into Analysis Services in VertiPaq mode and physically deleted the database while a user was trying to use it. The only reason this error was even noticed was because this actually happened during an early beta test of PowerPivot. So, while this is not a common scenario by any stretch of the imagination, it is an interesting observation that had occurred during the early days of PowerPivot beta testing. Also, this happens to be a pretty good way to show how the PowerPivot System Service ensures that the database is available when issues go awry.

ULS Logs

Another very powerful way to troubleshoot your environment is to review the SharePoint Unified Logging Service (ULS) logs. All services within your SharePoint environment will ultimately log their events directly into the ULS logs. This is important, because, as noted throughout this book, PowerPivot for SharePoint is reliant on other services within SharePoint — especially Excel Services.

So, while the Profiler trace does a great job of identifying issues within the Analysis Services engine itself, there is a whole set of infrastructure outside of the engine itself that you will often need to troubleshoot. Events from the SharePoint WFE, Excel Services, and PowerPivot System Service (among many others) are all recorded within the ULS logs.

The following are a few quick notes concerning the ULS logs:

➤ By default, the logs are located at `C:\Program Files\Common Files\Microsoft Shared\Web Server Extensions\14\LOGS`.

➤ The logs are automatically generated every 30 minutes and kept for 14 days. To change the configuration settings, go to SharePoint Central Administration ➪ Monitoring ➪ Reporting ➪ "Configure diagnostic logging."

➤ To review these logs, you should use tools like Excel or the ULS Viewer (`http://ulsviewer.codeplex.com/`). While the former is more colorful and familiar, the latter is a handy tool, especially when you want to open up multiple ULS logs at the same time.

➤ Remember that in an *existing* or *multi-server* farm configuration, you must review the ULS logs from both your WFE and App Servers. This gets a little bit more complicated when your farm includes more WFEs and App Servers (that is, identifying which servers you will need to review the ULS logs).

➤ Knowing *when* an event occurred is important, because, since the ULS logs record a lot of events, it often is not easy to discern which event belongs to which troubleshooting occurrence.

Because you know the time, go to the location of your ULS logs. Order the logs by the `Date Modified` column, and choose the log file with the date modified that occurs just after the actual event, as shown in Figure 9-7.

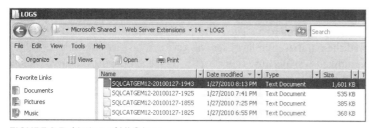

FIGURE 9-7: Listing of ULS logs

Sometimes when the error occurs, included within the error is a Correlation ID, as shown in Figure 9-8. This ID is stored in the last column of the ULS logs, allowing you to correlate multiple event occurrences to a single "process." Because of the complexity of SharePoint, this ID is not always populated, so most of the time it will still depend on detective work and going through the ULS logs to discover patterns associated with the error.

FIGURE 9-8: Error message with Correlation ID

For example, when referring to the previous database connectivity scenario, there was no large error message, and the users continued to work on. But, fortunately, one of the users knew what time the error had occurred (as noted in the previous section, the error occurred on 01/27/2010 19:50:03). So, let's find the same section within the ULS logs.

Looking back at the database connectivity issue in the Profiler trace of the Analysis Services engine on `1/27/2010 7:50:03pm`, Table 9-1 shows selected rows of interest (that is, Area and Message fields).

TABLE 9-1: Receive Pipeline Stages

NUM	AREA	MESSAGE
1	Excel Calculation Services	`Succeeded to initialize a chart.`
2	SSAS Mid-Tier Service	`Redirecting request for UserName=[SHAREPOINT\ system], UserAddress=[], Image=[http:// sqlcatgem12/PowerPivot Gallery/SDR Healthcare Audit.xlsx], Version=[1.0], Agent=[WCF Transport], Application=[], DatabaseId=[e87d1c95-c738-4676-b167- e322c8a473f7].`
3	Excel Services Application	`CDBConsHost::HandleOledbErrors - hr=80004005 text=Either the user, SHAREPOINT\system, does not have access to the SDR Healthcare Audit Sandbox e87d1c95-c738-4676-b167-e322c8a473f7 database, or the database does not exist.`
4	Excel Services Application	`Connection.MarkFree: Connection was found to be stale when used against the data provider. Connection=vltSBGSzVkiKtj9IXlJUCA==`
5	SSAS Mid-Tier Service	`Check whether "http://sqlcatgem12:80/ PowerPivot%20Gallery/SDR%20Healthcare%20 Audit.xlsx" is in the farm`
6	SSAS Mid-Tier Service	`Found an existing sandbox in its instance map but not in the engine instance and is looking for solutions - Database ID:e87d1c95-c738- 4676-b167-e322c8a473f7`
7	SSAS Mid-Tier Service	`Found an inconsistent state. Taking recovery measures - Database ID:e87d1c95-c738-4676- b167-e322c8a473f7`
8	SSAS Mid-Tier Service	`Allocating a new sandbox on SQLCATGEM12 - User:SHAREPOINT\system, DataSource: http:// sqlcatgem12:80/PowerPivot Gallery/SDR Healthcare Audit.xlsx, Version: 12/14/2009 19:57:33`

continues

TABLE 9-1 *(continued)*

NUM	AREA	MESSAGE
9	SSAS Mid-Tier Service	There is enough memory to load the new sandbox
10	SSAS Mid-Tier Service	A new database will be ImageLoaded for this request
11	SSAS Mid-Tier Service	Connection established to DataSource: http:// sqlcatgem12:80/PowerPivot Gallery/SDR Healthcare Audit.xlsx
12	SSAS Mid-Tier Service	Redirecting request for UserName=[SHAREPOINT\ system], UserAddress=[], Image=[http:// sqlcatgem12/PowerPivot Gallery/SDR Healthcare Audit.xlsx], Version=[1.0], Agent=[WCF Transport], Application=[], DatabaseId=[2fa2510a-19f1-4489-add8- b0c15613c17b].
13	Excel Services Application	ConnectionManager. CreateConnectionAndAddToList: Successfully created new connection, connection=23moeMxzTk +BB0zYsUE2rQ==, EmbeddedDataType=Embedded

Table 9-1 shows only 13 of the 170 available rows for the specific Correlation ID associated with this error — out of a total of 4,991 rows in the ULS log. But these rows definitely tell a story here. (In the following, the numbers inside the brackets refer to the "Num" column within Table 9-1.)

➤ Excel Services was able to render the workbook [1].

➤ A user clicks a slicer, and PowerPivot System Service tries to connect to a database [2].

➤ This connection fails. Excel Services is left without a connection and returns error to the user [3, 4].

➤ PowerPivot System Service is checking whether the workbook is even in its own SharePoint farm [5].

➤ It finds that it exists, according to its own metadata (Instance Map), but does not exist on the indicated Analysis Services Engine service [6] (because it was manually deleted).

➤ It then restores the database [7, 8, 9] via the ImageLoad command [10], and re-establishes connectivity [11, 12].

➤ Excel Services is now able to connect to the database again [13].

As you can tell from Table 9-1 (and implied heavily by the sheer number of entries within the ULS log), the ULS logs provide a very verbose recollection of events. Because there is a lot of information, it is important to use some handy tools to help you parse all this information (such as Excel or the ULS viewer described earlier).

The following PowerShell cmdlet provides a great way to consolidate ULS logs from a specific date range and specific area to your own log file. Follow these steps:

1. Go to Start ➪ Programs ➪ Microsoft SharePoint 2010 Products ➪ SharePoint 2010 Management Shell.

2. Enter the following to consolidate ULS Logs for the PowerPivot System Service into the log file `PPFS.log`:

```
Merge-SPLogFile -Path "C:\Program Files\Common Files\Microsoft Shared\
    Web Server Extensions\14\Logs\PPFS.log" -Area "SSAS Mid-Tier
    Service" -StartTime "2/1/2010 00:01"-EndTime "2/18/2010 22:30"
```

While some may consider using the PowerPivot Management Dashboard as a troubleshooting device, this is addressed later in this chapter in the section, "Monitoring PowerPivot Services." While it can reveal a lot of things like which workbooks are popular and which data refresh succeeded or failed, ultimately, you will still need to review the ULS logs or Profiler traces to better understand the events leading up to the event of interest.

TROUBLESHOOTING ISSUES

This section examines some of the more common troubleshooting issues experienced during installation, configuration, and management of PowerPivot. There are also some excellent online resources that you can reference to help you, including the following:

➤ "The Great PowerPivot FAQ" at `http://powerpivotfaq.com`.

➤ "PowerPivotGeek Reported Problems Section" at `http://bit.ly/67wBNo`.

➤ "PowerPivotGeek Troubleshooting Section" at `http://bit.ly/delaVe`.

➤ "SQL Server 2008 R2 PowerPivot for Excel" at `http://bit.ly/13n0MT`.

➤ "SQL Server 2008 R2 PowerPivot for SharePoint" at `http://bit.ly/4BKKDU`.

Also, there are some PowerPivot aggregator sites that include quite a bit of information, including the following:

➤ `PowerPivotPro.com`

➤ `PowerPivot-Info.com`

➤ `PowerPivotTwins.com`

There are plenty more resources available than those highlighted here, but these are a great starting point. While the troubleshooting problems discussed here cover the most common issues encountered to date, new ones most likely will appear, so ensure that you are familiar with the issues discussed here and the resources provided.

Installation

What follows are some of the more common installation-related issues.

Excel Client Installation Error

The Excel Client installation is a relatively straightforward process requiring Excel 2010, Office Shared Tools, and .NET 3.5 SP1. Yet, there are still some potential issues that have commonly arisen, usually surrounding the fact that you do not see the PowerPivot tab within the Office ribbon.

➤ If you are using Windows XP as your client, ensure that you install SP3, because this is the minimum client SKU supported for Excel 2010.

➤ When you install Excel 2010, ensure that you also install the Office Shared Tools. This feature contains Visual Studio Tools for Office (VSTO), which is required by PowerPivot. If you did not install VSTO, you'll need to uninstall Excel 2010 and PowerPivot for Excel, and then re-install Excel 2010 and Office Shared Tools before installing PowerPivot for Excel again.

➤ It is possible that the add-in is not enabled, so go to File ⇨ Options ⇨ Add-ins, and then Manage ⇨ COM Add-Ins ⇨ Go. In the COM Add-Ins window, check the `Microsoft.AnalysisServices.Modeler.FieldList.Addin.Integration` checkbox and click OK.

➤ If the add-in is disabled, it's possible that Excel disabled it because the add-in had crashed Excel a number of times.

➤ If the add-in did not load with the previous procedure with the error message `Not Loaded. The Managed Add-in Loader failed to initialize`, and you are not using Windows 7, ensure that you installed .NET Framework 3.5 SP1. (Windows 7 already has .NET 3.5 SP1.)

➤ If you install the x64 version of Excel, ensure that you also install the x64 version of the PowerPivot add-in. The same goes for x86. The key is not to have mismatched versions here.

PowerPivot for SharePoint Requires Server SKUs

While it may be possible to install PowerPivot for SharePoint on client SKUs (for example, Windows 7 Client), it is not recommended, because it requires a number of unsupported tweaks and configurations. Use only server SKUs with PowerPivot for SharePoint — with Windows Server 2008 and Windows Server 2008 R2 preferred.

PowerPivot for SharePoint Installation Errors

Chapters 2 and 8 extensively covered the installation steps for PowerPivot for SharePoint, single-server and existing farm installations, respectively. Before becoming too frustrated with the installation (especially the existing farm installation), ensure that you follow the actual installation guides supplied in this book. Good online installation guides can also be found at `http://powerpivotgeek.com/server-installation/` or `http://bit.ly/8yW18A`.

During a beta test period of PowerPivot for SharePoint, the vast majority of the installation errors revolved around not following the steps provided in these guides. So, before doing any install steps, it is *highly recommended* that you follow the steps in these guides.

 At the risk of overemphasizing this point, remember that, before you install PowerPivot for SharePoint, you should follow the guidance in Chapters 2 and 8, or any trustworthy documentation. To avoid a lot of headaches, grief, and sleepless nights, do this! A great example is the issue Lee Graber brought up in his posting at `http://bit.ly/6pLvuE` *("Could not load type 'Microsoft.AnalysisServices. SharePoint.Integration.ReportGalleryView'"). The most common reason why the PowerPivot Gallery failed to work was because they forgot to deploy the* `PowerPivotWebApp` *solution to a web application (as discussed in Chapter 8).*

Analysis Services VertiPaq Installation Error

As noted in Chapter 8, if there are any issues with the installation of SQL Server 2008 R2 Analysis Services in SharePoint Integrated mode, you will want to first review the SQL Server Setup logs. These logs can be found at `%programfiles%\Microsoft SQL Server\100\Setup Bootstrap\Log\`. For more information about these logs, refer to SQL Server Books Online, "How to: View and Read SQL Server Setup Log Files" at `http://msdn.microsoft.com/en-us/library/ms143702.aspx`.

Kerberos Is Not Required for PowerPivot for SharePoint

While you *can* install PowerPivot for SharePoint in a SharePoint farm with Kerberos authentication, Kerberos is *not* a requirement. There have been a number of rumors and statements noting that, because this is Analysis Services, you must turn on Kerberos in your existing farm multi-server topology because of the multi-hop scenarios.

As is extensively discussed in Chapter 10, while Analysis Services itself is not claims-aware, PowerPivot System Service is claims-aware, so the connection from WFE to Excel Services to PowerPivot System Service all occurs using the claims token. The last step — PowerPivot System Service to Analysis Services — is performed using Windows authentication via the Claims-To-Windows Token Service (c2wts). But there is no multi-hop occurrence here, just a single hop from PowerPivot System Service to Analysis Services, hence the reason why Kerberos is *not* required.

For more information, see Chapter 10. The key point here is that Kerberos is not required for PowerPivot for SharePoint.

Installing PowerPivot for SharePoint on a Domain Controller

This is a common approach when you want to install SharePoint on your own laptop and are not connected to a corporate network with its own separate domain controller. So, the solution is that you install PowerPivot for SharePoint on a machine that is also acting as its own domain controller at the same time (as SharePoint will not optimally work with non-domain accounts).

Before you proceed with this, be sure to read the section, "Off Network PowerPivot for SharePoint Scenario," later in this chapter. If you can connect to a domain network when you install PowerPivot for SharePoint, it may be easier to do the installation and follow the instructions in that section so that you can take your computer and workbooks off network.

However, if you really need to install on the same box as a domain controller, see the blog posting, "Installing PowerPivot for SharePoint on a domain controller" at `http://bit.ly/2miFey`.

So, why put the instructions into this discussion and ask you to view a blog posting? Well, the blogger, Dave Wickert (a long-time Analysis Services guru, and responsible for the PowerPivot backend infrastructure) is very technical by nature.

Yet, in the referenced posting, he managed to use the phrase "Quick like a bunny." This would be a rather funny thing to hear him say, let alone see him write. So, for the sake of trusting the author's sense of humor, you should review his blog posting.

Installation Verification

When you verify your PowerPivot for SharePoint installation, you should not just open the Excel workbook within the PowerPivot Gallery. As noted in other sections of this book, at this point, you have only engaged Excel Services itself. You must also click on a slicer to engage PowerPivot System Service and the Analysis Services Engine.

If this does not work, then you possibly have a connectivity issue between Excel Services and Analysis Services — more on this later in this chapter in the section, "Connectivity."

Usage

Let's now take a look at some interesting usage troubleshooting issues and some common solutions to the problems.

Unsupported Features in Excel Services

A common (but irritating) view within Excel Services is to see the "Unsupported Features" message shown in Figure 9-9. This message appears because PowerPivot itself makes use of custom Office Art shapes whose layout is controlled by the custom `FieldList` in the Excel client. Those shapes do not render

FIGURE 9-9: Unsupported Features message in Excel Services

in Excel Services, but they are also not needed in Excel Services, so you can simply click on the X at the right of the Unsupported Features message bar (not visible in Figure 9-9) to ignore this message.

> *For more information about these custom shapes, check out Lee Graber's comments in the Great PowerPivot FAQ at* `http://bit.ly/a7b3Ue.`

Cannot Use SharePoint Lists as Data Feeds

This error might be attributed to an improper installation. As noted in Chapter 8, to support SharePoint lists as a data feed, you must ensure that you also installed "Data Services Update for .NET Framework 3.5 SP1."

For more information, refer to the following links:

➤ "Data Services Update for .NET 3.5 SP1" blog posting (from the Astoria Team) at `http://bit.ly/b08Joq.`

➤ "ADO.NET Data Services Update for .NET Framework 3.5 SP1 for Windows 7 and Windows 2008 R2" at `http://bit.ly/bp99Ia.`

➤ "ADO.NET Data Services Update for .NET Framework 3.5 SP1 for Older OS" at `http://bit.ly/5TLL91.`

Failed to Download Excel Services Chart or Image, Yet Workbook and Slicers Are Still Working

Every so often, the issue shown in Figure 9-10 creeps up, and no one quite knows how or what happens. But before you do anything drastic, the key thing here is that if the workbook is still working, you are most likely not dealing with a corrupt workbook.

FIGURE 9-10: "Failed to download Excel Services chart or image"

Following are some courses of action when this situation occurs:

➤ Reboot the WFE with the Excel Services problem. In some cases when this problem occurred, some Windows update change and/or registry settings needed to be cleared out — but had not yet until a reboot occurred. So, as trite as the solution may sound, "reboot" and this problem should be solved.

➤ If this does not work, and the workbook is not corrupt, simply re-upload the workbook. This has the added benefit of fixing the thumbnails gallery in case there were problems with it, as well as fixing the chart or images.

➤ Chapter 8 includes instructions for increasing the maximum image size of Excel Services. Ensure that the images or charts you have do not exceed the default value that is currently set. Or, you can increase maximum size, as noted in the installation guide.

Warn on Data Refresh Message

When you are interacting with your PowerPivot workbooks (or, for that matter, any Excel workbooks) within your SharePoint farm, you may continually receive the refresh external data message shown in Figure 9-11. You typically will not see this in a single-server farm configuration of PowerPivot for SharePoint, but you may see this more often in your existing farm multi-server topology.

To avoid this error message, you must to turn off the "Warn on data refresh" message alert for Excel Services. To do this, go to Central Administration ➪ Manage Service Application ➪ Excel Service Application (for example, `ExcelServiceApp1`) ➪ Trusted File locations ➪ http:// within the External Data panel. Ensure that the Warn on Refresh ➪ "Refresh warning enabled" checkbox is unchecked, as shown in Figure 9-12.

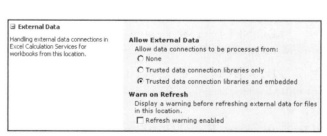

FIGURE 9-11: Refresh external data message

FIGURE 9-12: "Refresh warning enabled" checkbox unchecked

Downgrade and Then Upgrade User Permissions May Result in Unexpected Experience

Because IT administrators prefer not to give users access rights that are too expansive (but may downgrade permissions and then upgrade permissions again), this problem may occur on occasion. The problem that you may face is that the user whose account has been downgraded and then upgraded may not be able to refresh a workbook, even though that user is supposed to have permissions.

Following is a common scenario for this issue:

1. User A has full control, views Workbook A, and is able to refresh without any issues.

2. User A has been downgraded to Read permissions only, so when viewing Workbook A, nothing happens when the user attempts to refresh.

3. User A has been given Full Control rights again, but when the user again tries to refresh, still nothing happens

It will be necessary for the user to re-upload the Excel workbook altogether to get rights.

Upload of My Excel Workbook Takes a Long Time When Using Save As

When you use the Save As (or "Save to SharePoint") option from Excel to save your workbook, the save is done asynchronously via the Office Upload Center. When compared to saving via the SharePoint UI, it does take longer to save using the Save As option. This is especially noticeable when working with PowerPivot workbooks, which are typically much larger than your average Excel workbooks. But the advantage of using the Save As option is that the upload occurs asynchronously (that is, you can continue editing your workbook as it's being uploaded to SharePoint).

If the upload is taking a long time, open up the Office Upload Center to ensure that the upload is continuing to run in the background. To do this, go to the notification area in your task bar and click on the Microsoft Office Upload Center icon to view the Upload Center (Figure 9-13).

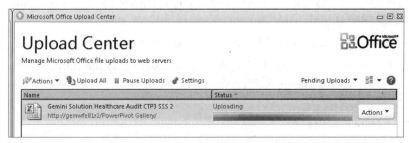

FIGURE 9-13: Office Upload Center uploading a PowerPivot workbook to SharePoint

Another advantage of using the Office Upload Center is that when you go off the network and then come back on, it will re-establish the connection and continue uploading. However, if clicking the Actions button for the affected workbook does not allow you to stop or modify the upload, you may want to perform a brute-force kill of the upload. To do this, follow these steps:

1. Kill the Office Upload Center process by using the task manager (MSOSYNC.exe).

2. Go to the C:\Users\<user>\AppData\Local\Microsoft\Office\14.0 location. Often, if there are issues with uploading through this method, you can delete the files in this directory.

You may also want to delete the files in the following directories:

➤ C:\Users\<user>\AppData\Local\Microsoft\Windows\Temporary Internet Files\ Content.MSO

➤ C:\Windows\ServiceProfiles\LocalService\AppData\Local\Temp\TfsStore

For more information, see the posting "Uploading PowerPivot for Excel workbook using 'Save As' vs. SharePoint UI" at http://bit.ly/7KIW9X.

Upload of My PowerPivot Workbook Results in "File Limit Exceeded"

You most likely will receive this error message because your PowerPivot workbook has surpassed the file size limits of Excel Services and SharePoint. By default, the maximum size of a document that can be uploaded to SharePoint is 50 MB. So, if you regularly surpass this maximum threshold, please follow the instructions in Chapter 8 for configuring file size limits.

Connectivity

As noted throughout this book, there are a lot of moving parts involved with PowerPivot for SharePoint. If any component is not working, the result may be the inability for PowerPivot to work.

This section provides an overview of some of the problems you may run into. The connectivity scenarios referred to here are the ones where you interact with Excel Services, and a problem results from connecting to the PowerPivot System Service and/or Analysis Services VertiPaq Engine or, for that matter, Excel Services itself.

Firewall

As noted in the installation guides, it is important to open up the firewall ports to enable the different services and components to communicate with each other. Following are some ports on which you should focus your troubleshooting efforts:

➤ *Excel Services* — Excel Services uses TCP/IP port 32843 to communicate.

➤ *Analysis Services Engine Service* — Include the program file itself under (default) `C:\Program Files\Microsoft SQL Server\MSAS10_50.POWERPIVOT\OLAP\bin\msmdsrv.exe` so that it can receive inbound communication.

➤ *SQL Browser* — To find the Analysis Services VertiPaq Engine service (or, for that matter, any named instance service), you will need to open up UDP port 1434.

➤ *SQL Server* — Ensure that TCP/IP port 1433 is open so that it is possible to communicate with the SQL Server.

 You should not enable these firewall ports if your installation is already working.

Additionally, if you want the capability to connect to the Analysis Services Engine service using SQL Server Management Studio (SSMS), you must open up ports 2382 and 2383 as well.

Excel Services Access Rights to the Content Database

Let's say that you set up or configured Excel Services without using the SharePoint Farm Administrator (from a security standpoint, this is a good idea). However, you then run into an error message that says, "The workbook cannot be opened." This may be caused by an Excel Services

Access rights issue. This is because, by default, the managed account for the Excel Services application pool does not have access to the SharePoint content databases — while the SharePoint Farm Administrator does.

To provide Excel Services with the necessary access rights, run the following PowerShell script:

```
$w = Get-SPWebApplication -identity $webapp
$w.GrantAccessToProcessIdentity("$svcacct")
```

In this script, $webapp is your Web application and $svcacct is the managed service account for the application pool that is running Excel Services.

To identify the service account, go to Central Administration ➪ Security ➪ Service Account. Under Credential Management, find the application pool that is running the Excel Services Application. For PowerPivot single-server install, this is the "Service Application Pool — SharePoint Web Services Default" or "Service Application Pool — SharePoint Web Services System," as shown in Figure 9-14.

FIGURE 9-14: Finding the application pool linked to Excel Services

Claims to Windows Token (Geneva) Service Issues

The issues related to the Claims to Windows token service typically revolve around the delegation error message, "The data connection uses Windows authentication and user credentials could not be delegated," as shown in Figure 9-15.

FIGURE 9-15: "User credentials could not be delegated error"

This error message is part of the reason why some may believe that Kerberos is required for PowerPivot. This is a generic delegation error message that would also occur if you had connection issues between Excel Services and a traditional Analysis Services server located on another box (that is, this is a multi-hop scenario that would require Kerberos). The message clearly states that the data connection uses Windows Authentication and user credentials could not be delegated, so this is an understandable presumption.

For more information about the use of Kerberos, see the components discussion in Chapter 10.

The key points to remember are that the SharePoint Security Token Service receives the Web request from the client to the WFE, and generates a new identity security token that represents the user (for example, it contains attributes such as username, policies, roles, and so on), as opposed to using the user's actual security context from Active Directory, LDAP, and so on. From this point on, the identity token (more commonly known as the *claims token*) is used to represent the user throughout the entire farm.

This means that when you go from the WFE to Excel Calculation Services to PowerPivot System Service, the claims token is used to identify the user because these are all claims-aware. While Analysis Services VertiPaq Engine Service is not claims-aware, the PowerPivot System Service takes care of that by re-hydrating the identity token and applying the Windows authentication rights of the PowerPivot System Service in order to connect to Analysis Services.

So, why would you receive a delegation error message? If the Claims to Windows Token Service (c2wts) is offline, the connection from the PowerPivot System Service to the Analysis Services in VertiPaq mode will fail because the claims token cannot be converted to a Windows token. As of SharePoint 2010, Excel Services only supports claims, so it is not capable of performing any delegation of Windows NT authentication to Analysis Services. Even if Excel Services supported NT authentication, it would not be capable of this delegation, because you would have a multi-hop scenario since you would be going from the WFE to multiple components on the App Server (therefore requiring Kerberos).

To solve this problem, you must log on to the SharePoint WFEs and SharePoint App Servers, and then ensure that the Claims to Windows Token Service (c2wts) is up and running, as shown in Figure 9-16. (Go to Central Administration ➪ System Settings ➪ "Manage Services on Server" and ensure that you have chosen the correct server indicated with the Server drop-down in the top

Service	Status	Action
Access Database Service	Stopped	Start
Application Registry Service	Stopped	Start
Business Data Connectivity Service	Stopped	Start
Central Administration	Started	Stop
Claims to Windows Token Service	Started	Stop
Document Conversions Launcher Service	Stopped	Start
Document Conversions Load Balancer Service	Stopped	Start
Excel Calculation Services	Started	Stop

FIGURE 9-16: Claims to Windows Token Service within the SharePoint Central Administration UI

right.) To do this, ensure that you turn on the service within the SharePoint UI. If you only turn it on within the Service Control Manager (that is, `services.msc`), in all likelihood, the service will be turned off by SharePoint to match the service state as indicated within the SharePoint UI.

SharePoint has health rules that check to ensure that all SharePoint services are running in the state defined by SharePoint. So, if the SharePoint UI has the Claims to Windows Token Service turned off, eventually, so will the service within the Service Control Manager.

 For some additional references on troubleshooting Excel Services to Analysis Services connectivity and delegation, see the postings at `http://bit.ly/cotGDb` *("Troubleshooting PowerPivot Excel Services connectivity") and at* `http://bit.ly/9QQ7Vt` *("Excel Services delegation").*

SQL Server Service Issues

After you click on your PowerPivot workbook within SharePoint, Excel Services should be able to render the workbook, provided it has access rights to the SharePoint content database. Once you click on a slicer, Excel Services reaches out to the PowerPivot System Service and, ultimately, the Analysis Services VertiPaq Engine Service. But you may get an unexpected error message, as shown in Figure 9-17.

The most common reason this error occurs is because of some configuration issue with Analysis Services VertiPaq Engine Service and/or SQL Server Browser (to make it possible to find the Analysis Services VertiPaq Engine Service). Possible solutions to this problem include the following:

FIGURE 9-17: Connection to external data source error

➤ Ensure that SQL Server Analysis Services (in VertiPaq mode) and SQL Server PowerPivot System Service are turned on for all of the SharePoint App Servers. Remember, this must be turned on within the SharePoint UI (similar to the Claims to Windows Token Service discussed previously), as opposed to the Service Control Manager, as shown in Figure 9-18.

Secure Store Service	Started	Stop
SharePoint Foundation Search	Stopped	Start
SharePoint Server Search	Stopped	Start
SQL Server Analysis Services	Started	Stop
SQL Server PowerPivot System Service	Started	Stop

FIGURE 9-18: PowerPivot Services within the SharePoint UI

➤ Ensure that SQL Server Browser is turned on and set to "automatic" on all of the SharePoint App Servers.

➤ As mentioned previously, you may want to first open up the firewall port for SQL Server Browser (UDP 1434), and then provide the Analysis Services Engine Service access through the firewall. Remember that ports 2382 and 2383 are not needed for PowerPivot to work within the SharePoint farm. They are just needed so that client tools such as SQL Server Profiler and SSMS can connect to the service.

 For more information on why it is so important to turn on Analysis Services within the SharePoint UI instead of the Service Control Manager, see the aptly named blog posting "Why you shouldn't stop/start Analysis Services from SCM when running in SharePoint Integration Mode" at `http://bit.ly/4yEBnx`.

Configuration Issues

This section examines configuration issues within the SharePoint farm infrastructure itself. While the error messages are similar to the ones examined in the previous sections, even after following the guidance outlined previously, you may still run into issues with your PowerPivot environment.

As noted earlier in this chapter, this is the time to open up SQL Server Profiler, Event Logs, and/or examine the ULS logs to see if you can understand the problem. What follows are some examples.

Services Are Not Running and/or Do Not Have Access Rights

Earlier, in the section "Excel Services Access Rights to the Content Database," you learned about how different managed accounts (that is, in this case Windows NT accounts) can and should be applied to different application pools so that the different services running within SharePoint (for example, PowerPivot System Service, Excel Services, and so on) can run under a different managed account than the SharePoint Farm Administrator. In that discussion, you learned that it was important for Excel Services to have rights to the content database.

But there are a lot of system resources within SharePoint that need access to these different services. So, if you are using different managed accounts for your different application pools (again, a good idea), ensure that the managed account you are using is also part of the `WSS_WPG` NT group on your SharePoint WFE and App Servers. This is aptly described by the following description of the `WSS_WPG` properties:

```
Members of this group have read access to system resources used
    by Microsoft SharePoint Foundation.
```

 For more information concerning the file and permissions for Office SharePoint Server 2007 (2010 is not all that different), see "Files and permissions for Office SharePoint Server 2007" at `http://bit.ly/DX2Nq` *and "Account permissions and security settings (Office SharePoint Server)" at* `http://bit.ly/7jwmXr`*.*

Cannot Access OLAP Backup Folder

When you try to click on a slicer within Excel Services after the workbook has been successfully rendered, in the Event Log, you may receive a message saying, "Cannot access OLAP Backup folder." In the ULS logs, you will see the following much more verbose error message for the area of `SSAS Mid-Tier Usage` (which is the PowerPivot System Service):

```
EXCEPTION:
System.ServiceModel.FaultException`1[System.ServiceModel.ExceptionDetail]:
    Access to the path 'C:\Program Files\Microsoft SQL Server\
    MSAS10_50.GEMINIBI\OLAP\Backup\Sandboxes\Default PowerPivot Service
    Application' is denied…
```

For whatever reason, when this occurs, the managed account that is running the application pool used by PowerPivot System Service does not have access to the `C:\Program Files\...\OLAP\Backup` folder. Recall from the "Troubleshooting Tools" section earlier in this chapter (and other discussions throughout this book) that the `OLAP\Backup` folder is used to store detached copies of the VertiPaq databases so they can be quickly re-attached upon request. If the PowerPivot System Service does not have access rights to this folder, databases cannot be attached or detached; therefore, you have no database access.

This often happens because the managed account running the application pool for the PowerPivot System Service no longer has access. In addition to this managed account being added to the `WSS_WPG` NT group, it should also be added to the `SQLServerMSASUser$<Server Name>$POWERPIVOT` NT group. It is the NT group that gives the necessary access rights and privileges for the Analysis Services Engine Service.

How to Retract PowerPivotFarm.wsp

When you're configuring a number of Web applications within your SharePoint farm, it is more than conceivable that one of the actions you will perform is to retract the `PowerPivotFarm.wsp`. The SharePoint solution package contains all of the PowerPivot customizations for your SharePoint farm, including the PSS Proxy. Perhaps you want to put this on another Web application, or perhaps it's for maintenance. Regardless of the reason, the point is that how you would normally expect to do this is to go to Central Administration ➪ System Settings ➪ Farm Management ➪ Manage Farm Solutions, click on `PowerPivotFarm.wsp`, and click Retract.

The problem is that if you do it this way, Central Administration may no longer work. To do this safely, use the following command to safely remove the PowerPivot Farm solution:

```
Stsadm.exe -o retractsolution -name powerpivotwebapp.wsp -local
        -url %ADMIN_WEBSITE%
```

Data Refresh Not Working If PowerPivot System Service and Farm Account Are Different

In order for the PowerPivot data refresh feature to work, the SharePoint Farm account and the PowerPivot System Service account must be the same account. The reason for this is because the SharePoint Farm account is the only account that is allowed to access the Secure Store Service (SSS) database. For data refresh to work, it will need access to the SSS to obtain the security rights, hence this requirement.

Off Network PowerPivot for SharePoint Scenario

Dave Wickert created a great blog posting called "Taking your PowerPivot server off the network," which you can find at: `http://bit.ly/b5epPS`. The basic scenario is that you installed PowerPivot for SharePoint onto your laptop, and now you're going to show your wonderful PowerPivot workbooks within the PowerPivot Gallery. Yet, now your laptop is no longer connected to a domain controller, so there is no way to do the conversion between the claim identity token to a Windows NT authentication (which occurs in the interaction between Excel Services, OLE DB provider, PowerPivot System Service, and Analysis Services Engine Service, as discussed in more detail in Chapter 10).

So, how do you work around this problem? You must ensure that you created and configured the `PowerPivotUnattendedAccount` as noted in the installation instructions of Chapters 2 and 8. Then, you must perform the following configuration changes.

To set the Excel Services Unattended Account, go to Central Administration ➪ Manage Service Applications ➪ Excel Service Application (for example, `ExcelServiceApp1`) ➪ Global Settings. Under the External Data pane, populate the Application ID text field with `PowerPivotUnattendedAccount`.

Next, change the Excel Services Authentication Settings for your workbooks. This will require you to change all workbooks that you want to work in this mode. To do this, follow these steps:

1. Click on the PivotTable of your workbook.

2. Go to PivotTable Tools ➪ Options ➪ Change Data Source ➪ Connection Properties.

3. Click on Definition. Click Excel Services, and then click on Authentication Settings.

4. As shown in Figure 9-19, select None. Click OK twice, and then save the workbook.

FIGURE 9-19: Excel Services Authentication Settings dialog

You will need to perform Step 4 for all workbooks, including the workbooks that power the PowerPivot Management dashboard if you want to demo them off network.

Now you can take your workbooks and SharePoint Server off network without worrying about domain controllers or claims to Windows token service.

Changing Passwords

Before you make any changes to your passwords, be aware that, as part of SharePoint 2010, SharePoint itself may be able to automatically handle password changes. The documentation can be found at "Plan automatic password change (SharePoint Foundation)" at `http://bit.ly/3kv6zL`. With this technique, you would still need to take care of resetting the passwords for services themselves (such as SQL Server, Analysis Services, and Reporting Services), but all the application pools, Web applications, and services can be configured through SharePoint itself.

However, in case you prefer to do it manually, or you must do it manually because changing passwords automatically does not work, Table 9-2 provides a handy checklist.

TABLE 9-2: Checklist for Changing Passwords

STEP	TASK	DESCRIPTION
1	Change Service Account passwords	Change the Service Account passwords using the Services Control Manager for the various services involved, including SQL Server, Analysis Services, and Reporting Services.

2	Update password for the account used by Central Administration Application Pool (all commands should be executed in the `%commonprogramfiles%\ Microsoft Shared\Web Server Extensions\14\ bin` folder)	Log in to the SharePoint WFE that hosts the Central Administration Web site using the Farm Administrator account. From an administrative command prompt window, type the following*:
		
		```stsadm -o updatefarmcredentials -userlogin DomainName\UserName -password NewPassword```
		
		On all other servers in the server farm, from an administrative command prompt window, type the following:
		
		```stsadm -o updatefarmcredentials -userlogin DomainName\UserName -password NewPassword -local```
		
		Restart IIS by typing the following in an administrative command prompt window:
		
		```iisreset /noforce```

3	Update the password for the Web applications application pool account	From an administrative command prompt, type the following: ```stsadm -o updateaccountpassword -userlogin DomainName\UserName -password NewPassword -noadmin```
4	Update the password for the Windows SharePoint Services Help Search Service account. This step is only necessary if you have SharePoint Search installed and enabled.	From an administrative command prompt, type the following: ```stsadm.exe -o spsearch -farmcontentaccessaccount DomainName\ UserName -farmcontentaccesspassword NewPassword```

continues

TABLE 9-2 *(continued)*

STEP	TASK	DESCRIPTION

5	Update the password for the Windows SharePoint Services Help Search Service default content access account. This step is only necessary if you have SharePoint Search installed and enabled.	From an administrative command prompt, type the following:
		
		`stsadm.exe -o spsearch`
		`-farmcontentaccessaccount DomainName\`
		`UserName -farmcontentaccesspassword`
		`NewPassword`
		
		At this point, you should be able to connect to the SharePoint Central Administration, if you could not before.

6	Configure Managed Accounts	Go to the SharePoint Central Administration ⇨ Security ⇨ Configure Managed Accounts. Go the account that requires the password change and click Edit. Within the Credential Management pane, check the Change Password Now checkbox, and change the password as appropriate. That is, choose "Use existing password" if the password has already been changed, and use the "Set account password to new value" if you need to change the password now.
7	Reset the application pools	It may be necessary to reset the application pools if the system is not running as expected. First, do a `iisreset` to see if the password change takes by entering the following command: `iisreset` If this does not work, open the IIS Manager ⇨ Application Pools and update each of the application pools whose identity has an account that needs its password changed. Once you do this, restart the application pool.

*If the `updatefarmcredentials` step fails to work, ensure that the SQL Server Service for your SharePoint databases and your SharePoint 2010 Timer service (both accessible from `services.msc`) are running. A common reason why this step does not work, especially on a single-server PowerPivot for SharePoint install, is because both services are running under the Farm Administrator account, and its password is no longer valid.

INSIDE POWERPIVOT

What is sometimes amazing about a password change is the number of details and individual steps required to update the SharePoint farm. What is even more amazing is that it took a pretty powerful brain trust to come up with the instructions!

So, kudos should be offered to the various people that were involved in this process, including Troy Starr (SharePoint Guru), Ashvini Sharma (Analysis Services and SSIS guru), and Leon Cyril (PowerPivot extraordinaire). Note the source for Steps 2 through 5 appearing in Table 9-2 is `http://support.microsoft.com/kb/934838`.

MONITORING POWERPIVOT SERVICES

One of the key issues concerning PowerPivot is controlling the chaos created by the use of spread-marts. IT professionals need a way to determine what workbooks are popular, what data sources are being accessed, what failures are happening, and so on. The PowerPivot Management dashboard shown in Figure 9-20 helps to provide this information. You can access this dashboard by going to Central Administration ➪ General Application Settings ➪ PowerPivot Management Dashboard.

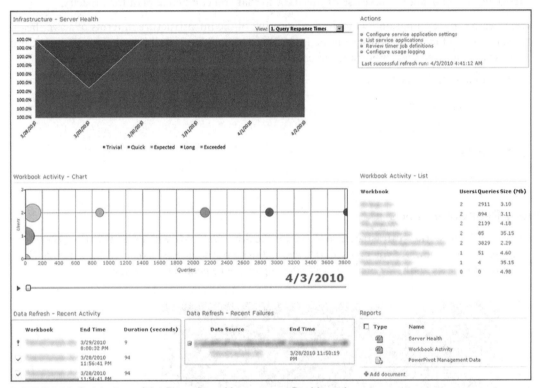

FIGURE 9-20 Quick view of the PowerPivot Management Dashboard

The PowerPivot Management dashboard can be broken down into the following main areas:

➤ *Infrastructure — Sever Health* — Provides a health view of your PowerPivot servers.

➤ *Workbook Activity* — Provides a high-level overview of the users and queries broken down by workbook.

➤ *Actions* — On the top right of the dashboard, the Actions menu allows an administrator to configure PowerPivot-specific settings within the SharePoint farm.

➤ *Data refresh* — Provides a breakdown of the recent activities and failures for PowerPivot data refresh.

➤ *Reports* — Allows a user to view the source Excel workbooks and databases for the PowerPivot Management dashboard.

Because of the amount of information provided in the PowerPivot Management dashboard, let's take an individual look at each Web part of the dashboard.

Monitoring Infrastructure (Server Health)

The PowerPivot Management dashboard provides you with the tools and data to better understand what reports are actually being viewed and used. As your enterprise becomes larger, it will become increasingly important to make use of this data so that you can better plan for capacity.

Let's begin this examination by tackling monitoring of the infrastructure in terms of server health, since this is the first chart you see on the PowerPivot Management dashboard. This Web part provides you with three very important indicators of your server health:

➤ Query Response Times

➤ Average Instance CPU

➤ Average Instance Memory

➤ Activity

➤ Performance

Query Response Times

Figure 9-21 shows the "Infrastructure — Server Health" Web part when selecting the *Query Response Times* view. As you can see, the vast majority of the queries executed took a trivial amount of time, with the "worst" queries running in the Expected time frame.

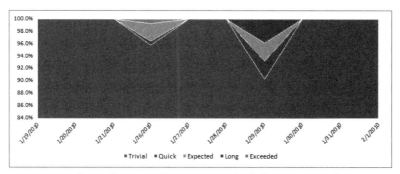

FIGURE 9-21: Query Response Times view in the "Infrastructure — Server Health" Web part

The purpose of this chart is to provide you with a quick overview of whether the vast majority of the queries are running as expected, or whether they are running slow. Once you start seeing more long-running queries (such as Long or Exceeded categories), you will want to consider determining which queries are running long and why (for example, is there a particular set of workbooks taking a long time). Or, perhaps you require more App Servers to handle the increased query load.

While having query response time categories of Trivial, Quick, Expected, Long, and Exceeded is great, what do these categories actually mean? To get some concrete definitions, go to Central Administration ➪ General Application Settings ➪ PowerPivot ➪ Configure Service Application Settings. The very last set of configurations under the Usage Data Collection pane contain the query response time definitions. Table 9-3 summarizes the default definitions.

TABLE 9-3: Query Response Time Category Definitions

CATEGORY	DEFINITION (UPPER LIMIT IN MILLISECONDS)
Trivial	0 < time < 500
Quick	500 < time < 1000
Expected	1000 < time < 3000
Long	3000 < time < 10000
Exceeded	>= 10000

Average Instance CPU

A fast way to determine if you have slow queries caused by your CPU load is to switch the Average Instance CPU view within the "Infrastructure — Server Health" Web part. As you can see in Figure 9-22, the line represents the SharePoint App Servers that has PowerPivot installed. The CPU usage is so small that it is barely registering in this view, so CPU is not a concern here.

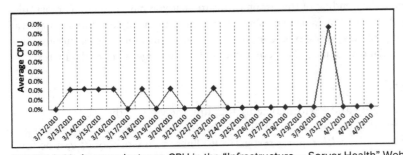

FIGURE 9-22 Average Instance CPU in the "Infrastructure — Server Health" Web part

While the view on this chart looks great, for environments with more PowerPivot workbooks that involve more complex calculations, this may not be the case. Understanding if you are pegging CPU in this view allows you to know the symptoms concerning slow query response times, which may include complex calculations, too many users accessing the system concurrently, and so on. Without reducing the number of users who can access the system and/or the complexity of calculations, having high CPU usage across all of your SharePoint App Servers with PowerPivot installed is an indicator that you need more PowerPivot-enabled SharePoint App Servers to handle your workload.

Average Instance Memory

Perhaps memory is a concern for your environment. After all, if the users have very large workbooks, a lot of your memory may be quickly used up by your environment — though this is unlikely, as, according to the Query Response Time, the queries are coming back pretty fast. If you were to take a quick look at the Average Instance Memory view, as shown in Figure 9-23, it would be apparent that memory is not an issue for this environment.

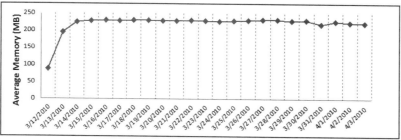

FIGURE 9-23 Average Instance Memory in the "Infrastructure — Server Health" Web part

As you can see, the example system is only using a maximum of roughly 250 MB. Yet, it is also interesting to note that, while there was so little CPU utilized (it barely registered), it only took 20 workbooks averaging 4.19 MB with only two users querying each workbook to use almost 250 MB of memory. (You'll learn more about how this was determined shortly.)

The lesson learned here is that it does not take much to use memory within PowerPivot. Remember, the VertiPaq engine is an in-memory BI engine that puts the entire column-store database into memory. So, it will be important to watch the trending of this graph to ensure that you have enough memory allocated for your SharePoint App Server(s). When you start getting close to the maximum memory available on your SharePoint App Servers, you should consider adding more memory and/or more servers to handle the larger volume of databases queried concurrently, and/or the larger sizes of databases.

Activity and Performance

While you can view the Activity and Performance by toggling the view within the Infrastructure — Server Health Web part, you will get a better view of this data by viewing the *Workbook Activity* and *Server Health* reports respectively. These two workbooks can be found on the bottom right of the PowerPivot Management dashboard under the heading Reports. (You'll learn more about this section of the PowerPivot Management dashboard later in this chapter in the section, "Reports.")

Workbook Activity

Let's take a detailed look at the dashboard Web parts concerning individual workbooks.

Chart

To get a good grasp of the workbook activity chart shown in Figure 9-24, you really need to play with it yourself. This isn't just a regular chart, but a Silverlight animation that allows you to view the changes in the number of queries (X-axis) by the number of users (Y-axis) over time. (Note the play button and sliding bar at the bottom of the chart.)

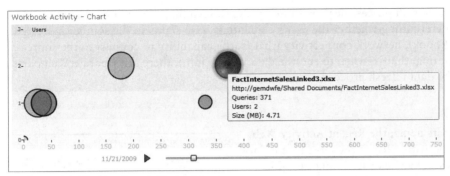

FIGURE 9-24: Workbook activity chart

But it isn't just all fun and games here. If you see an interesting pattern (such as the rightmost bubble indicating the most number of users and queries), you can pause the sliding window, hover over it, and see the attributes associated with the bubble, such as the name and location of the workbook, as well as the number of users, queries, and size. When you click on the bubble, you will also be able to edit the attributes of the workbook, including the title, managed key-

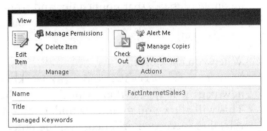

FIGURE 9-25: Editing the attributes of the workbook from the bubble

words, permissions, and so forth, as shown in Figure 9-25. If you click on the Name, you will also be able to configure the settings (for example, check out, alerts, manage permissions, and so on) of the workbook as well.

List

While the bubble chart is great, perhaps all you want is to view and sort the list of workbooks by their activity attributes (queries, users, and size). You can quickly do this by using the Workbook Activity — List Web part. Previously, when analyzing average instance memory, the number of users versus memory used (20 workbooks with an average size of 4.18 MB) was determined by referring to the Workbook Activity — List shown in Figure 9-26.

Data Refresh

One activity that has a lot going on in the background is the PowerPivot data refresh process. As noted

Workbook	Queries	Users	Size (Mb)
FactInternetSales3Linked.xlsx	516	3	4.76
ITOps.xlsx	1899	3	4.48
Gemini Solution Healthcare Audit CTP3.xlsx	243	2	4.98
FactInternetSales3.xlsx	59	2	4.68
FactInternetSales3GemDSQL2.xlsx	178	2	4.77
FactInternetSales3Linked.xlsx	1864	2	4.76
FactInternetSalesLinked3.xlsx	1013	2	4.77
Gemini3.xlsx	131	2	1.37
	29	1	1.37
FactInternetSales3.xlsx	46	1	4.56
1 2			

FIGURE 9-26: Workbook Activity — List

throughout this book, the data refresh process has a dedicated Timer Job to fire off data refresh processes for each workbook that has data refresh enabled. Once the data refresh process is completed, each workbook is populated with the latest set of information.

Because the data refresh process deals with many issues, including (but not limited to) access rights (that is, determining whether the user's credentials have rights to the sources indicated within the workbook), network connectivity (that is, the capability to connect to the source systems), and timing (that is, when to run the data refresh jobs), there are separate Web parts to help monitor the data refresh process.

Recent Activity

As indicated by its name, the Recent Activity Web part provides you with a list of the most recent data refresh activities. As you can see in Figure 9-27, within this Web part, most of the data refreshes have occurred without any issues. But there were a couple of issues that popped up, and from here you will want analyze why a particular data refresh event failed.

When you click on the `FactInternetSales3Linked.xlsx` workbook, a new page will appear that drills down to the details. This will allow you to quickly understand which refreshes succeeded or failed, and the potential reasons why a failure occurred. From the example page shown in Figure 9-28, you can tell the 12/31/2009 data refresh failed because there was an authentication issue between the workbook and its data source.

Data Refresh - Recent Activity

	Workbook	End Time	Duration (seconds)
!	Gemini Solution Healthcare Audit CTP3.xlsx	2/2/2010 9:31:36 AM	77
✓	FactInternetSales3Linked.xlsx	1/8/2010 4:16:08 PM	28
✓	FactInternetSales3Linked.xlsx	1/8/2010 4:00:28 PM	0
✓	FactInternetSales3Linked.xlsx	1/6/2010 5:15:48 PM	47
✓	FactInternetSales3Linked.xlsx	1/6/2010 5:08:47 PM	0
✓	FactInternetSales3Linked.xlsx	1/4/2010 3:01:48 PM	82
✓	FactInternetSales3Linked.xlsx	1/4/2010 2:54:33 PM	0
!	FactInternetSales3Linked.xlsx	12/31/2009 5:00:43 PM	16
✓	FactInternetSales3Linked.xlsx	12/29/2009 8:00:51 PM	24
✓	FactInternetSales3Linked.xlsx	12/29/2009 7:50:34 PM	0

1 2 3 4 5 6 7

FIGURE 9-27: "Data Refresh — Recent Activity" Web part

Name	FactInternetSales3Linked.xlsx
Current Status	Succeeded
Last Successful Refresh	01/08/2010 16:16:08
Next Scheduled Refresh	Unscheduled Configure Schedule ...

	Started	Completed	Time	Status	Comments
⊞	01/08/2010 16:15:40	01/08/2010 16:16:08	00:00:28	Succeeded	
	01/08/2010 16:00:28	01/08/2010 16:00:28	00:00:00	Succeeded	The data refresh schedule has been changed by GEMDOMAIN\Producer.
⊞	01/06/2010 17:15:01	01/06/2010 17:15:48	00:00:47	Succeeded	
	01/06/2010 17:08:47	01/06/2010 17:08:47	00:00:00	Succeeded	The data refresh schedule has been changed by GEMDOMAIN\geminiservice.
⊞	01/04/2010 15:00:26	01/04/2010 15:01:48	00:01:22	Succeeded	
	01/04/2010 14:54:33	01/04/2010 14:54:33	00:00:00	Succeeded	The data refresh schedule has been changed by GEMDOMAIN\Producer.
⊞	12/31/2009 17:00:27	12/31/2009 17:00:43	00:00:16	Failed	OLE DB or ODBC error: SQL Server Network Interfaces: The clocks on the client and server machines are skewed. ; 42000; OLE DB provider "SQLNCLI10" for linked server "gemdsql2" returned message "Cannot generate SSPI context".; 01000. The process operation ended because the number of errors encountered during processing reached the defined limit of allowable errors for the operation. An error occurred while the partition, with the ID of '9f217ca9-5116-4515-97a6-50684786a4b4', Name of 'DimGeography' was being processed. The operation has been cancelled.

FIGURE 9-28: Data refresh activities for a single workbook

Recent Failures

In Figure 9-28, notice that the failure occurred back on 12/31/2009, and, since then, the data refreshes for the `FactInternetSales3Linked.xlsx` workbook succeeded. Because of this, the PowerPivot Management dashboard also includes the Recent Failures Web part (Figure 9-29) that focuses only on the most recent data refresh failures. With this information in hand, you can go back to the Recent Activity Web part and drill down to the reason why a particular workbook data refresh failed.

FIGURE 9-29: "Data Refresh — Recent Failures" Web part

Reports

As shown in Figure 9-30, the Reports Web part within the PowerPivot Management dashboard contains the Excel workbooks that are the source for the PowerPivot Management dashboard charts.

FIGURE 9-30: Reports Web part

You can click on the workbook itself (for example, `Server Health.xlsx`) and you will see an Excel Services view of the same Query Response Times chart, as shown in Figure 9-31.

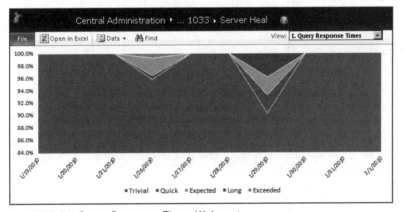

FIGURE 9-31: Query Response Times Web part

Once you click on Open in Excel, however, you are then connected to an Excel workbook that is connected directly to the `ITOps Sandbox` cube. So, if you want to analyze your PowerPivot farm metrics, you can make use of the same PowerPivot for Excel tool to understand the efficacy of your environment.

There are two pre-made reports (`Server Health.xlsx` provides Performance data, while `Workbook Activity.xlsx` provides Activity data) that populate the PowerPivot Management dashboard Web parts. They are also available for your own analysis. Also included is the `PowerPivot Management.odc` file that contains the link to the ITOps_<GUID> database. When you click on the .odc link, Excel 2010 will open up and connect to the cube, as shown in Figure 9-32.

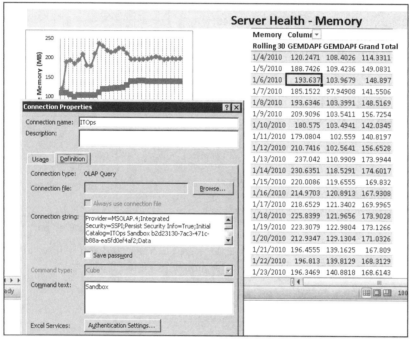

FIGURE 9-32: Opening the Server Health.xlsx file to perform ad hoc analysis against the IT Ops Sandbox

A quick peek inside the .odc file shows the following code snippet. Excel will connect by using the OLE DB for Analysis Services Provider (MSOLAP.4) using the PowerPivot Management Data.xlsx workbook as its source. This workbook contains only the source ITOps database. No charts or tables are included within this workbook.

```
<odc:Connection odc:Type="OLEDB">
  <odc:ConnectionString>
       Provider=MSOLAP.4;
       Initial Catalog=;
       Data Source=http://$SharePoint WFE$/
           PowerPivot Management/[GUID]/
           PowerPivot Management Data.xlsx;
       </odc:ConnectionString>
       <odc:CommandType>Cube</odc:CommandType>
       <odc:CommandText>Sandbox</odc:CommandText>
</odc:Connection>
```

 Note that this XML has been modified for readability.

You also have the capability to create your own reports based on the `ITOps Sandbox` database and its source. The source for the `ITOps` database is the `DefaultPowerPivotServiceApplicationDB[GUID]` SQL database, which should be on the same server as your SharePoint content and configuration databases. As noted in Chapter 11, you can also create your reports against the SQL source database.

Dashboard Settings

Meanwhile, do not forget that there are two important settings for your PowerPivot Management dashboard data. Go to Central Administration ➪ General Application Settings ➪ PowerPivot ➪ "Configure server application settings." Scroll down to the Usage Data Collection pane. Here you will notice the following:

➤ *Query Reporting Interval* — Data is refreshed for the dashboard every 300 seconds (by default).

➤ *Usage Data History* — By default, only 365 days of data is stored.

SECURITY

Let's now shift focus to security, and, in particular, how PowerPivot works within the context of Excel Services and SharePoint.

 This section does not examine SharePoint security in general, since this could take up an entire book in its own right.

Security Services

To begin this overview of security, let's discuss the security services utilized by PowerPivot, including the following:

➤ Secure Store Service

➤ Claims Token

Secure Store Service

The Secure Store Service is the service within SharePoint 2010 that enables you to safely and securely store credentials within your SharePoint environment. As noted throughout this book, PowerPivot uses the Secure Store Service to store credentials required for data refresh. The instructions provided in Chapter 8 include the steps on how to generate keys for the Secure Store.

As a general security best practice, you should have a policy to re-generate the key on a regular basis and store the pass phrase you used to generate the key in a separate secure location. The chance of an effective security attack is minimized against a system that has its security keys regularly changed. Additionally, before you generate the key, ensure that you back up the Secure Store database.

Claims Token

The purpose of the claims token (as part of the SharePoint Security Token Services within the context of Windows Identity Foundation) service was discussed a bit in Chapter 7 and will be discussed extensively in Chapter 10. The key point of the claims token is that you will no longer need to utilize Kerberos authentication in order to have a multi-layer farm consisting of multiple WFEs, App Servers, and dedicated SQL Server boxes. All communication within the SharePoint farm uses the claims token.

Also, a number of services running within SharePoint are claims-aware. For example, because PowerPivot for SharePoint is comprised of both PowerPivot System Service and Analysis Services, and because PowerPivot System Service is claims-aware, you will not need Kerberos authentication in order to enable PowerPivot for SharePoint. But if you are trying to connect to traditional Analysis Services on a separate server, then you would need to turn on Kerberos in order to handle the multi-hop communication between the WFE, Excel Services, and Analysis Services.

Site Access

When discussing security as it relates to site access, it's important to keep in mind several issues, including the following:

➤ Saving to SharePoint

➤ SharePoint Groups

➤ Document Specific Permissions

➤ More Sites

Save to SharePoint

In other parts of this book, you have learned about the differences between using the Excel Save As option versus the SharePoint UI to upload a workbook to SharePoint 2010. Another very powerful method for uploading a workbook is to publish it by using the "Save to SharePoint" option. To publish a workbook, click on File ➪ "Save & Send" ➪ "Save to SharePoint." From here, click on the Publish Options on the right side of the pane.

As shown in Figure 9-33, with this option, you can save to SharePoint the entire workbook (the default), specific sheets, or specific items in the workbook (choosing which option is defined by the drop-down list that currently says "Sheets"). In this example, only three sheets are being saved to SharePoint/Excel Services. When users open up the workbook in Excel Services, they will only be able to see the three worksheets that have been chosen.

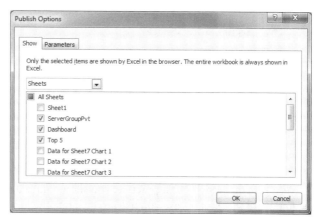

FIGURE 9-33: "Save to SharePoint" options

For more details, "Uncovering Publish to Excel Services in Excel 2010" (http://bit.ly/7imXvD) is a great post that will help you better understand publishing to Excel Services.

SharePoint Groups

Anyone who is familiar with SharePoint is probably familiar with the default SharePoint groups and their permissions. By default, the following three groups are created:

➤   Members (contribute permissions)

➤   Owners (full control)

➤   Visitors (read)

However, if users are placed in any of these groups, they can technically still download the Excel workbook rendered by Excel Services within your PowerPivot for SharePoint environment. In many cases, what you want is the user to have the capability to see the workbook within Excel Services but not actually download it.

This is important for PowerPivot for the following reasons:

➤   You want users to view the workbook, but not actually download and make undesired modifications. This prevents the dissemination of spreadmarts.

➤   With PowerPivot, all of the detailed data is actually stored within the workbook itself. You may want users to view the aggregate data but not actually look at the underlying raw data.

To accomplish this, Excel Services provides a SharePoint group called Viewers. An account in this group can open up the workbook, see the report, and even interact with the slicers, but cannot actually open the workbook in Excel. In the top part of Figure 9-34, notice that the Excel Services report does not have the "Open in Excel" button. This is because the user who opened this workbook was only in the Viewers SharePoint group, while the user who opened the lower workbook was in the Visitors SharePoint group.

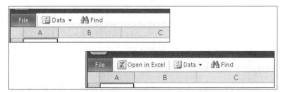

FIGURE 9-34 Toolbars of Viewers versus Visitors (SharePoint Groups)

To get access to the Viewers and other permissions, go to your site and click on Site Actions within the SharePoint ribbon. Then, click on Site Permissions.

Because you want to limit the actual dissemination of workbooks throughout the corporate landscape, following are common best practices concerning SharePoint groups:

➤   Place most of your users (for example, IW Consumers) who want to view these reports in the Viewers group so that you're in control of who can download the file.

➤ Limit the number of IW Producers who can upload or modify Excel workbooks within your farm (that is, Members group).

➤ Really limit the number of people who are placed in the Owners group, since they have full control of the site.

Document Specific Permissions

One of the options to limit user access to workbooks is to apply document-specific permissions within the PowerPivot Gallery. To access the document-specific permissions, enter the PowerPivot Gallery, click on Library within the SharePoint ribbon, and change the current view to All Documents. Click on the document for which you want to edit permissions, and then click on the Document Permissions button within the SharePoint Ribbon, as shown in Figure 9-35.

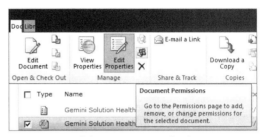

FIGURE 9-35: Edit permissions of a document

By default, the document will inherit the permissions of the PowerPivot site, as noted in Figure 9-36. In this particular case, you may want to stop inheriting permissions (the second button in the ribbon) in order to change permissions specific to this document.

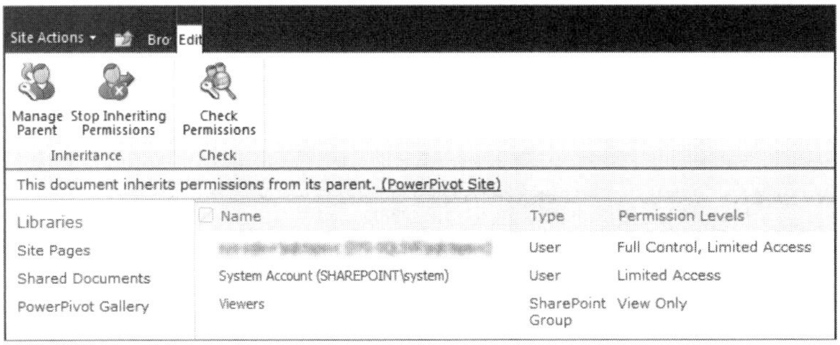

FIGURE 9-36: Manage permissions of a document

Once you click on the Stop Inheriting Permissions button, the ribbon will change and provide the option to Grant, Edit, and Remove user permissions or to Inherit permissions from the main site again, if so desired.

More Sites

You may find it easier to create a separate site within SharePoint instead of modifying the permissions of individual documents. This way, you can modify the permissions of the entire site (and all of the documents in it), instead of keeping track of custom permissions. To do this, click on Site Actions within the SharePoint ribbon, and click on New Site. Choose the PowerPivot Template, and fill in the Title and URL Name, and click Create.

Once you have created the site, click on Site Actions and click Site Permissions. You will have a view similar to Figure 9-36, except that these permissions will apply to the whole site you just created (as opposed to just a specific document). You will want to stop inheriting permissions and create a new set of SharePoint Groups that are specific to this site (click on the Create Group button within the SharePoint ribbon). Now, you will be able to create a site with a specific set of permissions for your set of users, team, management, and so on.

Infrastructure Access

When discussing security as it relates to infrastructure access, it's important to keep in mind several issues, including the following:

➤ Managed accounts

➤ Application pools

➤ PowerPivot accounts

Managed Accounts

The purpose of a managed account within SharePoint 2010 is to have one place to manage the account (for example, change passwords), and so that you can assign multiple service applications to that managed account. This avoids having to change the username and password for each service application.

To view your managed accounts, go to Central Administration ➪ Security ➪ "Configure managed accounts." This view quickly allows you to see which managed accounts you have, as well as information associated with password management (for example, password change schedule, next password change, and last password change).

But even more interesting is the Central Administration ➪ Security ➪ "Configure service account" page. As shown in Figure 9-37, this leads to the Credential Management page that notes which service applications are assigned to which managed account. Click on the drop-down list near the top of this page and you will see a list of farm accounts, Windows services, and application pools.

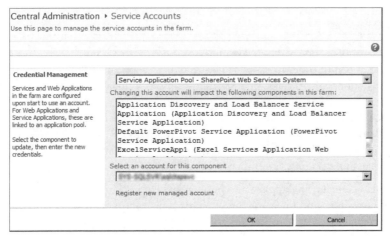

FIGURE 9-37: Multiple service applications assigned to a single application pool assigned to a managed account

From the context of PowerPivot, from here you can manage which managed account is running, for example, the Analysis Services Engine Service (Windows Service — SQL Server Analysis Services) or the Default PowerPivot Service Application (by default under the Service Application Pool — SharePoint Web Services Default). As noted previously, because these are managed accounts you can also automate the password change, making this much easier to manage.

Application Pools

As you can see from Figure 9-37, there are multiple service applications applied to a single application pool. Application pools are a configuration within IIS that allows multiple Web applications to be assigned to a single set of worker processes. Each application pool has its own allocated set of memory. Thus, different Web/service applications can operate within a smaller set of shared application pools.

In addition to using shared resources, other benefits to using application pools include the following:

➤ *Process isolation* — You have different Web service applications operating on different application pools. If one Web service application becomes overloaded, another one is not affected, because they have different worker processes.

➤ *Potential security benefit* — When you create separate application pools, the security benefit is that you can create them using different managed accounts with the least privileges. This way, if one application pool identity becomes compromised, other application pools are not necessarily compromised.

If you decide to assign different service applications with different managed accounts and permissions assigned to them, ensure that you have also done the basics, such as include the managed account within the WSS_WPG NT group (which provides read access to the SharePoint Foundation system resources) and provided the managed accounts with necessary privileges to access the different database rights required.

INSIDE POWERPIVOT

Configuring application pools is one of many examples of the cross-team collaboration that had to happen in order for PowerPivot to work. Application pools are themselves a construct of Web services, and SharePoint utilizes them to run a foundation of Web services. As noted in other chapters of this book, PowerPivot then makes use of Excel Services and SharePoint in order to function. Altogether, in order to get PowerPivot to work, collaboration was required with IIS, Windows Identity Foundation, SharePoint, SQL Server, Analysis Services, Excel Services, Excel, Office Workspace, and certainly a number of other teams.

The guidance information concerning application pools provided here came from the SharePoint gurus Troy Starr and Luca Bandinelli. This is just another small example of how many different teams worked together (in this example, SharePoint and SQLCAT) to build SharePoint and PowerPivot.

PowerPivot Accounts

After all this, when managing PowerPivot, you must be concerned with the following basic set of accounts:

➤ *PowerPivot Service Application* — This is a managed account that is assigned to the application pool for the PowerPivot Service Application. By default, refer to the managed account for the "Service Application Pool — SharePoint Web Services Default." Note that, by default, both Excel Services Application and Secure Store Service Application are assigned to this application pool as well.

➤ *Analysis Services VertiPaq Engine Service* — This is the Windows NT Service account that is assigned to run the Analysis Services in VertiPaq mode. Because of the number of health checks put in place, be sure to update the managed account associated with the engine service through the SharePoint UI. The benefits of doing this include having one location to look at all accounts, and using SharePoint automatic password change to manage the passwords for your account.

➤ *PowerPivotUnattendedAccount* — This is the data refresh account you set credentials against in Chapter 8. Remember, the connection for data refresh will occur based on the user-assigned credentials stored within the Secure Store Service. Therefore, the credentials you assign to this account should have the least privileges (for example, the capability to connect to database servers, but no actual database privileges). In this way, users do not choose the `PowerPivotUnattendedAccount` as their chosen credentials, removing a potential back door key to all of the source systems.

One thing you may have noticed as you're reading this is that there does not seem to be a lot of security information. This may imply that securing your PowerPivot for SharePoint environment is relatively straightforward and not very complex. However, that is not true, because there are a lot of best practices and guides to ensure that SharePoint itself is secure. What has been reviewed here is the potential impact of security by adding PowerPivot to a SharePoint farm. For more extensive information on SharePoint and Excel Services security best practices, refer to a SharePoint Ranger (domain expert), or other SharePoint Best Practices guides.

SUMMARY

This chapter took a roller coaster ride between the tools to troubleshoot PowerPivot, how to monitor PowerPivot Services, and some of the security aspects associated with PowerPivot for SharePoint. At this point in the book, you should have a pretty good idea of how to get your PowerPivot environment up and running, and how to use the tools to debug, monitor, and secure your environment.

In Chapter 10, though, you will learn much more about the architecture behind PowerPivot. All of the chapters up to now (including this one) have provided you with a lot of information to help you build your system from end-to-end. However, the next two chapters provide the foundational know-how for enterprise considerations.

10

Diving into the PowerPivot Architecture

WHAT'S IN THIS CHAPTER?

➤ Becoming familiar with the PowerPivot for Excel architecture

➤ Understanding Excel Services and PowerPivot for SharePoint

➤ Understanding the components and services that make up PowerPivot for SharePoint

➤ Becoming familiar with the use of claims token and Kerberos

At the end of Chapter 8, you were able to build up your PowerPivot for SharePoint multi-server installation. And, at the end of Chapter 9, you learned how to troubleshoot, monitor, and secure PowerPivot Services. Yet, how do you handle a large number of users who are querying and processing VertiPaq databases within your PowerPivot for SharePoint environment?

To help address these concerns, this chapter expands on the SharePoint services architecture flow originally discussed in Chapter 7 by diving even deeper into its components. You will learn some tips for capacity planning, and dealing with concurrency and data refresh issues. This chapter starts by reviewing the architecture details before diving into the capacity planning sections, because this will provide you with a better context on the issues concerning PowerPivot for SharePoint capacity planning.

 For a high-level overview video of PowerPivot for SharePoint enterprise best practices, you can also view the Academy Live video, "A Preview to PowerPivot Server Best Practices," by Denny Lee and Dave Wickert at http://bit.ly/5Qrq2y.

Let's begin with a review of the Excel client architecture. While this may be the simplest form of the architecture, it is also the basis of the architecture you will see behind the scenes with PowerPivot for SharePoint.

POWERPIVOT FOR EXCEL ARCHITECTURE

A simple high-level overview of the Excel architecture in relation to PowerPivot can be broken down into the core components of the PowerPivot Add-In — Analysis Services connectivity (AMO, ADOMD.NET, and MSOLAP), and the new Analysis Services Engine in VertiPaq mode as shown in Figure 10-1.

There are two ways for an Excel PivotTable to connect to traditional Analysis Services via the Microsoft OLE DB Provider for Analysis Services (MSOLAP). The most common way, shown in Figure 10-2, is for the PivotTable to connect via TCP/IP to Analysis Services. An example connection string for this type of connection is `SERVER=<$servername$>`.

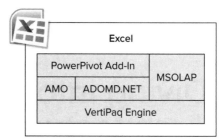

FIGURE 10-1: High-level PowerPivot for Excel component architecture

The PivotTable-to-Analysis Services Web scenario is to connect via HTTP with the MSOLAP provider to the data pump on a Web server, which itself will connect to Analysis Services (Figure 10-3). An example connection string for this type of connection is `SERVER=http://<$webserver$>/msmdpump.dll`. As a new feature of PowerPivot for SharePoint, when you connect to a PowerPivot workbook within SharePoint, it will also use the HTTP protocol. This is noted graphically as the dotted line from HTTP to SharePoint within Figure 10-3.

This leads to the Excel PowerPivot add-in. As noted in Figure 10-4, the PowerPivot add-in allows you to open up the PowerPivot Window and use the PowerPivot tools within the Office client ribbon to access the VertiPaq engine by way of AMO and ADOMD.NET. As well, the MSOLAP provider is updated to include an In-Process (In-Proc) protocol that allows an Excel PivotTable to access the In-Proc VertiPaq Engine data.

Recall that the VertiPaq engine is an in-process version of the Analysis Services Engine in VertiPaq mode, a new column-based, in-memory

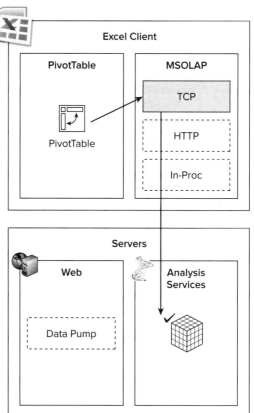

FIGURE 10-2: Excel Connectivity to Analysis Services via TCP/IP

storage mechanism that is incorporated within PowerPivot for Excel to support self-service BI. All of the calculations are performed in-memory, so there is virtually no disk I/O contention slowing down query performance. A column-based store has interesting properties concerning BI calculations, as well as compression, thus reducing the overall size of the data. In this case, the connection string for this type of connection is SERVER=$EMBEDDED$.

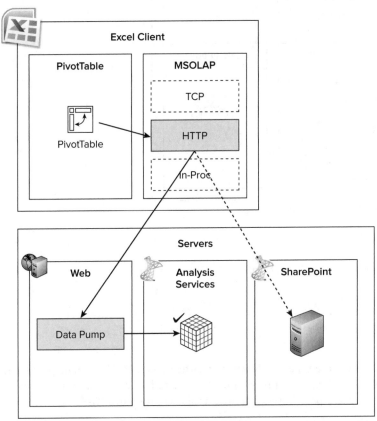

FIGURE 10-3: Excel connectivity to Analysis Services via HTTP/browser connectivity to PowerPivot workbook within SharePoint

But where is the data that the Excel PivotTable is accessing via the In-Proc protocol? As noted within the aptly titled blog posting "For Excel PowerPivot, the database is IN the workbook" (http://bit.ly/2odUpL), indeed, the PowerPivot database is embedded inside the Excel workbook. So, in the case of the In-Proc protocol, it allows the Excel PivotTable to access the data within itself.

So what is meant by the fact that the database is *in* the workbook? To better understand this, let's consider a typical PowerPivot for Excel workbook like the "SDR Healthcare Audit" Excel workbook noted in Figure 10-5. Copy the file and rename it with an extension of .zip instead of .xlsx.

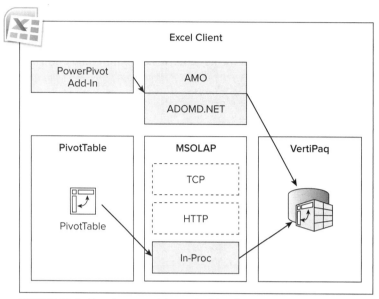

FIGURE 10-4: Excel connectivity to the VertiPaq engine via In-Proc protocol

Name	Date modified	Type	Size
SDR Healthcare Audit	11/3/2009 9:29 PM	Microsoft Excel Worksheet	5,089 KB
SDR Healthcare Audit	11/3/2009 9:29 PM	WinZip File	5,089 KB

FIGURE 10-5: Copy a PowerPivot workbook and rename it from .xlsx to .zip

The `.xlsx` extension represents the file type of a Microsoft Office Open XML format spreadsheet, which is a combination of XML and ZIP compression for file size reduction. So, like any other `.zip` file, open it up and you will see the Open XML structure, as shown in Figure 10-6.

Since it is an Excel file, open the `xl\customData` folder, and you'll notice that the bulk of the size of this workbook is all within the `item1.data` file (Figure 10-7).

Name	Type	Date modified	Size
_rels	Folder	1/1/1980 12:00 AM	
customXml	Folder	1/1/1980 12:00 AM	
docProps	Folder	1/1/1980 12:00 AM	
xl	Folder	1/1/1980 12:00 AM	
[Content_Types]....	XML Docum...	1/1/1980 12:00 AM	15,183

Name	Type	Date modified	Size
_rels	Folder	1/1/1980 12:00 AM	
itemProps1.xml	XML File	1/1/1980 12:00 AM	188
item1.data	DATA File	1/1/1980 12:00 AM	5,025,792

FIGURE 10-6: Open XML structure within the workbook

FIGURE 10-7: The item1.data file is the database within your Excel file

This is the embedded Analysis Services VertiPaq database. As noted in Chapter 7, this is the file extracted by the PowerPivot System Service and restored to an Analysis Services instance within your PowerPivot for SharePoint farm.

Going back to Excel, the fundamental idea is that the Excel PivotTable is able to access this PowerPivot embedded Analysis Services database file through the In-Proc protocol added to the MSOLAP provider, as shown in Figure 10-8. However, recall that this is an in-memory database. So, why is it accessing a file?

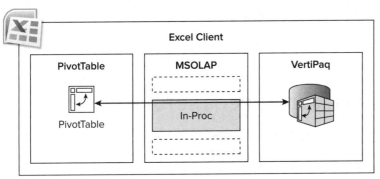

FIGURE 10-8: Simplified view of Excel PivotTable accessing the VertiPaq database

In fact, the engine is not accessing the file *per se*. What happens is that the In-Proc protocol performs the task of streaming the data from the embedded database into its own memory. So, while PowerPivot for Excel is accessing, modifying, and/or working with the data, it is, in fact, doing all of these tasks on data that is residing in memory.

As noted in the blog post "Understanding why an Excel PowerPivot workbook is so large" (`http://bit.ly/8y4Fp4`), the temporary cache of files used by PowerPivot Excel can be found in the `%TEMP%` folder. (Often, this is the `C:\Users\$MyName$\AppData\Local\Temp` folder.) Within this folder, you will find the most recent `IMBI_<GUID>` folder. Open it and you will find a structure similar to that shown in Figure 10-9.

Those who are familiar with the Analysis Services will recognize this as the Analysis Services data folder structure. Remember, this is the temporary cache of files stored onto disk. All of the calcula-

Name	Date modified	Type
ExcelMDX.0.asm	11/6/2009 11:28 PM	File folder
EXCELXLINTERNAL.0.asm	11/6/2009 11:28 PM	File folder
MS_c8b13dba-d8ae-4d8e-a547-34ac4b41...	11/6/2009 11:28 PM	File folder
System.0.asm	11/6/2009 11:28 PM	File folder
VBAMDX.0.asm	11/6/2009 11:28 PM	File folder
VBAMDXINTERNAL.0.asm	11/6/2009 11:28 PM	File folder
Administrators.0.role	11/6/2009 11:28 PM	XML Document
CryptKey.bin	11/6/2009 11:28 PM	BIN File
ExcelMDX.0.asm	11/6/2009 11:28 PM	XML Document
EXCELXLINTERNAL.0.asm	11/6/2009 11:28 PM	XML Document
master.vmp	11/6/2009 11:28 PM	VMP File
MS_c8b13dba-d8ae-4d8e-a547-34ac4b41...	11/6/2009 11:28 PM	XML Document
System.0.asm	11/6/2009 11:28 PM	XML Document
VBAMDX.0.asm	11/6/2009 11:28 PM	XML Document
VBAMDXINTERNAL.0.asm	11/6/2009 11:28 PM	XML Document

FIGURE 10-9: Cache folder structure for the PowerPivot data store

tions and modifications to the data are being performed in memory via the VertiPaq engine.

Once you have completed manipulating the data and saved your PowerPivot for workbook, the in-memory structure (cached in the `%TEMP%` folder) is then written to file. Excel streams the data from the in-process engine back to Excel, which will then place the data into the `item1.data` file stream within the workbook.

> *Another great client architecture blog is the one written by Dave Wickert. He created the original block diagram of the Excel client architecture at* `http://bit.ly/1WY74B`.

POWERPIVOT FOR SHAREPOINT ARCHITECTURE

Understanding the Excel architecture is important because it is the basis for the PowerPivot for SharePoint architecture review. This will ultimately help you better prepare for enterprise scenarios. The key breakdown for the architectural components here are as follows:

➤ Excel Services (a server-based Excel Rendering and Calculation Engine within SharePoint) is used to access PowerPivot data to calculate and display a PowerPivot workbook.

➤ Within PowerPivot for SharePoint, the Analysis Services instance within your SharePoint farm serves as an engine to host the PowerPivot data stored within the PowerPivot workbook.

➤ For both PowerPivot for Excel and PowerPivot for SharePoint, the updated Analysis Services OLE DB Provider (MSOLAP.4) allows for connectivity between the PivotTable and the database.

➤ A key component within PowerPivot for SharePoint is the PowerPivot System Service. It is responsible for connectivity to Analysis Services in VertiPaq mode, as well as PowerPivot-specific features such as data refresh.

Connection between the Excel PivotTable and the VertiPaq database is *through* the OLE DB Provider (MSOLAP.4) channel protocol. It simply directs the connections and end points together. Similarly, the PowerPivot System Services performs that task of connecting Excel Services to an Analysis Services instance within your SharePoint farm.

PowerPivot for SharePoint Services Architecture

Let's review the PowerPivot for SharePoint Services architecture discussed in Chapter 7. This review will be specific to the rendering of a PowerPivot workbook with a server action (for example, click on a slicer).

As shown in Figure 10-10, the activity flow starts with the IW Consumer user (labeled with the number 1 in the figure) who is using a browser to access a PowerPivot workbook within the PowerPivot-enabled SharePoint farm. Because an Excel workbook is being accessed, Excel Web Access (EWA) on the Web Front End (WFE) will be initiated and make a request to Excel Calculation Services (ECS) on the SharePoint App server (2).

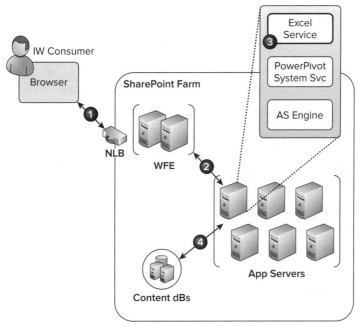

FIGURE 10-10: PowerPivot for SharePoint Services architecture review

Recall that the primary difference between a SharePoint App server and a WFE is that the latter will run the Web services for client access, while the former will run other service application services (for example, Excel Services, SharePoint Search, PowerPivot, and so on). From here, Excel Services will connect to the workbook's data by initially connecting to the PowerPivot System Service (3). It will then direct the Analysis Services engine in VertiPaq mode to extract and load the PowerPivot data from the workbook, if it has not already been done (4).

The PowerPivot System Service will then identify the location of the database if it has already been restored, or direct the Analysis Services engine in VertiPaq mode to extract the database from the workbook and restore it to one of the App Servers. It will then tell Excel Services which Analysis Services in VertiPaq mode instance to connect to so that it can perform its calculations (3). Upon completing its actions (for example, updating the query based on a selection change in a slicer), Excel Services sends this information back to EWA on the WFE (2), and then EWA will render the workbook to the user (1).

> *When a user checks out and saves the PowerPivot workbook, he or she will be interacting with the latest version of the workbook. However, all users who use the official version of the PowerPivot workbook (that is, before it was checked out) will see the older model to ensure a consistent view of the data. To achieve this, Excel and Analysis Services worked together to define how the connection is established. To achieve this, the workbook name and version name are used as part of the connection string. Because of this, you can see the changes you make periodically, and test deploy your newer solutions without impacting other users.*

Diving into Excel Services

In Figure 10-8, the basic principal was that the Excel PivotTable would connect to the VertiPaq database by way of the In-Proc protocol of the Analysis Services OLE DB driver. This is the same basic design when viewed in the context of Excel Services. To go through this concept, let's start with the components that make up Excel Services from a high level, as shown in Figure 10-11.

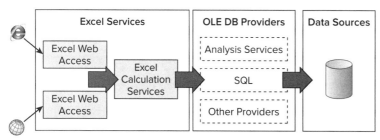

FIGURE 10-11: Excel Services connectivity to data source

Excel Services itself is made up of the following three different components:

➤ *Excel Web Access (EWA)* — This component performs the task of rendering an Excel workbook to the browser.

➤ *Excel Web Services (EWS)* — This component allows applications (that is, not a browser) to access and connect to an Excel workbook through a set of APIs.

➤ *Excel Calculation Services (ECS)* — This is the engine of Excel Services that performs all the workbook calculations.

A good reference for EWS can be found at: `http://bit.ly/SVje8`.

Whether you are connected by browser or some application, ultimately, EWA or EWS will connect to ECS in order for it to perform its calculations. ECS will then connect to the desired data source through an OLE DB provider (such as the SQL Server OLE DB provider, Analysis Services OLE DB provider, and so on), as shown in Figure 10-11.

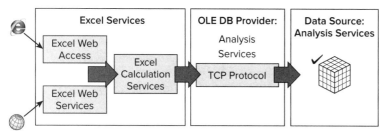

FIGURE 10-12: Excel Services connectivity to an Analysis Services database

So, let's update Figure 10-11 and address how Excel Services connects to a traditional Analysis Services database (Figure 10-12). As before, Excel Services will have either its EWA or EWS component connect to ECS. ECS will then connect to the Analysis Services OLE DB provider via the TCP protocol to the Analysis Services database.

So, taking these components and rolling back up to the services level, you now have the scenario shown in Figure 10-13. Here you can see how the Excel Services components work within the SharePoint farm. The figure has the EWA and EWS components on the WFE, and ECS is on the SharePoint App Server.

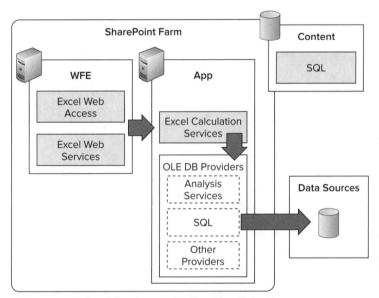

FIGURE 10-13: Excel Services within the SharePoint Farm

By default, when you install SharePoint and enable Excel Services, all three components are available on the server. However, recall that ECS is the Excel engine, so it will be more resource-intensive. Hence, the best practice is to enable Excel Calculation Services on the App Server while turning it off on the WFE. The EWA and EWS components will still be enabled on the WFE, because those components are tied to SharePoint Web services.

The Excel Services query request workflow is as follows:

1. The user requests an Excel workbook from the SharePoint WFE.

2. The EWA component on the SharePoint WFE makes a request to ECS on the SharePoint App server. Excel Services has its own load-balancing mechanism, so it will choose the ECS via round-robin, local, or workbook URL (the default), depending on how you have set this up.

For more information on this, refer to "Understanding Excel Services Load Balancing Options" at `http://bit.ly/6OFPD4`.

3. ECS connects to its OLE DB providers (for example, SQL or Analysis Services) to ultimately connect to the data source.

The Excel team has also gone to great lengths to provide more information about Excel and Excel Services. For more information, regularly review the blog at `http://blogs.msdn.com/excel/`. *For more information about the features of Excel Services, start with the blog postings "Excel 2010 Overview" at* `http://bit.ly/1Weu8X`, *"Excel Services in SharePoint 2010 Feature Support" at* `http://bit.ly/2WZMxU`, *and "Excel Services Architecture" at* `http://bit.ly/6QhLp4`.

Diving into PowerPivot Services

As shown in Figure 10-14, PowerPivot for SharePoint is actually made up of three different services:

➤ PowerPivot Web Service (located within WFE in the figure)

➤ PowerPivot System Service (located within App in the figure)

➤ Analysis Services in VertiPaq mode Engine Service (located within App in the figure)

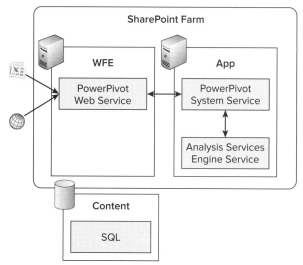

FIGURE 10-14: PowerPivot Services within a SharePoint farm

PowerPivot Web Service

Although Chapter 7 only discussed PowerPivot System Service and the Analysis Services Engine service, there is also the PowerPivot Web Service. This service allows applications such as Excel or Report Builder (or any client that is able to generate MDX, for that matter) to be re-directed to the appropriate PowerPivot System Service to work with data in a PowerPivot workbook. This is a component service installed on the WFE that allows for the redirection, and it is installed as part of the `PowerPivotWebApp.wsp`, as noted in Chapter 8. Because this component is installed as part of your Web application, it will only be installed on the SharePoint WFE servers within your SharePoint farm.

On the other hand, to install the PowerPivot System Service and Analysis Services Engine Service, as you may recall from Chapter 8, you must run a SQL Server 2008 R2 Analysis Services SharePoint Integrated Mode installation on each SharePoint App Server on which you want to have these services installed. The installation will automatically install both the PowerPivot System Service and the Analysis Services Engine Service on the desired App Server(s), because the Analysis Services Engine service in VertiPaq mode cannot work properly without the PowerPivot System Service.

PowerPivot System Service

So, what is the PowerPivot System Service? Similar to the In-Proc protocol directing traffic from the Excel PivotTable client to the VertiPaq database, this is the service that directs the Excel Services PivotTable to the Analysis Services Engine Service in VertiPaq mode. However, it also does much more than just directing traffic.

The PowerPivot System Service is also responsible for the following tasks:

➤ *Updating the instance map* — This is a table in the PowerPivot database (`PowerPivot ServiceApplicationDB[GUID]`) that tells which SharePoint application server (with PowerPivot installed) has which VertiPaq databases loaded at any point in time.

➤ *Connectivity* — Whenever Excel Services must connect to PowerPivot data already loaded on a SharePoint App Server (with PowerPivot installed), PowerPivot System Service will update and reference this instance map to connect Excel Services to the correct Analysis Services in VertiPaq mode service on the correct SharePoint App Server.

➤ *Attach/detach database* — If the database does not exist, the PowerPivot System Service will direct the Analysis Services engine in VertiPaq mode to extract the database from the Excel workbook being rendered by Excel Services, and attach it. Note that the extraction is performed by using the `OffGem.dll`, which allows the Analysis Services Engine in VertiPaq mode to extract the PowerPivot workbook data (that is, `item1.data`) from the Office Open XML custom data part to the Analysis Services data cache. From here, Excel Services loads its portion of the workbook while the Analysis Services engine makes use of `OffGem.dll` in order to grab the data and load (using the `ImageLoad` command) the `item1.data` file. The latter is initiated by the PowerPivot System Service. Chapter 6 provides more information on this.

> *By default, the Analysis Services data cache is the* `C:\Program Files\ Microsoft SQL Server\MSAS10_50.POWERPIVOT\OLAP\Backup` *folder. This folder contains actively loaded database folders, as well as a collection of detached databases, that can be quickly attached when requested. It is important to note that this cache can grow very large, and it has no predefined limits.*
>
> *However, the data cache will regularly have its files removed because of inactivity or during data refresh. If a VertiPaq database is not used for two days, it is detached to the data cache. If there are five days of non-use, then the VertiPaq database is deleted. In the case of data refresh, any old databases are immediately deleted from memory and hard disk upon completion of the task.*

➤ *Load balancing* — Similar to how Excel Services has its load-balancing mechanism to determine which App Server should perform its calculations, PowerPivot has its own mechanism to determine which server should load a newly requested workbook. The PSS Proxy is capable of making use of this information to determine to which SharePoint App Server it should attach the database. By default, the load-balancing method used is round-robin. But you also have the option to set it to health-based allocation mode, where the choice of the App Server to load the VertiPaq database is determined by how healthy the server is. An algorithm based on available resources is used to calculate a health score. The highest score is the healthiest server. More information concerning PSS and its interaction with the Proxy Endpoint is discussed in the section, "PowerPivot Services Interactions within the SharePoint Farm," later in this chapter.

➤ *Data refresh jobs* — When a user goes to the PowerPivot Gallery and schedules a data refresh job, it is ultimately executed by the PowerPivot System Service. It will use the credentials stored within the SharePoint Secure Store Service (originally entered in the Manage Data Refresh page for the PowerPivot workbook) so that it has access rights to the data required for the workbook. The PowerPivot System Service keeps the schedule and history and controls the flow of these data refresh jobs within the PowerPivot service application database.

➤ *Monitor Server Health* — The PowerPivot Health Statistics Collector Timer Job makes requests to the PowerPivot System Service to check Analysis Services system resource information, and stores that information for use by the PowerPivot Management dashboard.

➤ *Usage events* — The PowerPivot System Service also performs the task of pushing all of these usage events to the SharePoint and PowerPivot Service Application database(s).

Often, the SharePoint Web analytics service application is confused with the Web and usage events associated with PowerPivot. For server health events (including connection and response times) specific to PowerPivot, see the detailed discussion about the PowerPivot Management dashboard in Chapter 9. On the other hand, if you want to refer to Web and usage events for the entire SharePoint farm environment, then you would use the SharePoint Web Analytics Service application. For more information on how to review the SharePoint Web Analytics Services application (which uses the SharePoint usage events), refer to the blog, "Step-by-Step: Provisioning the Web Analytics Service Application on Microsoft SharePoint Server 2010 Beta," at: `http://bit.ly/5JshqN.`

Analysis Services Engine Service in VertiPaq Mode

For those familiar with traditional Analysis Services, from a high level, there are a lot of similarities between the Analysis Services instance that is running the VertiPaq mode in comparison to what is termed as traditional Analysis Services (MOLAP, HOLAP, ROLAP). If you're not familiar with traditional Analysis Services, check out the book *Professional Microsoft SQL Server Analysis Services 2008 with MDX* (Indianapolis: Wiley, 2009).

However, as noted in detail in previous chapters, this version of the Analysis Services Engine is in VertiPaq mode, which has the following significant differences:

➤ *Column-based store* — The VertiPaq engine is a column-based database engine, as opposed to the traditional row-based database engine. A column-based store can be optimal for data warehousing and BI scenarios because many aggregate calculations (for example, count, sum, and so on) are concerned with a select (that is, smaller) set of columns. Instead of obtaining all of the columns from your tables, including the ones you join with (that is, think star schema and joining to dimension tables that you need to group by), a column store such as the VertiPaq engine will only include the columns necessary to complete the calculation. This will ultimately use less resources and often results in faster queries, because less data must be processed to produce the result.

➤ *Compression* — VertiPaq has powerful compression capabilities, both because it is a column-based store, and because of repeatability within many BI systems. Most BI data sets are denormalized in the form of a star schema (or snowflake schema) for optimal query performance within a relational database management system (RDBMS). One of the characteristics of denormalization is that there are a lot of repeated values — namely the logical foreign key (FK) values to the dimension tables. Since there are not that many unique FK values, it is possible for the VertiPaq engine to organize and compress the data to a higher degree than Analysis Services in the past.

Note the use of the word "possible" here — in other words, not always. If your data set happens to have very high cardinality, and there are a lot of unique row values, there is less "compressibility" for a column-based store.

➤ *Data Dictionary* — As data is being imported into the VertiPaq engine (whether from the Excel client or during a data refresh), the re-organization to the column-based store occurs at the same time. This organization occurs in memory, which is why so much memory is used during a data import. One of the additional optimizations that occurs is that of the creation of data dictionaries, where the engine converts values into tokens (for example, 1 for Male, 2 for Female, and so on) for better compressibility.

What is interesting about this tokenization is that there is a slight difference in thinking when you import your data. It can be to your advantage to simply import the fact tables already joined to the dimension tables, so, instead of having the FK ID value, you have the actual descriptive value that the user would slice on. Since the engine tokenizes all of the values anyway, you would use less space by removing an unneeded key value, and you would remove the need to perform a join within the data.

➤ *In-memory* — With all of this compressibility and tokenization (as well as other optimizations) involved, the result is that many self-service BI scenarios can, in fact, be performed in-memory. With the possibility that tens or hundreds of millions of rows can be compressed into memory within the column-based store, why bother with disk I/O bottlenecks that may slow down performance? Instead, as discussed in previous chapters, your processor and memory resources are more optimally utilized so that you can get your answers faster. This does mean that your client and servers will require more memory and processor cores, but with the steadily decreasing cost of memory and processor cores, why not get the best bang for your buck, and get the answer faster instead?

There are a number of deep, technical SQL papers (which are applicable to Analysis Services) that discuss the topic of disk I/O and how it may impact query performance, including "Predeployment I/O Best Practices" (`http://bit.ly/3sseZL`*), "Disk Partition Alignment Best Practices for SQL Server" (*`http://bit.ly/2sdyAI`*), and "Accelerating Microsoft adCenter with Microsoft SQL Server 2008 Analysis Services" (*`http://bit.ly/ORKYF`*).*

PowerPivot Services Interactions within the SharePoint Farm

Earlier in this chapter, you learned about how Excel Services works within the SharePoint farm, and interacts with the services included as part of the PowerPivot for SharePoint installation. So, for a moment, let's focus back on the SharePoint App Server that holds ECS, which will ultimately connect to the Analysis Services in VertiPaq mode service to connect to the database.

To do this, Excel Services will first connect via the Analysis Services OLE DB Provider (MSOLAP.4). As noted in Figure 10-15, Excel Services queries are directed to a traditional Analysis Services cube by way of the TCP protocol. Any communication from the PowerPivot System Service to another SharePoint farm that is PowerPivot-enabled will use the HTTP protocol. Most importantly, Excel Services connects to the PowerPivot System Service in the same SharePoint farm through the channel protocol, which is analogous to the In-Proc protocol used by the Excel client to the database.

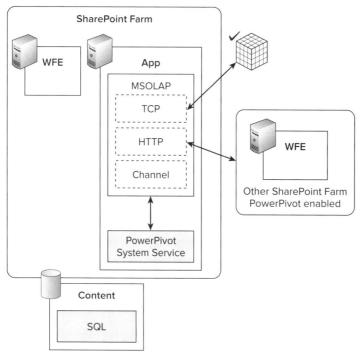

FIGURE 10-15 Overview of PowerPivot System Service and OLE DB provider interaction

Putting this together, let's review the interactions between Excel Services, PowerPivot Services, and the Analysis Services OLE DB provider (MSOLAP.4) to render a PowerPivot workbook within the SharePoint farm. Following is the work flow, with the numbers in parentheses corresponding to the numbers shown in Figure 10-16:

1. Using a browser, The IW Consumer makes a request to the SharePoint WFE for a desired PowerPivot for Excel workbook (1).

2. EWA takes this request (1) and submits it to ECS (2) on the SharePoint App Server.

3. Because ECS is making a request for a PowerPivot database, it will connect with the OLE DB Provider for Analysis Services (3).

4. Noting that the connection string is a PowerPivot workbook, it will connect to PowerPivot System Service (4) via the channel protocol of the MSOLAP driver (3).

5. As noted in Chapter 7 and in Figure 10-10, the system service will ultimately locate the VertiPaq database on one of the SharePoint App Servers within the farm (5).

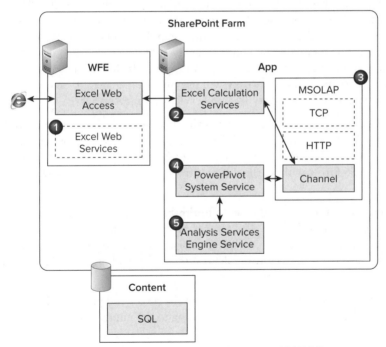

FIGURE 10-16: Detail of PowerPivot System Service and OLE DB Provider interaction

Load Balancing PowerPivot

The picture on how the various dependent services within PowerPivot all interact is *almost* complete. The process shown in Figure 10-16 works if you have only one WFE and one App Server. But, as is apparent for most SharePoint farms, you will have an environment involving multiple App Servers. In that case, how does the WFE know on which App Server to load a PowerPivot workbook's data?

To answer this question, let's start by reviewing the concept of a SharePoint proxy. Chapter 8 discussed the creation of a PowerPivot System Service proxy. (Within the single-server install described in Chapter 2, this is automatically done for you.) Within SharePoint, whenever you create a service application (for example, PowerPivot Service Application), there is a corresponding Service Application Proxy (for example, PowerPivot System Service Proxy, also known as PSS Proxy). A service application proxy allows the consumer of a service to communicate with the service application itself. In the case of the PSS Proxy, it allows the Analysis Services OLE DB Provider or PowerPivot Web Service to connect to the PowerPivot System Service.

> *For more information about the SharePoint Shared Service architecture, refer to Russ Maxwell's SharePoint Brew blog posting at:* `http://bit.ly/akdy1D` *("SharePoint 2010 Shared Service Architecture").*

The reason this proxy is important isn't just because of the communication path. It is the PSS Proxy that is the endpoint that determines which App Servers are available, and ultimately load balance the query connections. To do this, there is an instance map that is ultimately stored within the PowerPivot Service Application database that contains the map of which VertiPaq databases are loaded (or available to be loaded) on which SharePoint App Server. If the VertiPaq database is already attached and available to query, the PSS Proxy will use the instance map to determine the correct App Server and connect to the PowerPivot System Service on that App Server.

However, in the case of the VertiPaq database not being available when a user requests a PowerPivot workbook, it will extract the VertiPaq database and load it to the appropriate App Server Analysis Services in VertiPaq mode instance. When the load-balancing allocation method is set to round-robin (the default value), the PSS Proxy will use the instance map to determine the next App Server in rotation.

But, when the load-balancing allocation method is set to health-based, the PSS Proxy will connect to the App Server that has the highest health score. The algorithm for the health score is proprietary, but the basic principle is that it takes into account CPU, memory, and other resources to determine which App Server has the most resources available to support the loading and publishing of a VertiPaq database.

Figure 10-17 is an update to Figure 10-16, taking into account the proxy end points. Following is the work flow, with the numbers in parentheses corresponding to the numbers shown in Figure 10-17:

1. The user initially connects to Excel Web Access (that is, rendering an Excel workbook to a Web page) or Excel Web Service (that is, rendering to a non-browser application) that submits its request to ECS (1).

2. Because ECS is making a request for a PowerPivot database, it will connect with the OLE DB Provider for Analysis Services (2).

3. Before it makes its connection from the OLE DB Provider via the Channel protocol, it will make a connection to the PSS Proxy Endpoint (3). At this point, the proxy will determine the target PowerPivot System Service App Server.

4. Noting that the connection string is a PowerPivot workbook, it will connect to that App Server's PowerPivot System Service (4).

5. As noted in Chapter 7 and in Figure 10-10, the system service will ultimately locate the VertiPaq database on one of the SharePoint App Servers within the farm (5).

6. In the case of PowerPivot Web Service, it will connect directly to the PSS Proxy Endpoint to determine the target PowerPivot System Service App Server (6).

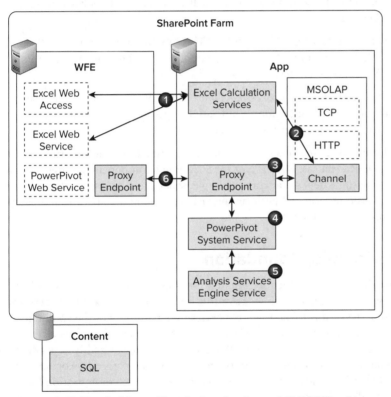

FIGURE 10-17: Detail of PowerPivot System Service and OLE DB Provider interaction

"Time" to Take a Break

Before we dive even further into the murky waters of the claims token and authentication, let's take a break and look at timer jobs. The purpose of SharePoint timer jobs is to allow tasks to be performed in an asynchronous manner. To get access to all of the timer jobs, go to SharePoint Central Administration ➪ General Application Settings ➪ PowerPivot Management Dashboard. On the top right, under Actions, click on "Review timer job definitions."

Following is a brief description of timer job definitions:

➤ *PowerPivot Usage Data Import Timer Job* — This job collects PowerPivot component usage information, and imports the data into the SharePoint logging database.

➤ *PowerPivot Usage Data Processing Timer Job* — With the Import Timer Job storing data in the SharePoint logging database, this job will extract the pertinent information to be stored within the PowerPivot Service Application database.

➤ *PowerPivot Data Refresh Timer Job* — Based on the definition of business hours, this timer job will fire off multiple asynchronous threads. Each thread will tell the PowerPivot System Service to process a PowerPivot workbook, including loading, processing, and packing the VertiPaq database back into the workbook. Also, it will store the database back into the SharePoint Content Database.

➤ *PowerPivot Health Statistics Collector Timer Job* — This job initiates the task of CPU and memory utilization statistics from the PowerPivot components, and imports the data into the PowerPivot Service Application database.

➤ *PowerPivot Management Dashboard Processing Timer Job* — With the PowerPivot Service Application database populated with resource utilization statistics, this job will now update the PowerPivot Management dashboard workbook.

➤ *PowerPivot Setup Extension Timer Job* — This timer job is used to upgrade or run patches to the SQL Server 2008 R2 (that is, PowerPivot for SharePoint components). Often, patches to PowerPivot will have some dependency (for example, schema changes to the SharePoint Content Database). This timer job will perform the task of running the upgrade and patches with minimal administrator interaction.

Diving into Windows Identity Foundation

Although the details surrounding Windows Identity Foundation (known as "Geneva"), which is a claims-based identity framework, are outside the scope of this book, it is important to understand some of the details concerning the claims token to gain a better understanding of the communication that occurs within the SharePoint farm. Because PowerPivot System Service itself is claims-aware, communication between Excel Services and the PowerPivot database is highly dependent on the Windows Identity Foundation being configured properly, and working correctly. Fortunately, most of the inner workings behind Windows Identity Foundation require no configuration for SharePoint or, for that matter, PowerPivot.

The key advantage of having your PowerPivot-enabled SharePoint farm utilize the claims token is that, for SharePoint 2010, you no longer need to utilize Kerberos to facilitate communication within the farm. There are some scenarios that will still require Kerberos, but for most of the PowerPivot-specific scenarios, Kerberos is no longer needed. This section provides a high-level overview of why.

 For more information about SharePoint and claims authentication, see "Plan for claims authentication (SharePoint Server 2010)" at `http://bit.ly/9VHopD`.

SharePoint Farm Communication

The Windows Identity Foundation has been included in SharePoint 2010 to allow the SharePoint farm to use claims tokens. If a service within the SharePoint farm is claims-aware, then it is possible for multi-hop communication to occur with that service within the SharePoint farm without requiring Kerberos authentication.

Traditionally, with SharePoint 2007, in order to have multiple servers within your SharePoint farm, you would need to enable Kerberos to address the multi-hop scenario. For example, if you were to look at Figure 10-18, the communication hop from the client using a browser (that is, from number 1 to number 3 in the figure), the SharePoint Servers would require Kerberos, because there was more than one hop from the client to the "Other SharePoint Servers."

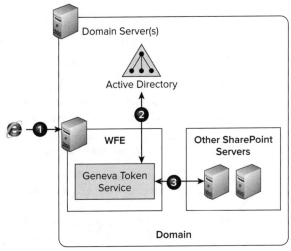

FIGURE 10-18: High-level overview of SharePoint Farm communication

With SharePoint 2010, Windows Identity Foundation is installed on every SharePoint server as part of the SharePoint Prerequisite Installer. Presuming Windows NT authentication inside and outside the SharePoint farm, following is a very simplified way of explaining the communication path. (The numbers in parentheses correspond to those in Figure 10-18.)

1. The client connects to WFE with Windows identity, presuming Windows authentication external to the SharePoint Farm (1).

2. With the connection to the WFE, Windows Identity Foundation Security Token Service is called into action. There is a trust relationship established between the WFE and the Active Directory attribute store (2). An identity (or claims) token is established that contains *attributes* of the Windows identity, but it is *not* the Windows identity. That is, a claims token is created to represent the user.

3. From this point forward, any communication within the SharePoint farm (provided that the services you are talking to are claims-aware) will use the claims token as the mechanism to identify the user.

When Kerberos Is Needed for SharePoint / SSAS Interactions

While Windows Identity Foundation simplifies some communication within the SharePoint farm, there are still scenarios where Kerberos is required. To keep the focus on Analysis Services, let's take a look at when Kerberos is needed for SharePoint / Analysis Services interactions.

As noted earlier, Analysis Services itself is not claims-aware. So, even though Windows Identity Foundation is available as part of SharePoint 2010, connections to Analysis Services via SharePoint will still require Kerberos.

Looking at Figure 10-19, the basic flow of communication from browser to Excel Services to Analysis Services is as follows (with steps corresponding to the numbers appearing in the figure):

1. The client browser connects to the SharePoint WFE. Windows Identity Foundation comes into play, and the identity (claims) token is created for the user.

2. The WFE connection to the App Server is now using a claims token — Kerberos is not required.

3. ECS connects to an Analysis Services instance that is not a claims-aware service within SharePoint and outside of the SharePoint farm. Therefore, Kerberos is required — specifically, Windows authentication using Kerberos-constrained delegation.

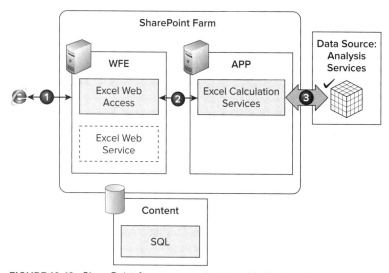

FIGURE 10-19: SharePoint farm communication with Analysis Services

However, in the case of PowerPivot for SharePoint, two key points are that PowerPivot System Service is installed (it is claims-aware), and Analysis Services is installed as a service within the SharePoint farm. These differences result in a different authentication flow from traditional Analysis Services.

Looking at Figure 10-20 the basic flow of communication from browser to Excel Services to Analysis Services is as follows (with steps corresponding to the numbers appearing in the figure):

1. The client browser connects to the SharePoint WFE. Windows Identity Foundation comes into play, and the identity (claims) token is created for the user.

2. The WFE connection to the App Server is now using a claims token — Kerberos is not required.

3. ECS connects to PowerPivot System Service, which is claims-aware.

4. The connection to the Analysis Services Engine service is a regular TCP/IP connection done within the context of the PowerPivot System Service. That is, the user's identity (claims) token has the Windows identity attributes of the PowerPivot System Service, so it can connect to the Analysis Services Engine using the latter's credentials.

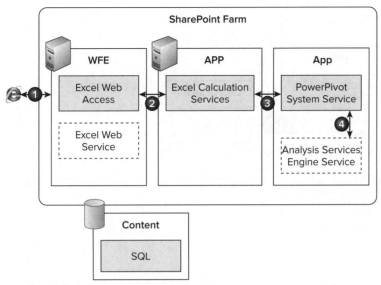

FIGURE 10-20: SharePoint farm communication with Analysis Services Engine Service

 This last step concerning user authentication is performed by the Claims to Windows Token Service (c2wts). If this service is configured incorrectly or not running, you will often receive Excel delegation errors within your PowerPivot for SharePoint environment (as noted in Chapter 9).

When Kerberos Is Needed for PowerPivot

As you can see from the previous discussion, as well as the discussion concerning Windows Identity Foundation/SharePoint claims token and Claims-to-Windows Token Service, Kerberos is not required for PowerPivot in most cases. Even in the data refresh scenario where the Analysis Services VertiPaq Engine is processing data from a source outside the farm, you do not need Kerberos. As noted in Figure 10-21, there is only one hop from Analysis Services in VertiPaq mode to the data source (such as a SQL database).

But, there are some data refresh scenarios that will require Kerberos authentication, such as the linked data source scenario. If the data refresh is against a data source that is linked to another data source (such as the one shown in Figure 10-22), Kerberos will be required because there are multiple hops between the Analysis Services VertiPaq Engine and the end-target data source (Data Source 2 in the figure). The type of Kerberos-constrained delegation required will be defined by the target end-point (Data Source 2). But note that the constrained delegation will be between the App Server, Data Source 1, and Data Source 2. It will not be with the entire SharePoint farm.

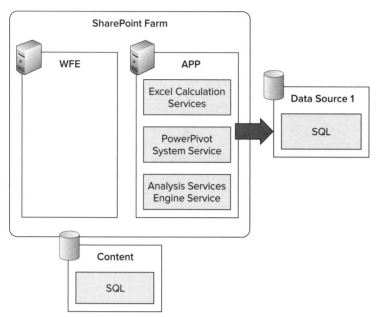

FIGURE 10-21: Data Refresh One-Hop Scenario does not need Kerberos authentication

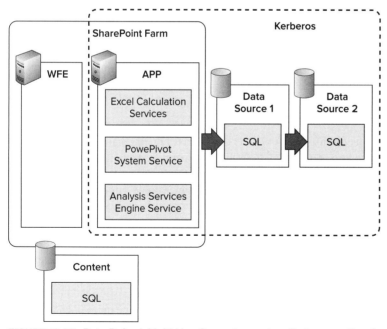

FIGURE 10-22: Data Refresh Multi-Hop Scenario requires Kerberos authentication

In general, outside of corner cases like linked data sources, Kerberos authentication is *not* required for PowerPivot. If turning on Kerberos authentication for your SharePoint farm becomes necessary, PowerPivot can still work. In that case, refer to the TechNet article, "Configure Kerberos authentication for the claims to Windows token service (SharePoint Server 2010)" (`http://bit.ly/9FHzOY`) to better prepare yourself for this scenario.

SUMMARY

This chapter took a deeper dive into the architectural components of PowerPivot for Excel and PowerPivot for SharePoint. For the latter, the discussion dove even deeper to review how Excel Services, PowerPivot Services, and Windows Identity Foundation work together to provide connectivity between the client and the Analysis Services Engine Service within the SharePoint farm.

This information should provide you with a better context for planning for enterprise considerations, which is the topic of Chapter 11.

11

Enterprise Considerations

WHAT'S IN THIS CHAPTER?

➤ Understanding best practices surrounding PowerPivot for SharePoint capacity planning

➤ Determining which SharePoint services to optimize for your PowerPivot for SharePoint environment

➤ Reviewing SharePoint upgrade considerations for PowerPivot

➤ Understanding why SharePoint Upload may be important for your PowerPivot for SharePoint environment

One of the main issues with any BI environment is how to plan and implement for an enterprise scenario. Getting yourself up and running for a departmental scenario is one thing. Adapting that environment to handle hundreds or thousands of concurrent users, querying tens or hundreds of workbooks with varying degrees of size and with a large number of PowerPivot workbooks being processed simultaneously, is a whole different (and more complex) problem to solve.

A key point that will be repeated throughout this chapter is that to handle an enterprise SharePoint environment, you should start with enterprise SharePoint books, material, and training. This chapter (and, for that matter, this book) will *not* be a replacement for enterprise SharePoint training because of the number of complex topics that can be associated with enterprise SharePoint deployments, including (but not limited to) SharePoint Search, FAST, deploying an external-facing SharePoint environment, and SharePoint customizations.

But what will be addressed in this chapter is the potential impact of PowerPivot on your enterprise SharePoint environment, and how you can better prepare and plan for it.

CAPACITY PLANNING

As noted, capacity planning for SharePoint is a pretty complex topic. Consequently, this is a topic that won't be deeply explored here because of the breadth and depth required to cover such a diverse topic. Nevertheless, this discussion provides some pointers and concepts surrounding capacity planning for SharePoint enterprise environments that are important to understand when measuring the impact of PowerPivot.

Resources

For starters, here are some resources that you will want to have handy in order to better understand the issues surrounding SharePoint:

➤ *Microsoft SharePoint Server 2010: Installation, Upgrade, Getting Started: TechNet* (`http://bit.ly/4xe15I`) — This TechNet site contains most of the Microsoft resources concerning how to install and work with SharePoint 2010. This is a good general reference portal that you should bookmark and regularly come back to.

➤ *SharePoint team blog* (`http://bit.ly/pd10`) — The SharePoint team blog covers a wide range of topics in-depth, so check out this blog on a regular basis, because you never know what wonderful hints and insight the team will reveal next.

➤ *Microsoft Office SharePoint Server 2007 Administrator's Companion (Redmond, Washington: Microsoft Press, 2009)* — This is a great book by Bill English to help you administer SharePoint.

➤ *Microsoft Office SharePoint Server 2007 Best Practices (Redmond, Washington: Microsoft Press, 2008)* — As the name implies, this book by Ben Curry and Bill English contains a lot of solid best practices from real-world deployments for SharePoint.

➤ *SharePoint 2010 Capacity Planning* (`http://bit.ly/74Z791`) — This SharePoint Saturday presentation in Denver (2009) is a great quick reference for SharePoint 2010 capacity planning.

➤ *SharePoint 2007 Performance and Capacity Planning Resource Center* (`http://bit.ly/2Sms5j`) — While this is for SharePoint 2007, this has a lot of solid whitepapers and guides.

➤ *25 Common Design Questions* (`http://bit.ly/7TWCHj`) — Ben Curry has provided answers to the top 25 common design questions concerning SharePoint 2007, most of which are applicable to 2010.

➤ *Bill's 5-min SharePoint Performance Recommendation* (`http://bit.ly/6hBVBa`) — This is a great read on a quick list of SharePoint performance recommendations.

➤ *Windows SharePoint Services Test Data Load Tool* (`http://bit.ly/6nLDrf`) — This is a test data load tool that will load up your SharePoint environment with data to allow for capacity testing.

➤ *PowerPivot Best Practices and Capacity Planning* — The SQLCAT team is currently writing this document based on customer lessons learned and best practices. Check the `http://sqlcat.com` Web site for reference.

The Windows SharePoint Services Test Data Load Tool is not specific to PowerPivot, but it is handy for understanding how well your environment can handle even larger concurrent query and data loads.

Recommended Hardware Requirements

The real questions you want to answer about budget and hardware allocation are, "What hardware do you need, and how much does it cost?"

Chapters 7 and 8 reviewed the minimal requirements to get up and running within a departmental or small farm scenario. But, in the case of enterprise considerations, you're talking about hundreds or thousands of concurrent users hitting the system. Remember, the key to SharePoint is that it is, by design, a scale-out farm system. This isn't to imply SharePoint cannot scale up — it can, and there are improvements in SharePoint 2010 that allow it to do this even better.

Nevertheless, the underlying infrastructure of SharePoint is a Web services architecture that is designed as a scale-out farm environment. What this means is that, for your SharePoint farm, you will want to have the same type of enterprise database commodity servers so that you can add, modify, and remove servers to the farm as necessary. As well, it becomes easier to repurpose servers (for example, switching an existing server from a WFE to an App Server) if all of the servers have the same configuration. But, unlike Web server farms, to fully utilize SharePoint 2010 services — especially PowerPivot — you must use enterprise database commodity servers, as opposed to your traditional Web commodity servers.

Memory

While the typically recommended amount of memory for test machines is 16 GB of RAM, the recommended amount of memory for production is 64 GB (or higher). The recommendation for more RAM is because PowerPivot itself uses a lot of memory. As will be noted later in this chapter in the section "Provisioning," the concurrent number of PowerPivot workbooks is a key data point for the amount of memory that is required.

When you open up an insightful PowerPivot for Excel workbook with hundreds of millions of rows, you can see the memory rapidly being consumed by Excel to support placing the VertiPaq database in memory. This was just for one database — you will need a lot more to support the tens or hundreds of concurrent PowerPivot users accessing tens or hundreds of different workbooks. The basic math concerning the amount of memory required is to add up all of the currently "in-use" databases across all servers and add a 10 percent to 20 percent buffer as overhead (such as for auto-detection).

Part of the reason for recommending 64 GB of RAM is the price point for enterprise commodity hardware. As of March 2010, you could purchase a Dell R900 with 64 GB RAM, 4-socket quad cores, plus local 15K RPM drives (and other bells and whistles) for approximately $17,500. Yet, going from 64 GB RAM to 128 GB RAM would cost an additional $9,000. Double that (the cost differential) and you have yourself another enterprise server.

If you come back to this book a year or two (or even more) later, the cost of memory will have dropped considerably, and, provided you had a lot of large PowerPivot workbooks, it may make sense to recommend large amounts of memory. However, at this time, go for the optimal enterprise architecture, which is 64 GB of memory.

64-Bit or 32-Bit

As noted in previous chapters, all SKUs of SharePoint 2010 are 64-bit to provide the operating system and any application or services running on them more addressable memory space to perform their tasks. So, from the standpoint of SharePoint, 64-bit is not even a recommendation — it's a requirement.

However, it is possible to place all of your SharePoint databases (for example, content, configuration, `PowerPivotServiceApplication`, and so on) onto SQL Server Express on 32-bit systems. Although it is possible, it's not a good idea for enterprise scenarios.

You want to scale your SQL databases up and out. For PowerPivot and its larger workbooks, you'll need to use a full version of SQL Server (that is, not SQL Express) in order to efficiently save these large workbooks as blobs within the database, or via Remote Blob Store (RBS). (You'll learn more about this later in this chapter during the discussion about databases.) Also, there is a large amount of usage and event data that is stored by the SharePoint and PowerPivot service databases that require the performance and manageability of enterprise SQL. This also means you will want to go to 64-bit for the SharePoint SQL databases.

Processor

As of March 2010, SQL Server Books Online recommends 4-socket, quad-core servers running at 2.6GHz. More cores are recommended because both Excel Services and PowerPivot use a lot of processors. Because the data is in memory, the processors do not have to worry about the latency to get data from disk. So, let the processors loose and let Excel Services and the Analysis Services Engine service calculate! The more complex the calculations, the more data you store, and/or the more PowerPivot workbooks you have, the more processors you'll want to have available to churn through that data.

As noted in the discussion on memory recommendations, you could potentially start with eight cores because of the price point for enterprise commodity hardware. As noted earlier, as of March 2010, you can purchase a Dell R900 with 64 GB RAM, 4-socket quad-cores, plus local 15K RPM drives (and other bells and whistles) for approximately $17,500. To add more cores, you'd need to purchase a new SKU with more sockets or upgrade to the newer multi-core chips. But, as noted later in this chapter, the onus of which SKU to purchase is partially dependent on the enterprise commodity standard of your IT department.

If you come back in a year or two, there will be a new standard for enterprise commodity hardware — probably more cores per CPU socket and more sockets — so this recommendation will change over time.

Disk

Fast disk is certainly recommended. Fast disk can mean a lot of things, so let's get down to some specifics here. Time and time again, people often focus on the disk size capacity, but little time is spent on disk speed. Yet, slow disk speed is often the main bottleneck to fast query performance. However, why would you need fast disk, since PowerPivot is the VertiPaq In-Memory BI database?

While a disk will have minimal effect for the PowerPivot database itself, you still have the temporary file caches (IIS, Excel Services, PowerPivot databases in the OLAP backup folder, `WebTempDir` folder, and so on), and the SQL databases holding PowerPivot events, logs, and workbooks. Slow disk speed will ultimately result in slower performance and increase query and processing times.

Since the focus for fast disk is disk speed, let's consider disk rotations and input/output processes (IOPs).

Exploring the Fast Disk Concept

The concept of fast disk is a deeply technical and complex one that could take up an entire book just to cover. So, while it is out of the scope of this book to address all of the issues concerning a fast disk, let's take a moment to highlight some general concerns and pointers that should help jump-start this issue.

Configuration

Because PowerPivot for SharePoint has so many different components, it may become important to lay out your disk into multiple volumes. This way, you can have a separate volume with its own separate physical disk (or disks) dedicated to providing I/O for each component. For example, consider the following volumes:

➤ *SharePoint content database* — This supports a lot of transactions to allow users to upload or download their PowerPivot workbooks, Word documents, Excel workbooks, PowerPoint presentations, or any other documents they would like to keep.

➤ *Analysis Services engine* — While the VertiPaq database is primarily in memory, the database temporary storage and cache is located (by default) in the `C:\Program Files\Microsoft SQL Server\MSAS10_50.MSSQLSERVER\OLAP\Backup` location.

➤ *Logging* — As you learned in Chapter 9, all of these components will populate Unified Logging Services (ULS) logs (SharePoint, PowerPivot, Excel Services, and so on) and IIS logs. By default, these log files are placed on the operating system drive (for example, `C:\`). It will be beneficial to place these logs on a separate volume not utilized by the databases.

Spindles

While the previously recommended configuration will help alleviate disk bottlenecks, it is also important to provide fast physical disks that make up these volumes. For starters, regardless of which type of disk system you are using (local, Direct Attach Storage, SAN, and so on), the key point is that the more spindles available for the system, the faster the disk system overall. Note that this rule of thumb does not come into play for solid-state drives.

Following are two general rules to keep in mind:

➤ *The more spindles the better* — Of course, cost is always an issue, but having more spindles means faster read/write speeds.

➤ *Ensure that you are purchasing a fast disk* — While capacity is important, the rotation speed of the disk is just as important — in many cases, more important. The cost of disk capacity continues to drop in price, but that does not necessarily translate into the speed of the disk. Faster physical disk rotation speeds (for example, greater than or equal to 10 K RPM) results in faster read/write speeds.

The underlying theme here is to have faster read/write speeds so that the disk can provide the chunks to the processor and memory fast enough to support your environment.

RAID Configuration

Within many enterprise environments, ensuring data redundancy and improving the performance of disks can be achieved by using a RAID (Redundant Array of Independent Disks) configuration. As a general rule, you should have a RAID 10 configuration to provide both mirroring and faster disk performance. While you may consider a RAID 5 configuration, the commonly referenced Write Penalty comes into play here. That is, if your users are uploading a lot of files, a RAID 5 configuration may not be optimal for your environment.

ENTERPRISE COMMODITY HARDWARE

There are some who would adamantly disagree with the definition of enterprise commodity hardware as 4-socket quad-cores and 64 GB of RAM. After all (as of March 2010), you can go one SKU up and get yourself 24 processors (4 socket x 6 cores) with 256 GB of RAM for around $42,500. If your definition of enterprise commodity hardware is this SKU, should you use the smaller SKU?

Of course not! Different enterprises will ultimately define enterprise commodity differently because of price point, discounts they can get, and/or hardware administration and maintenance. If your commodity SKU is larger than what is suggested here — use it! At the same time, if your definition of enterprise commodity is smaller, should you use a larger SKU?

In this case, yes! Don't misinterpret this. You may be able to do well with a smaller SKU and simply scale out. But, as a general rule, the enterprise commodity hardware required for SharePoint 2010 must be a lot more powerful than the SKU required for SharePoint 2007. Since you will very likely purchase a new set of hardware to support SharePoint 2010, you should use this more powerful SKU.

Provisioning

So, how much hardware do you need to support your environment? To answer that question, you must determine other factors such as your disk I/O requirements, how much memory you need, peak volume use, and so on. So, how do you know what's required?

One of the things to note about SharePoint capacity planning (which is similar to a lot of other BI or database capacity planning) is that it's about testing, extrapolating, and, very important, monitoring. This is important to note, because SharePoint has a lot of different variables that can make two different environments that look similar operate in very different ways.

This is especially important within the context of PowerPivot for SharePoint. Any number of variables can come into play in what resources (for example, memory, CPU, disk, network, and so on) are being utilized. Examples range from Excel Services spiking in CPU usage because of some complex trending calculation being performed, to Analysis Services using large amounts of memory because of the high cardinality and high row uniqueness. Therefore, the most straightforward way to determine what hardware and topologies you need is the methodology to test, extrapolate, and then monitor, as shown in Figure 11-1.

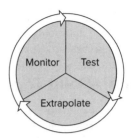

FIGURE 11-1 Provisioning by test, extrapolate, and monitor

As you saw earlier in this chapter in the section "Resources," a number of SharePoint capacity planning documents and books are available that cover in great detail the issues surrounding provisioning. So, while it is well outside the scope of this chapter to talk about general SharePoint provisioning, let's at least consider the impact PowerPivot will have on provisioning. There are a couple general rules of thumb that provide you a starting point for your planning, but will require you to test, extrapolate, and monitor to determine accuracy.

The first rule of thumb is that, for the enterprise commodity box currently recommended in this book, a SharePoint App Server running Excel Services and PowerPivot Services can handle approximately 50 different workbooks/databases concurrently. If the number must be higher, then it will be important to increase the number of App Servers to handle the workload.

Another rule of thumb concerns the metrics that you will need to measure in order to do your extrapolation and monitoring against. These have been summarized in Table 1-1. Over time, as you perfect your processes and policies, you will have more metrics that you will want to analyze and record to help you provision and plan your environment. However, at least this is a good starting point so that you can begin your planning.

TABLE 1-1 Capacity Planning — Provisioning

METRIC	DETERMINATION
Total number of users	This will allow you to have an idea of the total storage requirements. This will be calculated by the average number of files x average size of files x total number of users.
Total number of concurrent users (maximum)	This will provide you with the number of SharePoint WFEs required to support the number of users at any point in time.
Total number of PowerPivot users (total and concurrent)	This is similar to the previous two metrics in that you will see the impact on the number of PowerPivot users for your farm. This will help you determine the number of SharePoint App Servers (hosting Excel Services, Analysis Services, and PowerPivot System Service).
Number of files; average/maximum size of files	This is necessary to determine storage requirements for the SharePoint content database.
Data refresh options	This is the number of workbooks that require data refresh options. This will impact the amount of processing required to extract, populate, and store the database and workbook.

For the last metric concerning data refresh options, knowing this information prepares you for which data sources are being used. After all, just because the IW Producer has a driver to source X doesn't mean the driver is available in the SharePoint farm.

SharePoint Topologies

You should now have an idea of what to provision, and the resources required to support your PowerPivot-enabled SharePoint farm deployment. But what topology should you use? That is, how should you configure the WFEs, App Servers, and SQL servers within your environment? Note that you are not yet considering the number of each type of server, just the topology of the SharePoint farm.

So, where do you start? The best place is to refer to the "Topologies for SharePoint 2010" document for download at `http://bit.ly/6oNd3R`. This is an important overview document (in multiple formats) describing the topologies of SharePoint 2010. In addition to providing a general overview of the server roles and topology examples from limited deployments to large farm examples, it even provides guidance on which service should be applied to which server (Web Server or App Server). While PowerPivot is not included in these topology diagrams, as you can tell from previous chapters in this book (and in the next few sections), it is recommended that you place PowerPivot Services on the App Server.

But what types of farms are applicable within the context of PowerPivot for SharePoint? There is not supposed to be any difference between a regular SharePoint farm and a SharePoint farm that is PowerPivot-enabled. Yet, there are different modes of thinking about PowerPivot, so let's discuss them.

Single-Server Farm

What's great about the single-server farm deployment shown in Figure 11-2 is that it is (in comparison) the simplest deployment of your PowerPivot for SharePoint scenario. As noted in Chapter 2, when installing SQL Server 2008 R2 Analysis Services in SharePoint Integrated mode, the installer will not only install and configure all of the PowerPivot components, it will also configure many of the SharePoint farm components — including (but not limited to) IIS, Excel Services, and SharePoint farm configurations.

This topology is great for small and/or departmental deployments where the number of users and the number of PowerPivot workbooks are limited (for example, if less than 64 GB of PowerPivot workbooks are opened concurrently). But this isn't a very good farm scenario, as you have limited ways to scale the service — the main one being to scale up (that is, add more memory or processors). Since this is a single server, you cannot have high availability (that is, there is going to be downtime on the server), and any disaster recovery will definitely result in downtime.

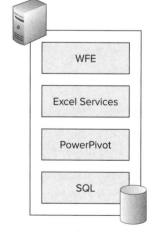

FIGURE 11-2 Single-server farm deployment

However, since it is easier to deploy, it allows your department or business unit to get up, tested, and running on PowerPivot faster.

Single-Server Farm with Dedicated SQL Server

So, let's say that you now have your single-server SharePoint farm set up, but you know that you'll eventually want to scale out this environment to handle the large number of users (especially concurrent users) who want to play with PowerPivot. How do you do this?

For starters, get the SQL databases from your single-server deployment onto their own dedicated server. As noted previously, you'll want to provide enough resources (for example, RAM, more CPU cores, dedicated disk, and so on) so that you can continue to use this one dedicated server to handle the greater workload when you add more WFEs and App Servers to your SharePoint farm (to support more users, features, and PowerPivot workbooks). Therefore, the topology is created with a dedicated SQL Server for your single-server farm, as shown in Figure 11-3.

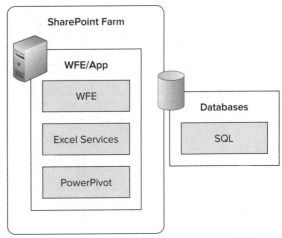

FIGURE 11-3 Single-server farm with dedicated SQL Server deployment

What's great about this deployment is that it becomes much easier to set up and configure your dedicated SQL server for high availability (for example, SQL clustering) and disaster recovery (for example, log shipping, replication, mirroring, and so on). An easy way to create this topology is to perform the PowerPivot for SharePoint Single-Server Install (as described in Chapter 2), and then migrate the SharePoint databases to a separate dedicated SQL Server. For more information on these configurations, see the section "SharePoint Databases," later in this chapter.

There is nothing to prevent you from starting your deployment with this topology. If you prefer this topology, the instruction guide to do a "Single Server Install with Dedicated SQL Server" can be found in SQL Server Books Online, or at `http://bit.ly/5X5Rwy`. If you prefer to start with the single-server deployment and then migrate your SQL databases to a separate dedicated server, follow the instructions from TechNet with the article "Move all databases (Office SharePoint Server)" at `http://bit.ly/SemgU`. While these instructions are for SharePoint 2007, as of this writing, the SharePoint 2010 instructions had not yet been provided.

Whether you started from here or migrated to this point, you are now in a position to scale out your SharePoint farm to handle larger workloads when they come.

Multi-Single WFE/App Server with Dedicated SQL Server

There are two ways to view interpret Figure 11-4 concerning your scale-out SharePoint deployment:

➤ Multiple, individual, single-server deployments

➤ Multiple, single, complete servers in the same farm

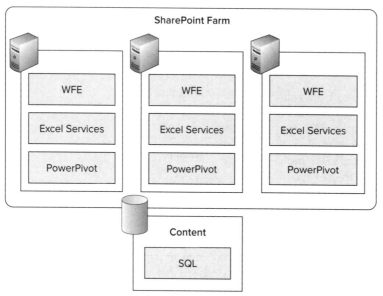

FIGURE 11-4 Multiple single-server deployments with dedicated SQL Server

 What should not be debatable is the part of Figure 11-4 showing the dedicated SQL Server. For more information on this, see the earlier section, "Single-Server Farm with Dedicated SQL Server."

The first interpretation is that there are multiple *individual* single-server deployments that point to the same dedicated SQL Server. This approach would result in each of the three *individual* single servers having its own content and configuration databases. That is, there would be three different content databases, three different configuration databases, three different `PowerPivotService` Application databases, and so on. Also, this would mean that there are three different SharePoint Web URLs to go to. This is not the typical SharePoint environment, and you should not be going down this route.

It is possible that you may arrive at this topology because of a fast consolidation. For example, say that you had three different departments (for example, HR, Sales, and Finance) with their own PowerPivot environments. They all need a dedicated SQL Server to handle the large files they are working with, so they all migrate their databases to this more powerful dedicated SQL Server to handle the workload. While, from an individual team and consolidation standpoint, this makes sense, it may not from an IT administrative perspective.

From another perspective, Figure 11-4 shows three WFE/App Servers pointing to the same set of SharePoint databases. This way, if you go to any of those three servers (via their own URLs), you get access to the same data and configuration. The same site, lists, and documents are available to you, regardless of which server you access. Once you add a load balancer in front of the servers, then you can hit the load balancer alias, which will load balance to any of the three servers without users needing to know which server to specifically query.

This configuration is more complex because it does involve an existing farm installation. While the first single-server setup was a "new farm" and the migration of the SQL databases involved their own separate steps, the addition of the other two servers will follow the "existing farm" instructions. However, while it is a little bit more complex of an installation, it does support the key fact that you will be able to evenly distribute the load across all three servers, provided you have a load balancer to do this for you. Also, it is relatively easy to rebuild a single-server instance in comparison to the other options (which will be noted shortly).

The concern with this topology for PowerPivot-centric deployments is that it doesn't take into account the fact that the WFEs use less hardware resources than the App Server components (that is, Excel Services and PowerPivot Services). It is not uncommon to see PowerPivot-centric deployments where there are only one or two WFEs, while there are three or more App Servers to handle the load.

The concern for SharePoint farm deployments in general (regardless of whether PowerPivot is enabled or not) is similar, except that the differentiation is greater. There are many resource-intensive SharePoint services that require multiple App Servers dedicated to their own set of tasks. Because of this, let's examine farm topologies that involve the distribution of App Servers and dedicating sets of App Servers to a set of services.

Existing Farm with App Servers That Have PowerPivot Only

One of the topologies for a PowerPivot-centric SharePoint farm deployment under consideration would be to have the App Servers only have PowerPivot Services. This is a rather tempting option, since, from current environments, it is apparent that Excel Services and PowerPivot Services utilize the vast majority of resources. Why not then just spread the workload between the WFEs and App Servers by having Excel Services on the WFE and PowerPivot Services on the App Servers, as shown in Figure 11-5?

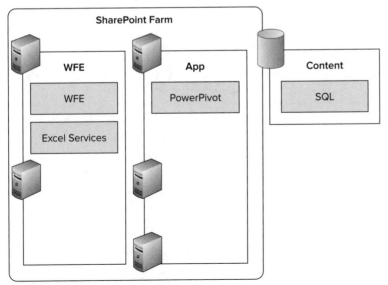

FIGURE 11-5 Farm topology with App Servers dedicated to PowerPivot Services only

This approach is interesting and will work if your farm is dedicated to PowerPivot only and the vast majority of your workload is because of PowerPivot. Yet, this topology most likely will *not* be common for the following reasons:

➤ Most calculations for PowerPivot are not overly complex. So, while there is a lot of memory utilized (the databases are in-memory, after all), in comparison, the models are not as CPU-intensive.

➤ Excel Services can be both memory-intensive and CPU-intensive, since they must perform calculations.

Note, these statements are generalizations — there are times when PowerPivot will be more CPU-intensive (for example, processing, many concurrent queries, and so on) and Excel Services will be more memory-intensive (for example, any complex calculations requiring creation of hash tables such as distinct calculations, and so on). But the whole point is that *in general*, having App Servers dedicated just to PowerPivot Services may not be a good use of available resources.

Existing Farm with App Servers That Have Excel Services and PowerPivot

This now leads to the optimal PowerPivot-enabled SharePoint farm topology, which is also in the spirit of SharePoint farm topologies in general. That is, have separate WFEs and App Servers where the WFEs perform Web rendering duties, while the App Servers perform their service tasks. Since the focus here is that of a PowerPivot-enabled SharePoint farm, the two key services that are on the App Servers are Excel Services and PowerPivot Services, as shown in Figure 11-6. Because there is a lot of chatter between these two sets of services, having them on the same server will reduce bottlenecks surrounding network latency.

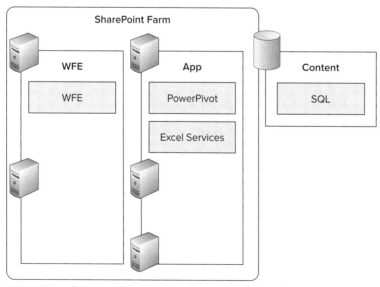

FIGURE 11-6 Farm topology with App Servers with Excel Services and PowerPivot services

You may be able to place more services on your App Servers than just Excel Services and PowerPivot Services. But that will be best determined from testing, extrapolating, and monitoring. That is, you must go back to your provisioning plan to determine the required resources within this topology.

THE IMPACT OF NETWORK LATENCY

If you recall the services architecture from Chapter 7, or the components architecture from Chapter 10, you would have noticed that there is a lot of communication occurring between different services and components within your SharePoint farm. For example, to render a PowerPivot for Excel workbook to the browser, the one-way communication path is WFE (Excel Web Access) ⇨ Geneva Claim Token ⇨ ECS ⇨ OLE DB Provider (Channel) ⇨ PowerPivot System Service ⇨ PowerPivot system service identity ⇨ Analysis Services Engine Service.

That's not to mention all of the trips to the SQL databases (metadata, workbook, and so on) within this communication path. As your farm becomes larger, network bandwidth and latency become your bottlenecks.

So, it is important to ensure that you have 1 Gigabit (or the newer 10 Gigabit) network infrastructure to support your SharePoint farm. This isn't just the network cards in your servers, but also the routers and even the cables you are using to connect the servers (for example, Cat 5e or Cat 6).

In some cases, if network bandwidth is really a bottleneck for your WFEs (you should verify this first), you may want to have multiple network interface cards (NICs) — one set to support network throughput to the clients and another set to connect to the SharePoint databases and/or App Servers.

SHAREPOINT WFES

As previously mentioned, PowerPivot for SharePoint does not have a very large impact on the WFE. Considering how little CPU and memory is utilized by the WFE as shown in Figure 11-7, you might be tempted to simply keep your SharePoint farm deployment limited to a single server. After all, in this particular example of a small departmental deployment (less than 20 unique users, with approximately 30 unique PowerPivot Excel workbooks), average daily memory utilization was less than 0.5 GB, and less than 1 percent CPU for the WFE. It is important to note that these results are reflected for a PowerPivot for SharePoint deployment where the only thing the WFE was doing was rendering PowerPivot workbooks.

This is not very intensive on the WFE, and it is common to see one WFE and three App Servers on a SharePoint farm, since the App servers require more resources. But it is important to remember that SharePoint can (and will) be used in far more ways than just PowerPivot. There will also be searches, lists, and other documents that must be rendered, and that will all take its toll on the WFE.

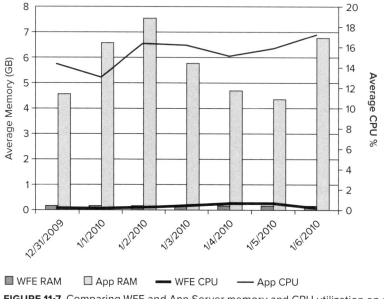

FIGURE 11-7 Comparing WFE and App Server memory and CPU utilization on a small PowerPivot for SharePoint farm deployment

Therefore, the key point here is that PowerPivot for SharePoint by itself has little impact on the SharePoint WFE. The one exception to this rule is during the upload of a file into SharePoint. Specifically, PowerPivot for Excel workbooks are typically much larger than your average Excel workbook.

As noted in the setup and configuration instructions in Chapter 8, an optional step is to increase the maximum size of a document to be stored within SharePoint to 2,047 MB (that is, 2 GB). If you're working with a large enterprise, your workbooks will be much larger than the default values, so it is highly recommended that you follow those steps. Also, more network and CPU resources are used to get the file from the client to the WFE, and then from the WFE to the content database. This is discussed in more depth later in this chapter in the section "Upload Considerations."

SHAREPOINT APP SERVERS

The exact opposite can be said for the SharePoint App Servers when compared to the WFEs. As noted in Figure 11-7, there are significantly more memory and CPU resources utilized by the App Server when compared to the WFE. Within your App Servers, Excel Services is utilizing CPU in order to perform its calculations. Meanwhile, the Analysis Services in VertiPaq mode is using a lot of memory.

The reason for the higher resource utilization by the SharePoint App Servers is because both Excel Services and Analysis Services are using memory and CPU resources to perform their tasks. Remember, Figure 11-7 is a pretty small departmental deployment, so even the high was less than 18 percent average CPU utilization and 7 GB RAM.

Nevertheless, the point is that when this SharePoint farm must be deployed for the entire enterprise (corporate-wide), that's about two orders of magnitude more users — and resources. So, what can you do to help improve performance outside of adding more App Servers? Following are some tips broken down by the key services on the App Server.

Excel Calculation Services

There are a number of things that affect Excel Services within your PowerPivot for SharePoint environment. The first issue is that of increasing the maximum size of an Excel workbook that can be rendered by Excel Services. In Chapter 8, one of the optional instructions was to increase the maximum size. For your enterprise PowerPivot scenario, this is highly recommended, since these workbooks typically are much larger than the default maximum size.

Another key point that has been called out throughout this chapter is the separation of Excel Calculation Services (ECS) so that it is operating on the SharePoint App Servers, while the Excel Web Access (EWA) and Excel Web Services (EWS) reside on the WFE, as shown in Figure 11-8.

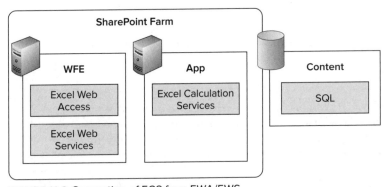

FIGURE 11-8 Separation of ECS from EWA/EWS

To do this, you must ensure that SharePoint has been installed as "Server Farm and Complete" (as indicated in Chapter 8) so that all of the Excel Services components are installed on both the WFE and the App Servers. When you go to your SharePoint farm WFE and click on Central Administration ⇨ Application Management ⇨ Manage Service Applications, you will notice that the Excel Services application is up and running, as shown in Figure 11-9.

FIGURE 11-9 Central Administration, Manage Service Applications View

This is the Excel Services application where any changes to this service application affect all of the servers in the farm — you will not be touching this service. However, if you go to Central Administration ⇨ System Settings ⇨ "Manage services on server" and you're currently on the server itself, then you can turn off ECS for your specific WFE, as shown in Figure 11-10. This way, the ECS is operating only on your SharePoint App Servers, while EWA/EWS are running on your WFEs.

FIGURE 11-10 Central Administration, "Manage services on server" view for ECS on a WFE

 For a more complete understanding of the resource requirements to support Excel Services, see the TechNet article "Determine resource requirements to support Excel Services" at `http://bit.ly/4MoDmB`. *This document provides an in-depth look at the resource requirements, topologies, and even performance testing for Excel Services.*

PowerPivot System Service

For PowerPivot System Service, there is not a lot you must do to ensure that this service is up and running, and that it's ready for the enterprise. If you were to make any changes to this service, you would do it through SharePoint Central Administration ⇨ Application Management ⇨ Manage Service Applications. Choose your `PowerPivotServiceApplication`, go to the right set of dialogs under Actions, and you can then configure service application settings. While there are many different settings (such as connection pools and usage data collection), the two primary settings that you will want to focus on within your enterprise environment are that of load balancing and data refresh.

Load Balancing

For load balancing, there are two different options in terms of distributing the query workload from the client to the different App Servers that have PowerPivot services installed. You select from these options in the drop-down shown in Figure 11-11.

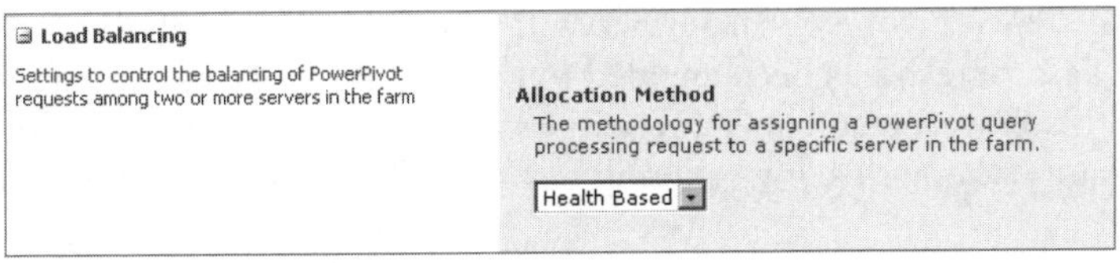

FIGURE 11-11 Load Balancing in PowerPivot Settings

By default, the allocation method is Round Robin, where the server is chosen in a round-robin fashion. If the PowerPivot servers are under a large amount of load caused by large volumes of concurrent users, using the Round Robin method will utilize fewer resources, because it uses a much simpler mapping and algorithm (in comparison to Health Based) to determine the next server.

But you should use the Health Based allocation method, which determines how healthy the App Server is, if you have reason to suspect the App Servers will undergo memory pressure. Health-based algorithms are used to provide a health score of the server; whichever server has the highest score ends up receiving the query. If one of your App Servers is under heavy stress, health-based allocation will ensure that new user queries will be distributed among the remaining servers.

Data Refresh

As noted in Chapters 7 and 10, another key task of the PowerPivot System Service is to perform data refresh on the workbook within the PowerPivot Gallery. These settings can be controlled by the PowerPivot Settings within the Central Administration, as shown in Figure 11-12.

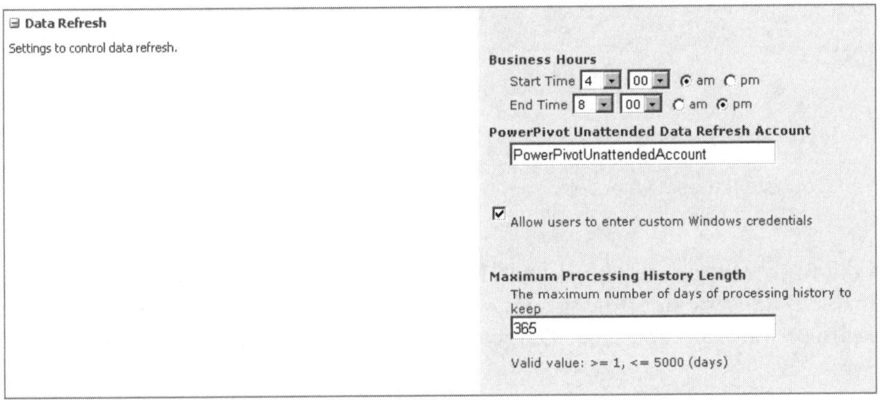

FIGURE 11-12 PowerPivot Settings for data refresh

The settings by themselves are not overly complex, but there are a number of issues that should be addressed by following the options included within the data refresh settings.

Data Refresh: Business Hours

The business hours indicated here are the working day hours when the data refresh will not occur. The indicated business hours ensure that the PowerPivot System Service and the Analysis Services are dedicated for querying purposes. However, during non-business hours (for example, from 8:00 p.m. to 4:00 a.m.), the PowerPivot System Service will invoke its Timer Job to go through each workbook where data refresh has been enabled to kick off the workbook's own job to refresh the data. By default, this PowerPivot Timer Job will kick off in the non-business hours, and check every minute (by default) whether each workbook has started and/or finished its data refresh job.

To control the PowerPivot Timer Job, go to Central Administration ⇨ General Application Settings ⇨ PowerPivot Management Dashboard ⇨ Actions (top right) ⇨ "Review timer job definitions." Click on the PowerPivot Data Refresh Timer Job, and then you can define how often this Timer Job executes, as shown in Figure 11-13. Remember, this is how often the PowerPivot Data Refresh Timer Job is executed (whose task is to check if the jobs are executed), not the actual refresh job for a particular workbook.

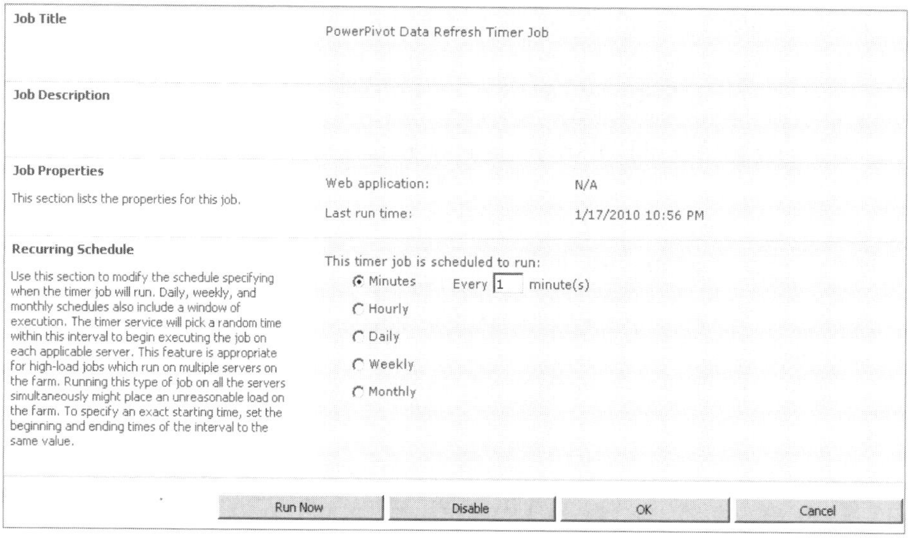

Job Title	
	PowerPivot Data Refresh Timer Job

Job Description

Job Properties

This section lists the properties for this job.

Web application:	N/A
Last run time:	1/17/2010 10:56 PM

Recurring Schedule

Use this section to modify the schedule specifying when the timer job will run. Daily, weekly, and monthly schedules also include a window of execution. The timer service will pick a random time within this interval to begin executing the job on each applicable server. This feature is appropriate for high-load jobs which run on multiple servers on the farm. Running this type of job on all the servers simultaneously might place an unreasonable load on the farm. To specify an exact starting time, set the beginning and ending times of the interval to the same value.

This timer job is scheduled to run:

- ⦿ Minutes Every `1` minute(s)
- ○ Hourly
- ○ Daily
- ○ Weekly
- ○ Monthly

[Run Now] [Disable] [OK] [Cancel]

FIGURE 11-13 PowerPivot Data Refresh Timer Job

To control when the workbook gets refreshed itself, the IW Producer who created and controls the workbook will enable Data Refresh for the specific workbook. In the process, the IW Producer can also indicate the earliest start time and schedule the frequency (lowest granularity is day) to perform the data refresh.

There are a number of enterprise concerns that you should take into account concerning the concept of "business hours." Do not forget that business hours is in relation to the time used by your servers and SharePoint setting, which may or may not match the time of your users.

First of all, you must determine if there truly exists a concept of business/non-business hours in your enterprise, if your analysts are globally located. This is most likely not the case, so this implies a potentially larger impact on your source systems, and that data refresh may, in fact, be running at all hours of the day (depending on which source systems have their own availability times).

Because of this, you must better monitor these workbooks (more information on this appears in Chapter 9) to ensure that the data refresh process does not result in a bad user experience (for example, slow user queries). This also implies that you may need more resources (that is, more powerful servers and/or more servers), so that it's possible to have concurrent queries and concurrent data loading on the same App Servers.

The larger concern, however, is the impact on your source systems. Different source systems may have different query availability. In some cases, the data refresh may have to be done during business hours, since the source system is only available at this time. Therefore, it will be important that you limit the number of IW Producers who have the capability to enable data refresh. Also, you must work closely with those IW Producers so that you and they are aware of which systems are available at what times.

In enterprise-speak, this means you must create a set of processes and policies so that IW Producers are not improperly enabling data refresh and setting suboptimal start times. But note, even with the capability of IW Producers to set the earliest start time and schedule frequency, it is ultimately up to you to set the PowerPivot Data Refresh Timer Job and the PowerPivot Settings.

Data Refresh Accounts

Another Data Refresh configuration setting of concern is that of the accounts. As noted in Chapters 7 and 8, the `PowerPivotUnattendedAccount` is the account that you create based on an existing Windows authentication (or other authentication method) account. This account will run the data refresh thread by processing the VertiPaq database within the Excel workbook. To get access to the source data, you will need the credentials stored within the Secure Store Service to access the data.

From an enterprise perspective, this brings up a couple of important points about the accounts. The first is that the `PowerPivotUnattendedAccount` should not be a farm administrator account or an account that has a lot of access rights. Actually, the best practice is that it should be an account with virtually no rights at all, except the capability to log in to other servers as a guest or with minimal access rights. Remember, it's the service account credentials associated with the PowerPivot System Service account running the data refresh threads, and typically it's the user accounts stored within the Secure Store Service that have the rights to the actual data.

Since it's the user's accounts that have access rights, the issue is that, with people leaving, password changes, and access rights, how do you know if there are issues with the data refresh? The first line of defense is the user who can store credentials and indicate who needs to be notified by email if a refresh fails within the data refresh dialog of the report itself, as shown in Figure 11-14. While this is good, an IT Pro knows that you cannot always depend on the user to know and/or inform you if a problem exists.

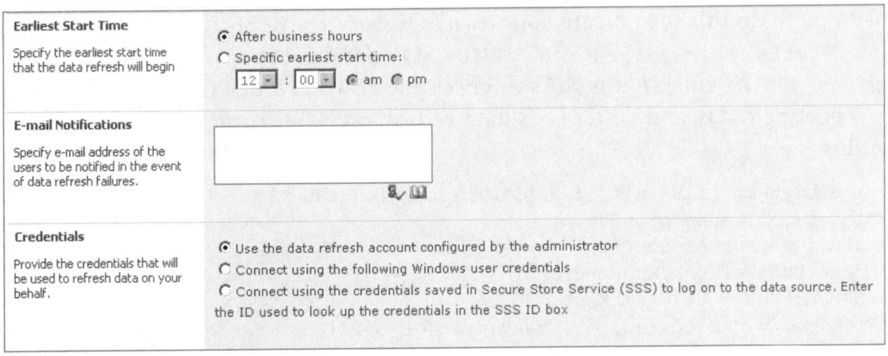

FIGURE 11-14 PowerPivot Gallery Workbook Data Refresh dialog

Detecting Data Refresh Issues

While user access rights are a key concern for data refresh issues, there are a number of scenarios that can prevent the data refresh from working correctly, including (but not limited to) source systems being offline, network interruptions, SharePoint farm/service account password resets, and so on. Regardless of the cause of your failure, you must understand what is going on within the environment. While having PowerPivot System Service "auto-magically" take care of the processing without any need for manual intervention, you experience a sense of loss of control and understanding of what is going on with the data refresh.

Therefore, the primary option is to refer to the Data Refresh Web parts within the PowerPivot Management Dashboard (Central Admin ⇨ General Application Settings ⇨ PowerPivot Management Dashboard). Typically, this is at the bottom of the dashboard, as shown in Figure 11-15. While this is a great feature, one of the enterprise considerations concerning data refresh is the sheer number of reports that you will have to assess.

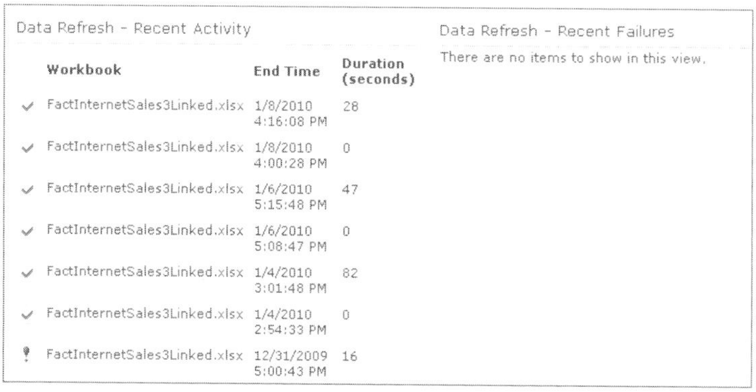

Data Refresh – Recent Activity				Data Refresh – Recent Failures
Workbook	**End Time**	**Duration (seconds)**		There are no items to show in this view.
✓ FactInternetSales3Linked.xlsx	1/8/2010 4:16:08 PM	28		
✓ FactInternetSales3Linked.xlsx	1/8/2010 4:00:28 PM	0		
✓ FactInternetSales3Linked.xlsx	1/6/2010 5:15:48 PM	47		
✓ FactInternetSales3Linked.xlsx	1/6/2010 5:08:47 PM	0		
✓ FactInternetSales3Linked.xlsx	1/4/2010 3:01:48 PM	82		
✓ FactInternetSales3Linked.xlsx	1/4/2010 2:54:33 PM	0		
❢ FactInternetSales3Linked.xlsx	12/31/2009 5:00:43 PM	16		

FIGURE 11-15 Data Refresh Web Parts within the PowerPivot Management dashboard

While the dashboard shown in Figure 11-15 notes that there were no recent failures, in most enterprise scenarios involving tens or hundreds of reports that need to be refreshed, there will almost always be some failures. So, it is recommended that you build a process to be alerted or notified when reports fail — that is, the system tells you the report has failed, instead of you having to go look at the system.

A quick-and-easy way to do this is to create your own SQL Services Reporting Services report against the `PowerPivotServiceApplication_<GUID>` SQL database that is the underlying source for the `ITOps_<GUID>` cube that is the source for the PowerPivot Management Dashboard. A sample query reporting today and yesterday's data refresh events against the SQL database would look like this:

```
select f.FriendlyName, r.Result, f.RunStartTime, f.RunEndTime, f.[Source],
     f.[Catalog], f.ConnectionString
  from DataRefresh.RunDetails f
    inner join DataRefresh.RunResults r
      on r.ResultKey = f.ResultKey
where RunEndTime >= dateadd(dd, -1, cast(cast(GETDATE() as varchar(11)) as
```

```
             smalldatetime))
      order by
           f.FriendlyName
```

This simple source can be used to create (for example) a SQL Services Reporting Services report displaying notification alerts and/or subscriptions so that you can be informed on data refresh issues, as shown in Figure 11-16.

FIGURE 11-16 Simple SSRS Data Refresh Report based on data refresh events

 To find out more information and get a sample of this report, see the PowerPivot Data Refresh SSRS Report at `http://bit.ly/7FP1km.`

Data Refresh and 2 GB Limit

Another issue of concern is the 2 GB limit for your PowerPivot workbook. Both PowerPivot for Excel and SharePoint prevent you from creating or storing a workbook that is larger than 2 GB in size. (Note that this typically means your actual database is 4 GB in size.) However, once you upload your workbook to SharePoint and enable data refresh, the new data being added to your workbook during the refresh may force the workbook to cross the 2 GB threshold. When this happens, the data refresh will fail to complete its task.

Whether you are the IW Producer of the report or the IT Pro administrating the environment, you must work together to best resolve this issue. Potential solutions range from reducing the number of columns or rows of data, importing the data in a different way to reduce the size, pushing the solution to traditional Analysis Services, and/or partitioning the workbook (for example, having a workbook for each year of data).

Data Refresh and Drivers

Another key issue for data refresh is whether the drivers exist for your SharePoint environment. For example, say that your IW Producer must import data from a third-party database. Say that the IW Producer has the driver installed on his or her own client computer in order to perform the initial download of data. This does not mean that the SharePoint farm and the PowerPivot System Service have access to that driver when the data refresh is enabled.

Therefore, you will want to build processes and policies that prevent errors like this from happening, in addition to the alerts and reports to review all of the reports where data refresh has failed.

SSAS Engine Service

As you will recall from Chapter 7 and Chapter 10, the SQL Server Analysis Services (SSAS) engine is the same Analysis Services Engine that is used for traditional Analysis Services (for example, MOLAP, HOLAP, ROLAP). There is a setting within the Analysis Services Engine when it is installed in SharePoint Integrated Mode that turns on the VertiPaq engine. An IT Professional familiar with Analysis Services may be tempted to configure and tweak the various settings within the Analysis Services Engine service in an attempt to improve query concurrency, performance, or just out of sheer interest.

However, for SQL Server 2008 R2 Analysis Services, any tweaking and/or changes to the registry or the msmdsrv.ini file are not supported. This may change for future releases of SQL Server, but in its current form for self-service BI, these actions are not supported.

The vast majority of configuration and control of the VertiPaq Engine is performed by the PowerPivot System Service. Even standard tools such as Visual Studio 2008 Business Intelligence Development Studio (BIDS) and SQL Server Management Studio have not been updated yet to properly connect to a VertiPaq engine (outside of the SQL Profiler, as noted in Chapter 9). Creating these as services within SharePoint allows for less manual intervention and less need for tweaking.

So, what are things that you can do to help tweak or improve performance? To put it rather lightly, not much. There are only a few things you must do to ensure your SSAS engine (in VertiPaq mode) is working properly. And you can only do these tasks from SharePoint Central Administration.

Resource Allocation for Your App Servers

Recall that the databases are in-memory, which means that, to determine how much memory you will need for your App Servers, you use the sum of all the databases in use. Add 10 percent to 20 percent overhead for the memory mapping necessary for auto-detection.

If there are memory pressure issues, unused databases will be detached and stored in the OLAP backup folder (c:\Program Files\...\OLAP\backup) as a temporary cache, so they can retrieve the database from this folder instead of extracting it from Excel. Your tool is the PowerPivot Management dashboard, which will report the memory and CPU utilization for all servers that have PowerPivot Services installed.

Concurrent Users Querying the Same Workbook

One of the key issues you will be concerned with is the capability of a single VertiPaq in-memory database to handle concurrent users because only one instance of the workbook model will ever be deployed. You will also use the PowerPivot Management Dashboard to determine if there are a lot of concurrent users querying this one workbook.

If this is occurring, you may want to build a traditional Analysis Services cube to handle the query workload for this report. This way, you can have more control, and it will be capable of handling a heavier workload. A not-very-elegant workaround to this issue is to create multiple copies of the same workbook (for example, one for HR, Sales, or Finance), and have different sets of users go to their assigned workbooks. The load-balancing mechanism should ensure that each workbook, while containing the same data, will be on a different App Server to spread the workload. Do this only if you think it's absolutely necessary, as it may be easier just to create a new traditional SSAS cube instead.

SHAREPOINT DATABASES

SharePoint 2010 officially supports using SQL Server 2005, SQL Server 2008, and SQL Server 2008 R2 for its own databases. But it is highly recommended that you use SQL Server 2008 R2, since it is faster than its predecessor, and you can potentially take advantage of features like Remote Blob Store (RBS) to store the larger PowerPivot for Excel workbooks in an RBS provider (instead of as a blob within the database).

The performance factor is important because of the large file sizes and more extensive SharePoint and PowerPivot logging that require a more robust database to handle the transactional workload. This is especially important when you switch to a dedicated SQL Server to host your SharePoint databases, because this one server will need to handle all the transaction requests from all of the services and servers in the entire farm.

Sizing

There are various recommendations on what should be the maximum size of a database — especially the SharePoint content databases. Some articles and books indicate that you should keep the content database size to 100 GB. But, in reality, the determining factor for this is how well you can back up and restore the database if there are disaster-recovery issues.

 You can find out more of the specifics on database sizing specific to SharePoint in the book Microsoft SharePoint 2010 Administrator's Companion *(Redmond, Washington: Microsoft Press, 2009).*

Scaling Out

Once you determine your optimal database size, you must be able to scale out. In the case of your content database, you can easily add more content databases from the Central Administration. To do so, go to Central Administration ➪ Application Management ➪ "Manage content databases," and then click the "Add content database" button. Not only can you easily add more content databases through the Central Administration user interface (UI), but you can even add databases to different servers.

Maintenance

Since these are standard SQL databases, you must treat them as such. If you want to ensure high availability for your SharePoint databases, then you should make use of the clustering feature. If you want to ensure that you can handle disaster recovery, you must set up times to back up the databases and/or make use of logging/database mirroring to have an available copy of the data in case disaster strikes.

These maintenance concepts require far deeper and more extensive technical detail in order to provide adequate guidance, and, therefore, are outside the scope of this book. Nevertheless, check out the site `sqlcat.com`, *which provides in-depth articles on these and other SQL server topics based on enterprise customer findings.*

Remote Blob Store

As noted throughout this book, one of the major concerns with PowerPivot for Excel workbooks is the sheer size of them. The default max size of files being uploaded to SharePoint is 50 MB. Meanwhile, files may grow to 2 GB in size. While you can update the SharePoint and Excel Services configurations to handle 2 GB workbooks, ultimately, these workbooks are stored as a blob within a SQL Server database.

Storing blobs directly within a SQL Server database tends to have a higher overhead. This is the reason why, throughout the last few chapters, there have been various references to Remote Blob Storage (RBS). It can help reduce the overall overhead against the SQL Server because the file is no longer stored within the actual SQL database.

While it may look like you are storing the file within the database, with RBS enabled, the file is actually stored in an RBS provider. One such example of an RBS provider is the `FILESTREAM`. This means that while SharePoint thinks it is storing and accessing the file within/from the SQL database, in reality, the RBS provider is making use of the RBS `FILESTREAM` provider (in this case) to store the file directly onto the file system. While there is a negligible overhead for this redirection, there are performance improvements in binary file storage (for example, a SharePoint user uploads files faster).

For more information about RBS and how to install/configure it, see `http://bit.ly/5t65dW`. *For more information on the potential advantages of using RBS for your PowerPivot for SharePoint environment, see* `http://bit.ly/9BW9Wx`.

UPGRADE AND PATCHING CONSIDERATIONS

Two important areas not to be forgotten when discussing the enterprise environment are upgrades and patches to the SharePoint deployment. Let's take a look at each of these in a bit more detail.

Upgrading from SharePoint 2007 to 2010

As you have read thus far, this chapter covers how PowerPivot impacts enterprise considerations. Upgrading your SharePoint 2007 farm to SharePoint 2010 is a very complex endeavor. This section hardly covers all of the facets of this, and it is highly recommended that you heavily reference the Upgrade and Resource Migration Center (`http://bit.ly/3Yzk10`) and/or contact your SharePoint Ranger (that is, subject matter expert).

Briefly, following are the primary reasons for the complexities surrounding such an upgrade:

➤ SharePoint 2010 has three times more services than the 2007 version. It is a foundation for many services and components requiring more resources, and where services require their own set of servers to handle the workloads.

➤ The great thing about SharePoint in general is the capability to customize it to your specifications. Many portions of SharePoint, from the UI to how services operate, have changed, potentially forcing the reconstruction of any customizations that you previously created.

Thus, you should always tackle the following fundamental action items when upgrading from SharePoint 2007 to SharePoint 2010:

➤ Upgrade to SharePoint 2007 SP2

➤ Run the Pre-Upgrade Checker Tool (`http://bit.ly/5cYyTI`)

The Pre-Upgrade Checker Tool will go through your entire farm and will produce a report that notes the status of your environment from upgrade readiness to unsupported customizations. To run this Pre-Upgrade Checker Tool, from a command prompt (run as an Administrator), navigate to the `%Common Program Files%\Microsoft Shared\Web Server Extensions\14\bin` and run the following command:

```
stsadm.exe -o preupgradecheck
```

So, how does PowerPivot impact your upgrade from SharePoint 2007 to SharePoint 2010? Following are some primary concerns:

➤ Since PowerPivot Services and Excel Services use a lot of memory and CPU cycles, you will most likely need new hardware, as opposed to doing an in-place upgrade on existing hardware.

➤ While, with SharePoint 2010, it is possible to use SQL Server 2005 64-bit as your SQL Server, it is recommended that you use SQL Server 2008 or SQL Server 2008 R2 as your database. In addition to faster performance, SQL Server 2008 provides you with the option to use RBS, so you can save the larger PowerPivot for Excel workbooks to an RBS provider, instead of as a blob within the database.

➤ PowerPivot does not support inter-farm shared services, which means that the App Servers running PowerPivot Services must reside in the same farm where the content is actually stored.

Upgrade and Patch Management

As many of you may have experienced with SharePoint 2007, performing an upgrade and patching of the farm was haphazard at times, especially when it involved schema changes to the content databases. The good news is that, for SharePoint 2010, there is an "Upgrade and Patch Management" page within the Central Administration (Central Admin ⇨ Upgrade and Patch Management), as shown in Figure 11-17.

FIGURE 11-17 SharePoint Central Admin "Upgrade and Patch Management"

With a combination of various PowerShell scripts and this page, you can monitor and control your upgrade and patch management mechanisms. You can even manage specific database upgrade status by clicking the "Review database status" link, with the results as shown in Figure 11-18.

Central Administration ▸ Manage Databases Upgrade Status

Use this page to view the upgrade status for databases in the farm.

SQL Instance	Database	Type
GemSQLR2	SharePoint_AdminContent_71f1a029-03d7-498d-b15a-8711483fdfb5	Content Database
GemSQLR2	WSS_Content	Content Database
GemSQLR2	PowerPivotServiceApplication1_b6bf667d890146e48e1dff43f5ebf03f	GeminiServiceDatabase
GemSQLR2	Secure_Store_Service_DB_f97a7044b1704223bcfc5a9a4d78a949	SecureStoreServiceDatabase
GemSQLR2	SharePoint_Config	Configuration Database
GemSQLR2	StateService_f541320304134367ad5e7a70821ab88b	StateDatabase
GemSQLR2	User Profile Service Application_ProfileDB_00fa47483a384a7dbcc0ed44ae599ab9	ProfileDatabase
GemSQLR2	User Profile Service Application_SocialDB_bc5f3c5027134c1c8d4b41df986c92db	SocialDatabase
GemSQLR2	User Profile Service Application_SyncDB_1321525cc32f407da8db10a712ef32f9	SynchronizationDatabase
GemSQLR2	WSS_Logging	SPUsageDatabase

FIGURE 11-18 Manage Database Upgrade Status from the SharePoint Upgrade and Patching Management Central Admin interface

 For more information on upgrade and patch management, see the book Microsoft SharePoint 2010 Administrator's Companion *(Redmond, Washington: Microsoft Press, 2009).*

So, how does PowerPivot impact upgrading and patching within your SharePoint 2010 farm? Recall that the PowerPivot Management dashboard includes the option to "Review timer job definitions." The job of interest is the PowerPivot Setup Extension Timer Job, as shown in Figure 11-19.

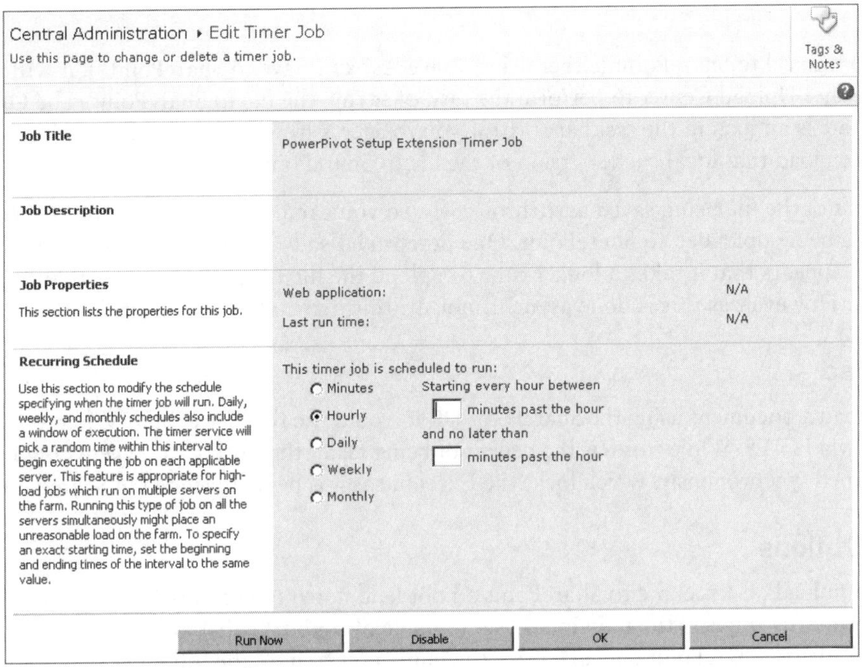

FIGURE 11-19 PowerPivot Setup Extension Job

By default, this job will run hourly to determine if there are any PowerPivot components that require patching. This is a common method within SharePoint where services are typically patched via scheduled Timer Jobs. This reduces manual intervention, especially within the context of timing (for example, databases going offline, a patch having to occur after a database schema upgrade, and so on) and manual labor (going through each server and running patching deployment would not be terribly enjoyable). Note there is the Run Now button (located at the bottom of Figure 11-19), so, just in case you want to manually perform the patching of the PowerPivot components, you can do so as well.

UPLOAD CONSIDERATIONS

The reason for focusing on SharePoint upload considerations is because SharePoint has been optimized for the download scenarios (that is, users downloading files from SharePoint to their own local desktop). So, while download scenarios may have been optimized, the opposite direction is not as optimized (comparatively, anyway). With the advent of larger PowerPivot for Excel workbooks (that is, up to 2 GB), there is potentially a much larger impact on the SharePoint WFEs.

Save As Versus Upload

So, let's start off with some quick definitions. When an IW Producer has created a workbook, he or she can either save the Excel workbook using Save As to the SharePoint site within Excel itself, or save and close the workbook and upload the workbook using the SharePoint UI. What may not be known (or realized) is that there are two different mechanisms of saving that occur when you choose one method or the other. The issues and description of these two methods are described in detail in the blog posting at http://bit.ly/7KIW9X, but let's get to the heart of the issue.

Excel Save As

Once you save from Excel to SharePoint (either using "Save As" or "Save to SharePoint"), it will make use of the Office Upload Center to perform the task of saving the file to SharePoint. The Office Upload Center (there is an icon in the taskbar tray for you to access it) will save the file to a local cache first, and then load that local cache version of the file to SharePoint.

This has the benefit of the file being saved asynchronously, so you can continue to edit and work with the file as it is being uploaded to SharePoint. One potential disadvantage with using Save As is that, from tests, it appears that it takes a longer time to upload the file using this method than from the SharePoint UI. However, as this is done asynchronously, this may not be a concern for you.

SharePoint Upload

If you were to upload a document using the SharePoint UI, it would use the SharePoint Web interface to upload the files via HTTP. While this has the benefit of being faster than using the Save As option, this task is performed synchronously, which locks the Excel file as it is being uploaded to SharePoint.

Comparing the Options

These methods to upload an Excel file to SharePoint do not lend much to enterprise considerations, since the choice primarily impacts the individual user (outside of support calls). But if you have a lot of users uploading files to SharePoint concurrently, it is important to note the following:

➤ Uploading by the SharePoint UI is faster, but also uses more network bandwidth. Using this method is advantageous when you have high-bandwidth and low-latency environments (for example, within the corporate network LAN), since you are not as concerned about network bottlenecks.

➤ If you are concerned about network bottlenecks (for example, corporate WANs, other high-latency/low-bandwidth scenarios, and so on), you may want to make it a standard to use Save As. By using the Office Upload Center, while it may be slower in comparison, it is asynchronous, and less bandwidth is utilized, as smaller chunks of data are sent across the wire.

In the end, there isn't any policy that you can use to enforce what users do to save their Excel workbooks to SharePoint. However, if you are concerned about a particular network environment scenario, you may be able to at least influence your users to go one way or the other to give them (and yourself) a smoother experience.

Effect of Bandwidth on Upload

The previous discussion touched a bit on the impact of network bandwidth. Following are a couple of analyses that focus in on this issue.

As you can see in Figure 11-20, in a standard corporate environment where the connection to the SharePoint farm is a 100 Mbps line, it takes approximately 20 minutes to perform the upload. Yet, if you were to do this using a cable modem (for example, with a 1 Mbps upload speed), it would take more than 3 hours and 40 minutes to perform the same upload. Fortunately, this upload is done asynchronously, so the user may not be affected much even if it takes that long to upload the file.

Switching to within your corporate LAN, the breakdown shown in Figure 11-21 is between 100 Mbps and 1 Gbps. You will notice the steady increase in duration because the file is larger in size. But, instead of taking almost 7 minutes, the same 1.3 GB file can be uploaded in a little more than 2 minutes using a 1 Gbps line.

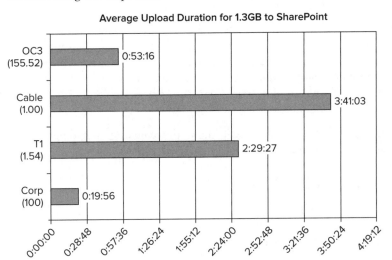

FIGURE 11-20 Average upload duration for a 1.3 GB file to SharePoint broken out by network bandwidth using Excel Save As

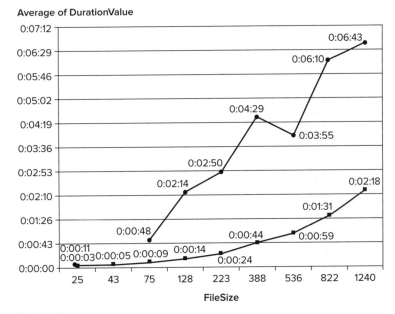

FIGURE 11-21 Average upload duration for a 1.3 GB file to SharePoint broken out by network bandwidth using SharePoint Upload

LargeChunkFileSize Configuration

If you're using the SharePoint UI in a corporate environment, you're probably okay with the upload performance. However, you may also be interested in any configurations within SharePoint itself that may improve upload performance for the Excel Save As option.

One possible configuration option that may help is the `LargeChunkFileSize` parameter within SharePoint. This parameter changes the size of chunks that SharePoint receives from the client. The premise is that, if you receive fewer larger chunks, you may be able to upload the file faster. However, the Save As option using the Office Upload Center is already creating smaller chunks of data, and the chunks are primarily chunks of blob binary data, as opposed to chunks of XML text data (like most other Excel or Office documents).

But, as you can see from Figure 11-22, there is minimal-to-no improvement in upload performance when you change the default to `LargeChunkFileSize` (500).

SharePoint Upload Versus File Copy

So, what else can you do to improve upload performance if this is a serious problem? Recall that, when SharePoint performs its upload, it's using the HTTP protocol to perform the transfer of the file from the local computer to the SharePoint server. A more simplistic version (to the user) is to "upload" the file from a client box to the SharePoint WFE by using the UNC path so that it looks like it's a file copy.

For example, instead of uploading the file to `http://mySharePoint/PowerPivot%20Gallery/`, you can copy the file to the UNC path of `\\mySharePoint\PowerPivot%20Gallery` if you have Windows 7 or Desktop Experience turned on for Windows Server 2008 and 2008 R2. This copying methodology makes use of Web-based Distributed Authoring and Versioning (WebDAV) protocol, which is a set of extensions to HTTP included within the operating system of the client and server. However, the copy via WebDAV is only going to be nominally faster than Save As or using SharePoint UI upload, since all three methods are using different flavors of HTTP.

But what if you are able to copy the files (that is, a regular file copy) to a directory on the SharePoint WFE? From there you could do a local upload from the UI, or build your own Powershell script using the SharePoint Object Model (OM) to automatically upload the files. How much faster would the file copy be in comparison to HTTP (WebDAV)?

As you can tell from the 1.3 GB file transfer rate shown in Figure 11-23, it took almost seven minutes to perform the file copy when using WebDAV, while it took the file copy less than a minute. Because this is considerably faster than the HTTP methods, if upload times are a concern for your environment, and you have resolved the security issues of having users copy files directly to the WFE or to a staging area within the same lab infrastructure as your SharePoint farm, you may want to consider building a process/mechanism to automatically upload these files from the said staging area.

Typically, there is only a small group of IW Producers who will be creating these large workbooks — often in batches. To get these files uploaded faster from disparate locations, you may want to take advantage of the speed of a regular file copy.

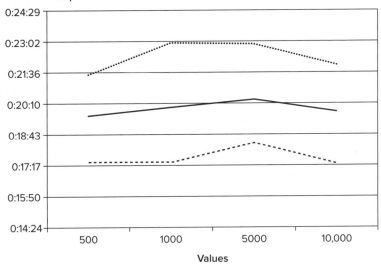

Average of UploadFileTime
Minimum of UploadFileTime
Maximun of UploadFileTime

Values
——— Average of UploadFileTime
- - - - - Minimum of UploadFileTime
••••••••• Maximum of UploadFileTime

FIGURE 11-22 Upload time of 1.3 GB file with different LargeChunkFileSize values

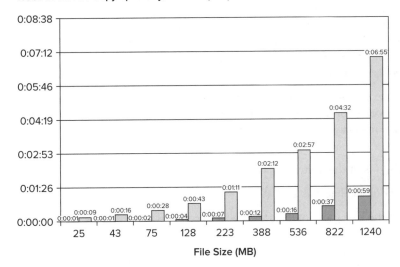

WebDav vs. File Copy Speed by File Size (1Gb)

■ File Copy   □ Web Dav

FIGURE 11-23 WebDav versus FileCopy speed by file size

Impact of Online Edit

When you open up an Excel workbook within SharePoint, behind the scenes, it is Excel Services and PowerPivot Services that are doing all of the calculations. But what about when you want to edit your Excel file?

The traditional way to edit a file within SharePoint is through the "All documents" view. Yet, within the PowerPivot Gallery, by default, the view is created by the Silverlight control. To check out and edit the file using the standard SharePoint menus, you must switch from the current PowerPivot view back to the "All Documents" view.

You can find more information about Online Editing in the posting
`http://bit.ly/8oO5Tp`.

From the PowerPivot Gallery, the more natural way of doing this is to open the workbook within the browser and click on the "Open in Excel" button. From there, you are given the option to edit the file within Excel.

For example, let's say that you already set the PowerPivot Gallery library settings to ensure that you check out the file every time your files are edited, as shown in Figure 11-24.

You'll notice that there is a checkbox called "Use my local drafts folder" when you want to check out and edit the file. If this checkbox is not checked, the Excel file will actually reside on the SharePoint WFE, instead of on your local client box. As noted in the "SharePoint WFEs" section earlier in this chapter, there is a potential impact when you upload or edit a file. Every time you upload a

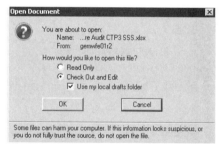

FIGURE 11-24 Editing an Excel file from within Excel Services

file, it will go from Excel to the WFE, which will receive the file and perform the task of storing the file within the content database, as shown in Figure 11-25.

The same thing happens when you do an online edit of the file, except that even more resources are utilized because the "master copy" of the workbook actually resides in temporary folders of the WFE. This can be even more intensive if users are constantly saving when they are doing an online edit of their Excel file.

To better describe this, let's look at the following scenario:

1. A user opens workbook in SharePoint.

2. The user checks out the Excel workbook and begins to edit it. The file is not saved to the local drafts but rather on the WFE.

3. The user clicks on slicer 1.

4. The user clicks on slicer 2.

5. The user clicks Save in Excel.

6. The user clears slicer 2.

7. The user clears slicer 1.

8. The user clicks Save in Excel.

9. The user changes a report filter.

10. The user clicks Save in Excel.

11. The user closes Excel.

12. The user returns to PowerPivot Gallery.

13. The user opens the workbook in SharePoint.

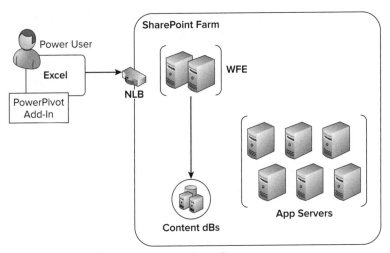

FIGURE 11-25 Architecture for uploading a file

This is a relatively simple scenario commonly performed by anyone who wants to edit a PowerPivot workbook. In terms of resources utilized, if these actions were performed with the "Use my local drafts" checkbox checked, there would be no impact on the WFE or content database until the user saves *and* checks in the file. Clicking on Save in this sequence of steps would only result in the user saving the file to a local drafts folder on the user's own computer. It is not until the user checks in the file that there would be an impact on the farm.

However, if the user had not checked the "Use my local drafts" checkbox, every time the user clicked on Save, the workbook would then be saved from the WFE to the SharePoint content database. If you have a large workbook (for example, 2 GB), this means that every time you click on Save, 2 GB are transferred from the WFE to the content database each and every time, thus hogging up network and CPU resources.

Figure 11-26 shows the results from a perfmon trace that was performed for the previously noted sequence of steps. The perfmon trace was recorded on the SharePoint SQL Server (holding the content database that would ultimately store the workbook) of a three-server farm with one WFE, one App Server, and one dedicated SQL Server.

In the graph, the first and last spikes represent the "Bytes Sent" from the SharePoint content database to the WFE/App Servers. You will notice that these spikes are attributed to when a user is opening the workbook within Excel Services, thus requiring the extraction of the workbook from the SharePoint content database. The three middle spikes are associated with each time the user clicked on Save when performing an online edit of the workbook. These spikes are the "Bytes Received" — that is, the workbook in its entirety saved to the SharePoint content database.

What this reveals is that, when you're working with PowerPivot workbooks (which are generally larger than your average document), you may want to force users to check out the file, as well as strongly encourage users to save the file to their local drafts. That way, the PowerPivot workbook resides on their local desktops and does not unnecessarily add more resource load to your SharePoint farm and the network infrastructure in between.

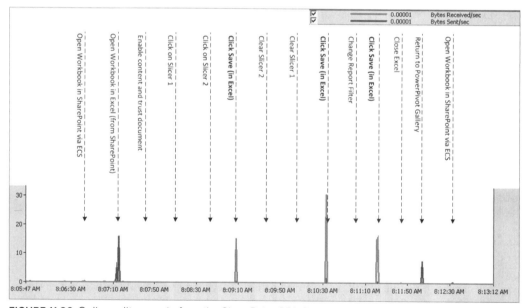

FIGURE 11-26 Online edit scenario from the SharePoint SQL Server (content database)

CHECK OUT AND EDIT

One of the ways to reduce the impact on the SharePoint WFE is to ensure that users who are editing the Excel workbook are doing so on their local box. This does require more client resources, but, as most PowerPivot for Excel workbooks require more powerful client resources to import the data, this most likely is not a cause for concern. There is also the concern that people will not have the same version of the Excel file, because different people will download the file to their client box, and then you are back to spreadmart chaos.

One of the ways to solve this problem is to force users to check out the file when they are about to edit. To do this, you can go to the PowerPivot Gallery and click on Library ➪ Settings ➪ Library Settings within the Office Ribbon. In the Document Library Settings page, go to the General Settings pane and click on Versioning Settings. The very Last Option is the Require Check Out dialog. Ensure that the radio button is set to "Yes," and then all of your workbooks will require a user to check out the file in order to edit it.

It is important to note that doing this will result in multiple versions of the same file; the user will be editing the most current version. The drawback to this approach is that, if you allow versioning, you may require more disk space for your SharePoint Content database because multiple versions of this file are stored. You can control the number of versions in the same Versioning Settings dialog noted in the previous paragraph.

SUMMARY

This chapter expanded your understanding of the impact of PowerPivot and SharePoint architectures when working with enterprise scenarios. This chapter did not delve deeper into issues ranging from SharePoint capacity planning to Excel Services optimization because these topics deserve their own chapter (or book) by themselves. Yet, this chapter did identify and provide enterprise considerations on how PowerPivot effects the IT environment.

When considering the hardware requirements, you should not just consider optimal performance, but also the corporate IT enterprise database server standard. Unless this standard is horribly underpowered, it is most likely possible to standardize your PowerPivot for SharePoint environment around these corporate IT standards. But, in addition to the individual resource components, you have learned about the holistic view of your SharePoint farm (that is, topology) so that you can better provision and plan out your PowerPivot for SharePoint farm.

To help the latter, you learned about the individual server components of a PowerPivot for SharePoint environment (for example, WFE, App, Database, and so on), and about optimization techniques for each one. The greatest impact of PowerPivot on a SharePoint farm is the SharePoint App Server, which, in effect, is an enterprise Analysis Services server in its own right.

Concerning upgrading and patching your SharePoint farm, this chapter discussed the difficulties surrounding an upgrade, because it involves both software and hardware changes. Nevertheless, SharePoint provides some interesting tools that make upgrade and patch management easier than before.

Finally, this chapter discussed issues surrounding uploading to SharePoint. While this topic may not seem to amount to much at first, PowerPivot impacts this topic because it creates larger-than-average files, and SharePoint is rightly optimized for download scenarios. Because of this, you learned about the various impacts of bandwidth, upload methodologies, and the impact of online edit. Building policies around how you upload these files may reduce the overall impact on your SharePoint farm.

Putting this all together, you should now be a little better prepared to plan, test, and implement for your enterprise scenarios.

Do not forget to download the online chapter and appendix that provides example PowerPivot scenarios, as well as code downloads (for example, database, sample workbook, and so on). You may find this material at this book's companion Web site, www.wrox.com.

PART IV
Appendix

▶ **APPENDIX A:** Setting Up the SDR Healthcare Application

Setting Up the
SDR Healthcare Application

In Chapters 3 through 6 of this book, you work through an extended example of how to create and publish a PowerPivot workbook. This example involves a fictional healthcare company, SDR Healthcare, and involves doing analysis and reporting on the data in that company's audit database, and other external data sources.

To simulate importing data from multiple data sources, some setup of those data sources is needed before starting the application. In the real world, those data sources would already be there. But, for this example, they are not. This appendix provides instructions on how to set up the initial environment before starting to work on the example. These instructions assume that PowerPivot for SharePoint is already set up. Instructions for a simple single-machine setup can be found in Chapter 2. Instructions for a more detailed multi-machine setup can be found in Chapter 8.

SETTING UP THE SQL SERVER AUDIT DATABASE

The main analytical data for the application comes from a SQL Server database. This data is included in the SDRAudit.bak file included in this book's downloadable files.

To restore the backup onto a SQL Server 2008 R2 instance, follow these steps:

1. Start SQL Server Management Studio.

2. Connect to the server on which you want to restore the database.

3. Right-click on the Databases folder for that server in the Object Explorer window, and select Restore Database.

4. In the "Source for restore" section of the dialog, select From Device. Click the edit field button (the button with the "…" caption).

5. In the Specify Backup dialog, click the Add button.

6. Specify the full name (including the path) of the SDRAudit.bak file in the "File name" field and click the OK button.

7. Click OK in the Specify Backup dialog.

8. Click on the Restore checkbox in the "Select the backup sets to restore" section of the dialog.

9. In the "To database" drop-down in the "Destination for restore" section of the dialog, select "SDRAudit" and click OK. SQL Server Management Studio will restore the database. Once the restore is completed, click OK on the completion message box.

SETTING UP THE DATABASE GROUP NAME SHAREPOINT LIST

The Database Group Name table in the SDR Healthcare application comes from a SharePoint 2010 list that is imported as a data feed. In order for the SharePoint functionality of exporting a list as a data feed to work, you must install the Data Services Update for .NET Framework 3.5 SP1 on your SharePoint server. You can find this update at the following locations:

➤ For Windows Server 2008, go to the following:

```
http://www.microsoft.com/downloads/details.aspx?familyid=
    4B710B89-8576-46CF-A4BF-331A9306D555&displaylang=en
```

➤ For Windows Server 2008 R2, go to the following:

```
http://www.microsoft.com/downloads/details.aspx?familyid=
    79d7f6f8-d6e9-4b8c-8640-17f89452148e&displaylang=en
```

This book's download files include a `DatabaseGroupName.xlsx` file that contains a worksheet page with the data needed for the Database Group Name SharePoint list. To import that data into SharePoint, follow these steps:

1. In your SharePoint 2010 installation, navigate to the Lists section of the site, as shown in Figure A-1.

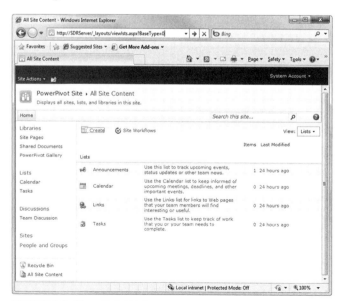

FIGURE A-1: SharePoint Lists page

2.   Click on the Create button.

3.   In the Create dialog, navigate to the Import Spreadsheet item and click on it. On the right side of the dialog, click the Create button.

4.   Fill in the name and, optionally, the description of the new list. In this case, enter **DatabaseGroupName.**

5.   Click on the Browse button and navigate to the location of the DatabaseGroupName.xlsx file.

6.   Click the Import button.

7.   In the Import to Windows SharePoint Services list, select Range of Cells. In the Select Range field, ensure that all the cells with data on the DatabaseGroupName sheet are selected (that is, $A\$1:\$C\$23$). Click on the Import button.

After the import completes successfully, you will have a new SharePoint list called DatabaseGroupName (Figure A-2) that can be used as a data feed with PowerPivot.

FIGURE A-2: The DatabaseGroupName SharePoint list

SETTING UP THE CLIENT ADDRESS TO STATE REPORT

The final external data source needed for the SDR Healthcare application is a Reporting Services report that is also imported as a data feed. Before setting up that report, however, you must set up SQL Server 2008 R2 Reporting Services. The following steps show how to do it:

1. Launch SQL Server 2008 R2 setup.

2. In the main setup page, select "New Installation or add features to an existing installation."

3. Click OK on the Setup Support Rules page.

4. On the initial Setup Support Files page, click Install.

5. On the second Setup Support Rules page, click Next.

6. On the Installation Type page, select "New installation or add shared features" and click Next.

7. On the Product Key page, either select "Specify a free edition" and choose Evaluation, or select "Enter the product key" and enter your product key. Click Next.

8. On the License Terms page, accept the license terms. You may also select to send feature usage data to Microsoft. Doing this allows Microsoft to do a better job of prioritizing features and fixes in future versions. Doing this is recommended.

9. On the Setup Role page, select SQL Server Feature Installation and click Next.

10. On the Feature Selection page, select only Reporting Services and click Next.

11. On the Installation Rules page, click Next.

12. On the Instance Configuration page, select "Default instance" and click Next. Click Next on the Disk Space Requirements page.

13. On the Server Configuration page, supply an Account Name and, if needed, a Password. Click Next. Click Next on the Reporting Services Configuration page.

14. On the Error Reporting page, you have the opportunity to elect to send error information to Microsoft. Doing this gives Microsoft required information to fix problems for later releases and service packs. Doing this is recommended.

15. Click Next on the Installation Configuration Rules page.

16. Click Install on the Ready to Install page.

After Reporting Services is installed, it must be configured. The following steps describe how to configure the Report Server:

1. Go to Start ➪ All Programs ➪ Microsoft SQL Server 2008 R2 ➪ Configuration Tools. Click Reporting Services Configuration Manager. The Reporting Services Configuration Connection dialog opens.

2. Specify the server name (Machine Name) and Report Server instance. Click Connect.

3. Select the Database tab on the left side of the dialog, and click Change Database.

4. Ensure that "Create a new Report Server database" is selected and click Next.

5. Enter a correct Database Server instance name (that is, the machine and instance on which you want to host your Report Server database) and click Next.

6. Enter a database name of your choice. Ensure that you select SharePoint Integrated Mode as the Report Server Mode and click Next.

7. In the Authentication Type drop-down, select Windows Credentials and specify the account that will be used to connect to the Report Server database. Click Next.

8. On the Summary page, click Next and then click Finish after the configuration wizard completes.

9. Select the Web Service URL tab on the left side and click Apply.

You should now see the "The URL was successfully reserved" message at the bottom of the page.

 Do not close this dialog, as you will need the information to complete the next step, integrating Reporting Services with SharePoint.

To integrate Reporting Services with SharePoint, follow these steps:

1. Install the SQL Server 2008 R2 Reporting Services Add-in for Microsoft SharePoint Technologies 2010. The file for this component is `rsSharePoint.msi` and can be found on the SQL Server 2008 R2 installation media in the `1033_ENU_LP\x64\Setup` folder. (This path assumes an English SQL Server install. If your SQL Server is a different language, look for it in the corresponding `<code page>_<language>_LP` folder). Click through the pages, accepting the license agreement and other defaults.

2. After the add-in is installed, open the SharePoint Central Administration Web site. Click General Application Settings on the left, and then select Reporting Services Integration.

3. In the Report Server Web Service URL field, enter the Web Service URL that you reserved earlier.

4. In the Authentication Mode section of the dialog, specify Windows Authentication and specify the account/password you want to use. Then click OK.

At this point, you should have Reporting Services configured to host the report needed for the "Client Address to State" report. The following steps set up that report:

1. Restore the database backup for the data that will be used for the report. This backup file is in the same location as the `SDRAudit.bak` file you restored at the start of this appendix and is called `mappingtable.bak`. Use the same procedure that you used to restore the `SDRAudit.bak` file to restore `mappingtable.bak`.

2. Open the `ClientAddressToState.rdl` file in a text editor and find the line that specifies the data source connection string for the report. It should look like Figure A-3.

Replace the value of the Data Source property (`sdrserver\powerpivot`) with the instance name of the server that contains the `mappingtable` database you restored in the previous step. Save the file.

3.   Upload the `ClientAddressToState.rdl` file to a document library on the SharePoint server that you installed Reporting Services on. You can test whether this procedure worked by opening the report from the SharePoint document library. If all is well, you should see a report titled `ClientAddressToState`, as shown in Figure A-4.

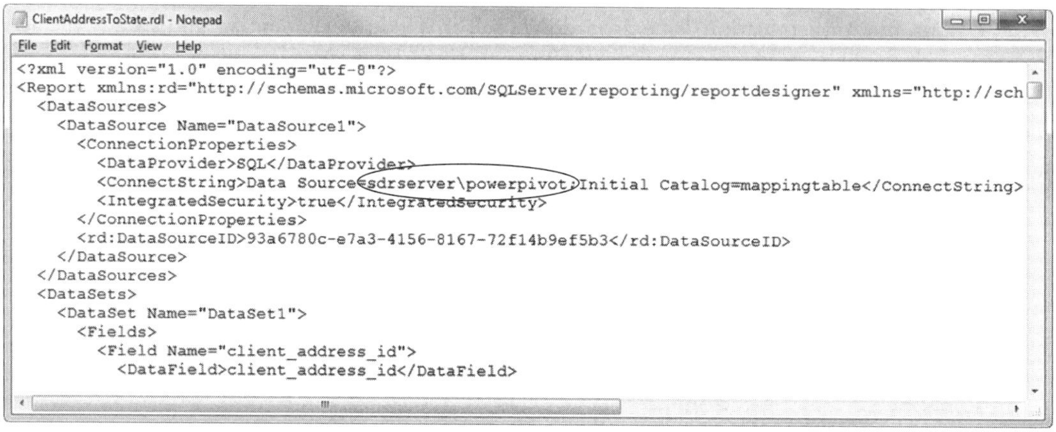

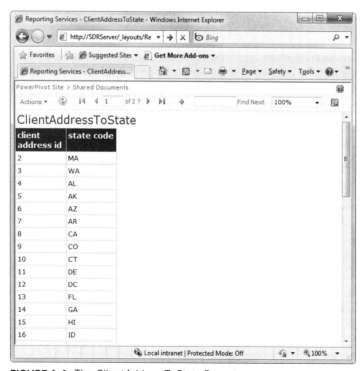

FIGURE A-3: ClientAddressToState.rdl file contents

FIGURE A-4: The ClientAddressToState Report

You have now set up the initial data sources for the SDR Healthcare application and are ready to work through the steps of creating the application, which starts in Chapter 3.

INDEX